STAR⇄CROSSED!!

02

JUNKO

C O N T E N T S

S T O R Y

High-schooler Azusa Asahina, with her gorgeous looks and excellent grades, is beloved by all in her school as the perfect girl. ...But it's all a cover for her true identity: an out-of-control idol otaku! Her unwavering dedication gets her caught up in an accident during the concert of her favorite idol, Chikashi Chida, and they end up...switching bodies?! While the two struggle to keep up appearances, they resign themselves to sharing the secret with Chikashi's manager, Matsumoto. Fully apprised of the situation, Matsumoto's grand plan is... to transfer Chikashi into Azusa's high school?! So begins the school life a fan usually dreams of! ☆

CHARACTER

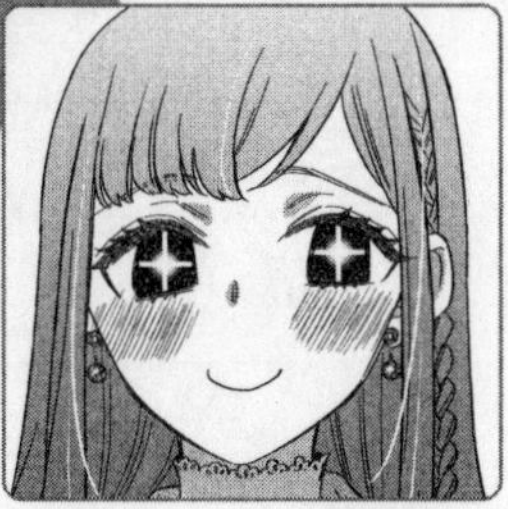

Azusa Asahina

A picture-perfect high school girl—with the looks, grades, and student council president title to match. In reality, she's a rabid fangirl who's crafted an elaborate image to be a worthy superfan of her favorite idol, Chikashi Chida.

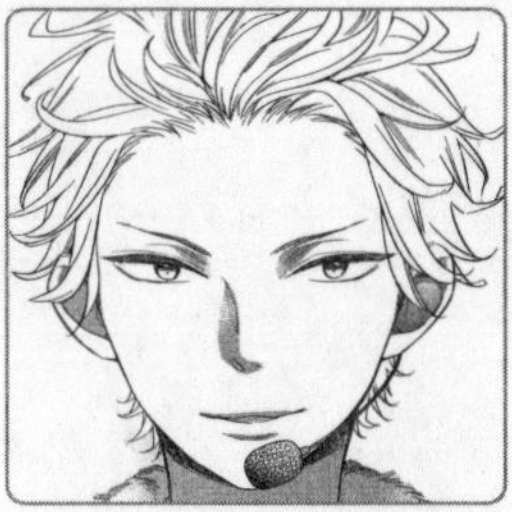

Chikashi Chida

A member of the four-man idol group P4U, and Azusa's favorite. He died in an accident during a concert, but was restored to life by God. He's put off by Azusa's idol obsession.

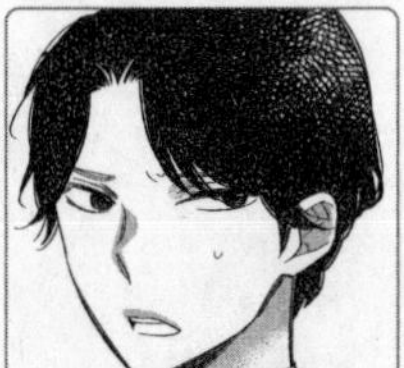

Matsumoto

P4U's manager. Loves cats.

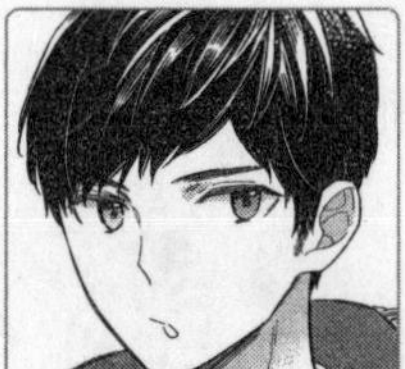

Fumi

Azusa's childhood friend. May be in love with Azusa?

P4U

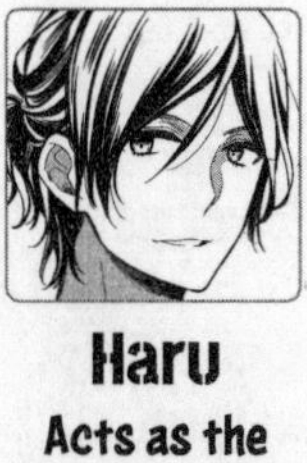

Haru

Acts as the group's leader.

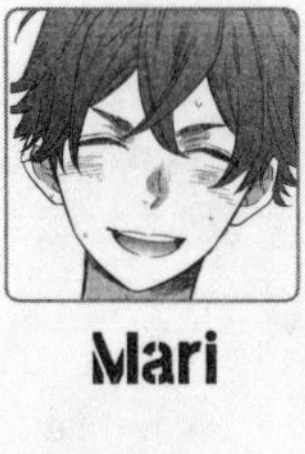

Mari

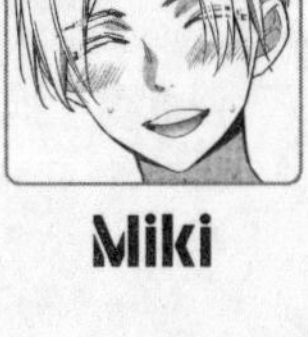

Miki

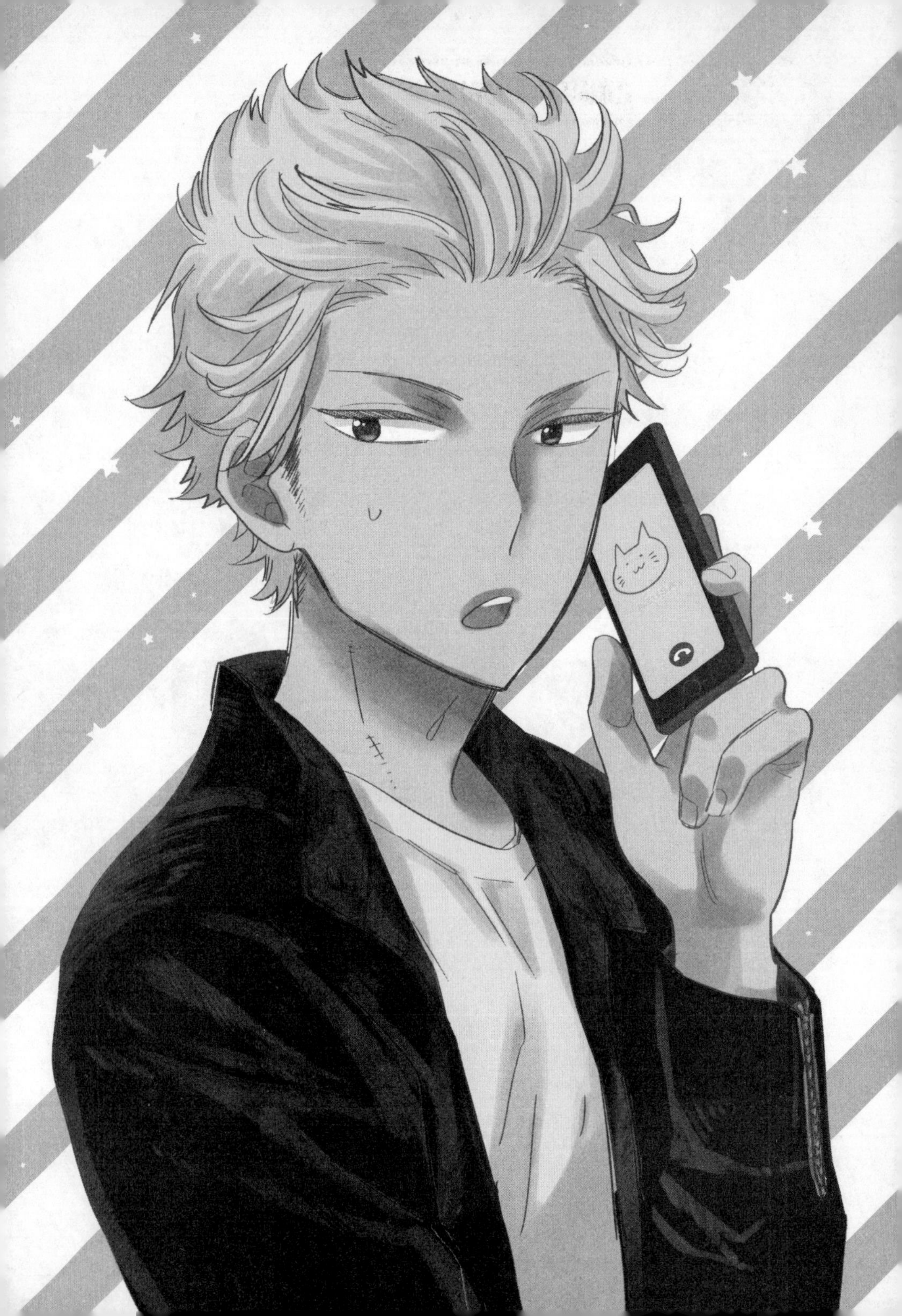

STAGE. 4 | WHAT A SLOPPY SETUP!

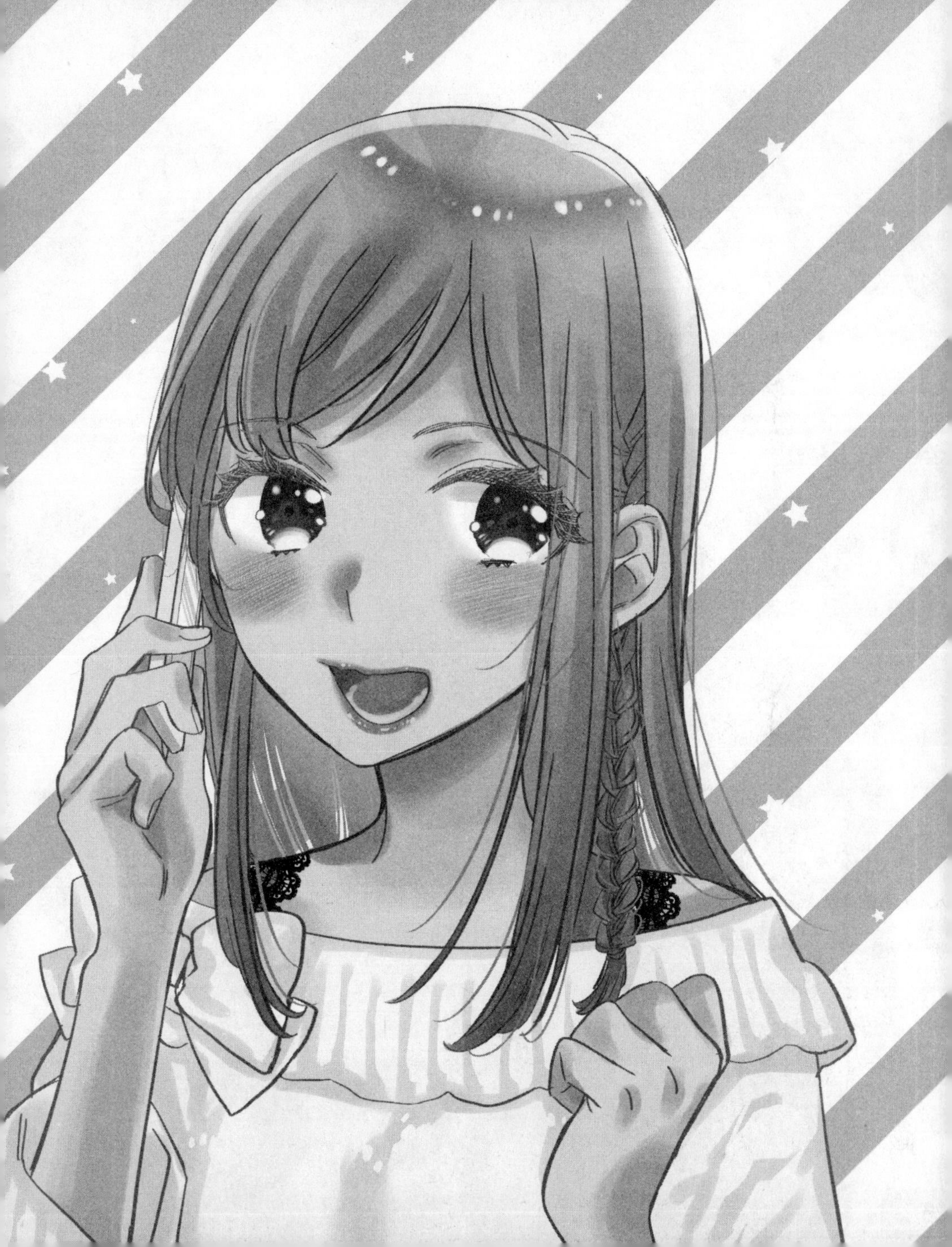

R⇄CROSS

D!! STAR

AR⇄CROS

CROSSED.

⇄CROSSE

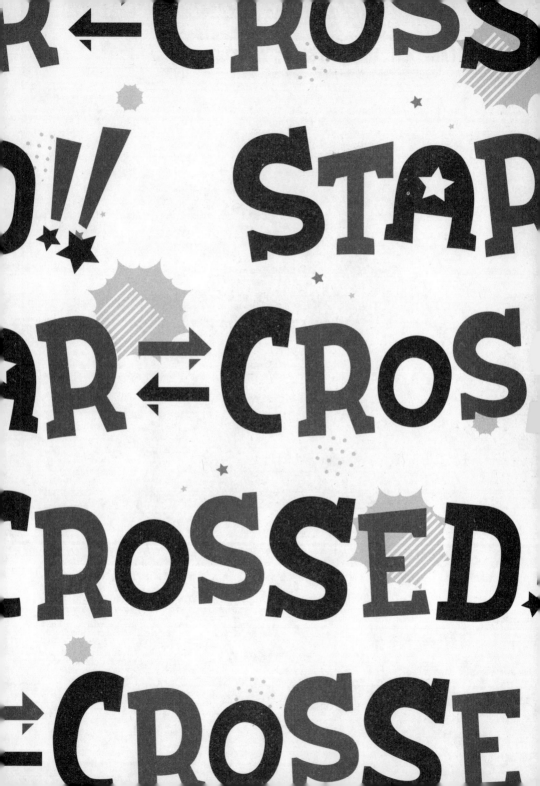

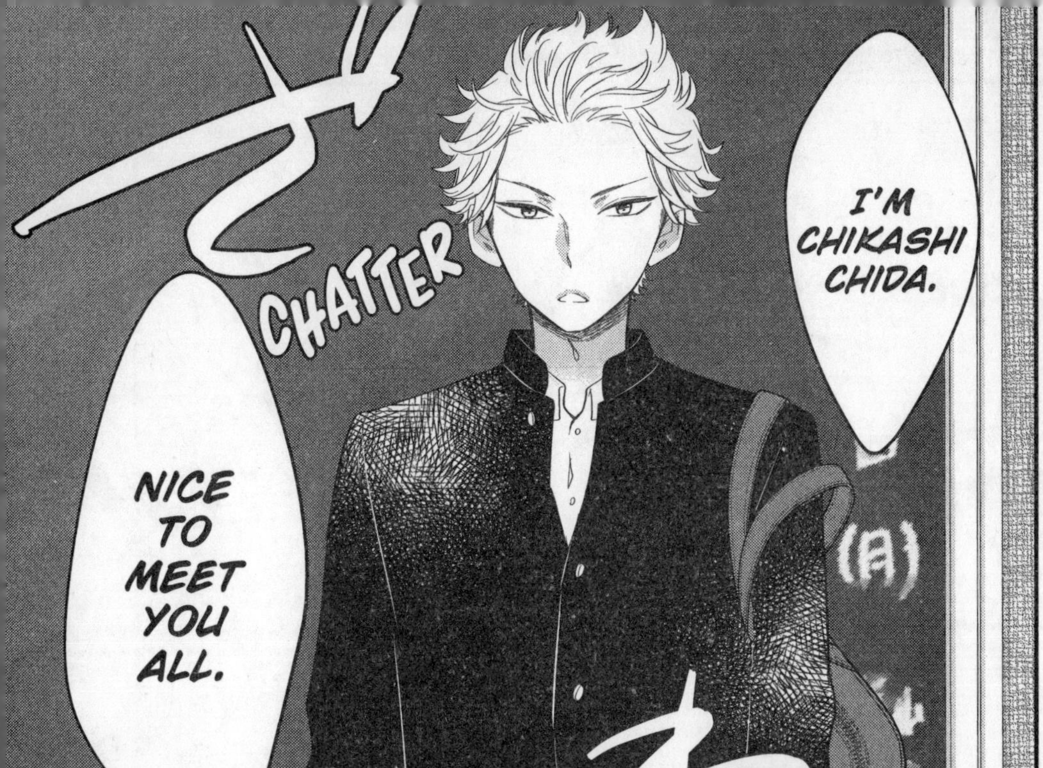
I'M CHIKASHI CHIDA.
CHATTER
NICE TO MEET YOU ALL.
BOARD: XXBER XXTH (MONDAY)

STAR⇄CROSSED!!

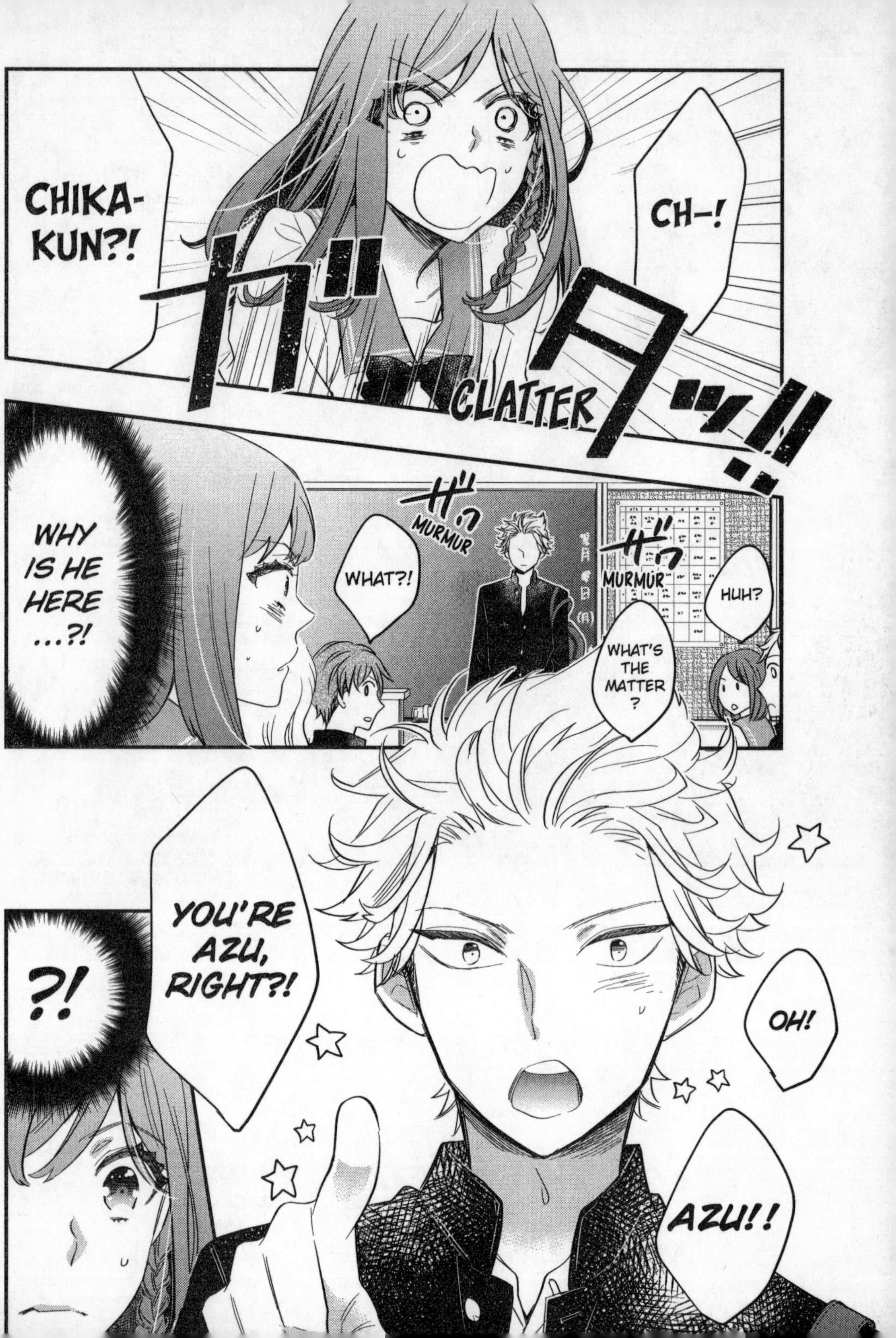
CH–!
CHIKA-KUN?!
ガタッ!!
CLATTER
HUH?
WHAT'S THE MATTER?
MURMUR
MURMUR
WHAT?!
WHY IS HE HERE ...?!
OH!
AZU!!
YOU'RE AZU, RIGHT?!
?!

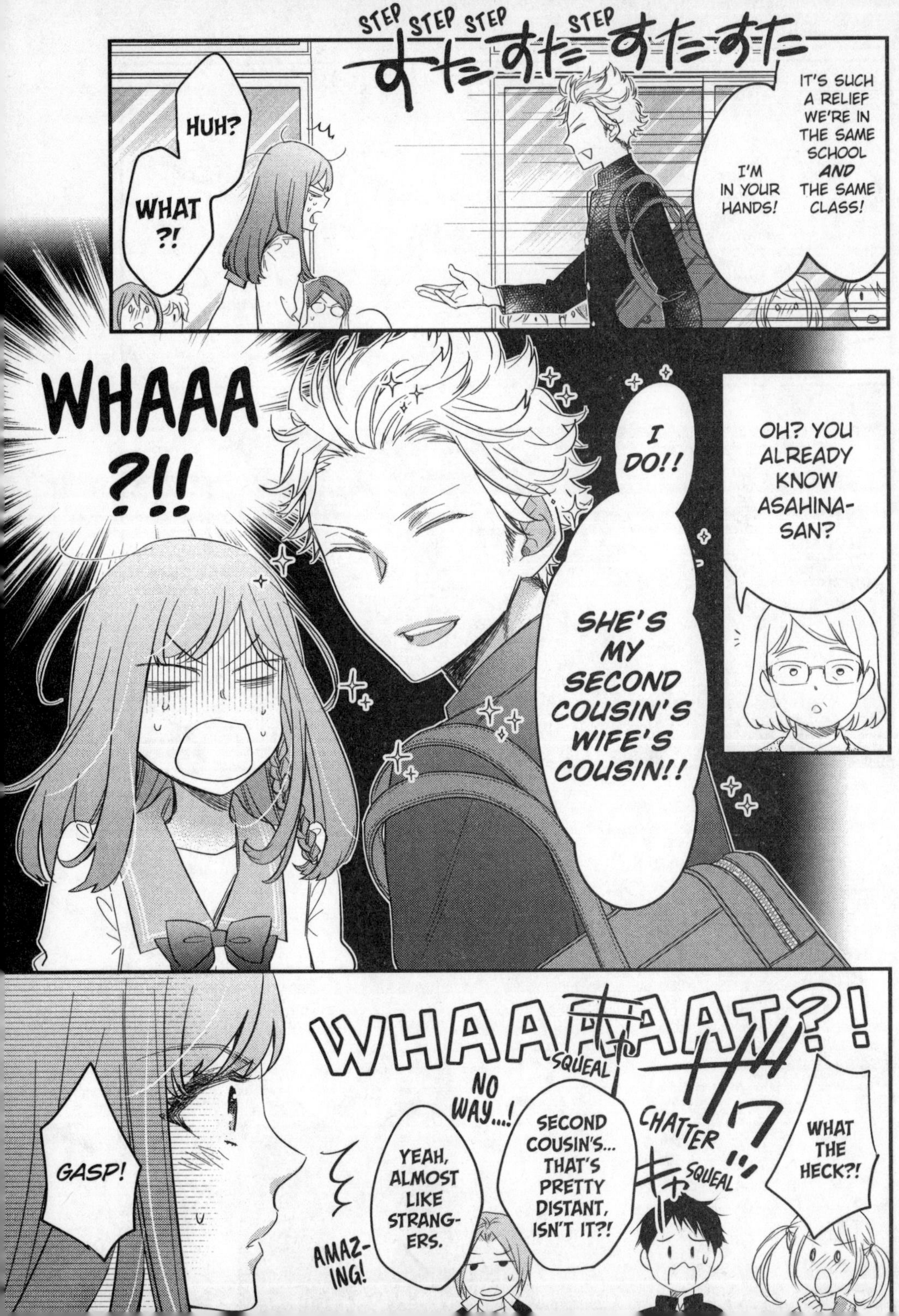
STEP STEP STEP STEP
すたすたすたすた
IT'S SUCH A RELIEF WE'RE IN THE SAME SCHOOL AND THE SAME CLASS!
I'M IN YOUR HANDS!
HUH?
WHAT?!
OH? YOU ALREADY KNOW ASAHINA-SAN?
I DO!!
SHE'S MY SECOND COUSIN'S WIFE'S COUSIN!!
WHAAA?!!
WHAAAAAT?!
WHAT THE HECK?!
CHATTER
SQUEAL
SQUEAL
SECOND COUSIN'S... THAT'S PRETTY DISTANT, ISN'T IT?!
NO WAY...!
YEAH, ALMOST LIKE STRANGERS.
AMAZ-ING!
GASP!

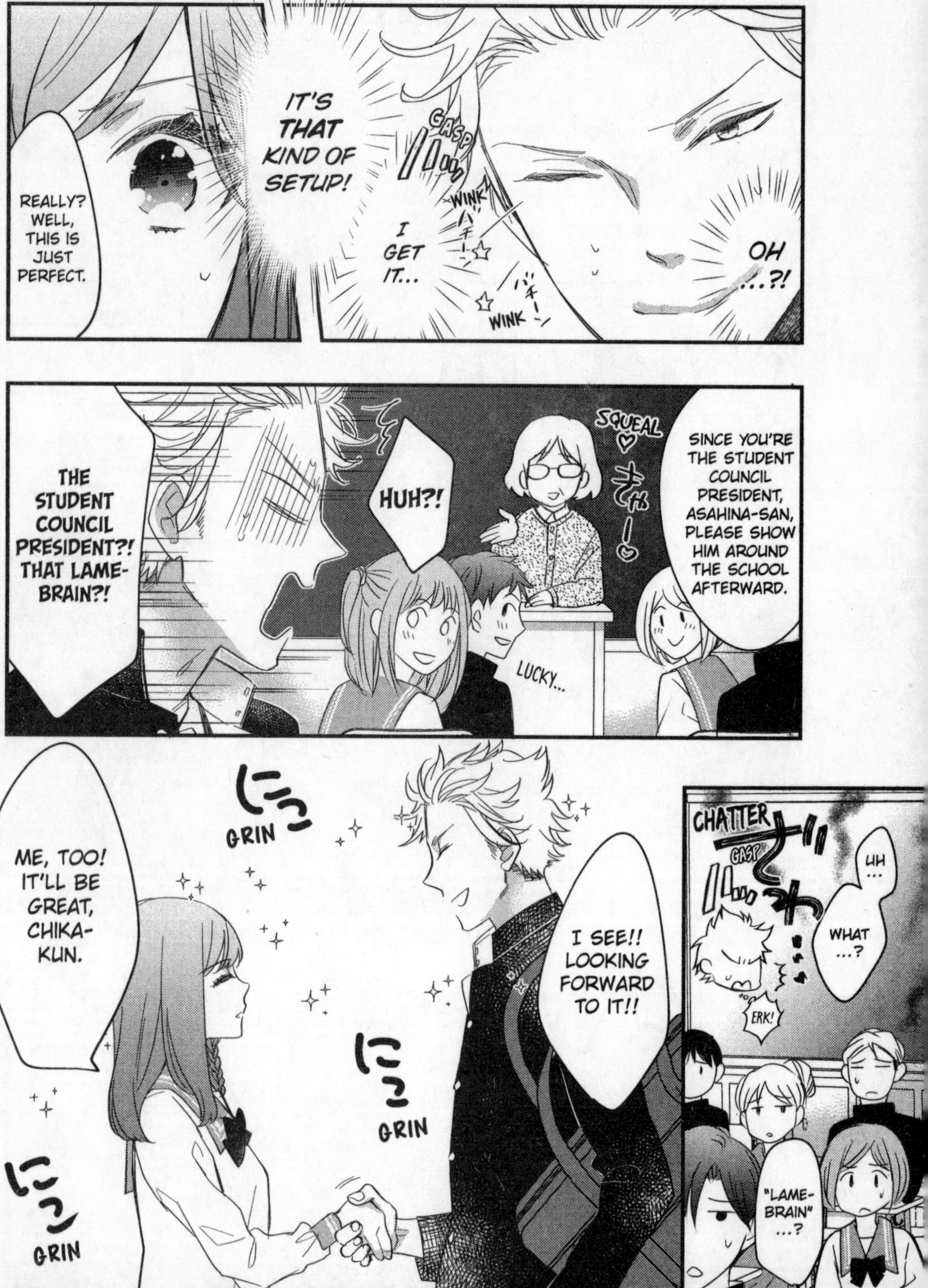
OH ...?!
WINK
WINK
I GET IT...
IT'S THAT KIND OF SETUP!
GASP
REALLY? WELL, THIS IS JUST PERFECT.
SINCE YOU'RE THE STUDENT COUNCIL PRESIDENT, ASAHINA-SAN, PLEASE SHOW HIM AROUND THE SCHOOL AFTERWARD.
SQUEAL
LUCKY...
HUH?!
THE STUDENT COUNCIL PRESIDENT?! THAT LAME-BRAIN?!
CHATTER
GASP
UH ...
WHAT ...?
ERK!
"LAME-BRAIN" ...?
I SEE!! LOOKING FORWARD TO IT!!
GRIN
GRIN
ME, TOO! IT'LL BE GREAT, CHIKA-KUN.
GRIN

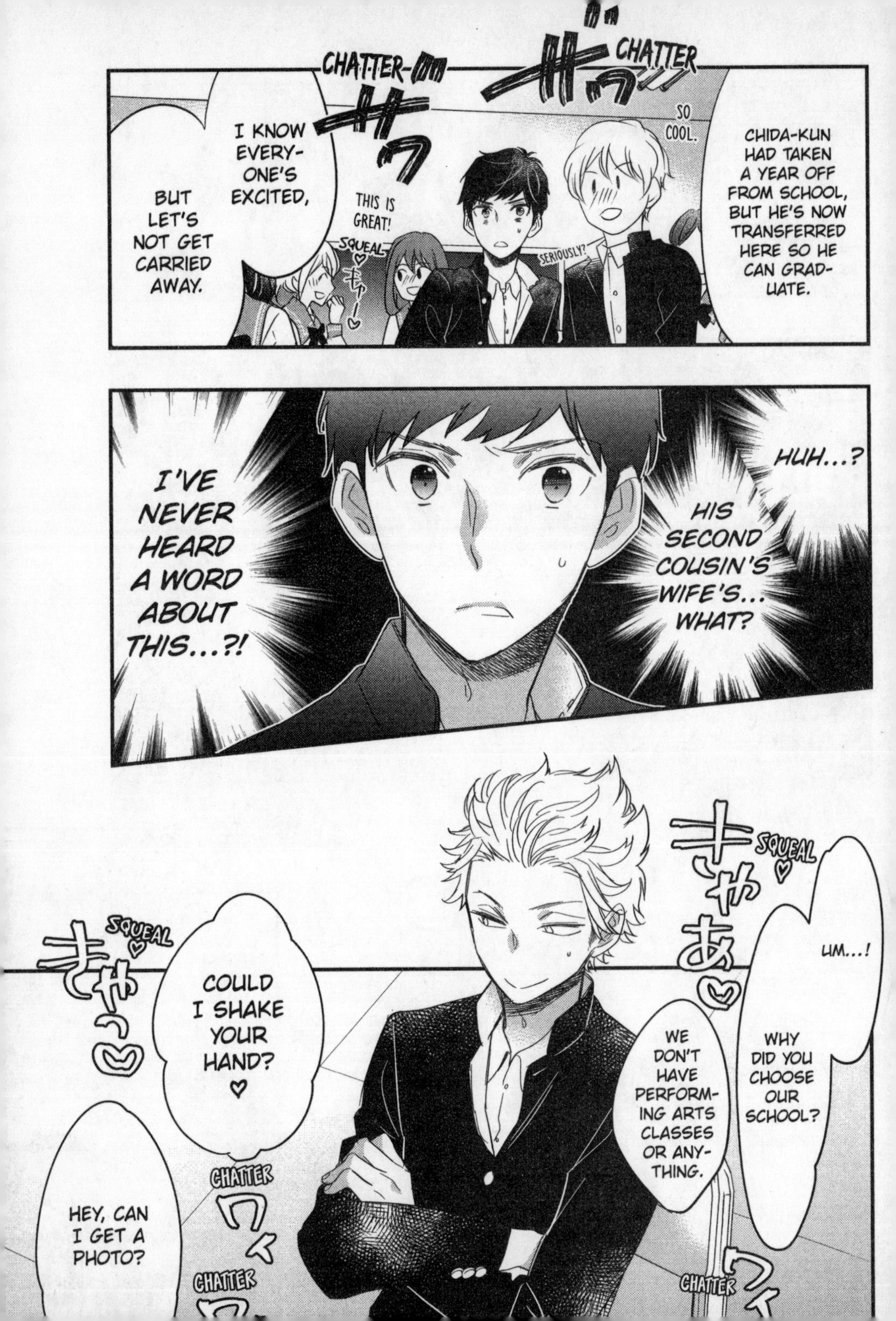
CHATTER
CHIDA-KUN HAD TAKEN A YEAR OFF FROM SCHOOL, BUT HE'S NOW TRANSFERRED HERE SO HE CAN GRADUATE.
SO COOL.
SERIOUSLY?
THIS IS GREAT!
SQUEAL ♡
I KNOW EVERYONE'S EXCITED,
BUT LET'S NOT GET CARRIED AWAY.
CHATTER-CHATTER
HUH...?
HIS SECOND COUSIN'S WIFE'S... WHAT?
I'VE NEVER HEARD A WORD ABOUT THIS...?!
SQUEAL ♡
UM...!
WHY DID YOU CHOOSE OUR SCHOOL?
WE DON'T HAVE PERFORMING ARTS CLASSES OR ANYTHING.
CHATTER
SQUEAL ♡
COULD I SHAKE YOUR HAND? ♡
CHATTER
HEY, CAN I GET A PHOTO?
CHATTER

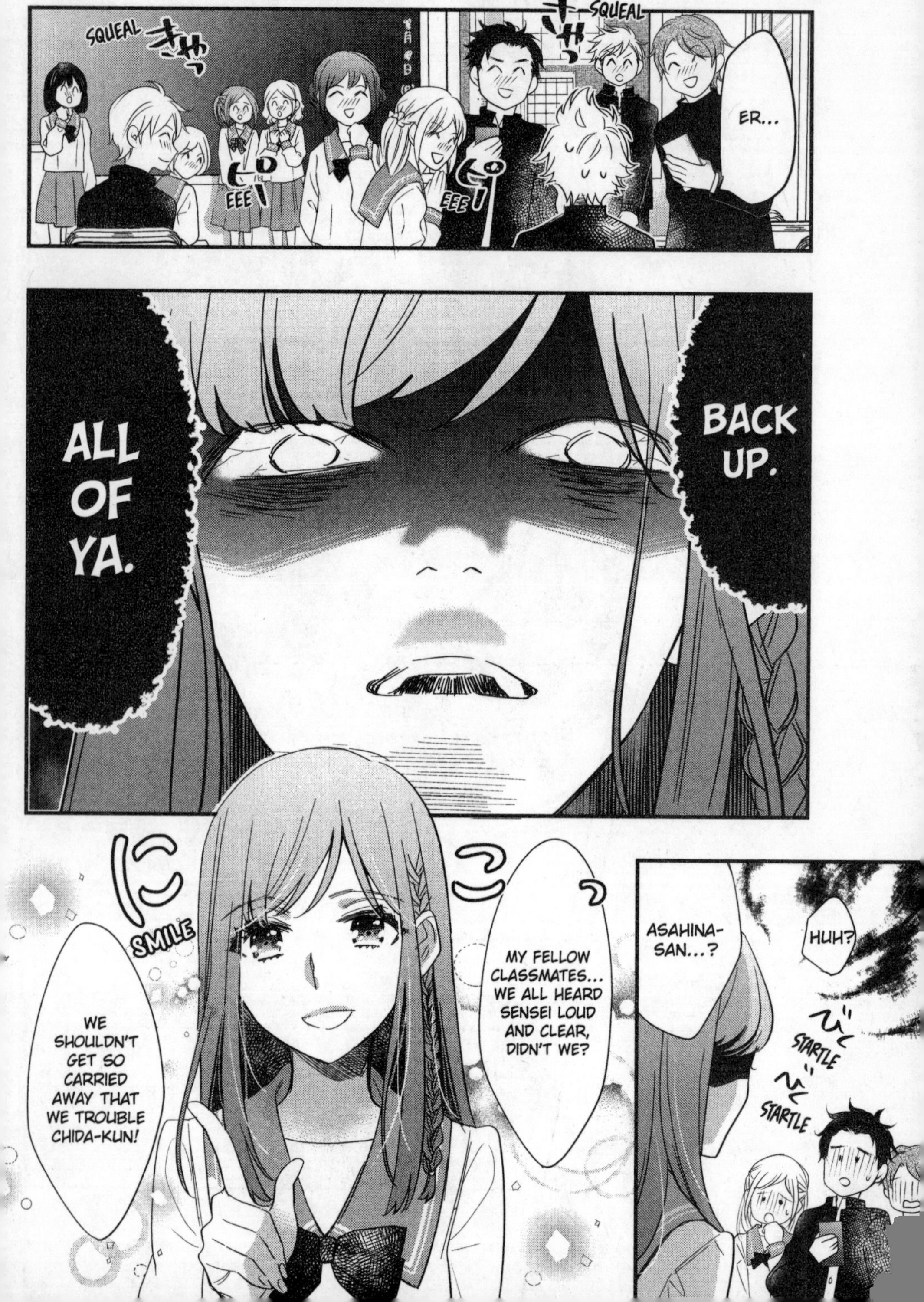
SQUEAL
ER...
EEE
SQUEAL
EEE
BACK UP.
ALL OF YA.
HUH?
ASAHINA-SAN...?
STARTLE
STARTLE
MY FELLOW CLASSMATES... WE ALL HEARD SENSEI LOUD AND CLEAR, DIDN'T WE?
SMILE
WE SHOULDN'T GET SO CARRIED AWAY THAT WE TROUBLE CHIDA-KUN!

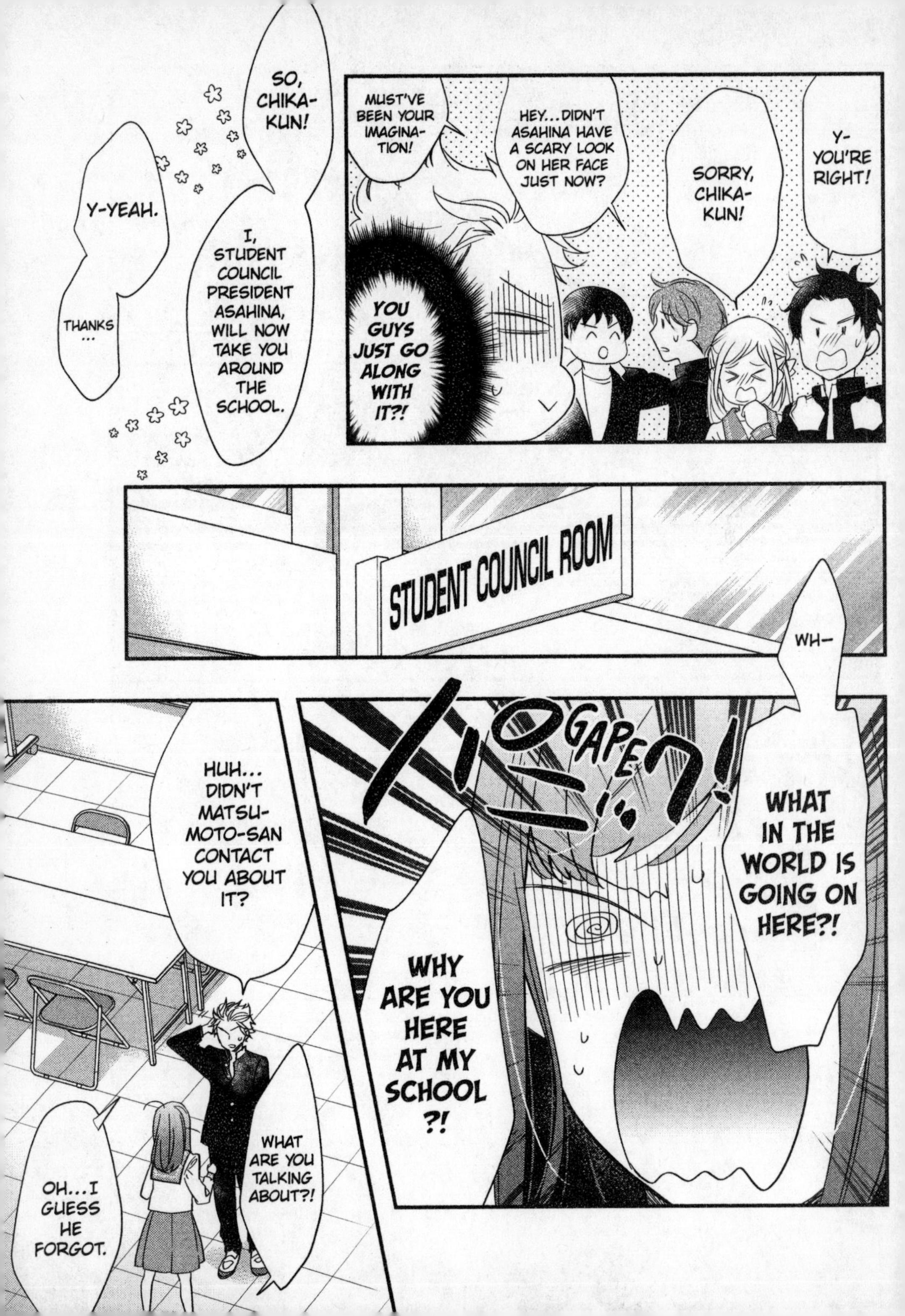
Y-YOU'RE RIGHT!
SORRY, CHIKA-KUN!
HEY...DIDN'T ASAHINA HAVE A SCARY LOOK ON HER FACE JUST NOW?
MUST'VE BEEN YOUR IMAGINATION!
YOU GUYS JUST GO ALONG WITH IT?!
SO, CHIKA-KUN!
I, STUDENT COUNCIL PRESIDENT ASAHINA, WILL NOW TAKE YOU AROUND THE SCHOOL.
Y-YEAH.
THANKS...
STUDENT COUNCIL ROOM
WH—
GAPE
WHAT IN THE WORLD IS GOING ON HERE?!
WHY ARE YOU HERE AT MY SCHOOL?!
HUH... DIDN'T MATSUMOTO-SAN CONTACT YOU ABOUT IT?
WHAT ARE YOU TALKING ABOUT?!
OH...I GUESS HE FORGOT.

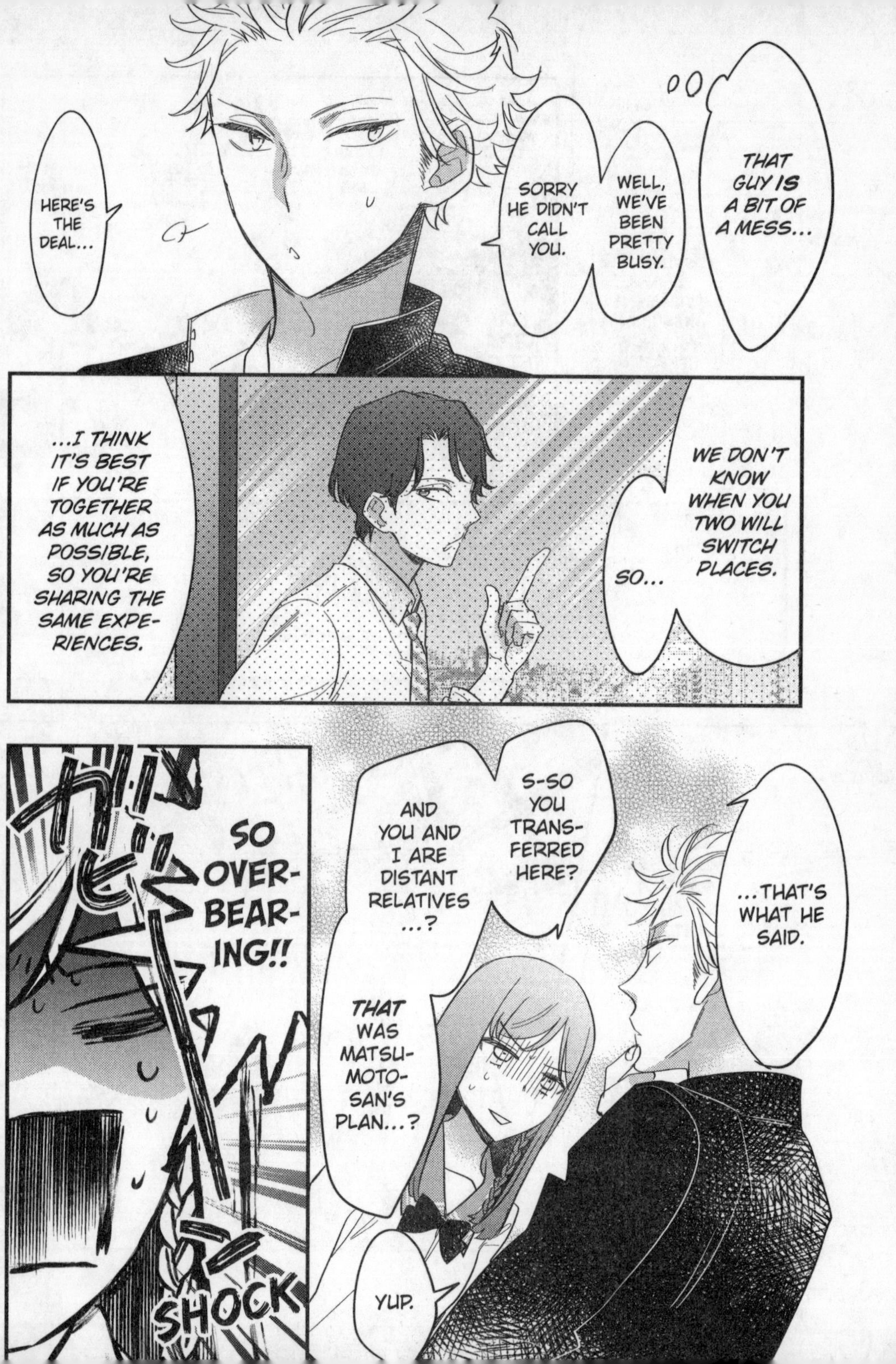
THAT GUY IS A BIT OF A MESS...
WELL, WE'VE BEEN PRETTY BUSY.
SORRY HE DIDN'T CALL YOU.
HERE'S THE DEAL...
WE DON'T KNOW WHEN YOU TWO WILL SWITCH PLACES.
SO...
...I THINK IT'S BEST IF YOU'RE TOGETHER AS MUCH AS POSSIBLE, SO YOU'RE SHARING THE SAME EXPERIENCES.
...THAT'S WHAT HE SAID.
S-SO YOU TRANSFERRED HERE?
AND YOU AND I ARE DISTANT RELATIVES ...?
THAT WAS MATSUMOTO-SAN'S PLAN...?
YUP.
SO OVERBEARING!!
SHOCK

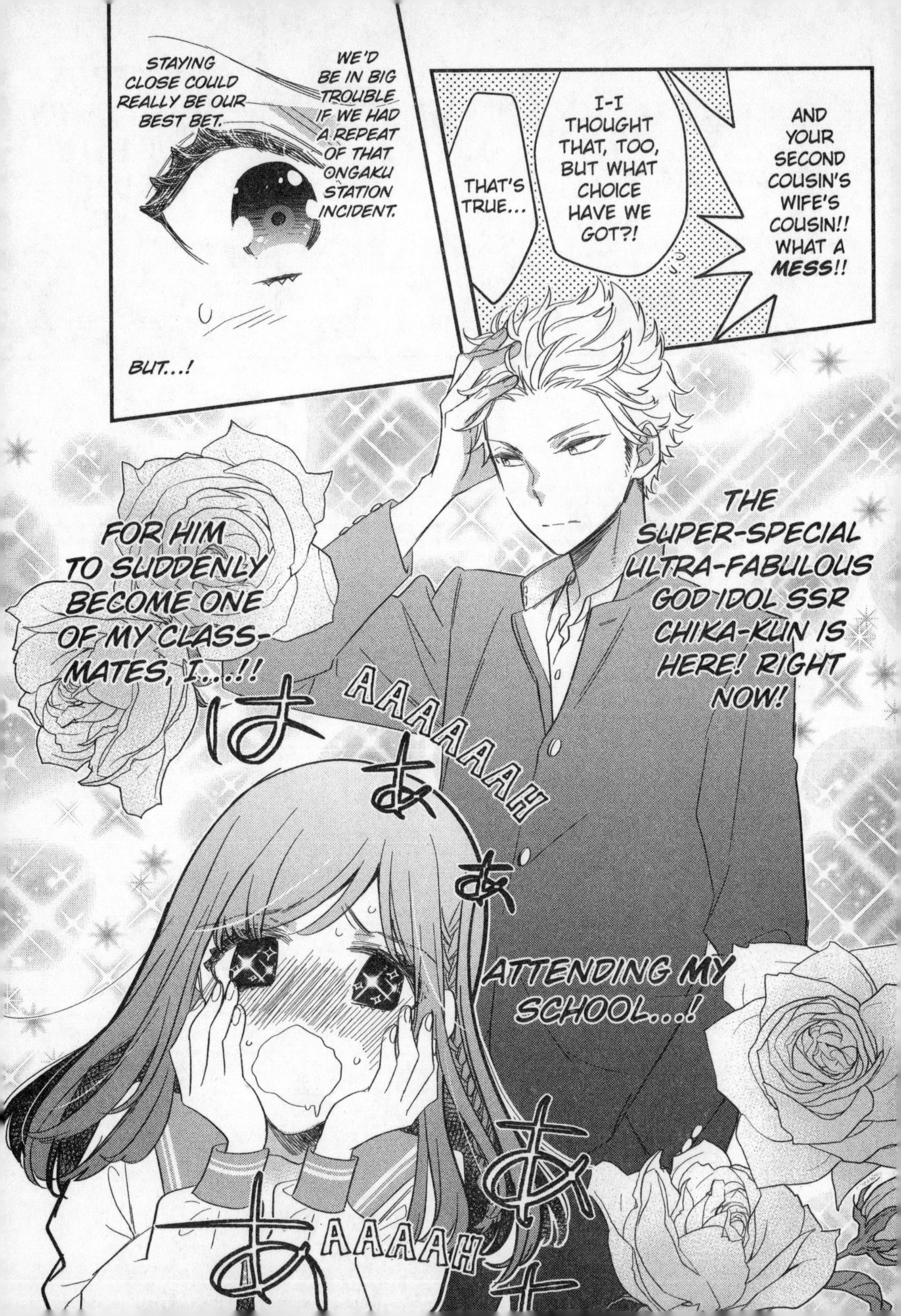
AND YOUR SECOND COUSIN'S WIFE'S COUSIN!! WHAT A MESS!!
I-I THOUGHT THAT, TOO, BUT WHAT CHOICE HAVE WE GOT?!
THAT'S TRUE...
WE'D BE IN BIG TROUBLE IF WE HAD A REPEAT OF THAT ONGAKU STATION INCIDENT.
STAYING CLOSE COULD REALLY BE OUR BEST BET.
BUT...!
THE SUPER-SPECIAL ULTRA-FABULOUS GOD IDOL SSR CHIKA-KUN IS HERE! RIGHT NOW!
ATTENDING MY SCHOOL...!
FOR HIM TO SUDDENLY BECOME ONE OF MY CLASSMATES, I...!!
AAAAAAAAH
AAAAAH

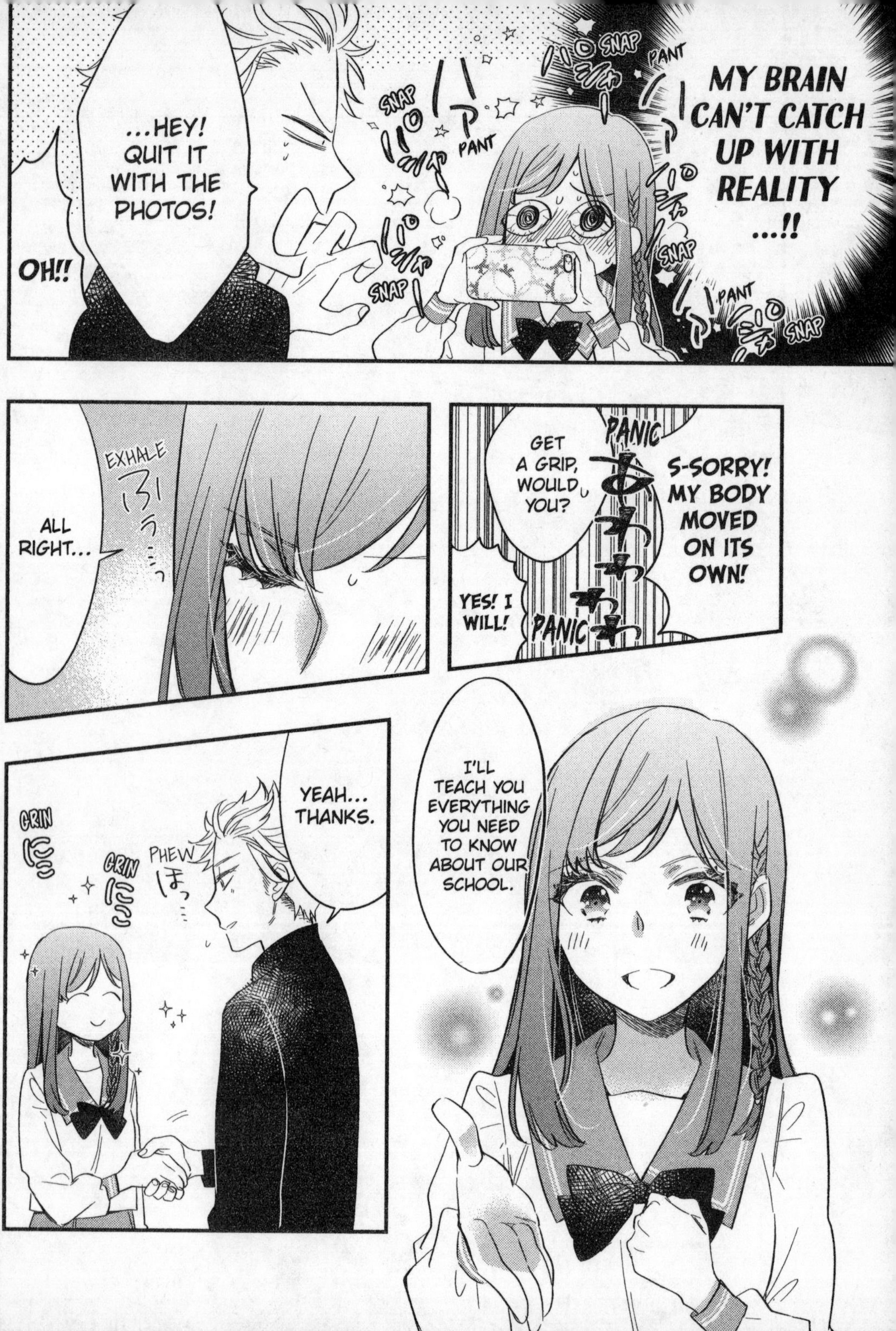
MY BRAIN CAN'T CATCH UP WITH REALITY ...!!
SNAP
PANT
SNAP
PANT
SNAP
PANT
SNAP
PANT
SNAP
SNAP
...HEY! QUIT IT WITH THE PHOTOS!
OH!!
S-SORRY! MY BODY MOVED ON ITS OWN!
PANIC
GET A GRIP, WOULD YOU?
YES! I WILL!
PANIC
EXHALE
ALL RIGHT...
I'LL TEACH YOU EVERYTHING YOU NEED TO KNOW ABOUT OUR SCHOOL.
YEAH... THANKS.
PHEW
GRIN
GRIN

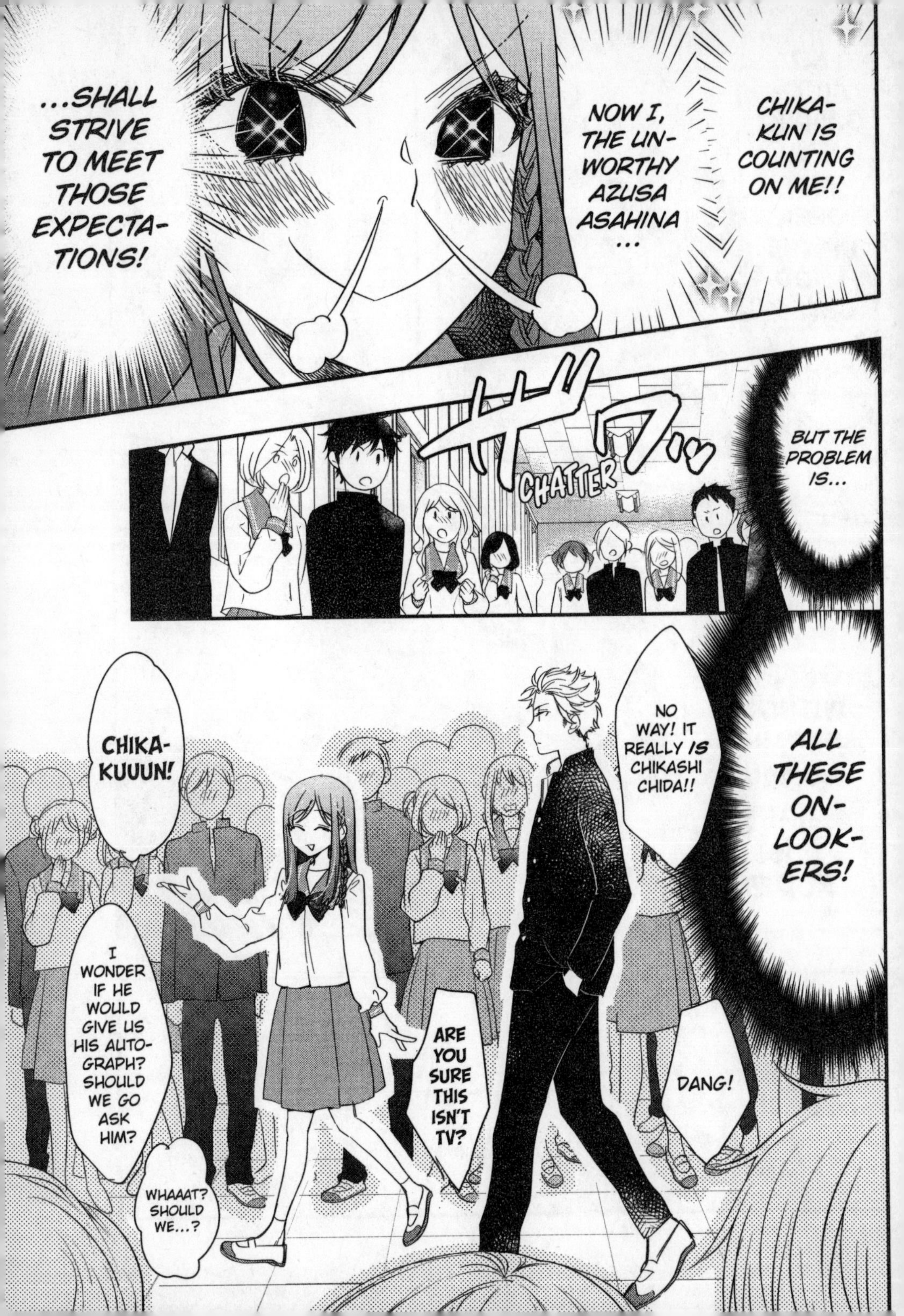
CHIKA-KUN IS COUNTING ON ME!!
NOW I, THE UNWORTHY AZUSA ASAHINA ...
...SHALL STRIVE TO MEET THOSE EXPECTATIONS!
BUT THE PROBLEM IS...
ザワ♥
CHATTER
ALL THESE ONLOOKERS!
NO WAY! IT REALLY IS CHIKASHI CHIDA!!
DANG!
ARE YOU SURE THIS ISN'T TV?
CHIKA-KUUUN!
I WONDER IF HE WOULD GIVE US HIS AUTOGRAPH? SHOULD WE GO ASK HIM?
WHAAAT? SHOULD WE...?

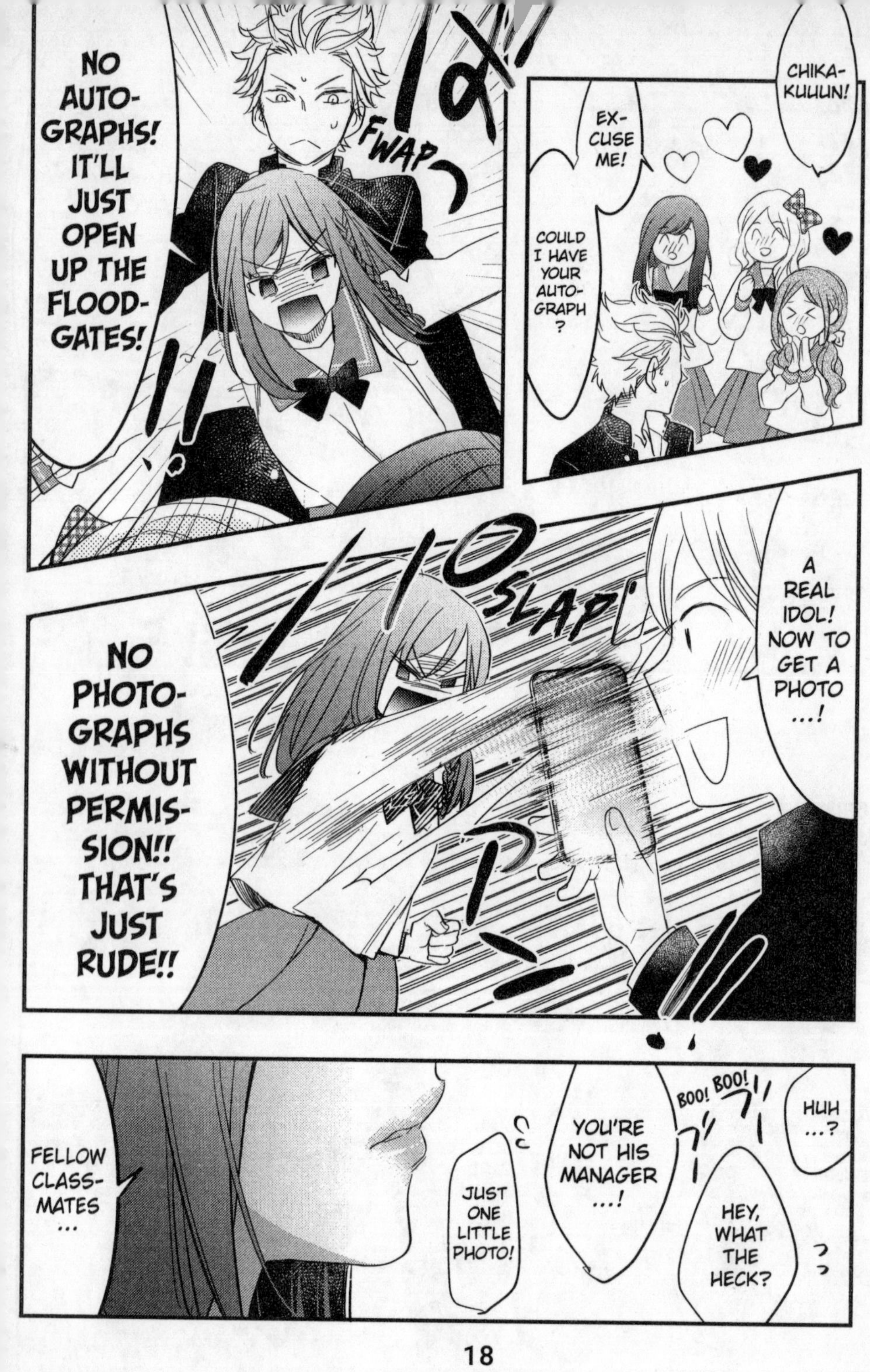
CHIKA-KUUUN!
EX-CUSE ME!
COULD I HAVE YOUR AUTO-GRAPH?
FWAP
NO AUTO-GRAPHS! IT'LL JUST OPEN UP THE FLOOD-GATES!
A REAL IDOL! NOW TO GET A PHOTO ...!
SLAP
NO PHOTO-GRAPHS WITHOUT PERMIS-SION!! THAT'S JUST RUDE!!
HUH ...?
BOO! BOO!
HEY, WHAT THE HECK?
YOU'RE NOT HIS MANAGER ...!
JUST ONE LITTLE PHOTO!
FELLOW CLASS-MATES ...

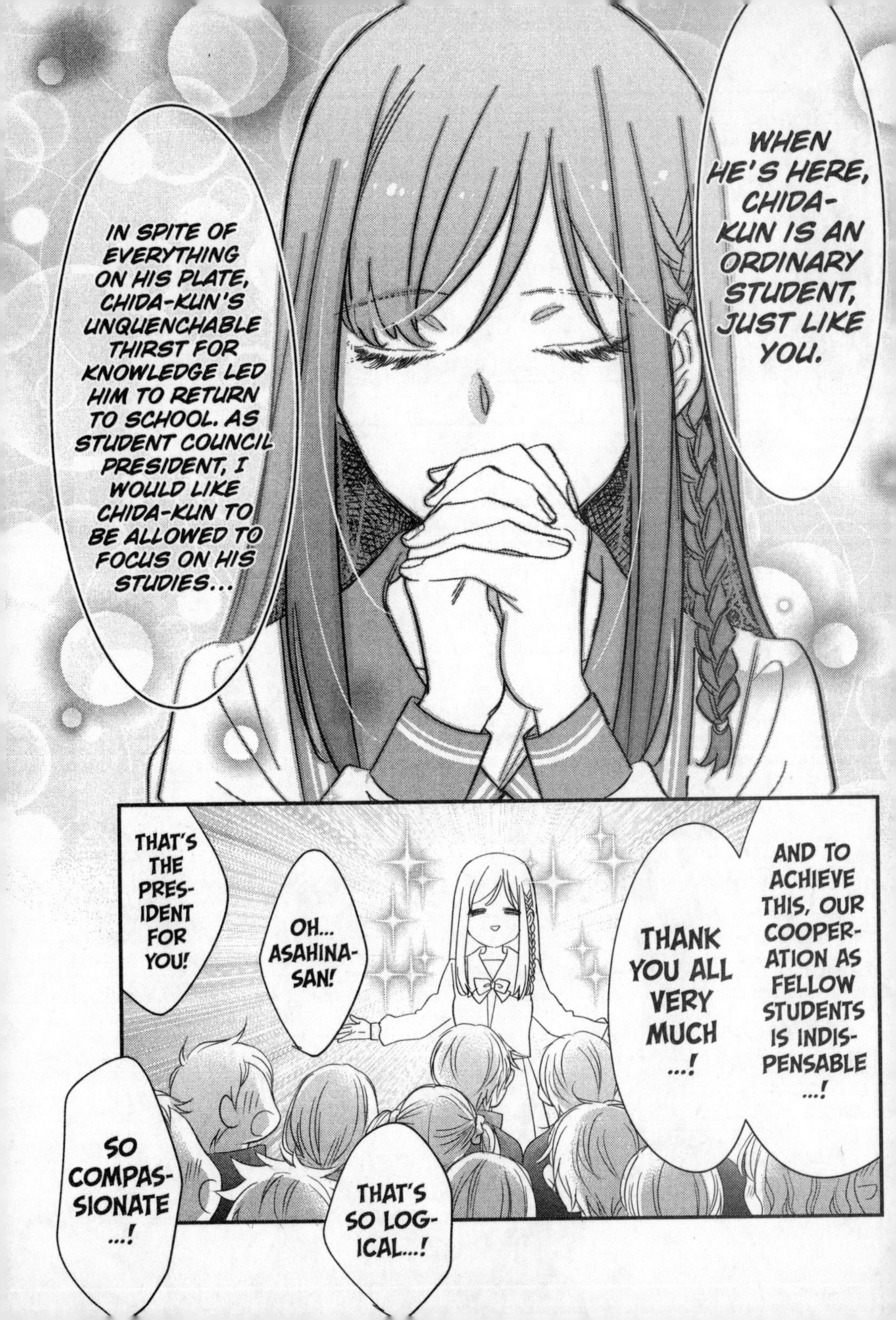
WHEN HE'S HERE, CHIDA-KUN IS AN ORDINARY STUDENT, JUST LIKE YOU.
IN SPITE OF EVERYTHING ON HIS PLATE, CHIDA-KUN'S UNQUENCHABLE THIRST FOR KNOWLEDGE LED HIM TO RETURN TO SCHOOL. AS STUDENT COUNCIL PRESIDENT, I WOULD LIKE CHIDA-KUN TO BE ALLOWED TO FOCUS ON HIS STUDIES...
AND TO ACHIEVE THIS, OUR COOPERATION AS FELLOW STUDENTS IS INDISPENSABLE ...!
THANK YOU ALL VERY MUCH ...!
THAT'S THE PRESIDENT FOR YOU!
OH... ASAHINA-SAN!
THAT'S SO LOGICAL...!
SO COMPASSIONATE ...!

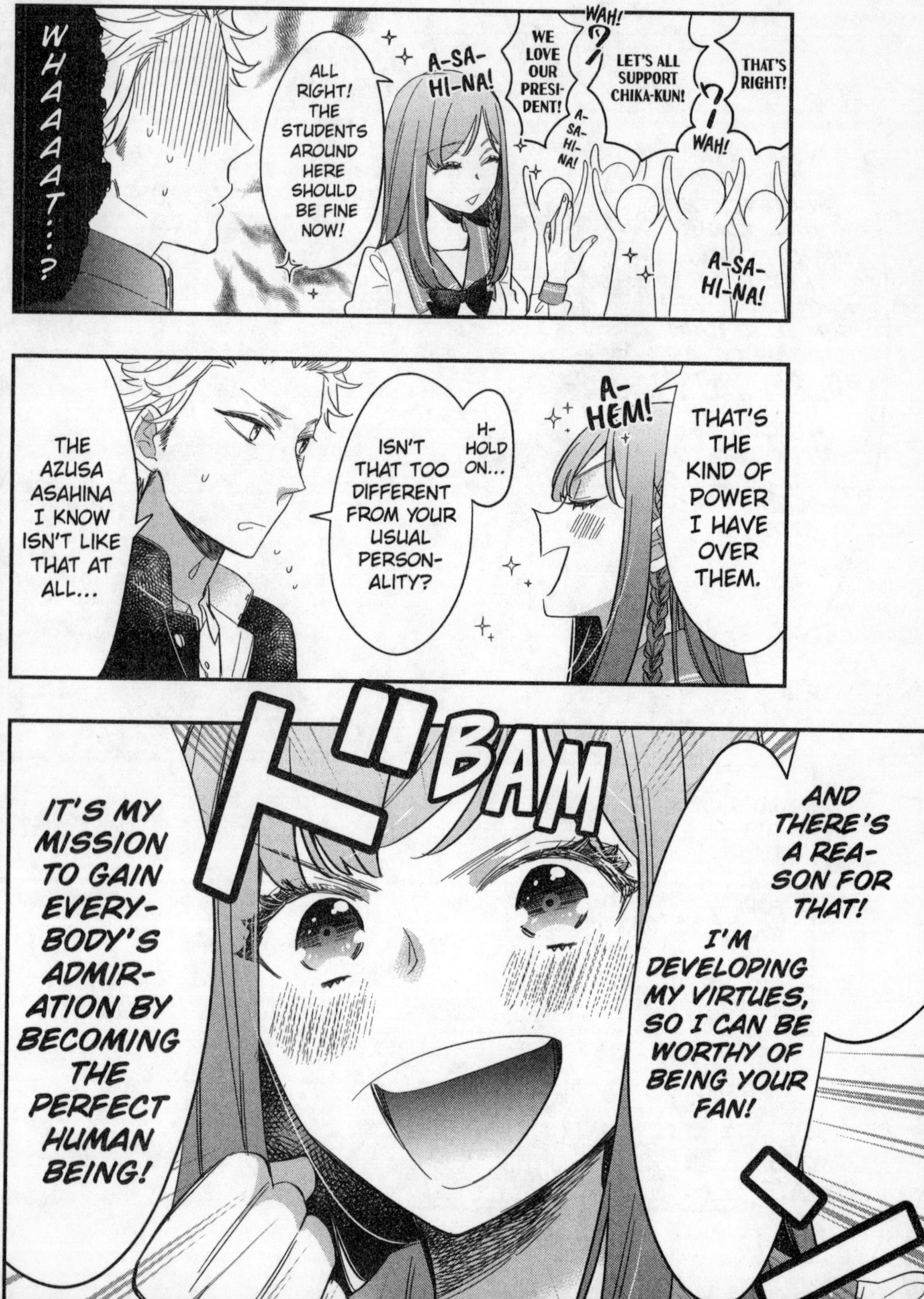
THAT'S RIGHT!
WAH!
LET'S ALL SUPPORT CHIKA-KUN!
WAH!
WE LOVE OUR PRESIDENT!
A-SA-HI-NA!
A-SA-HI-NA!
A-SA-HI-NA!
ALL RIGHT! THE STUDENTS AROUND HERE SHOULD BE FINE NOW!
WHAAAAAT...?
THAT'S THE KIND OF POWER I HAVE OVER THEM.
A-HEM!
H-HOLD ON...
ISN'T THAT TOO DIFFERENT FROM YOUR USUAL PERSON-ALITY?
THE AZUSA ASAHINA I KNOW ISN'T LIKE THAT AT ALL...
AND THERE'S A REA-SON FOR THAT!
I'M DEVELOPING MY VIRTUES, SO I CAN BE WORTHY OF BEING YOUR FAN!
BAM
IT'S MY MISSION TO GAIN EVERY-BODY'S ADMIR-ATION BY BECOMING THE PERFECT HUMAN BEING!

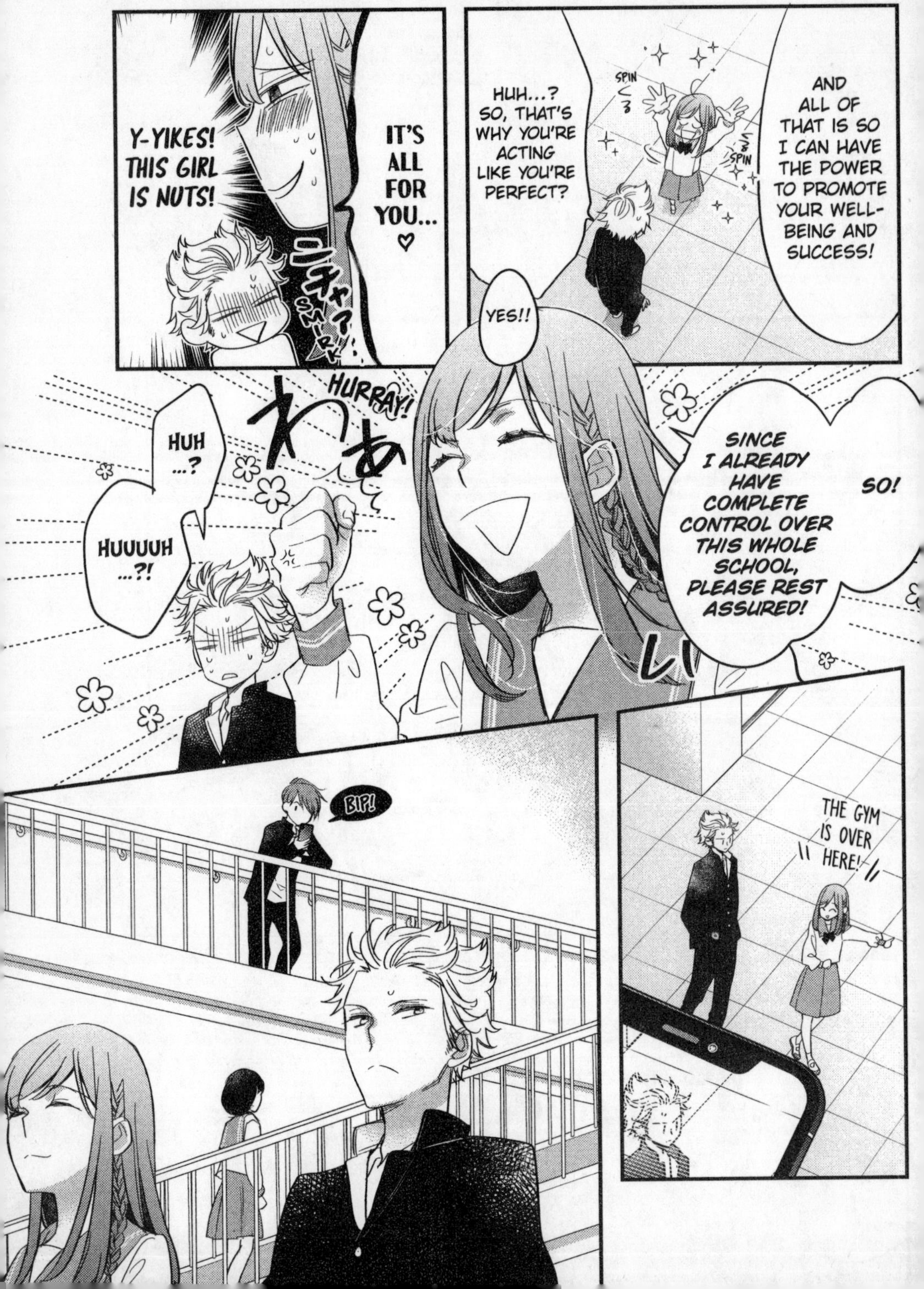
AND ALL OF THAT IS SO I CAN HAVE THE POWER TO PROMOTE YOUR WELL-BEING AND SUCCESS!
SPIN くる
SPIN くる
HUH...? SO, THAT'S WHY YOU'RE ACTING LIKE YOU'RE PERFECT?
YES!!
IT'S ALL FOR YOU... ♡
Y-YIKES! THIS GIRL IS NUTS!
ニチャア SMIRK
SO!
SINCE I ALREADY HAVE COMPLETE CONTROL OVER THIS WHOLE SCHOOL, PLEASE REST ASSURED!
い
わあ HURRAY!
HUH ...?
HUUUUH ...?!
THE GYM IS OVER HERE!
BIP!

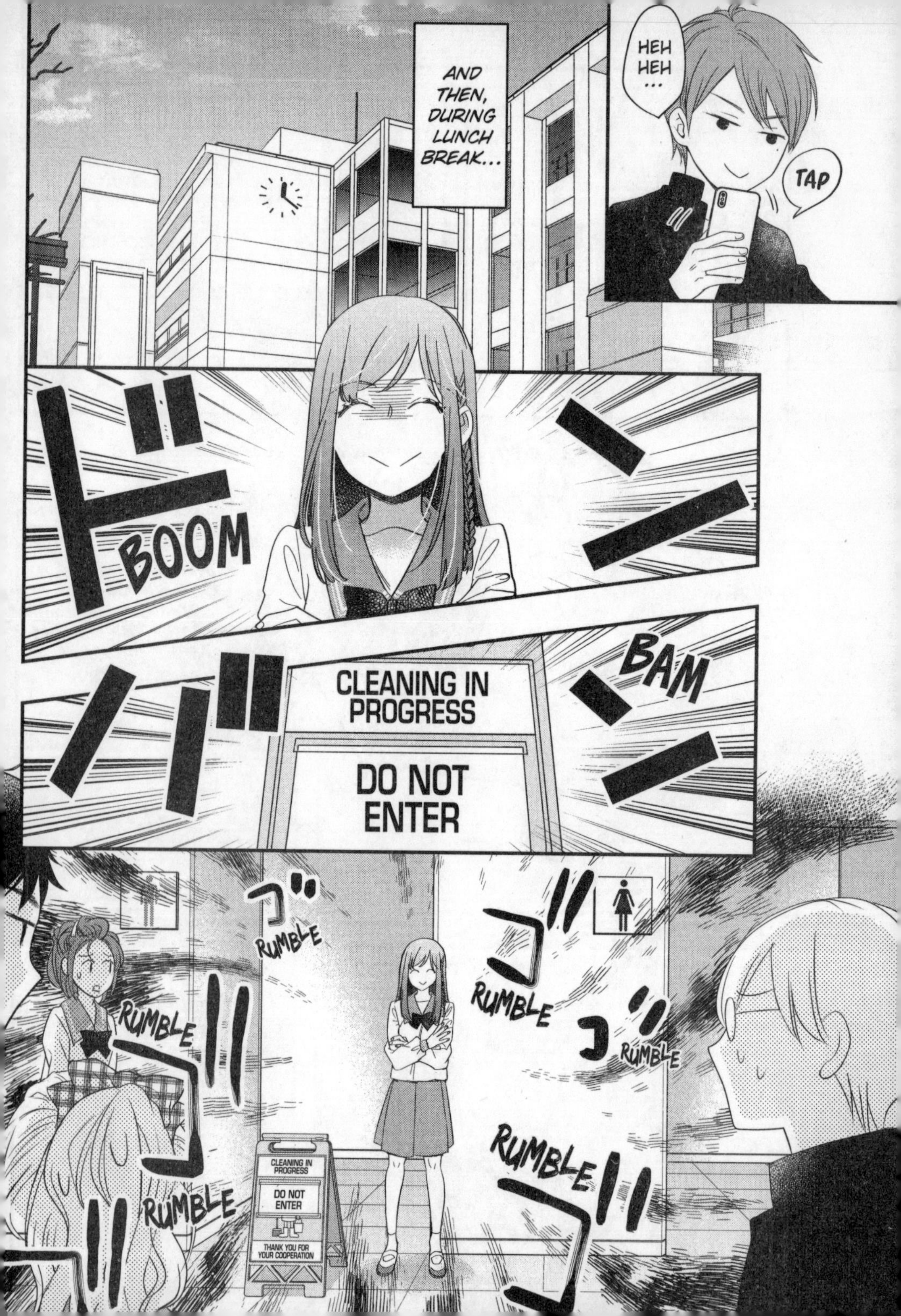

HEH HEH ...
TAP
AND THEN, DURING LUNCH BREAK...
BOOM
BAM
CLEANING IN PROGRESS
DO NOT ENTER
RUMBLE
RUMBLE
RUMBLE
RUMBLE
RUMBLE
RUMBLE
CLEANING IN PROGRESS
DO NOT ENTER
THANK YOU FOR YOUR COOPERATION

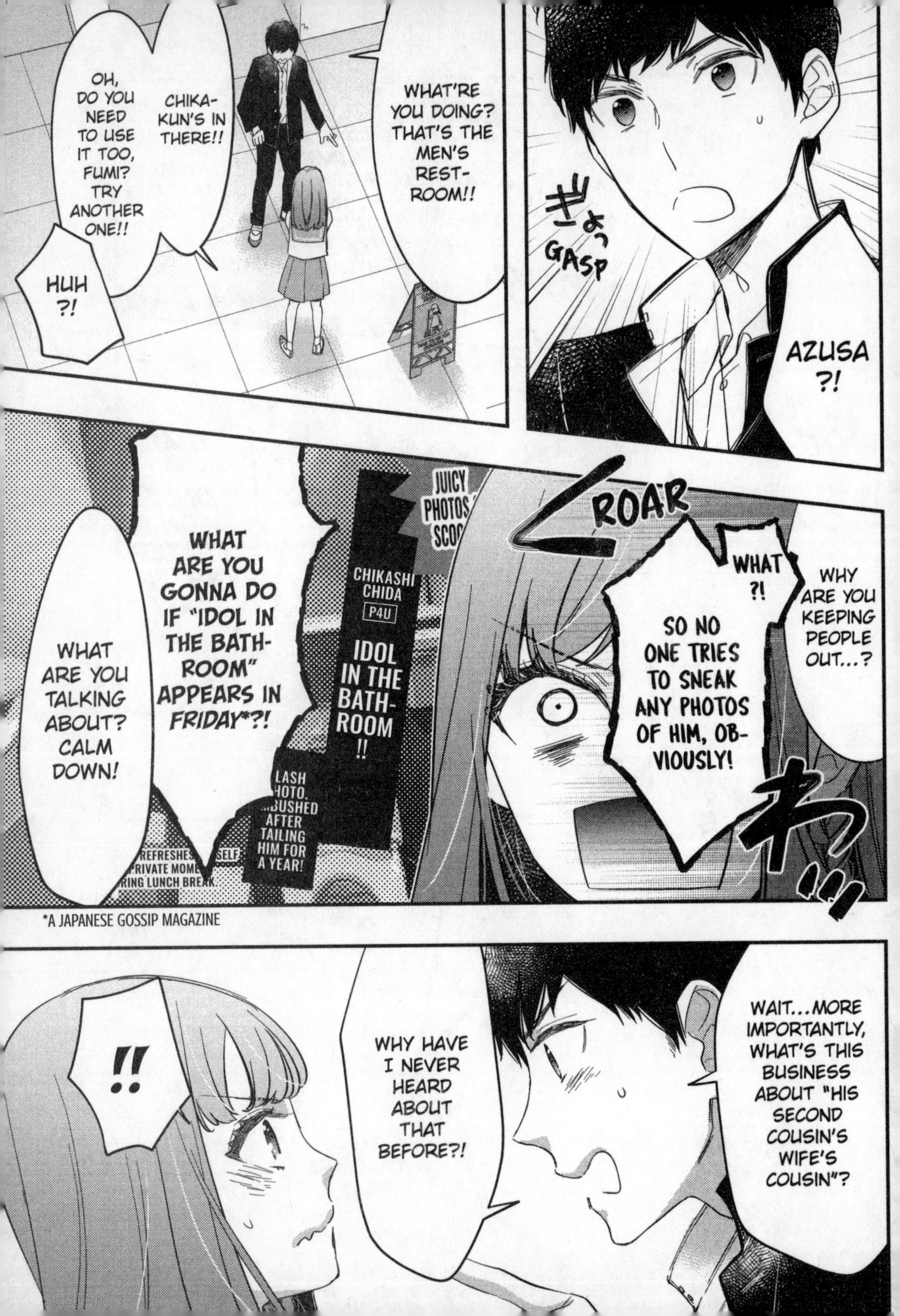
ぎょっ
GASP
AZUSA?!
WHAT'RE YOU DOING? THAT'S THE MEN'S REST-ROOM!!
CHIKA-KUN'S IN THERE!!
OH, DO YOU NEED TO USE IT TOO, FUMI? TRY ANOTHER ONE!!
HUH?!
WHY ARE YOU KEEPING PEOPLE OUT...?
ROAR
WHAT?!
SO NO ONE TRIES TO SNEAK ANY PHOTOS OF HIM, OBVIOUSLY!
わっ
JUICY PHOTOS
CHIKASHI CHIDA
P4U
IDOL IN THE BATH-ROOM!!
AFTER TAILING HIM FOR A YEAR!
WHAT ARE YOU GONNA DO IF "IDOL IN THE BATH-ROOM" APPEARS IN FRIDAY*?!
WHAT ARE YOU TALKING ABOUT? CALM DOWN!
WAIT...MORE IMPORTANTLY, WHAT'S THIS BUSINESS ABOUT "HIS SECOND COUSIN'S WIFE'S COUSIN"?
WHY HAVE I NEVER HEARD ABOUT THAT BEFORE?!
!!

*A JAPANESE GOSSIP MAGAZINE

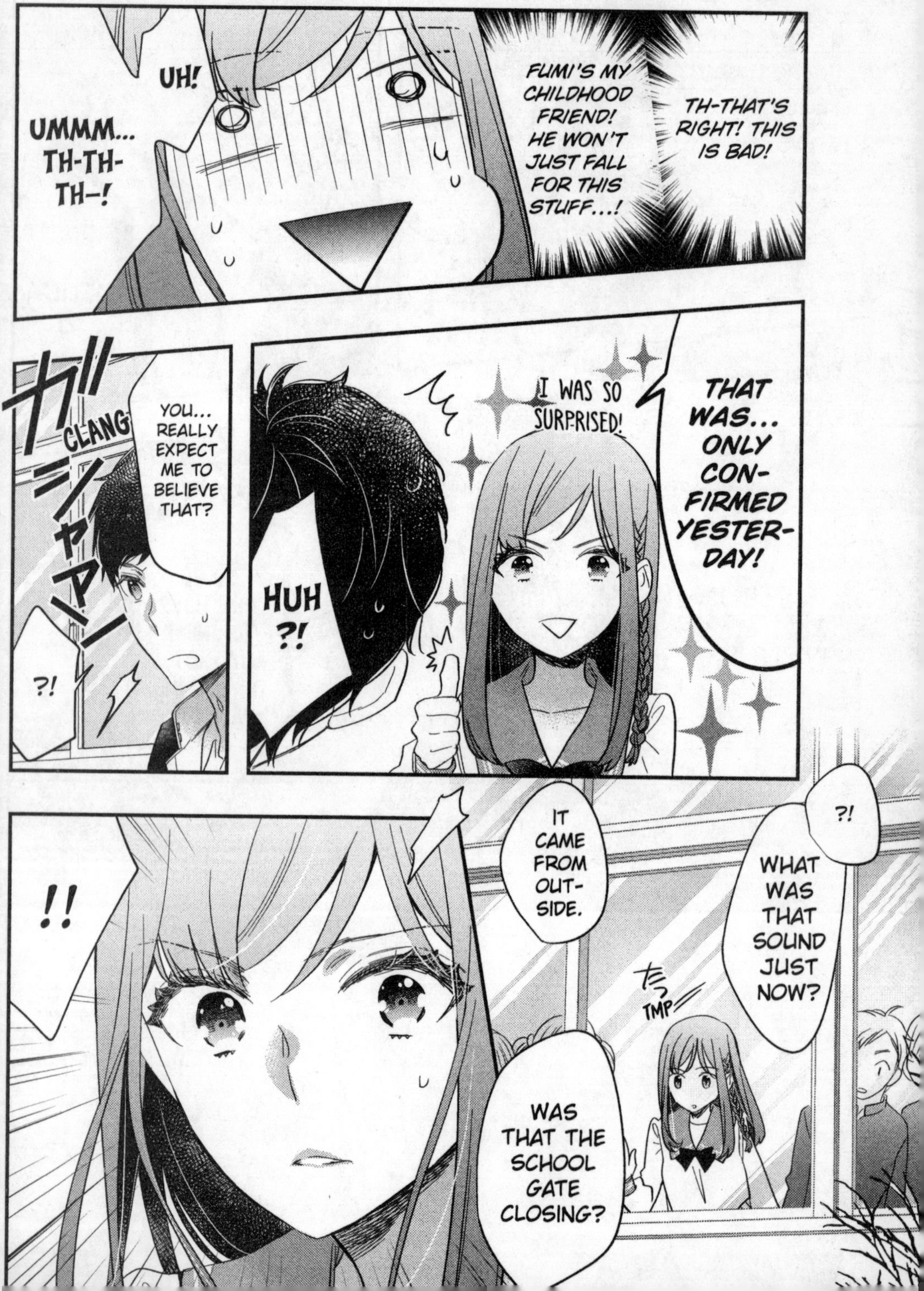
TH-THAT'S RIGHT! THIS IS BAD!
FUMI'S MY CHILDHOOD FRIEND! HE WON'T JUST FALL FOR THIS STUFF...!
UH!
UMMM... TH-TH-TH–!
THAT WAS... ONLY CON-FIRMED YESTER-DAY!
I WAS SO SURPRISED!
HUH?!
YOU... REALLY EXPECT ME TO BELIEVE THAT?
CLANG
?!
?!
WHAT WAS THAT SOUND JUST NOW?
TMP
IT CAME FROM OUT-SIDE.
WAS THAT THE SCHOOL GATE CLOSING?
!!

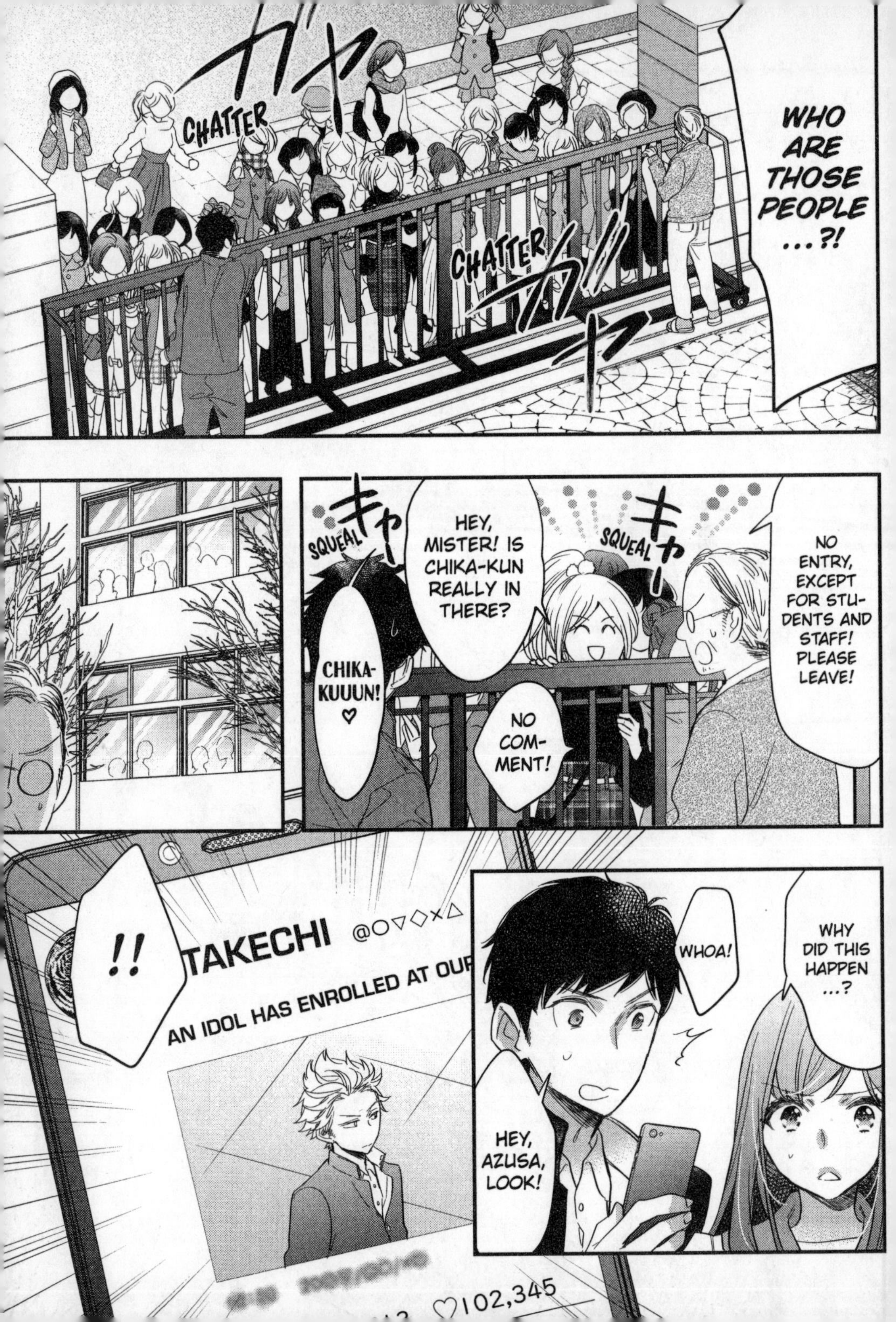
WHO ARE THOSE PEOPLE ...?!
CHATTER
CHATTER
NO ENTRY, EXCEPT FOR STUDENTS AND STAFF! PLEASE LEAVE!
SQUEAL
HEY, MISTER! IS CHIKA-KUN REALLY IN THERE?
SQUEAL
CHIKA-KUUUN! ♡
NO COMMENT!
WHY DID THIS HAPPEN ...?
WHOA!
HEY, AZUSA, LOOK!
!!
TAKECHI @○▽◇×△
AN IDOL HAS ENROLLED AT OUR
♡102,345

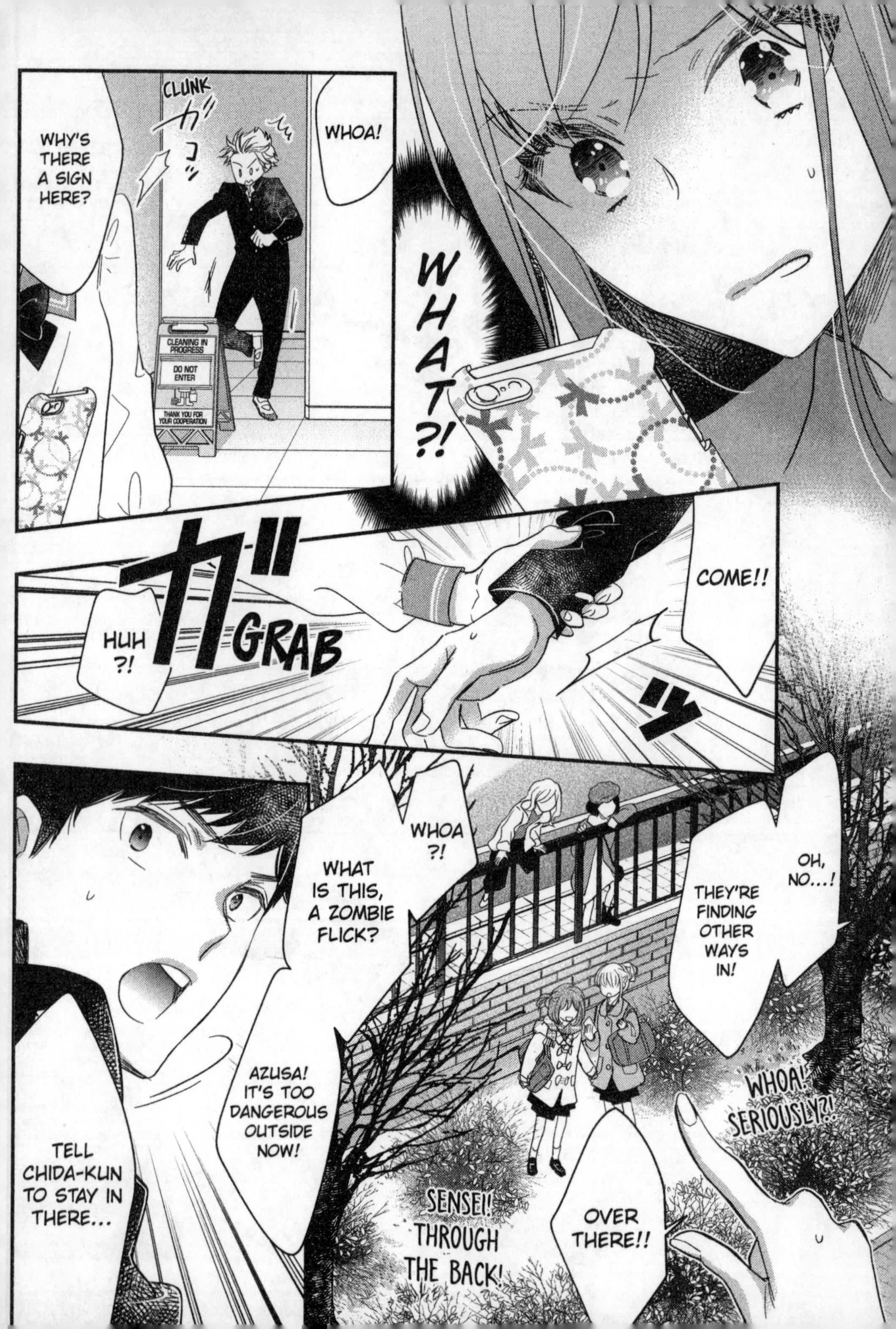
WHAT?!
WHOA!
CLUNK
WHY'S THERE A SIGN HERE?
CLEANING IN PROGRESS
DO NOT ENTER
THANK YOU FOR YOUR COOPERATION
COME!!
GRAB
HUH?!
OH, NO...!
THEY'RE FINDING OTHER WAYS IN!
WHOA?!
WHAT IS THIS, A ZOMBIE FLICK?
WHOA! SERIOUSLY?!
OVER THERE!!
SENSEI! THROUGH THE BACK!
AZUSA! IT'S TOO DANGEROUS OUTSIDE NOW!
TELL CHIDA-KUN TO STAY IN THERE...

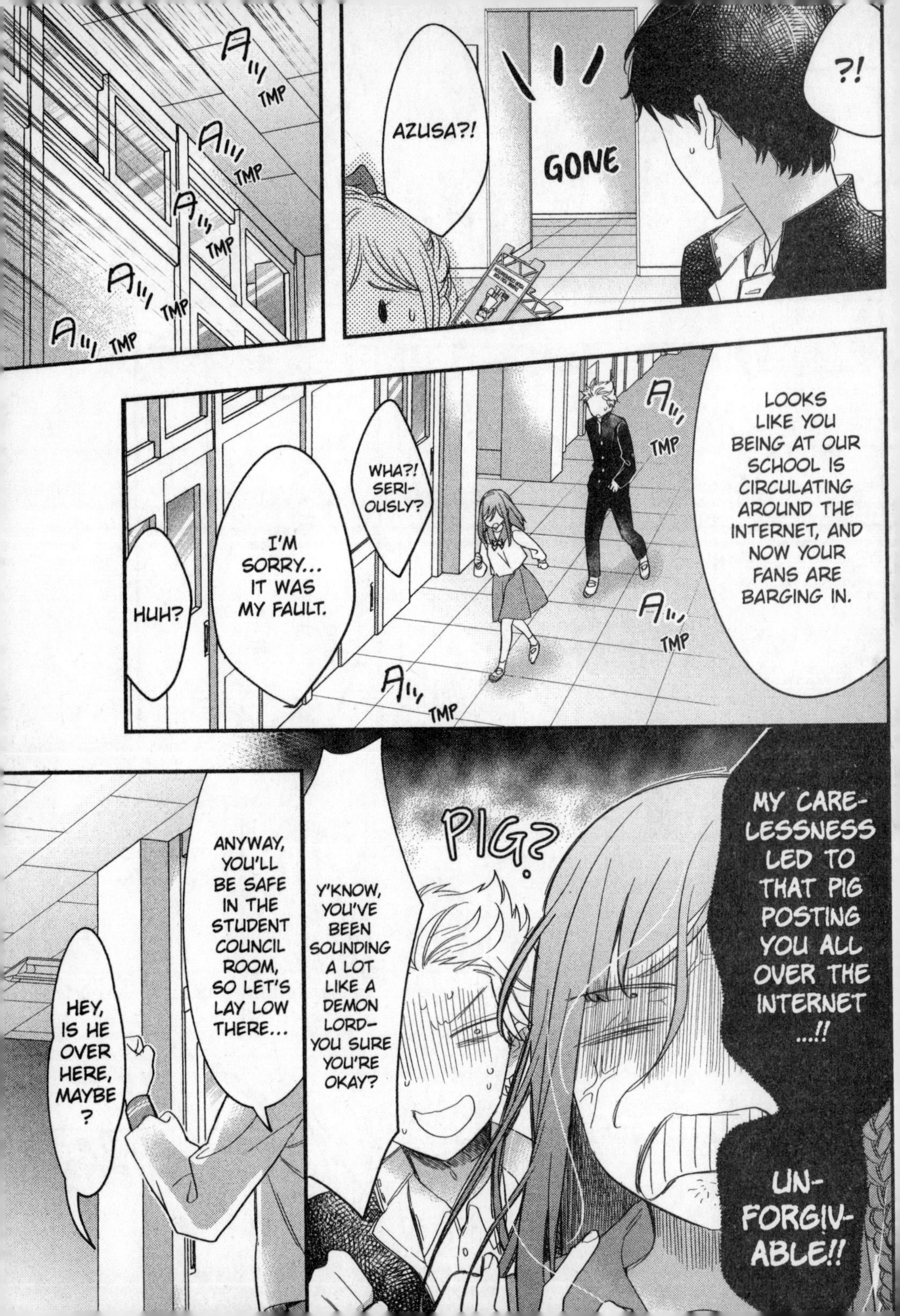
?!
GONE
AZUSA?!
A TMP
A TMP
A TMP
A TMP
A TMP
LOOKS LIKE YOU BEING AT OUR SCHOOL IS CIRCULATING AROUND THE INTERNET, AND NOW YOUR FANS ARE BARGING IN.
A TMP
A TMP
A TMP
WHA?! SERI-OUSLY?
I'M SORRY... IT WAS MY FAULT.
HUH?
MY CARE-LESSNESS LED TO THAT PIG POSTING YOU ALL OVER THE INTERNET ...!!
PIG?
UN-FORGIV-ABLE!!
Y'KNOW, YOU'VE BEEN SOUNDING A LOT LIKE A DEMON LORD– YOU SURE YOU'RE OKAY?
ANYWAY, YOU'LL BE SAFE IN THE STUDENT COUNCIL ROOM, SO LET'S LAY LOW THERE...
HEY, IS HE OVER HERE, MAYBE ?

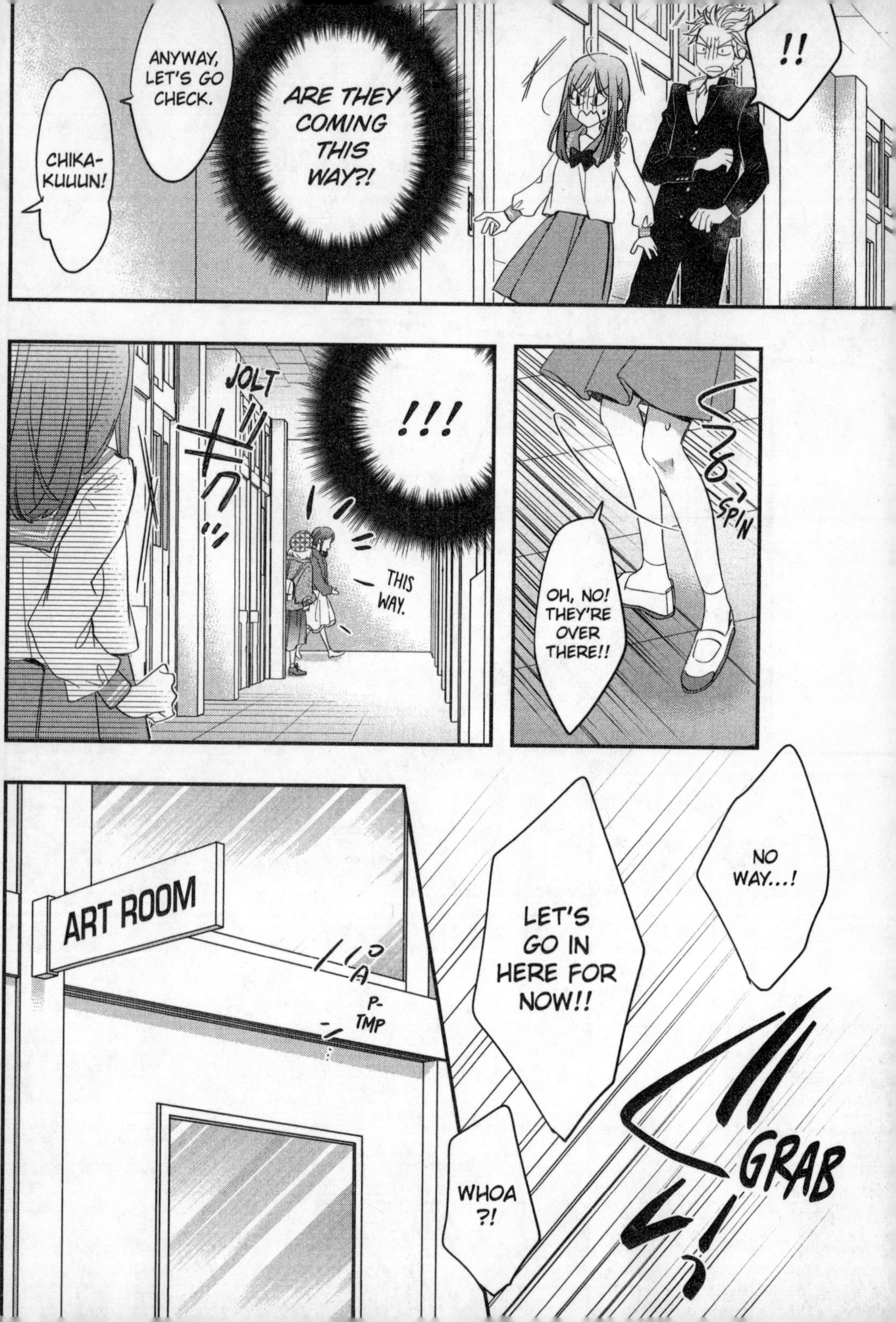
!!
ARE THEY COMING THIS WAY?!
ANYWAY, LET'S GO CHECK.
CHIKA-KUUUN!
SPIN
OH, NO! THEY'RE OVER THERE!!
!!!
JOLT
THIS WAY.
NO WAY...!
LET'S GO IN HERE FOR NOW!!
GRAB
WHOA ?!
ART ROOM
P-TMP

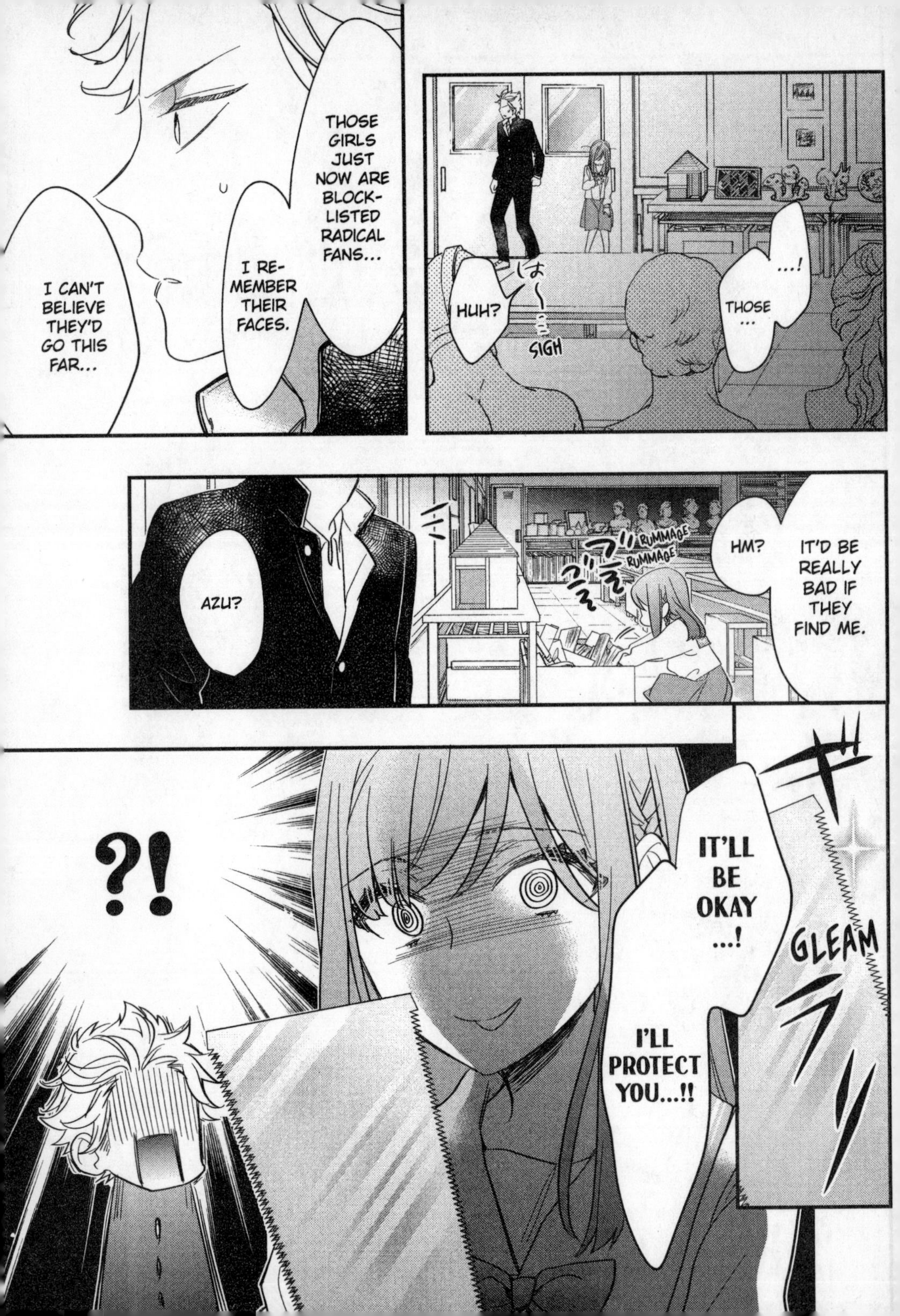
...!
THOSE ...
HUH?
SIGH
THOSE GIRLS JUST NOW ARE BLOCK-LISTED RADICAL FANS...
I RE-MEMBER THEIR FACES.
I CAN'T BELIEVE THEY'D GO THIS FAR...
IT'D BE REALLY BAD IF THEY FIND ME.
HM?
RUMMAGE RUMMAGE
AZU?
IT'LL BE OKAY ...!
GLEAM
I'LL PROTECT YOU...!!
?!

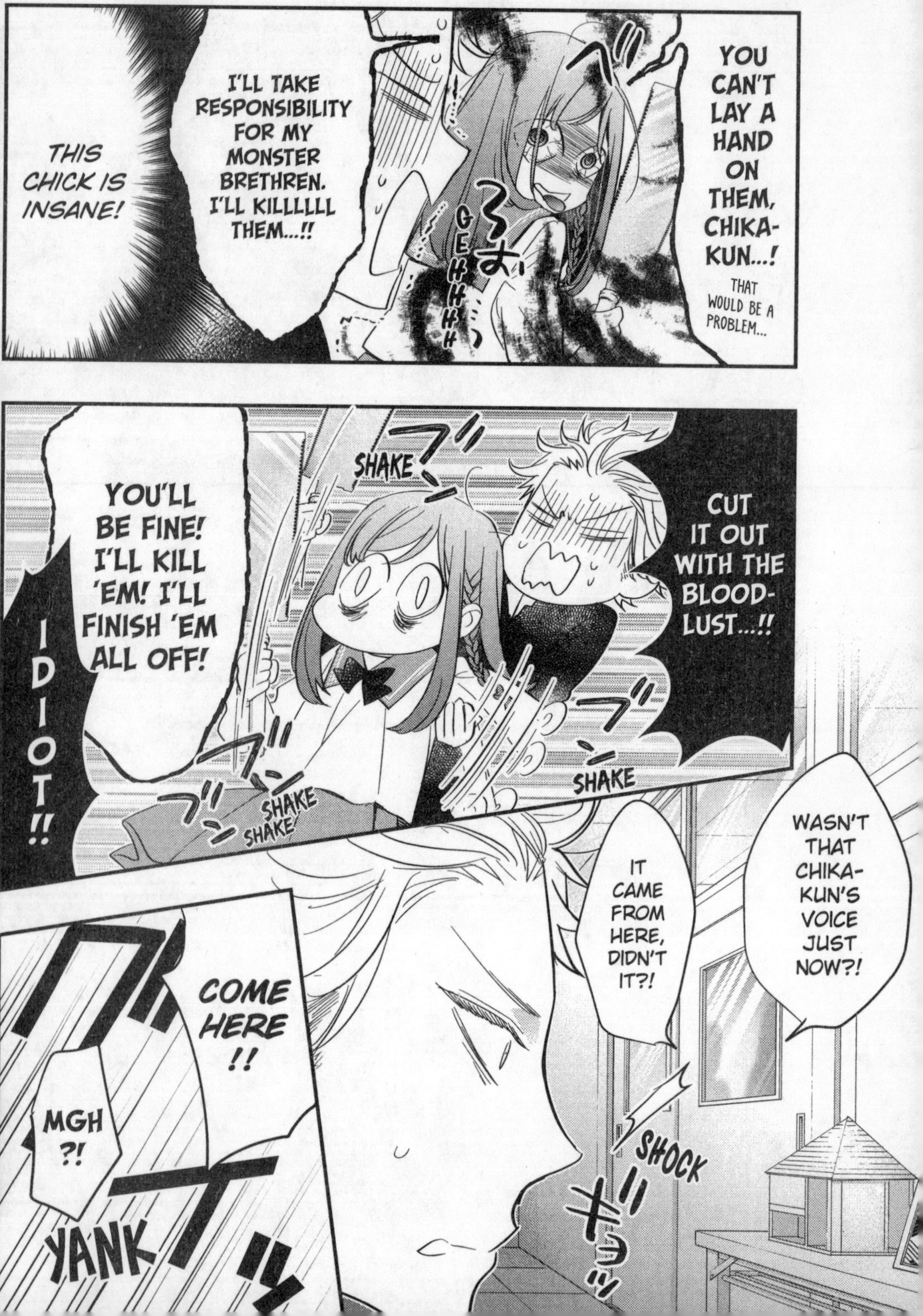
YOU CAN'T LAY A HAND ON THEM, CHIKA-KUN...!
THAT WOULD BE A PROBLEM...
GEHHHHHH
I'LL TAKE RESPONSIBILITY FOR MY MONSTER BRETHREN. I'LL KILLLLLL THEM...!!
THIS CHICK IS INSANE!
CUT IT OUT WITH THE BLOOD-LUST...!!
SHAKE
YOU'LL BE FINE! I'LL KILL 'EM! I'LL FINISH 'EM ALL OFF!
IDIOT!!
SHAKE
SHAKE
SHAKE
WASN'T THAT CHIKA-KUN'S VOICE JUST NOW?!
IT CAME FROM HERE, DIDN'T IT?!
SHOCK
COME HERE!!
MGH?!
YANK

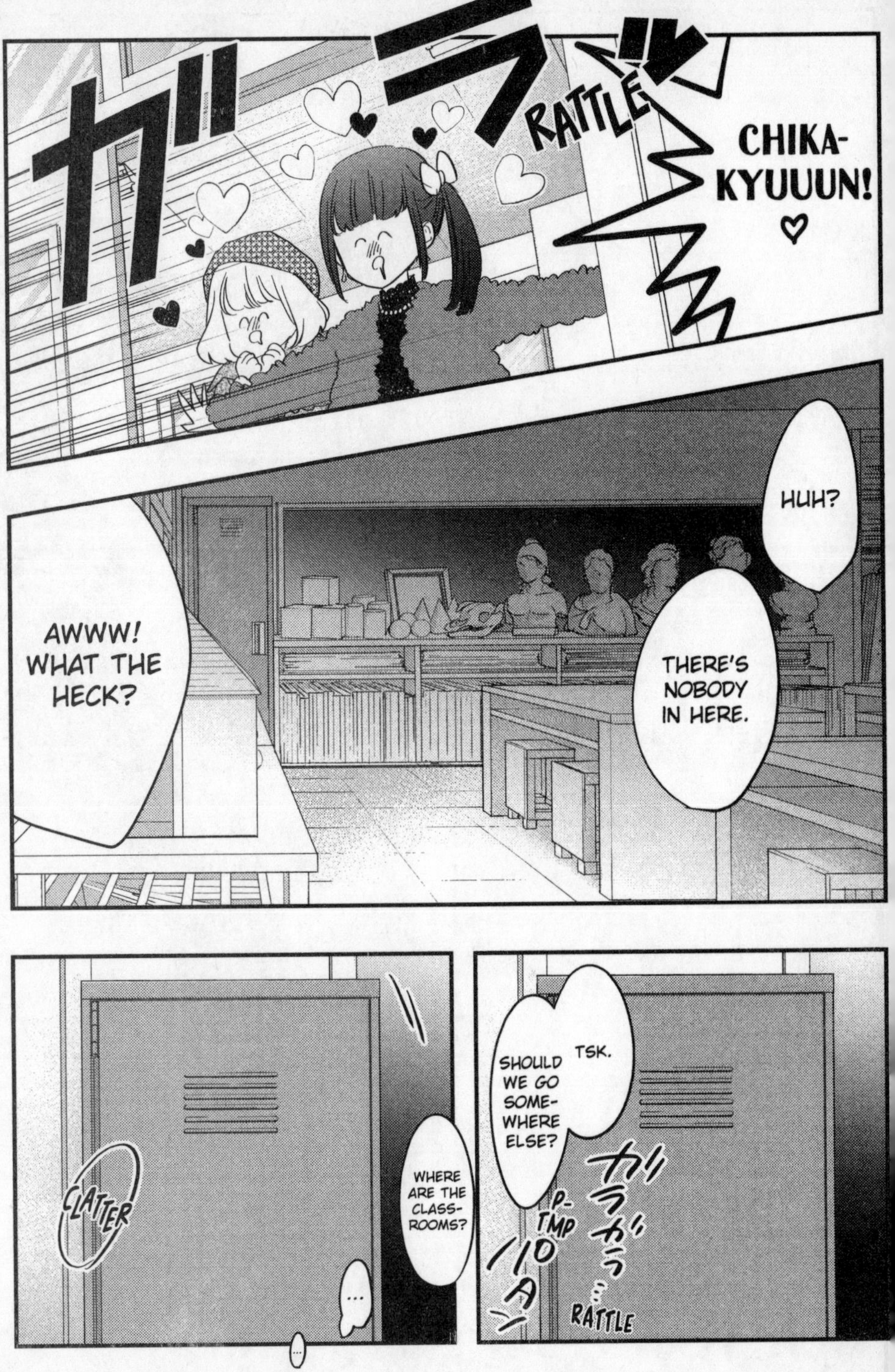
RATTLE
CHIKA-KYUUUN! ♡
HUH?
THERE'S NOBODY IN HERE.
AWWW! WHAT THE HECK?
TSK.
SHOULD WE GO SOME-WHERE ELSE?
WHERE ARE THE CLASS-ROOMS?
P-TMP
RATTLE
...
CLATTER
...

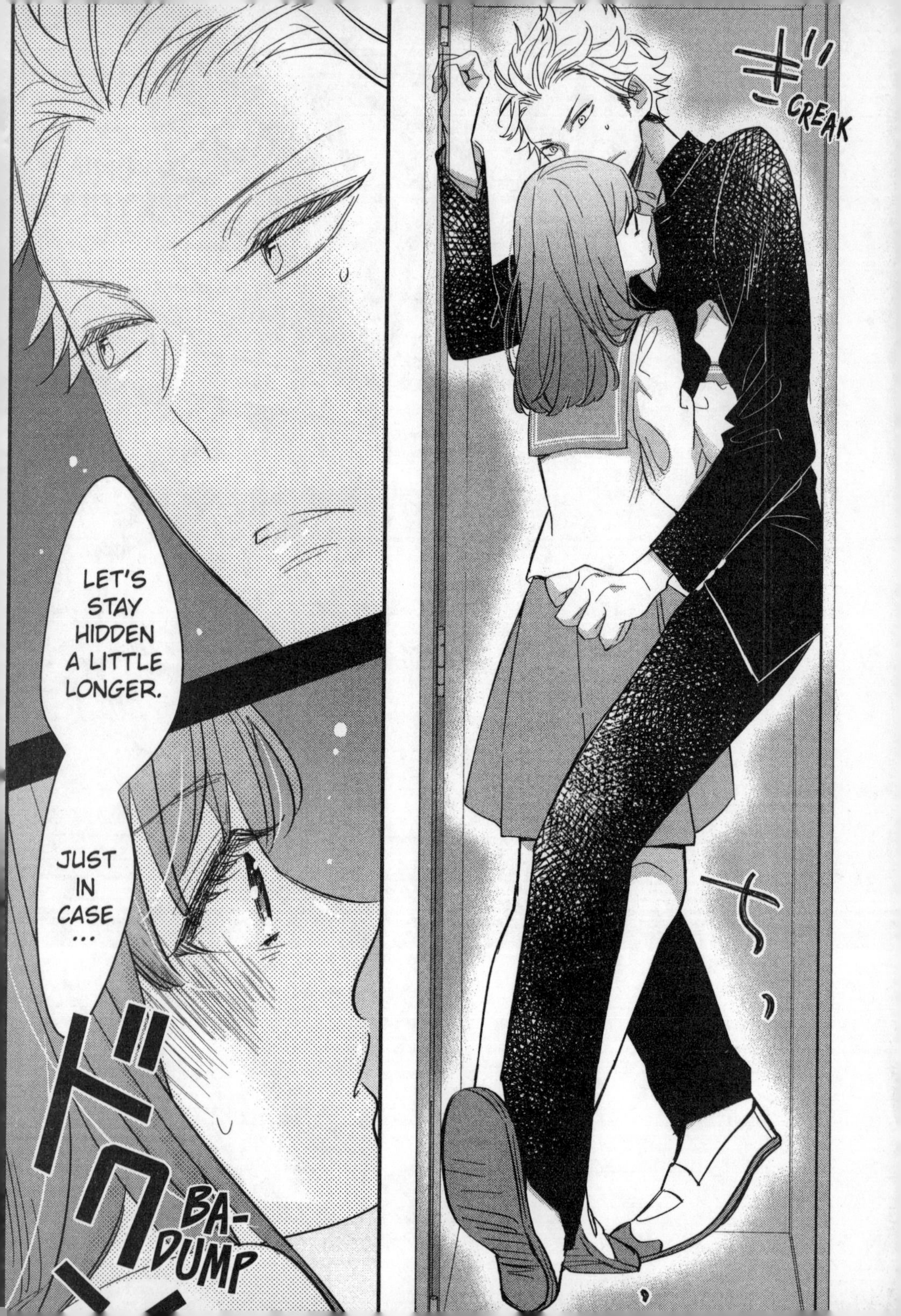
CREAK
LET'S STAY HIDDEN A LITTLE LONGER.
JUST IN CASE...
BA-DUMP

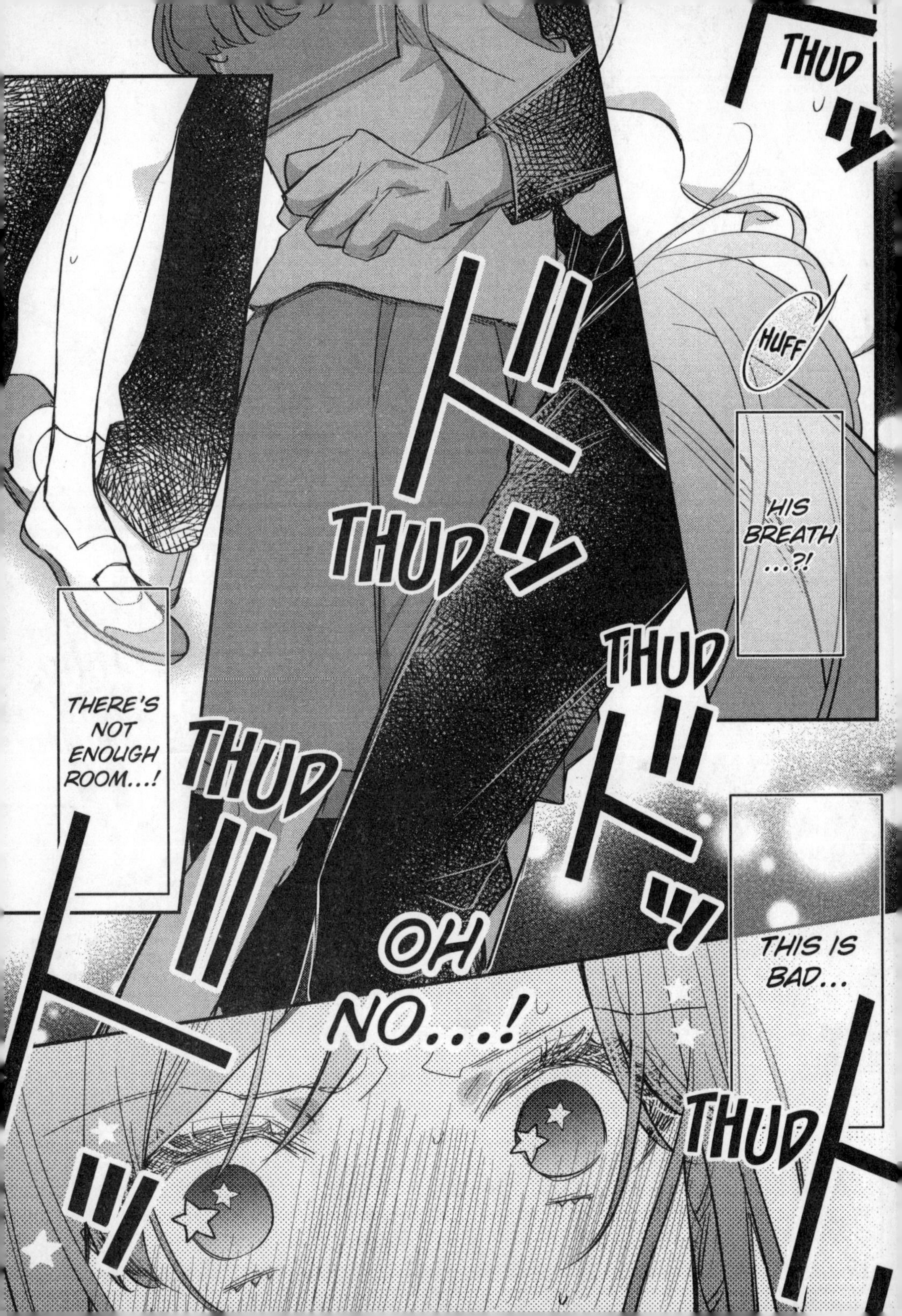
THUD
HUFF
HIS BREATH...?!
THUD
THERE'S NOT ENOUGH ROOM...!
THUD
THUD
THIS IS BAD...
THUD
OH NO...!

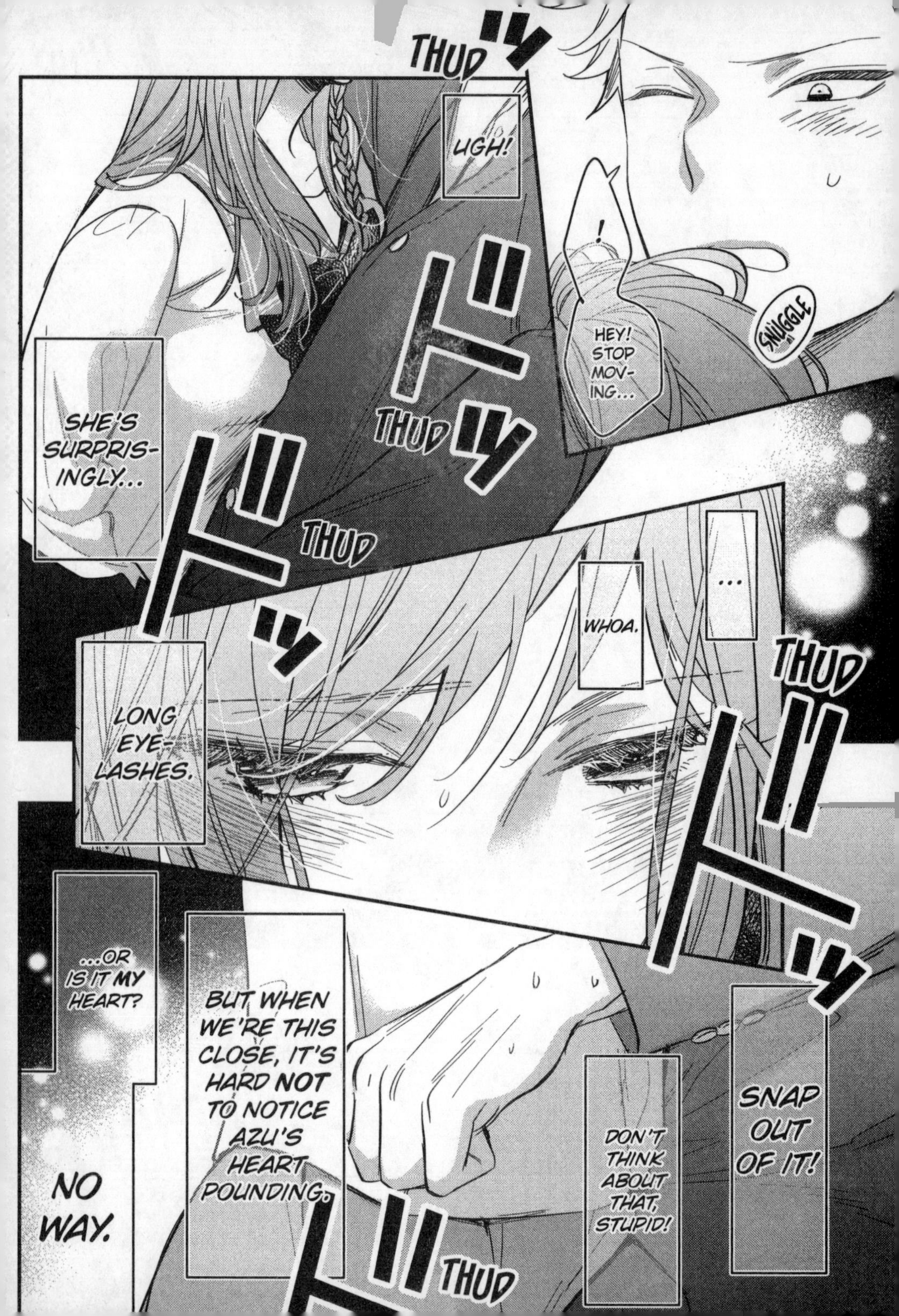
THUD
!
HEY! STOP MOVING...
SNUGGLE
UGH!
THUD
THUD
SHE'S SURPRISINGLY...
...
WHOA.
THUD
LONG EYELASHES.
SNAP OUT OF IT!
DON'T THINK ABOUT THAT, STUPID!
BUT WHEN WE'RE THIS CLOSE, IT'S HARD NOT TO NOTICE AZU'S HEART POUNDING.
...OR IS IT MY HEART?
NO WAY.
THUD

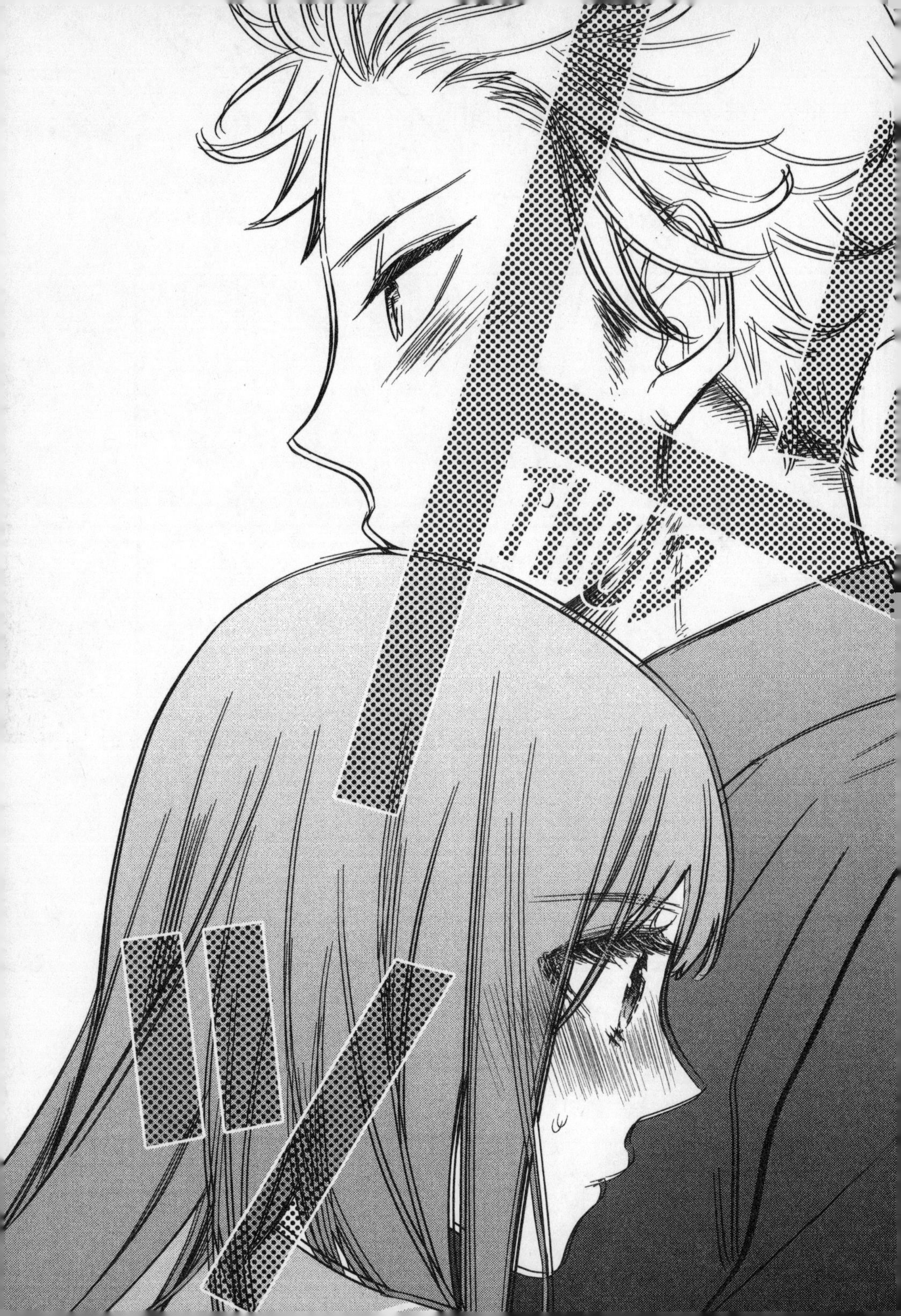
THUP

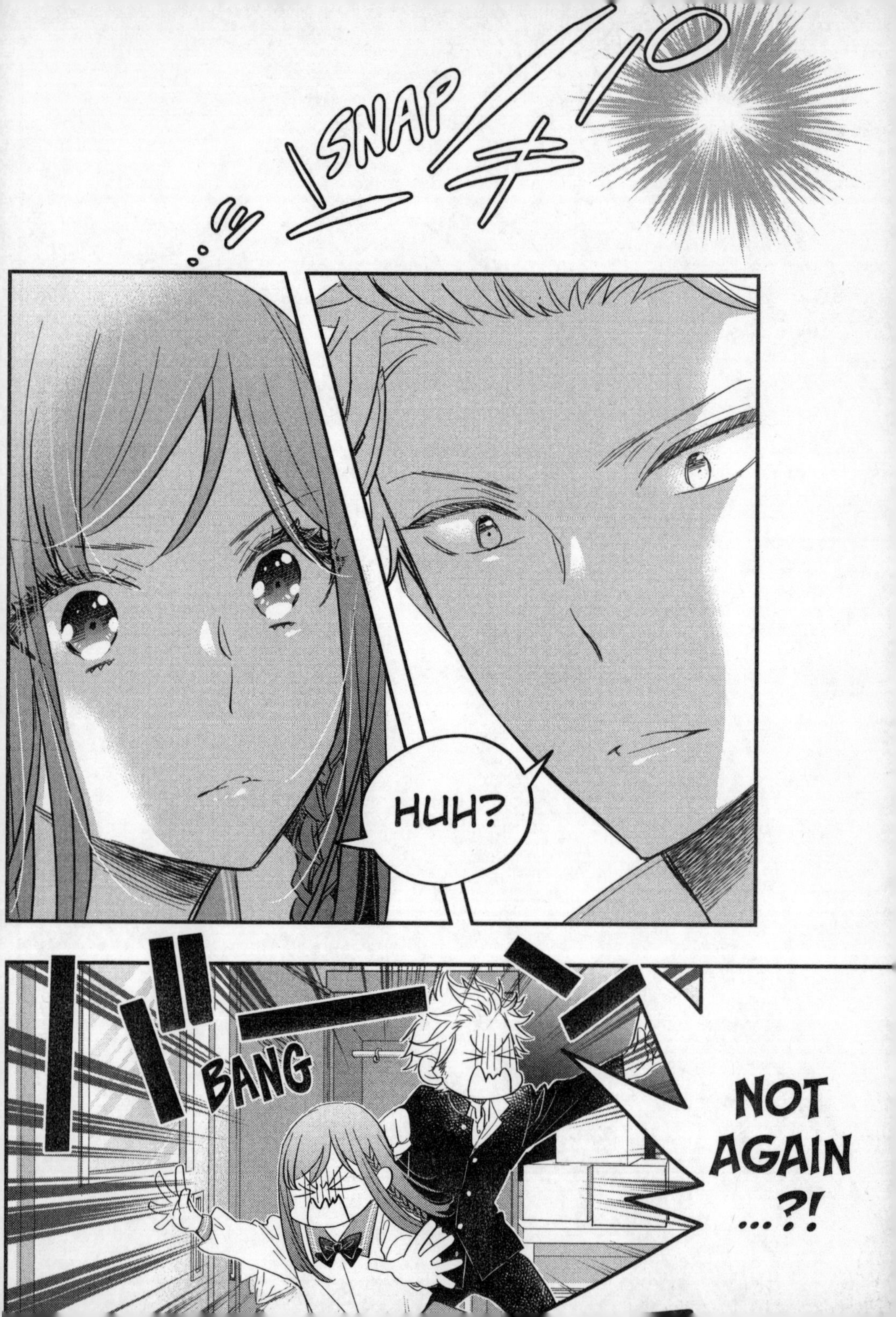
SNAP
...?!
HUH?
BANG
NOT AGAIN ...?!

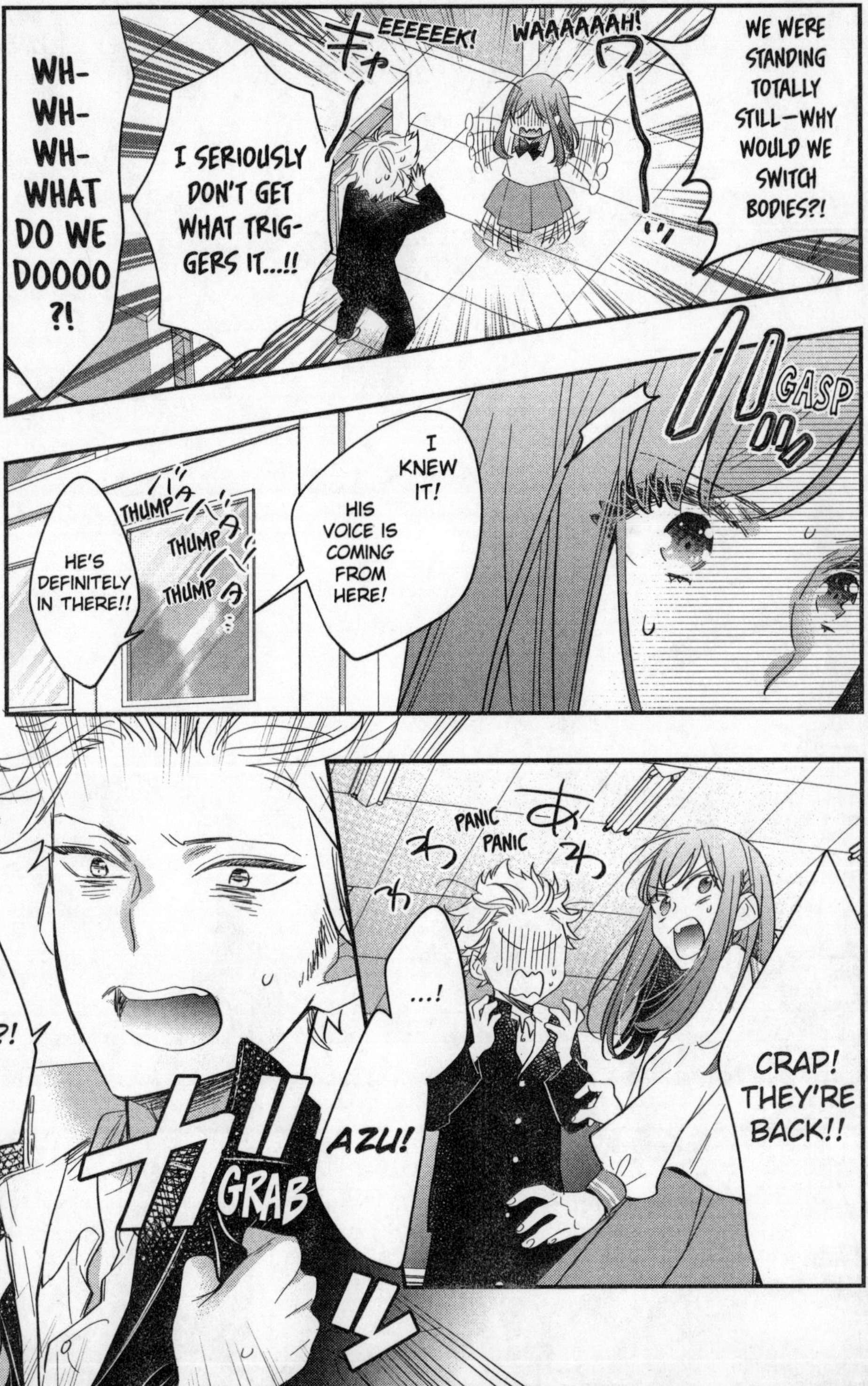
WE WERE STANDING TOTALLY STILL—WHY WOULD WE SWITCH BODIES?!
WAAAAAAH!
EEEEEEK!
I SERIOUSLY DON'T GET WHAT TRIG-GERS IT...!!
WH-WH-WH-WHAT DO WE DOOOO?!
GASP
I KNEW IT!
HIS VOICE IS COMING FROM HERE!
THUMP
THUMP
THUMP
HE'S DEFINITELY IN THERE!!
CRAP! THEY'RE BACK!!
PANIC
PANIC
...!
AZU!
GRAB
YES?!

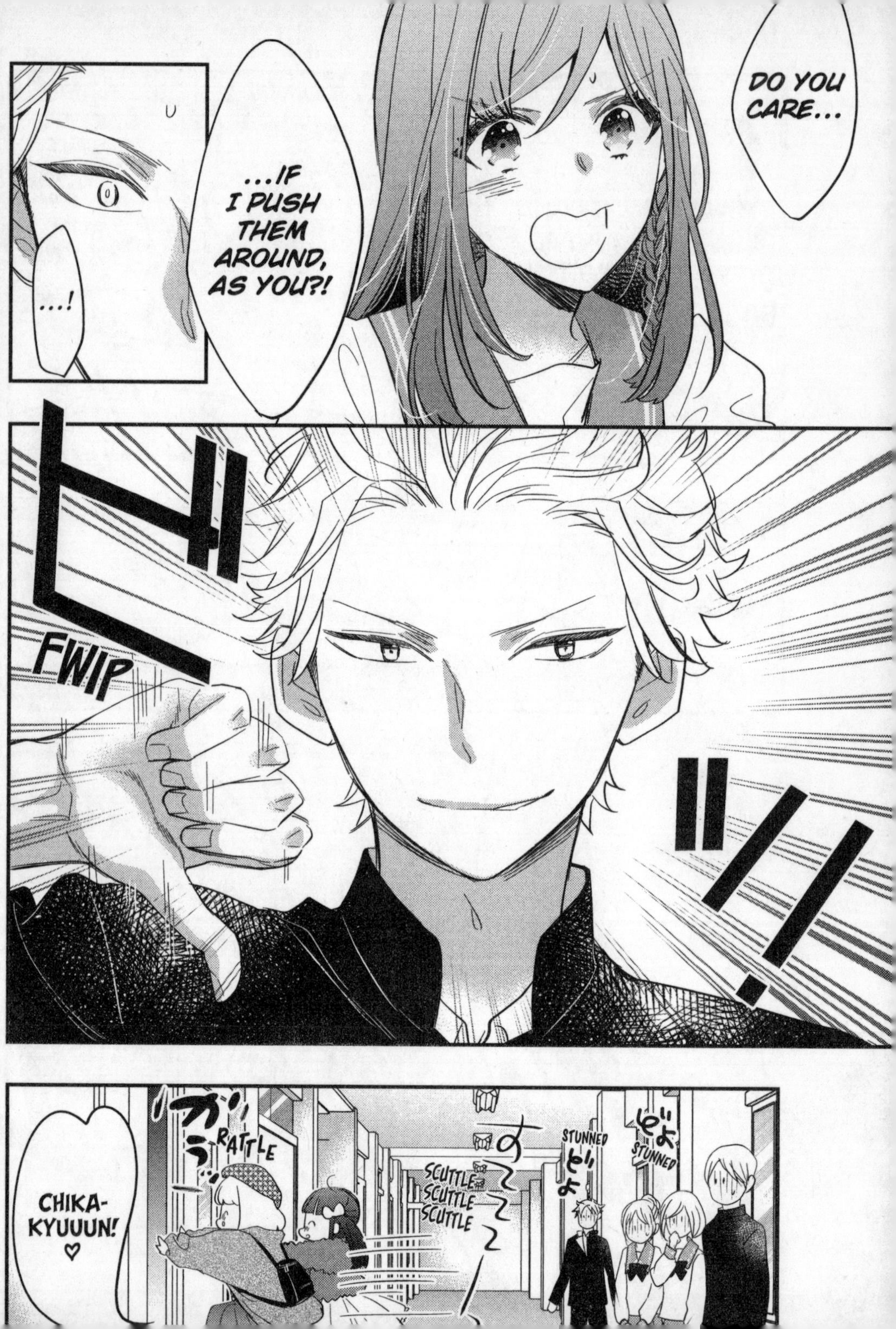
DO YOU CARE...
...IF I PUSH THEM AROUND, AS YOU?!
...!
FWIP
!!
STUNNED
STUNNED
SCUTTLE SCUTTLE SCUTTLE
RATTLE
CHIKA-KYUUUN! ♥

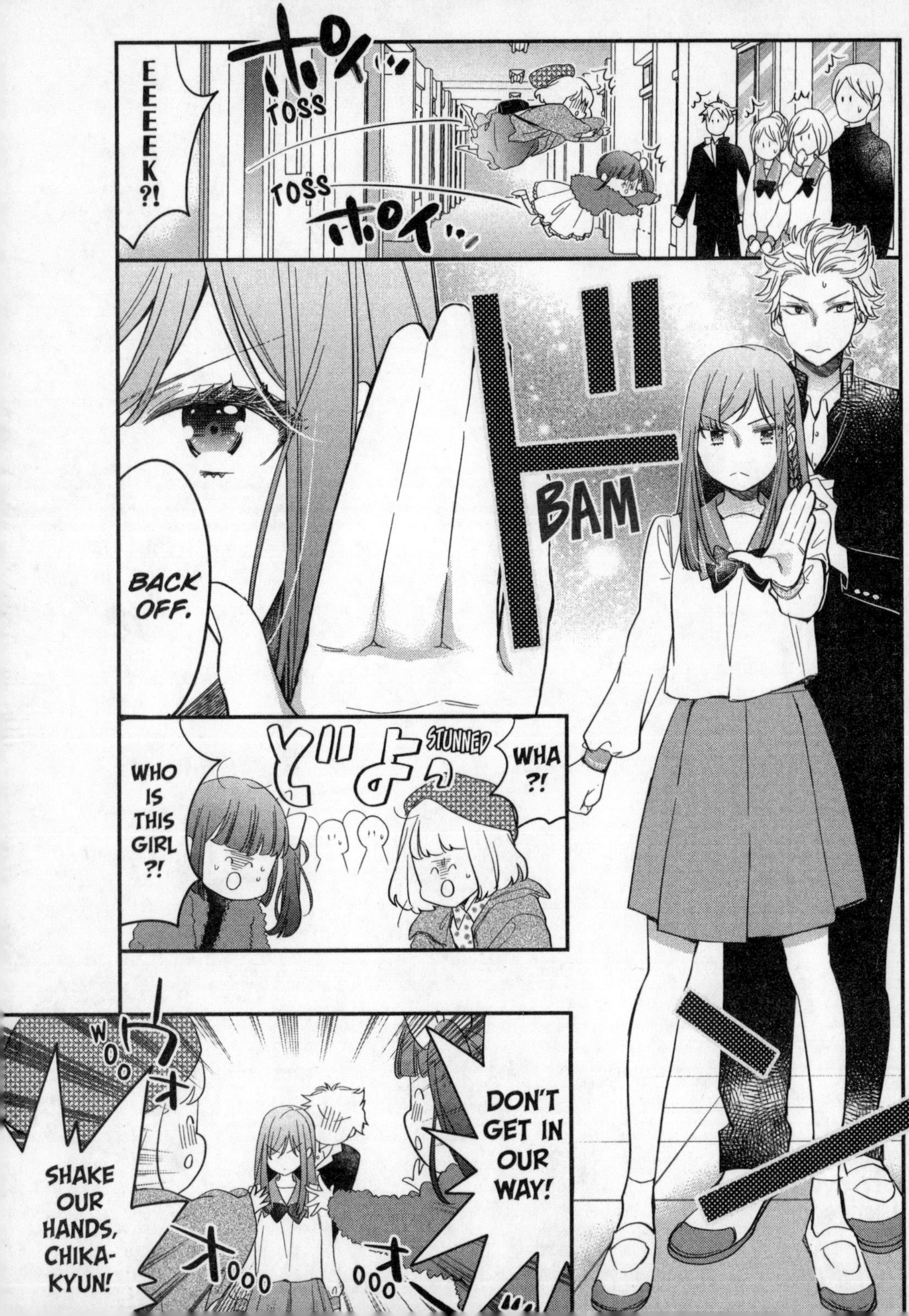

TOSS
TOSS
EEEEEK?!
BAM
BACK OFF.
STUNNED
WHA?!
WHO IS THIS GIRL?!
DON'T GET IN OUR WAY!
WOOO
SHAKE OUR HANDS, CHIKA-KYUN!
OOO
OOO

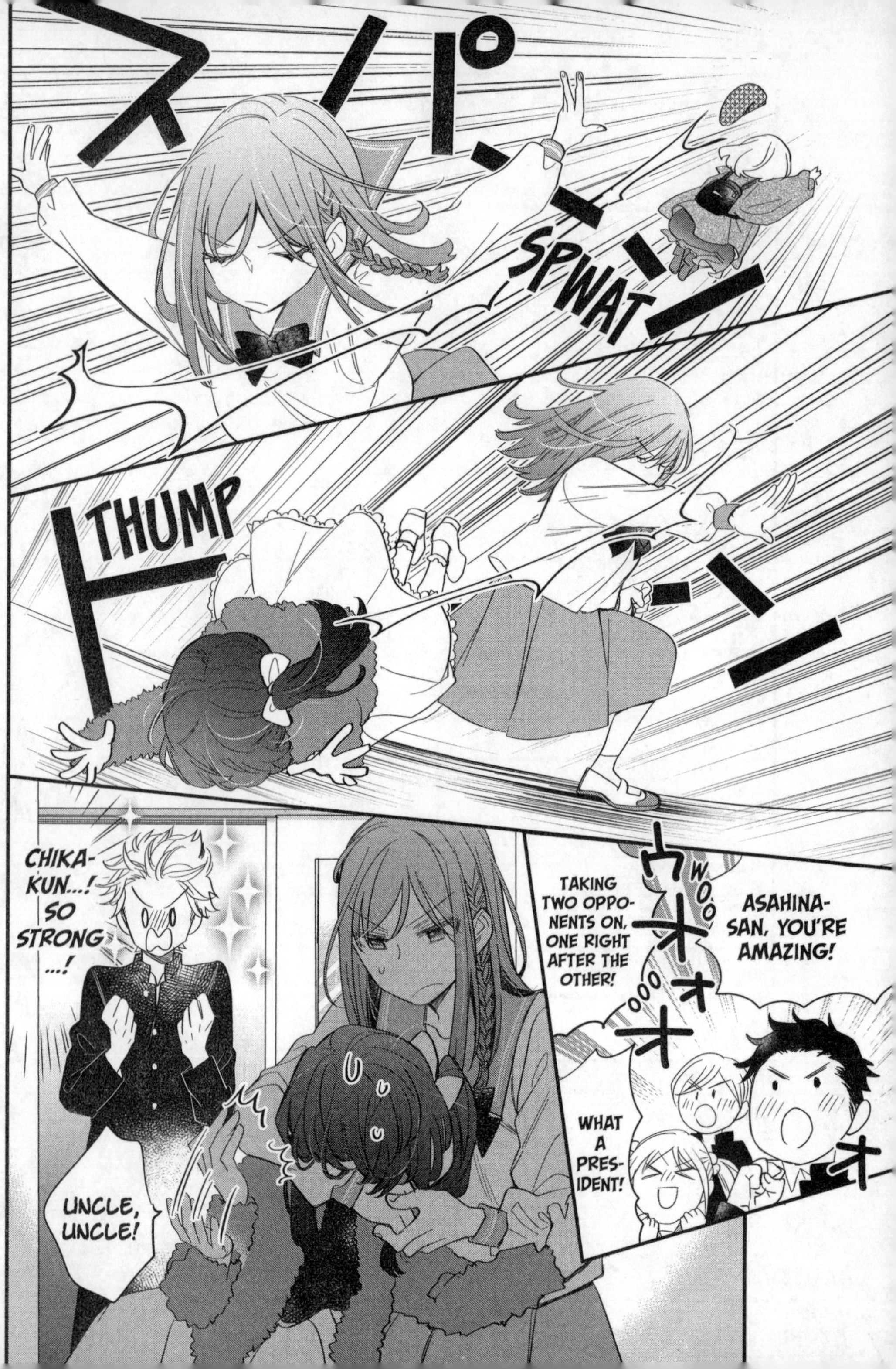
スパーン
SPWAT
ドーン
THUMP
ASAHINA-SAN, YOU'RE AMAZING!
ウオオオ
WOOO
TAKING TWO OPPONENTS ON, ONE RIGHT AFTER THE OTHER!
WHAT A PRES-IDENT!
CHIKA-KUN...! SO STRONG ...!
UNCLE, UNCLE!

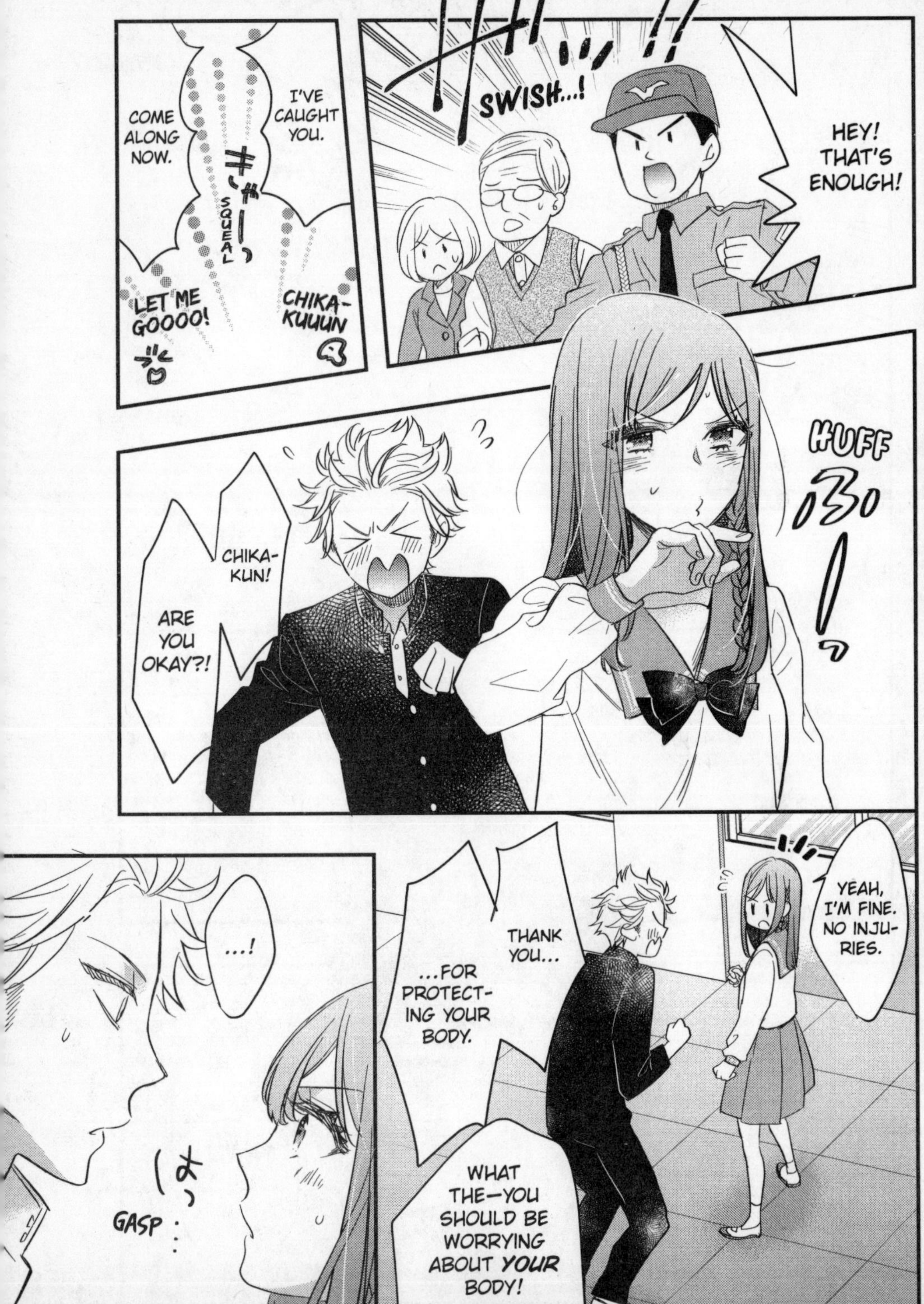
SWISH...!
HEY! THAT'S ENOUGH!
I'VE CAUGHT YOU.
COME ALONG NOW.
SQUEAL
CHIKA-KUUUN
LET ME GOOOO!
HUFF
CHIKA-KUN!
ARE YOU OKAY?!
YEAH, I'M FINE. NO INJU-RIES.
THANK YOU...
...FOR PROTECT-ING YOUR BODY.
WHAT THE—YOU SHOULD BE WORRYING ABOUT *YOUR* BODY!
...!
GASP

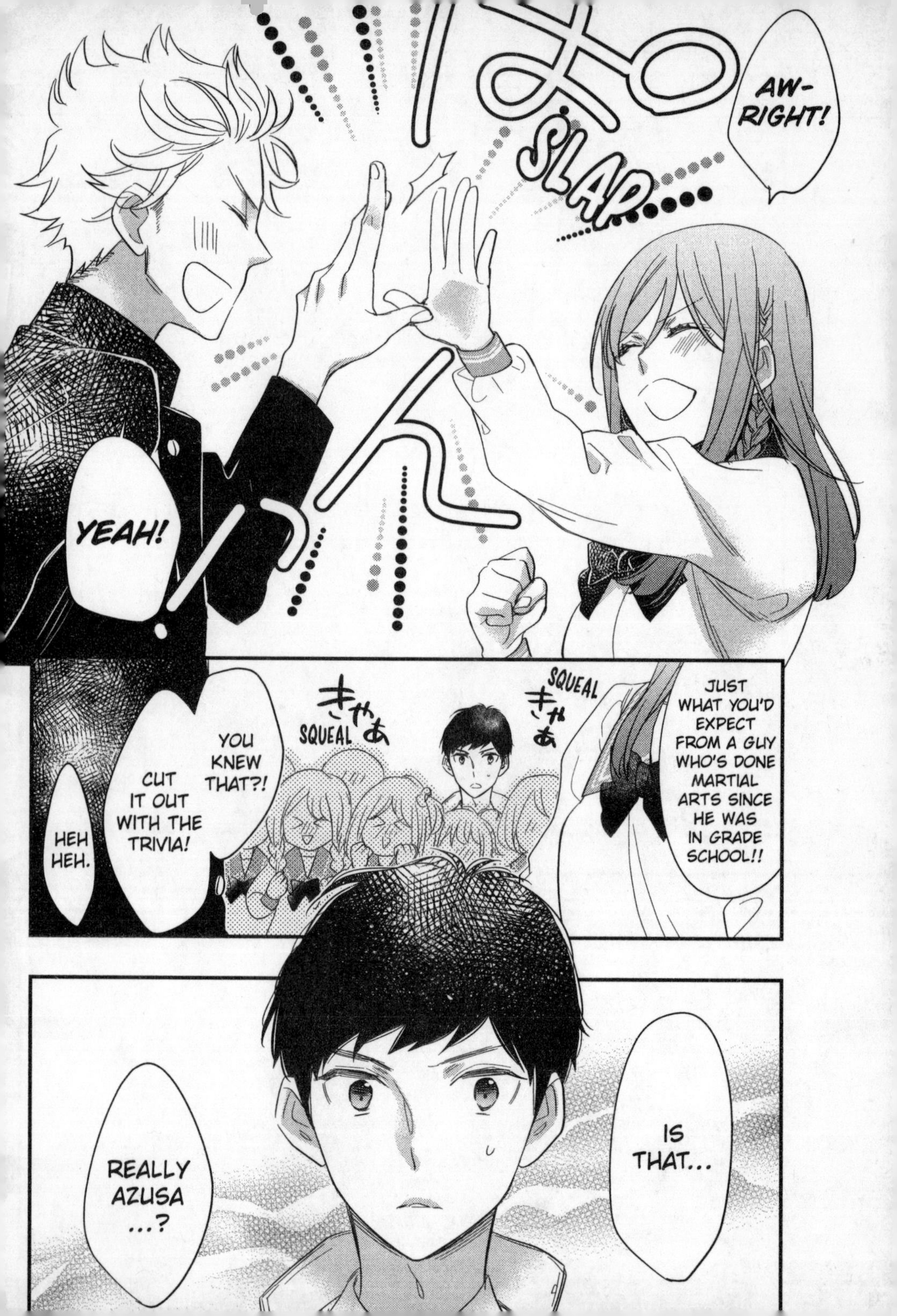
AW-RIGHT!
SLAP
YEAH!
JUST WHAT YOU'D EXPECT FROM A GUY WHO'S DONE MARTIAL ARTS SINCE HE WAS IN GRADE SCHOOL!!
SQUEAL
きゃあ
SQUEAL
きゃあ
YOU KNEW THAT?!
CUT IT OUT WITH THE TRIVIA!
HEH HEH.
IS THAT...
REALLY AZUSA ...?

R⇄CROSS

D!! STAR

AR⇄CROS

CROSSED

⇄CROSSE

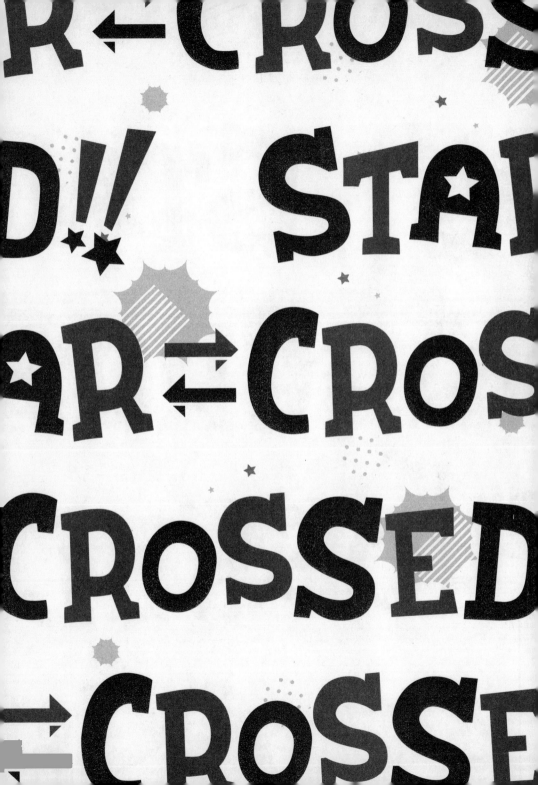

R⇄CROSS

D!! STAR

AR⇄CROS

CROSSED

⇄CROSSE

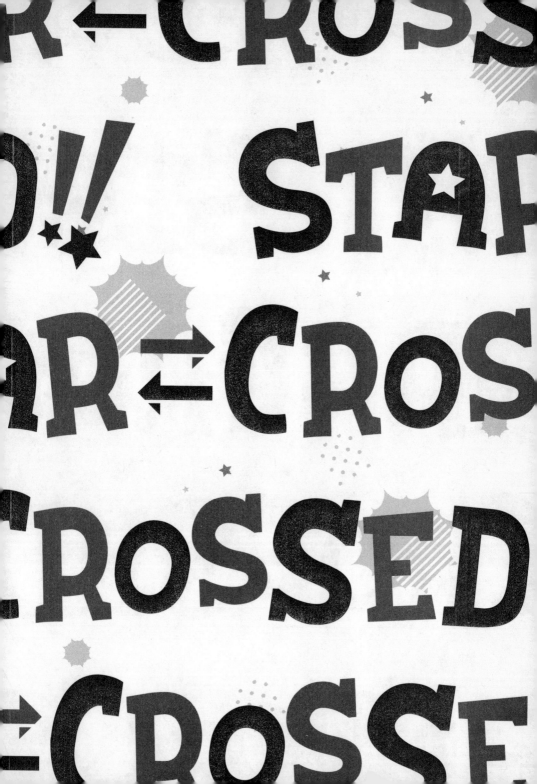

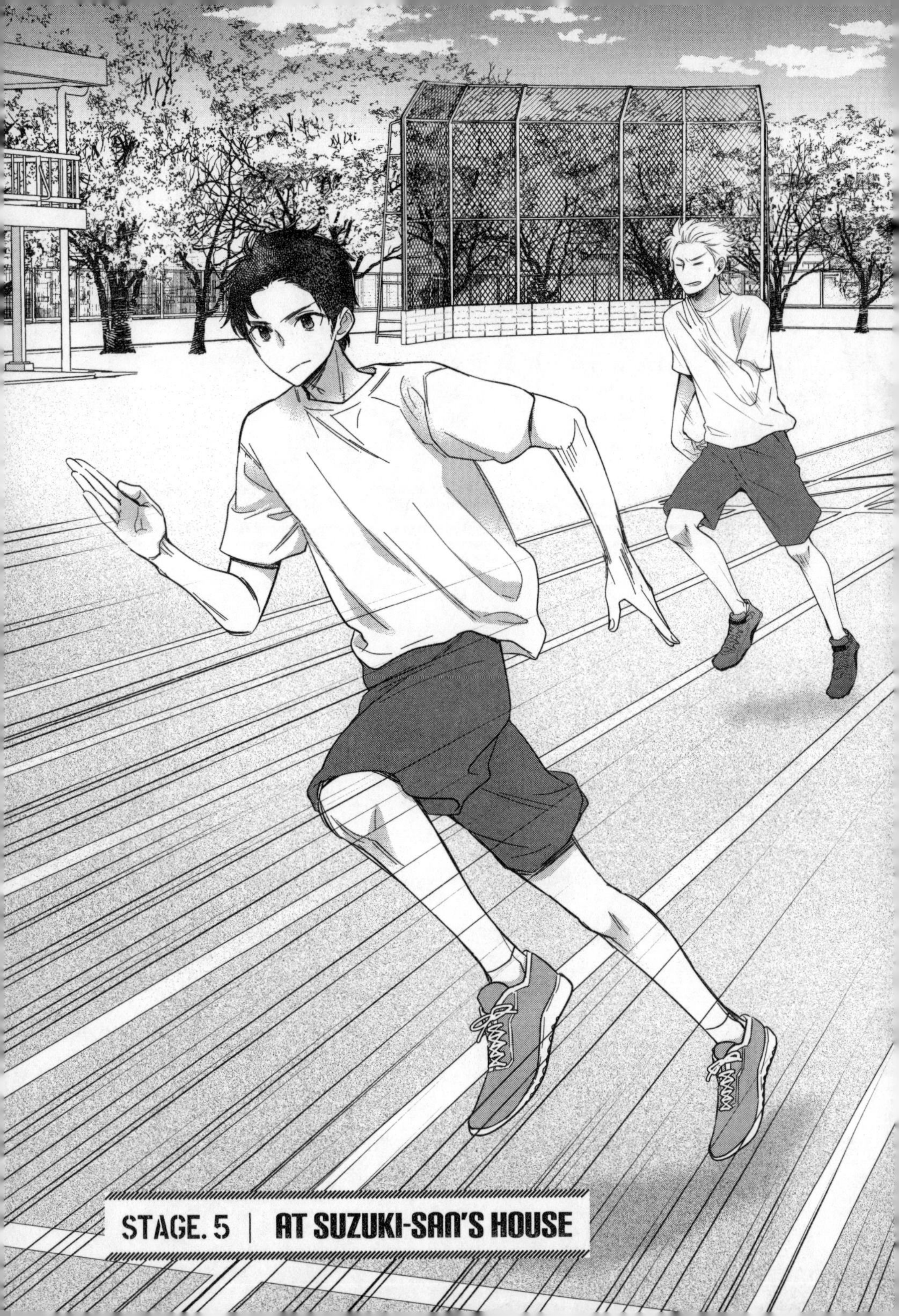
STAGE. 5 | AT SUZUKI-SAN'S HOUSE

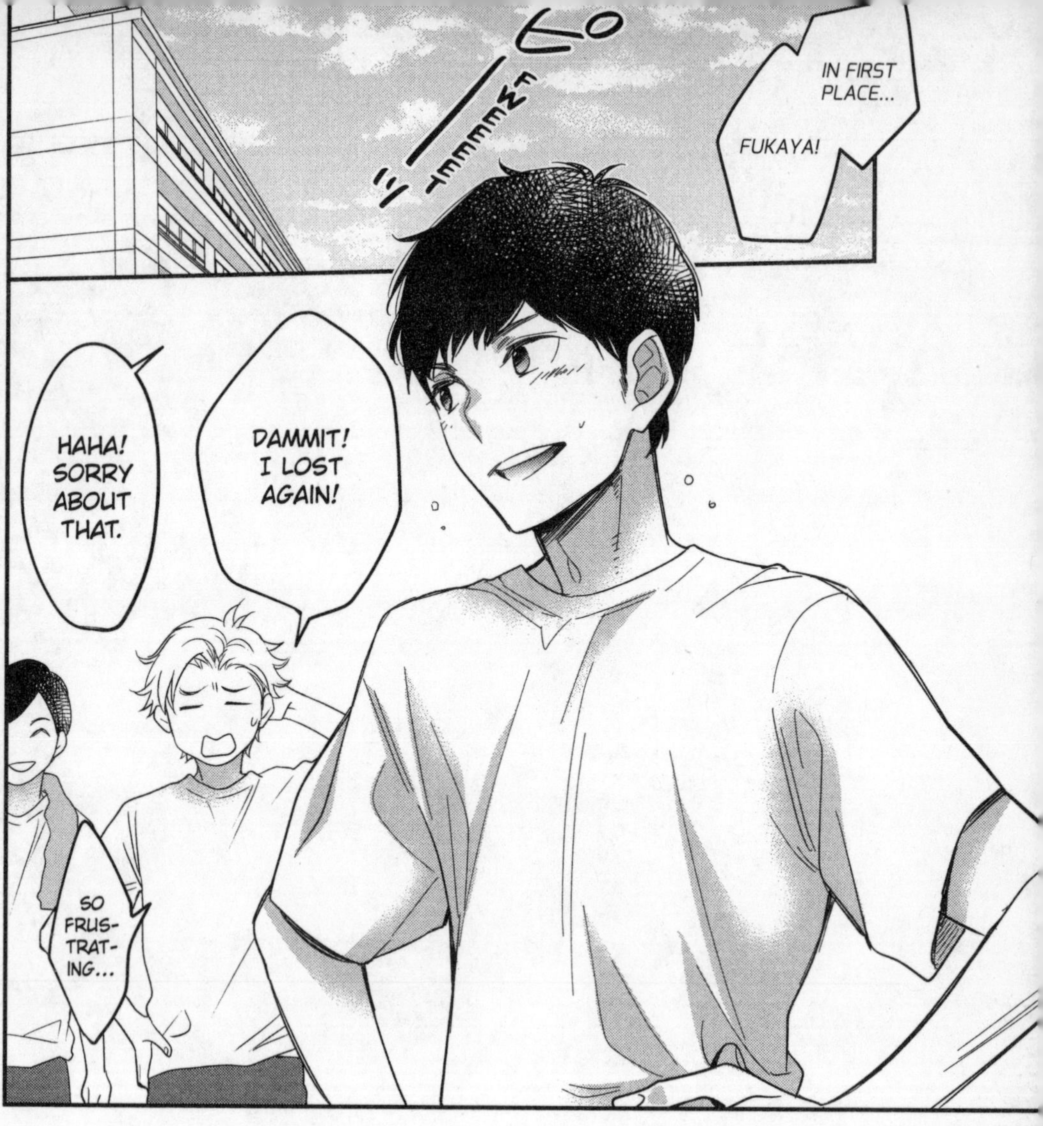
IN FIRST PLACE...
FUKAYA!
DAMMIT! I LOST AGAIN!
HAHA! SORRY ABOUT THAT.
SO FRUS-TRAT-ING...

STAR⇄CROSSED!!

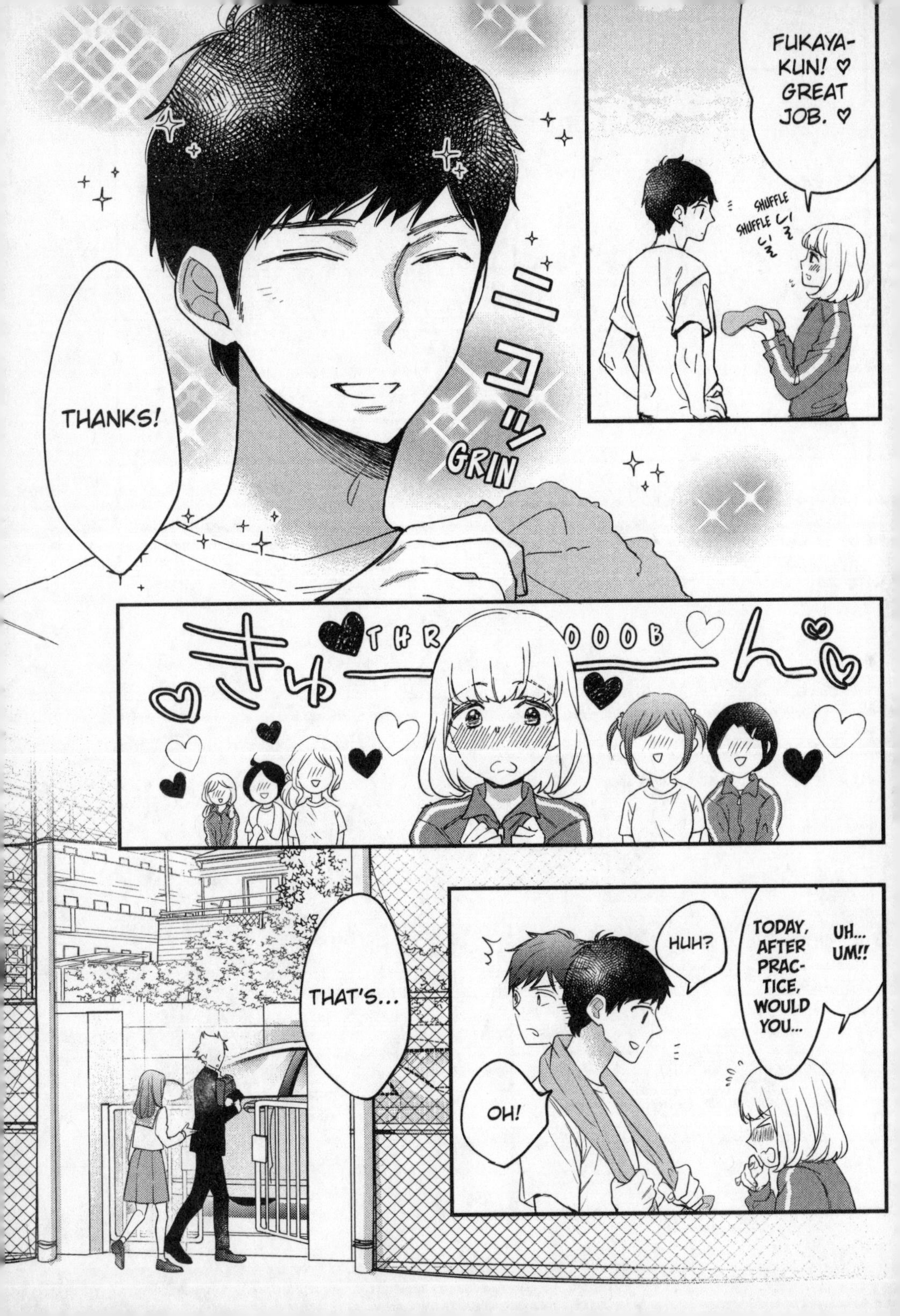
FUKAYA-KUN! ♡ GREAT JOB. ♡
SHUFFLE SHUFFLE
THANKS!
ニコッ
GRIN
きゅーーん
THR OOOB
UH... UM!!
TODAY, AFTER PRAC-TICE, WOULD YOU...
HUH?
OH!
THAT'S...

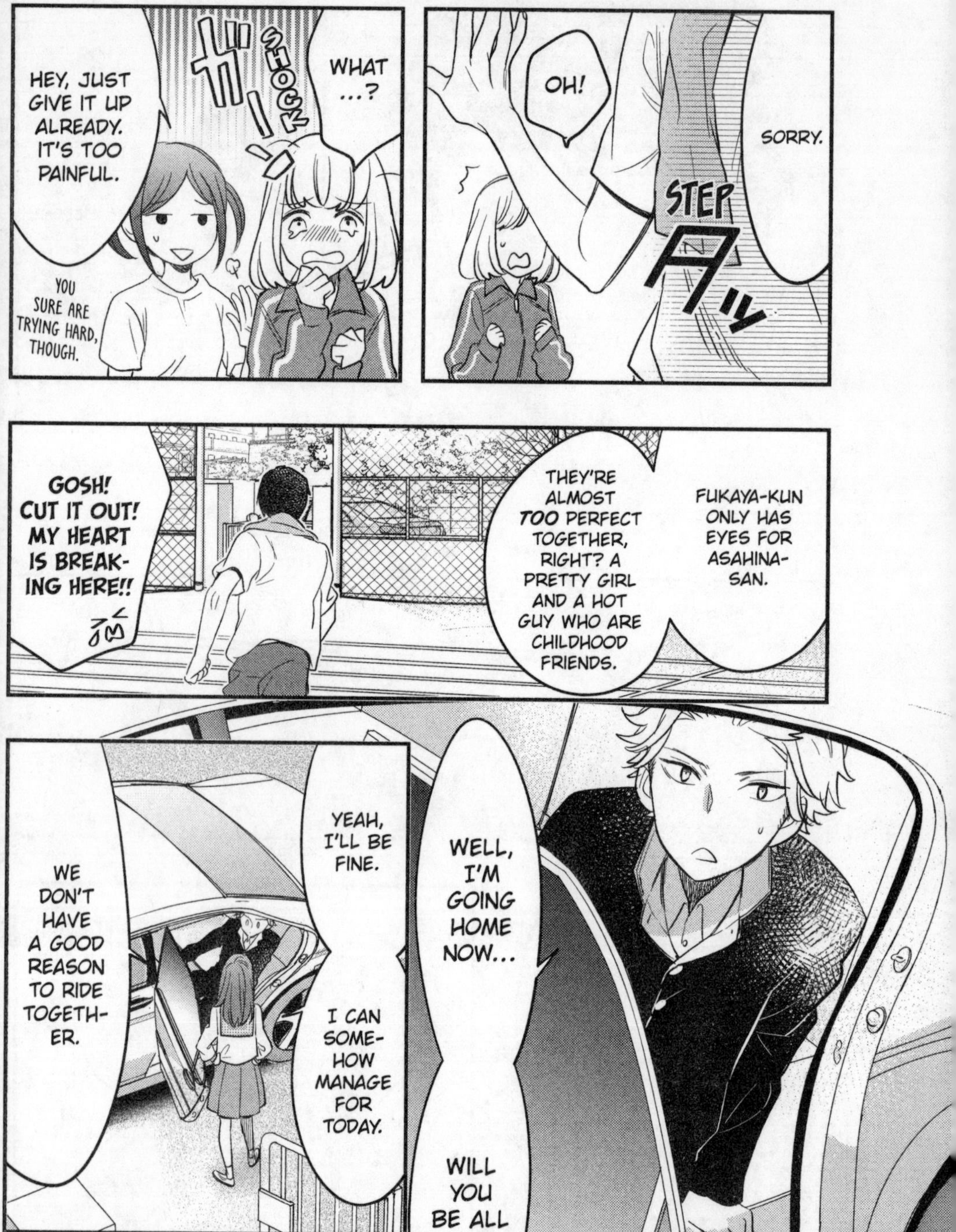
OH!
SORRY.
STEP
WHAT ...?
SHOCK
HEY, JUST GIVE IT UP ALREADY. IT'S TOO PAINFUL.
YOU SURE ARE TRYING HARD, THOUGH.
FUKAYA-KUN ONLY HAS EYES FOR ASAHINA-SAN.
THEY'RE ALMOST *TOO* PERFECT TOGETHER, RIGHT? A PRETTY GIRL AND A HOT GUY WHO ARE CHILDHOOD FRIENDS.
GOSH! CUT IT OUT! MY HEART IS BREAKING HERE!!
WELL, I'M GOING HOME NOW...
WILL YOU BE ALL RIGHT?
YEAH, I'LL BE FINE.
I CAN SOMEHOW MANAGE FOR TODAY.
WE DON'T HAVE A GOOD REASON TO RIDE TOGETHER.

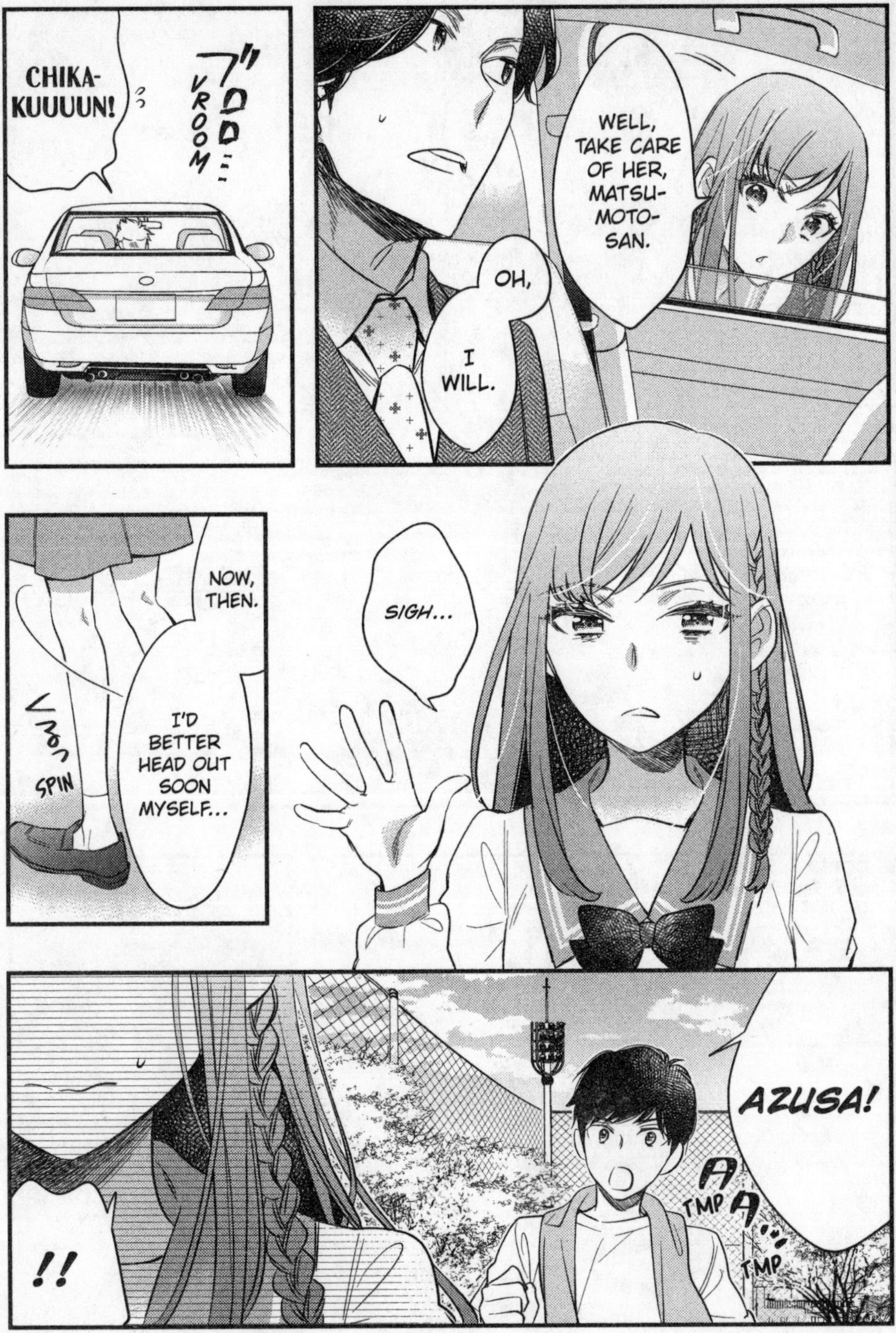
WELL, TAKE CARE OF HER, MATSU-MOTO-SAN.
OH,
I WILL.
VROOM
CHIKA-KUUUUN!
SIGH...
NOW, THEN.
I'D BETTER HEAD OUT SOON MYSELF...
SPIN
AZUSA!
TMP
TMP
!!

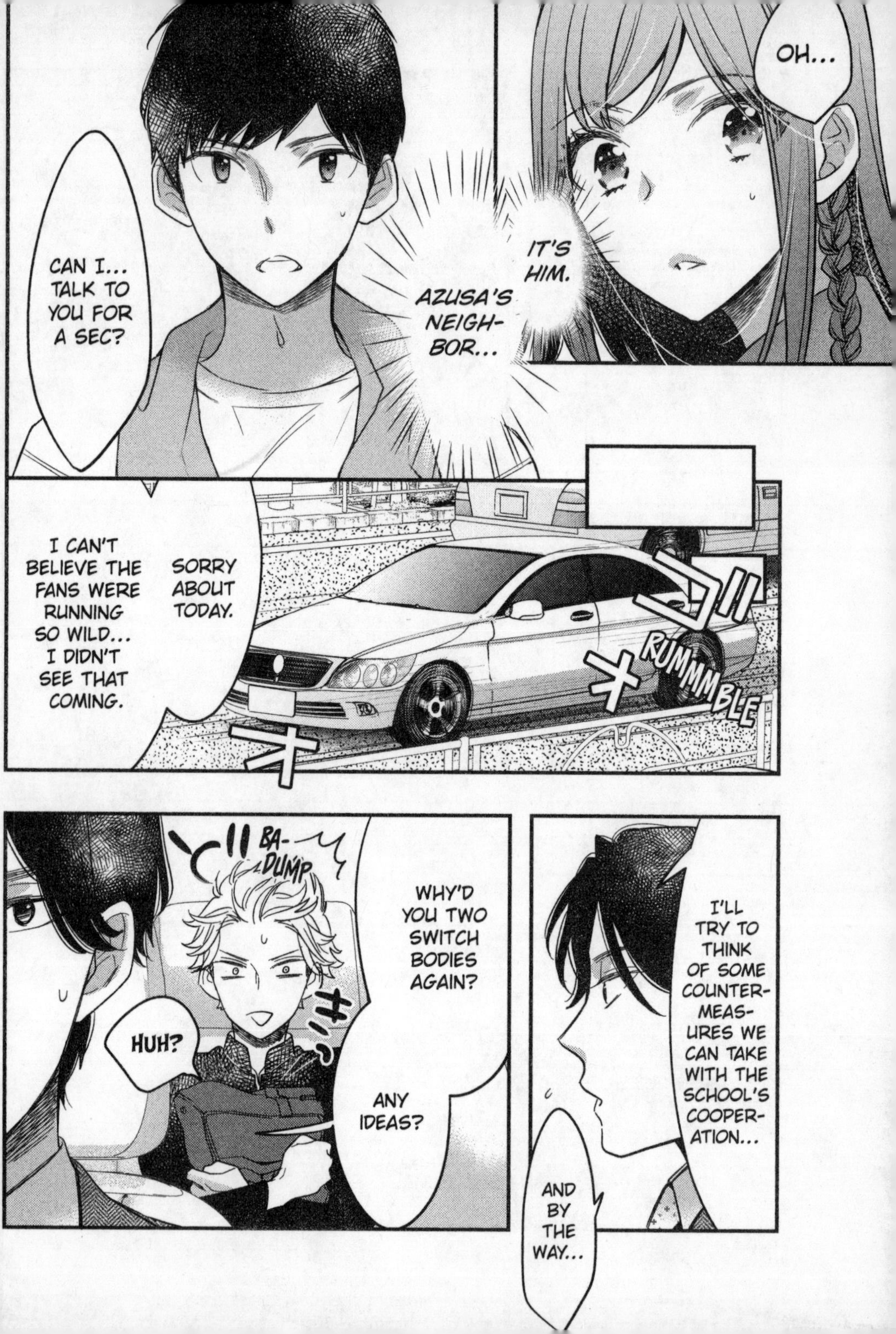
OH...
IT'S HIM.
AZUSA'S NEIGH-BOR...
CAN I... TALK TO YOU FOR A SEC?
RUMMMBLE
SORRY ABOUT TODAY.
I CAN'T BELIEVE THE FANS WERE RUNNING SO WILD... I DIDN'T SEE THAT COMING.
I'LL TRY TO THINK OF SOME COUNTER-MEAS-URES WE CAN TAKE WITH THE SCHOOL'S COOPER-ATION...
AND BY THE WAY...
WHY'D YOU TWO SWITCH BODIES AGAIN?
BA-DUMP
HUH?
ANY IDEAS?

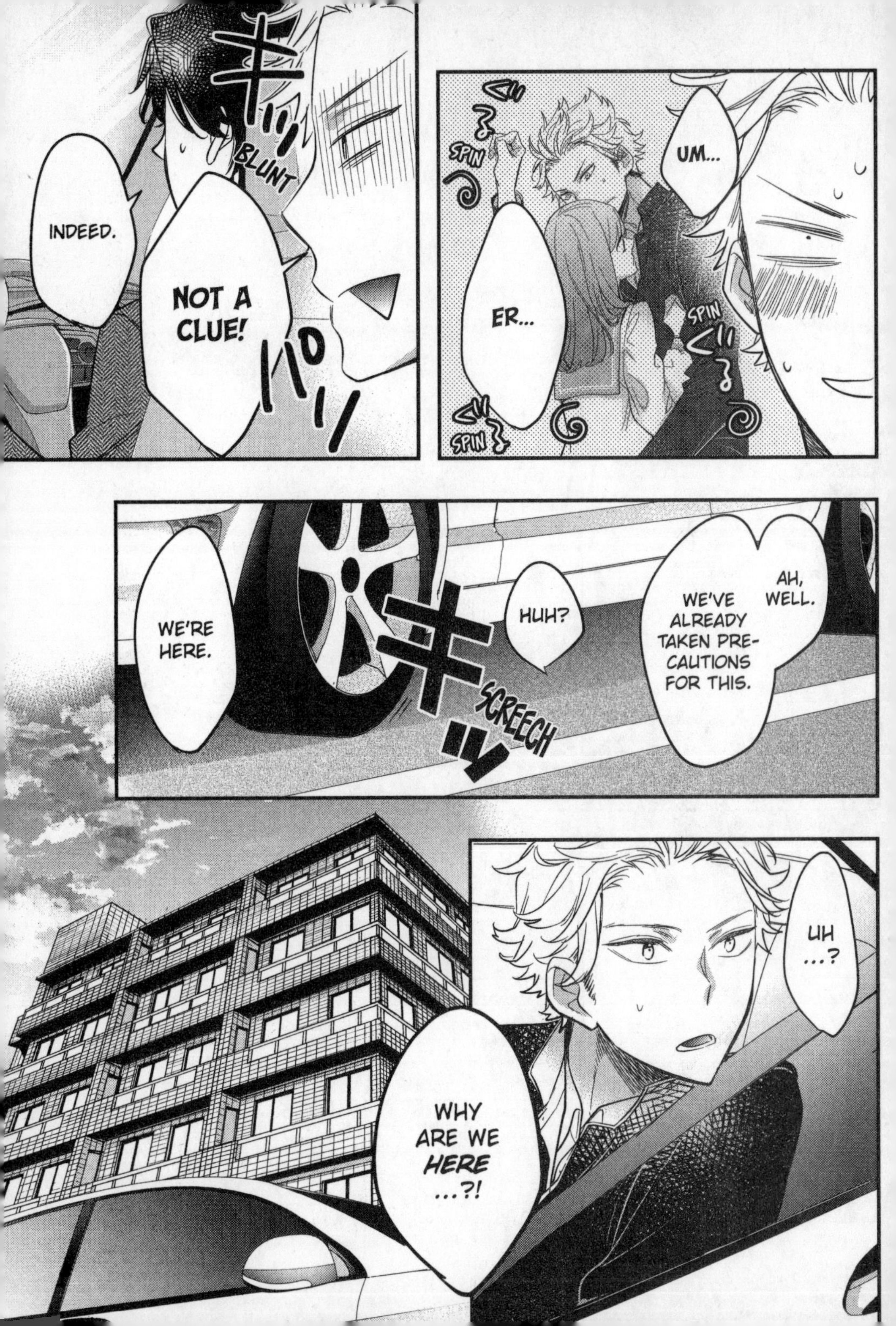
UM...
SPIN
ER...
SPIN
SPIN
BLUNT
NOT A CLUE!
INDEED.
AH, WELL.
WE'VE ALREADY TAKEN PRE-CAUTIONS FOR THIS.
HUH?
SCREECH
WE'RE HERE.
UH ...?
WHY ARE WE *HERE* ...?!

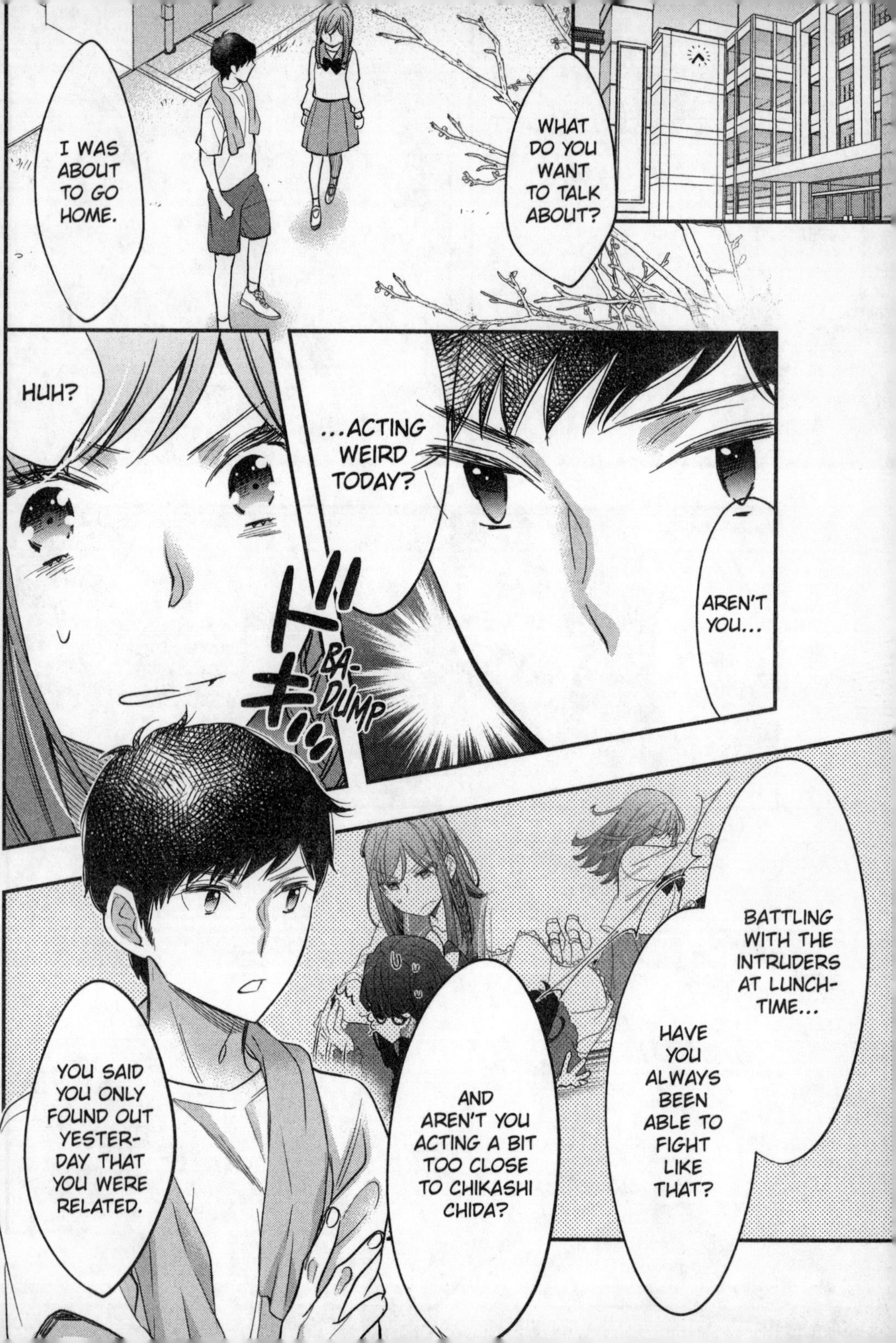
WHAT DO YOU WANT TO TALK ABOUT?
I WAS ABOUT TO GO HOME.
AREN'T YOU...
...ACTING WEIRD TODAY?
BA-DUMP
HUH?
BATTLING WITH THE INTRUDERS AT LUNCH-TIME...
HAVE YOU ALWAYS BEEN ABLE TO FIGHT LIKE THAT?
AND AREN'T YOU ACTING A BIT TOO CLOSE TO CHIKASHI CHIDA?
YOU SAID YOU ONLY FOUND OUT YESTER-DAY THAT YOU WERE RELATED.

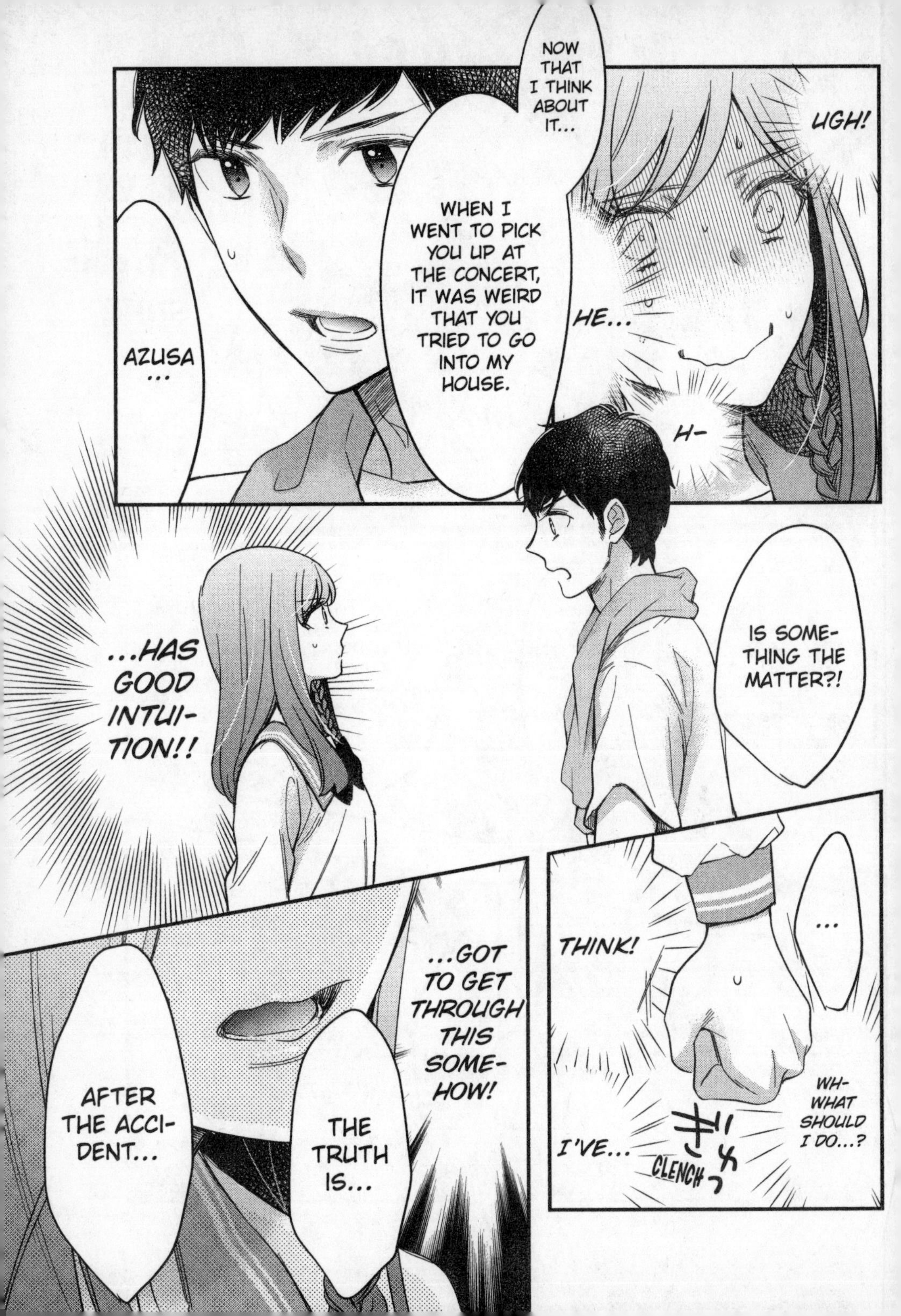
UGH!
HE...
H-
NOW THAT I THINK ABOUT IT...
WHEN I WENT TO PICK YOU UP AT THE CONCERT, IT WAS WEIRD THAT YOU TRIED TO GO INTO MY HOUSE.
AZUSA ...
IS SOMETHING THE MATTER?!
...HAS GOOD INTUITION!!
...
THINK!
WH- WHAT SHOULD I DO...?
I'VE...
CLENCH
...GOT TO GET THROUGH THIS SOMEHOW!
THE TRUTH IS...
AFTER THE ACCIDENT...

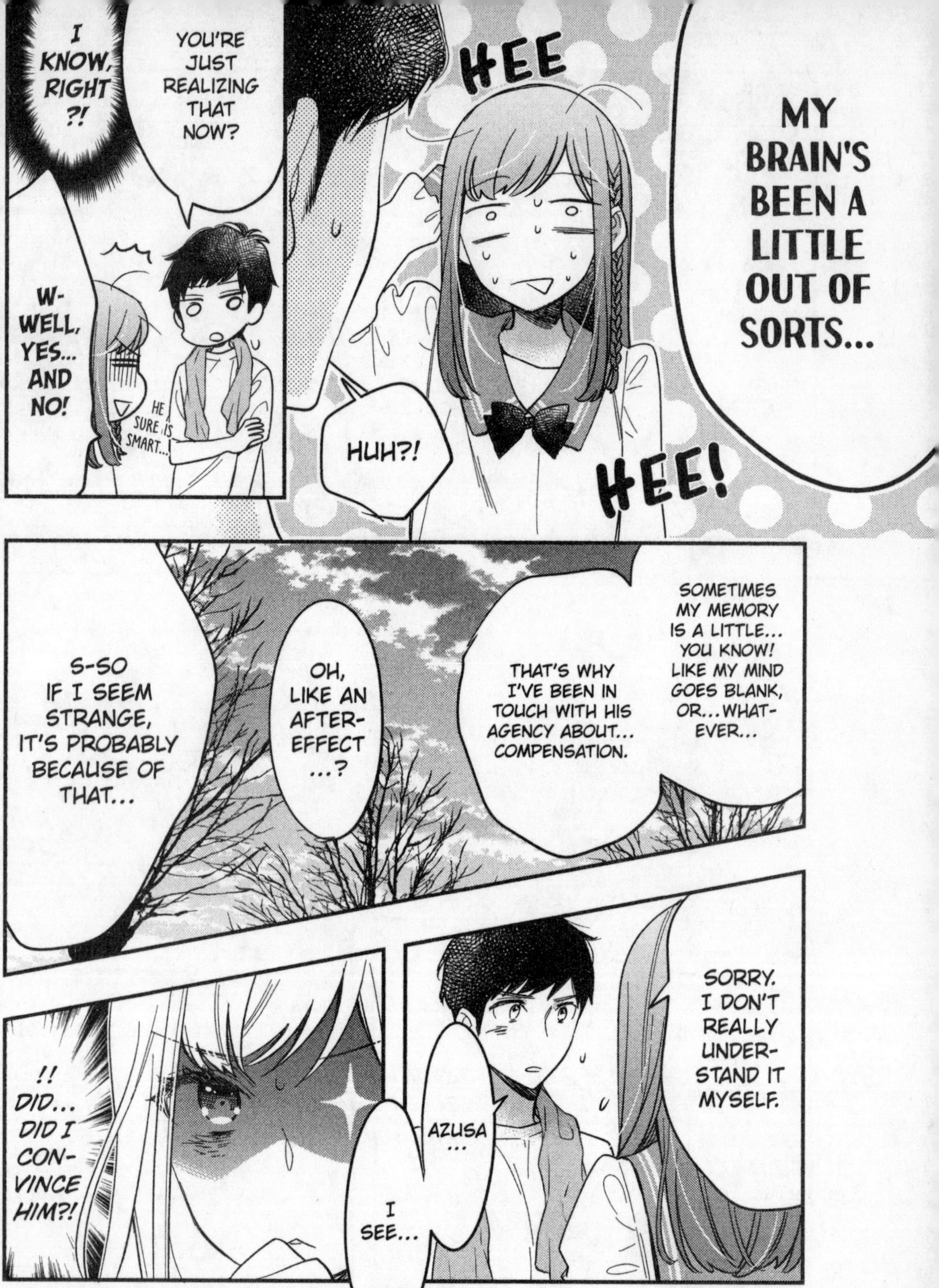
MY BRAIN'S BEEN A LITTLE OUT OF SORTS...
HEE
HEE!
HUH?!
YOU'RE JUST REALIZING THAT NOW?
I KNOW, RIGHT?!
W-WELL, YES... AND NO!
HE SURE IS SMART...
SOMETIMES MY MEMORY IS A LITTLE... YOU KNOW! LIKE MY MIND GOES BLANK, OR...WHATEVER...
THAT'S WHY I'VE BEEN IN TOUCH WITH HIS AGENCY ABOUT... COMPENSATION.
OH, LIKE AN AFTER-EFFECT ...?
S-SO IF I SEEM STRANGE, IT'S PROBABLY BECAUSE OF THAT...
SORRY. I DON'T REALLY UNDER-STAND IT MYSELF.
AZUSA ...
I SEE...
!! DID... DID I CON-VINCE HIM?!

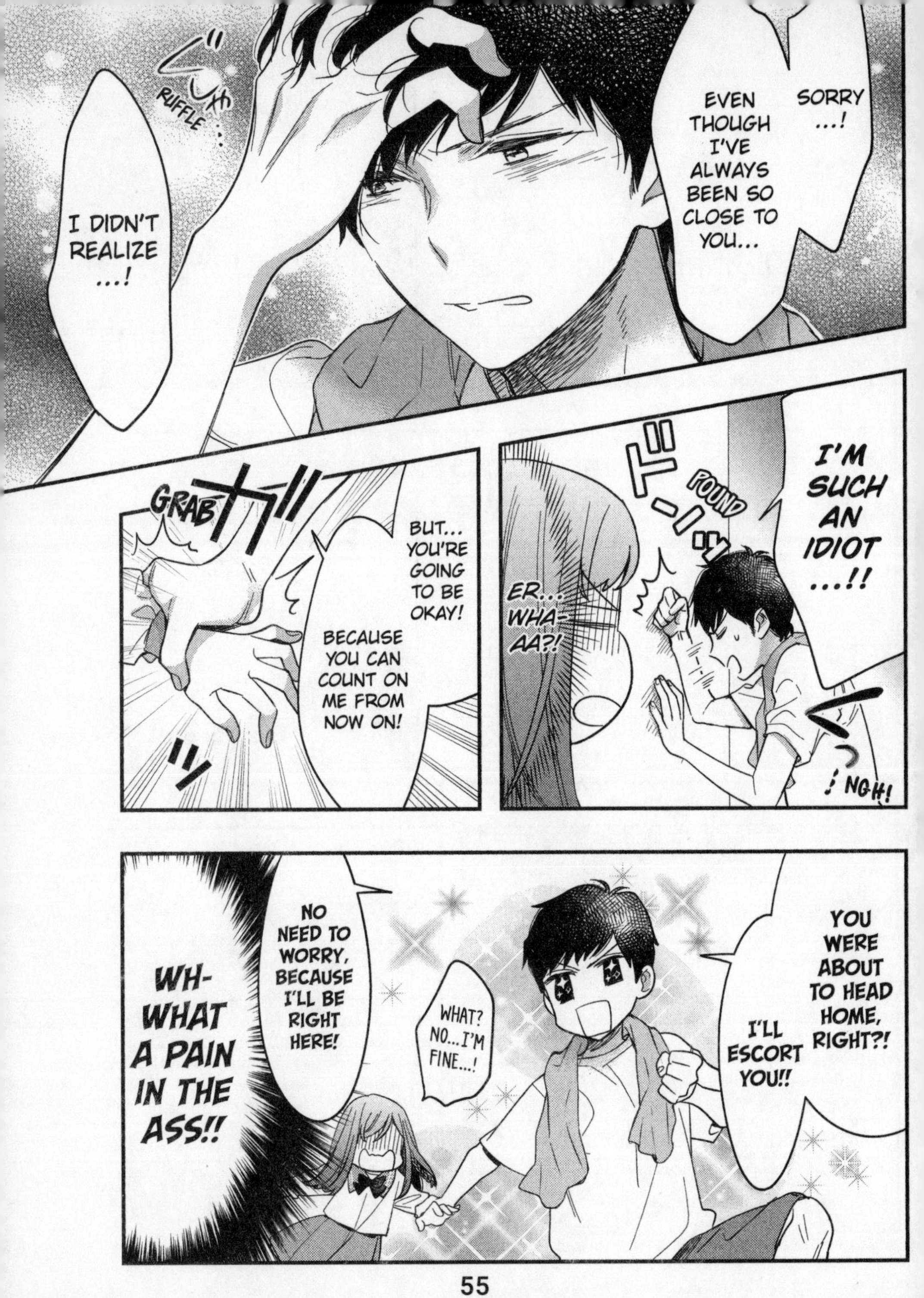
SORRY ...!
EVEN THOUGH I'VE ALWAYS BEEN SO CLOSE TO YOU...
RUFFLE
I DIDN'T REALIZE ...!
I'M SUCH AN IDIOT ...!!
POUND
ER... WHA-AA?!
NGH!
GRAB
BUT... YOU'RE GOING TO BE OKAY!
BECAUSE YOU CAN COUNT ON ME FROM NOW ON!
YOU WERE ABOUT TO HEAD HOME, RIGHT?!
I'LL ESCORT YOU!!
NO NEED TO WORRY, BECAUSE I'LL BE RIGHT HERE!
WHAT? NO... I'M FINE...!
WH-WHAT A PAIN IN THE ASS!!

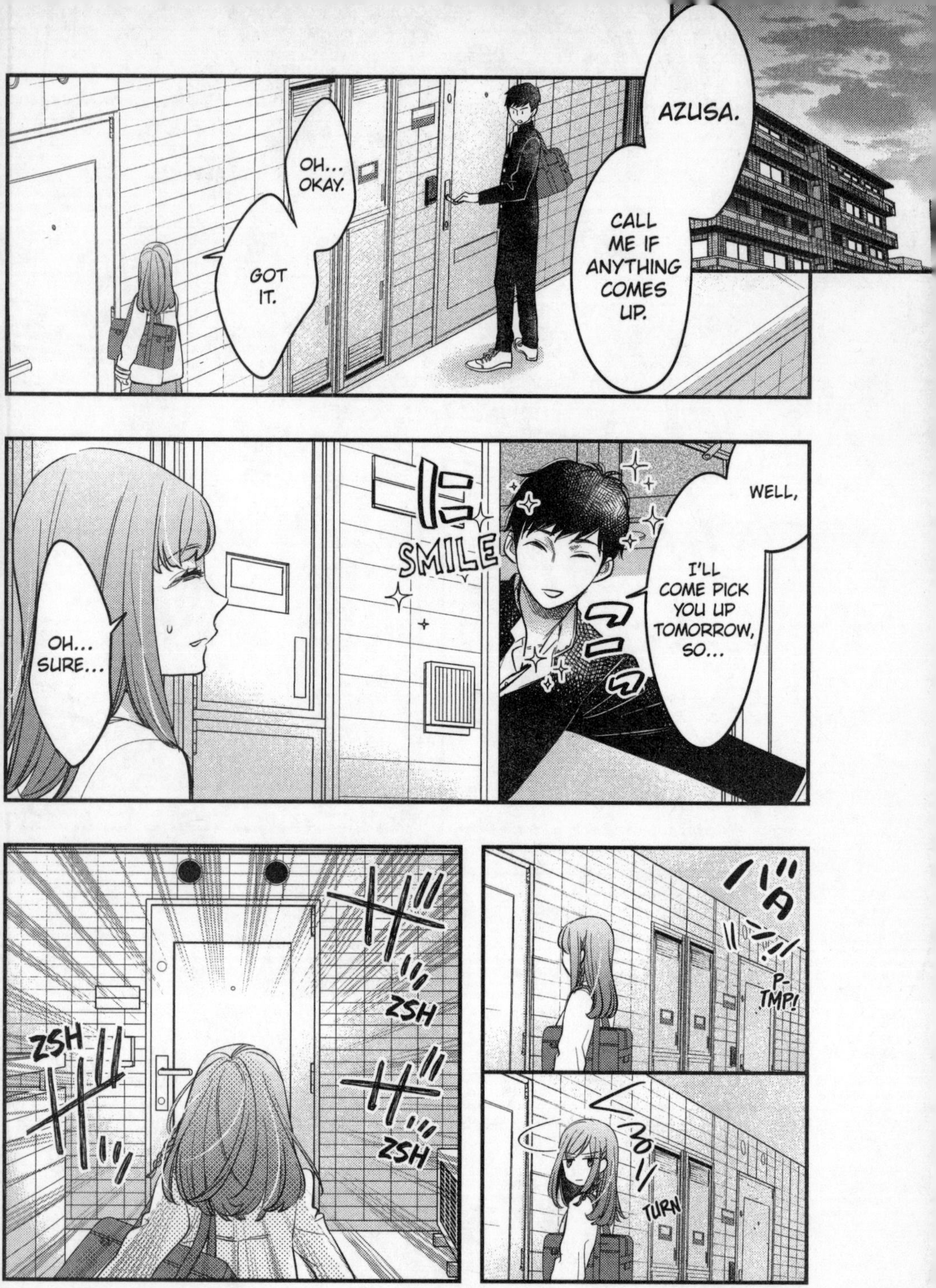
AZUSA.
CALL ME IF ANYTHING COMES UP.
OH... OKAY.
GOT IT.
WELL,
I'LL COME PICK YOU UP TOMORROW, SO...
SMILE
OH... SURE...
P-TMP!
TURN
ZSH
ZSH
ZSH

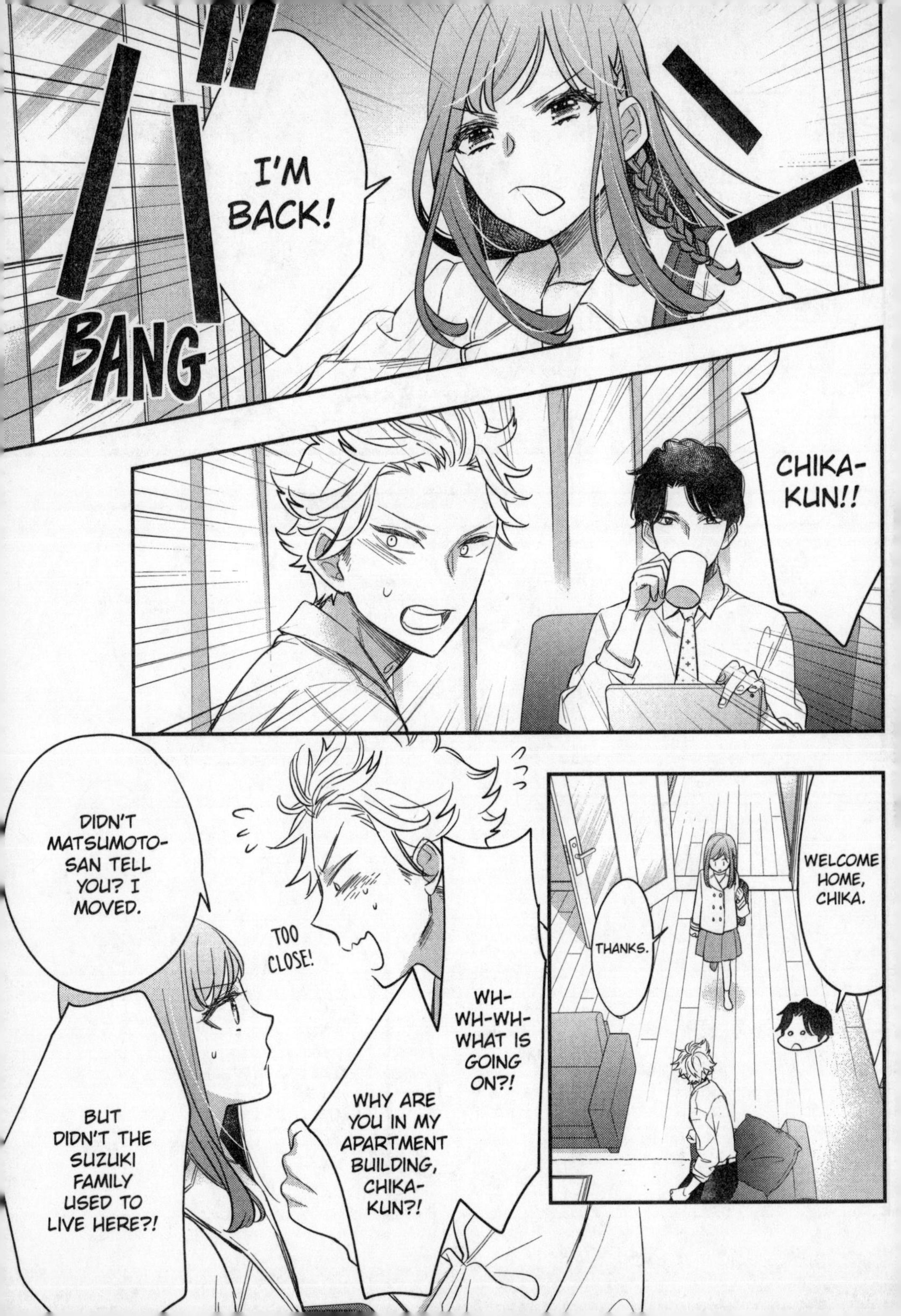
I'M BACK!
BANG
CHIKA-KUN!!
WELCOME HOME, CHIKA.
THANKS.
WH-WH-WH-WHAT IS GOING ON?!
WHY ARE YOU IN MY APARTMENT BUILDING, CHIKA-KUN?!
TOO CLOSE!
DIDN'T MATSUMOTO-SAN TELL YOU? I MOVED.
BUT DIDN'T THE SUZUKI FAMILY USED TO LIVE HERE?!

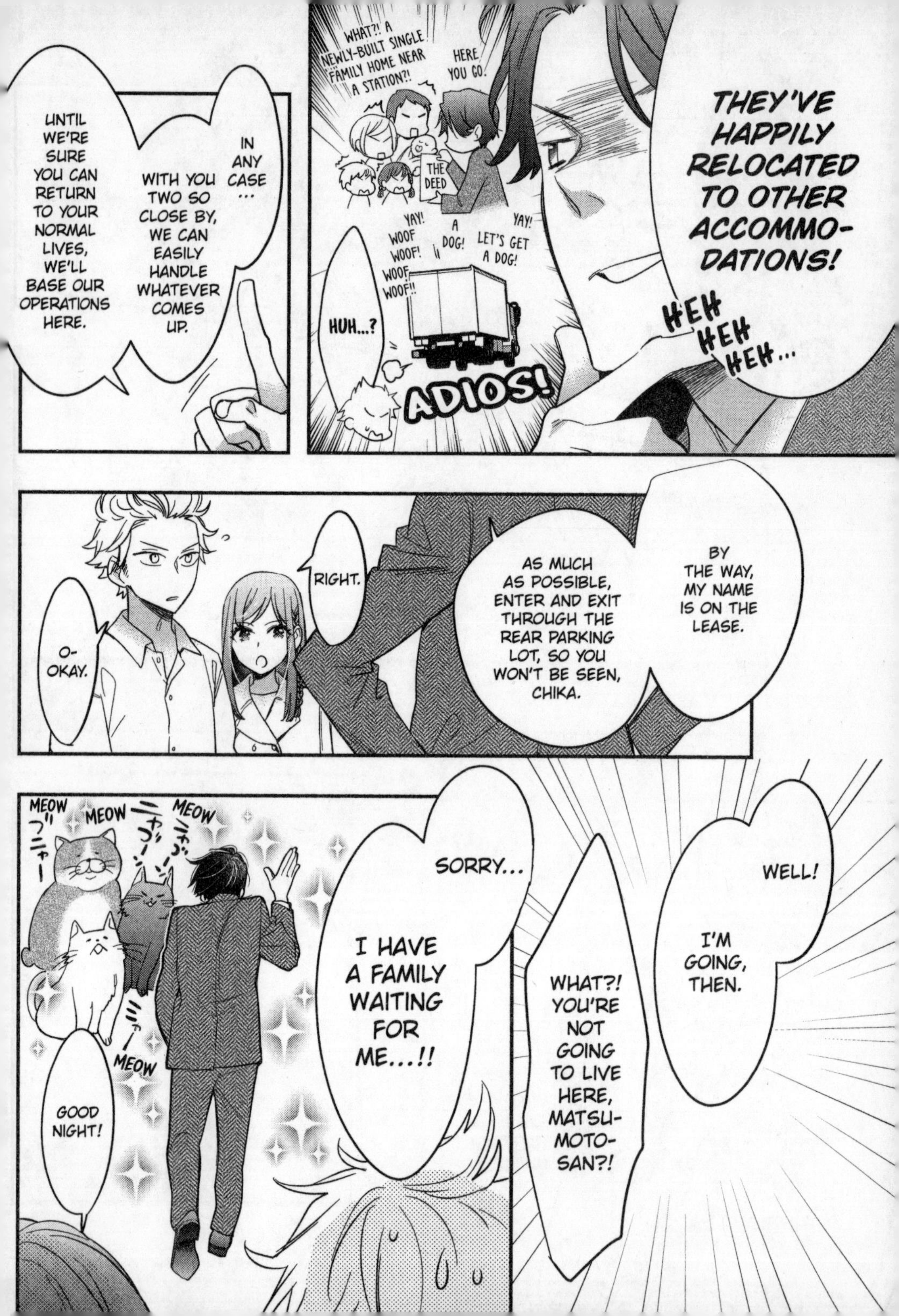
THEY'VE HAPPILY RELOCATED TO OTHER ACCOMMODATIONS!
HEH HEH HEH...
WHAT?! A NEWLY-BUILT SINGLE FAMILY HOME NEAR A STATION?!
HERE YOU GO.
THE DEED
YAY! LET'S GET A DOG!
A DOG!
YAY! WOOF WOOF!
WOOF WOOF!!
HUH...?
ADIOS!
IN ANY CASE...
WITH YOU TWO SO CLOSE BY, WE CAN EASILY HANDLE WHATEVER COMES UP.
UNTIL WE'RE SURE YOU CAN RETURN TO YOUR NORMAL LIVES, WE'LL BASE OUR OPERATIONS HERE.
BY THE WAY, MY NAME IS ON THE LEASE.
AS MUCH AS POSSIBLE, ENTER AND EXIT THROUGH THE REAR PARKING LOT, SO YOU WON'T BE SEEN, CHIKA.
RIGHT.
O-OKAY.
WELL!
I'M GOING, THEN.
WHAT?! YOU'RE NOT GOING TO LIVE HERE, MATSUMOTO-SAN?!
SORRY...
I HAVE A FAMILY WAITING FOR ME...!!
MEOW
MEOW
MEOW
MEOW
GOOD NIGHT!

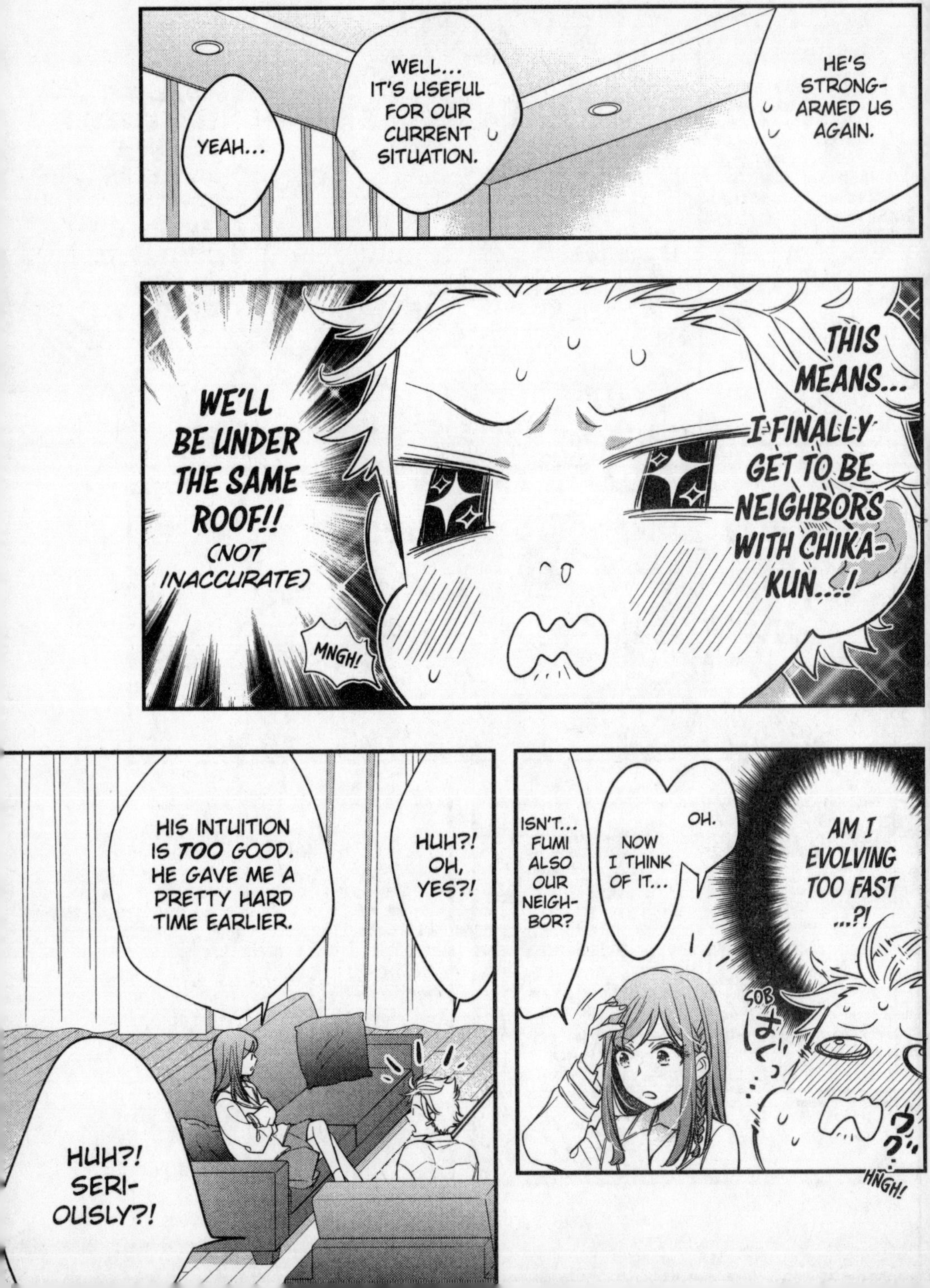
HE'S STRONG-ARMED US AGAIN.
WELL... IT'S USEFUL FOR OUR CURRENT SITUATION.
YEAH...
THIS MEANS... I FINALLY GET TO BE NEIGHBORS WITH CHIKA-KUN...!
WE'LL BE UNDER THE SAME ROOF!!
(NOT INACCURATE)
MNGH!
AM I EVOLVING TOO FAST ...?!
OH.
NOW I THINK OF IT...
ISN'T... FUMI ALSO OUR NEIGHBOR?
SOB
HNGH!
HUH?! OH, YES?!
HIS INTUITION IS TOO GOOD. HE GAVE ME A PRETTY HARD TIME EARLIER.
HUH?! SERI-OUSLY?!

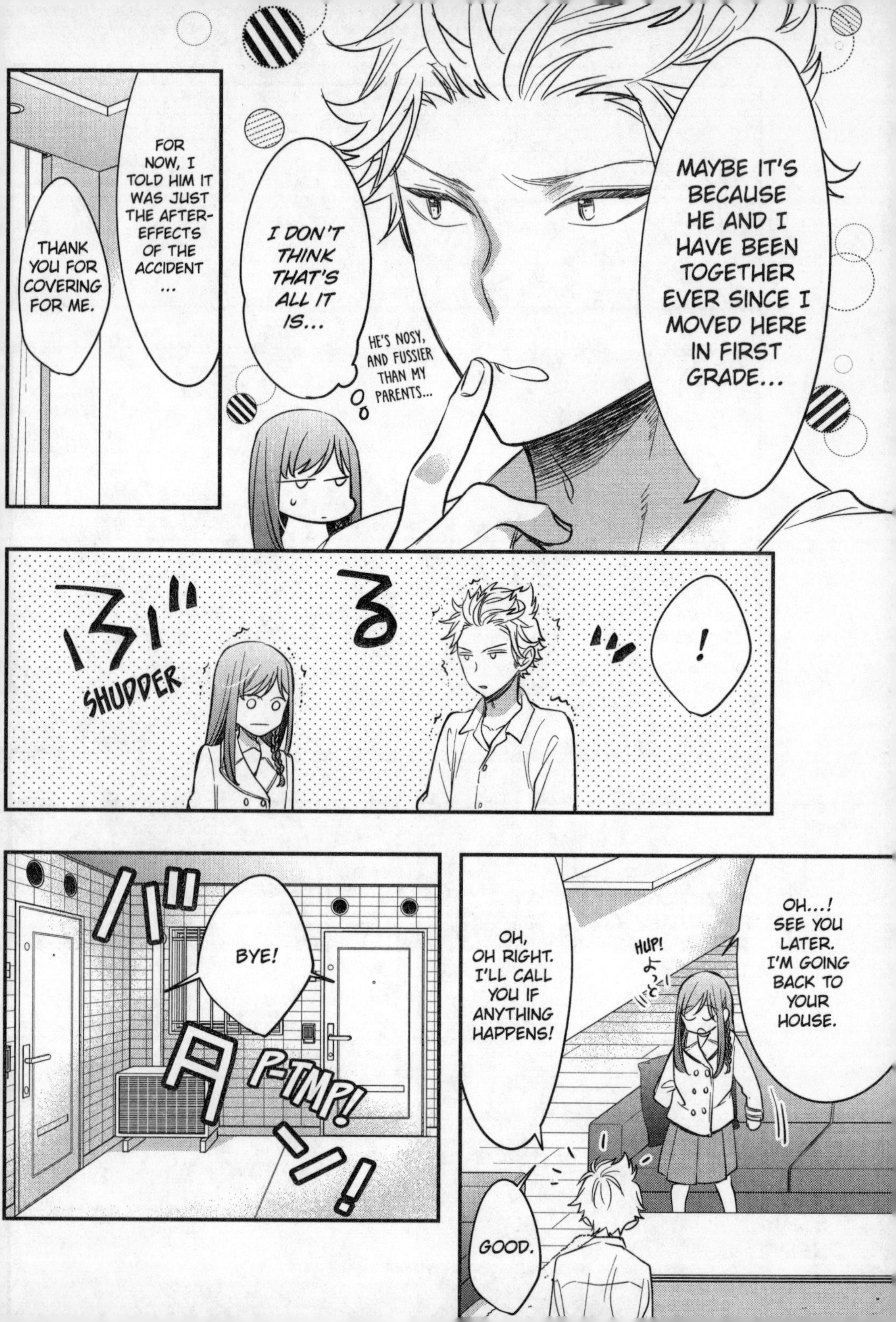
MAYBE IT'S BECAUSE HE AND I HAVE BEEN TOGETHER EVER SINCE I MOVED HERE IN FIRST GRADE...
I DON'T THINK THAT'S ALL IT IS...
HE'S NOSY, AND FUSSIER THAN MY PARENTS...
FOR NOW, I TOLD HIM IT WAS JUST THE AFTER-EFFECTS OF THE ACCIDENT...
THANK YOU FOR COVERING FOR ME.
!
SHUDDER
OH...! SEE YOU LATER. I'M GOING BACK TO YOUR HOUSE.
HUP!
OH, OH RIGHT. I'LL CALL YOU IF ANYTHING HAPPENS!
GOOD.
BYE!
P-TMP!

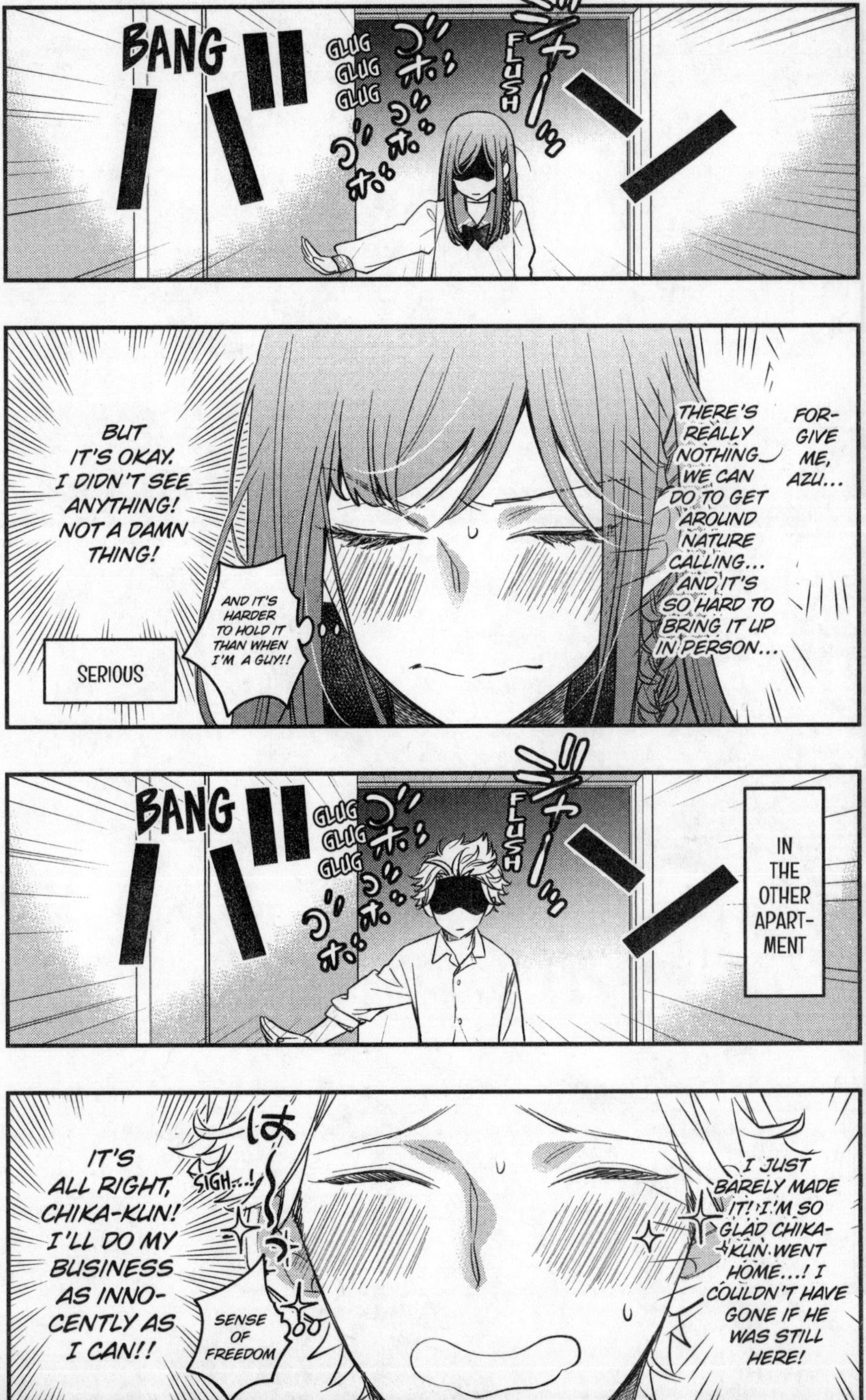
FLUSH
GLUG GLUG GLUG
BANG
FORGIVE ME, AZU...
THERE'S REALLY NOTHING WE CAN DO TO GET AROUND NATURE CALLING... AND IT'S SO HARD TO BRING IT UP IN PERSON...
AND IT'S HARDER TO HOLD IT THAN WHEN I'M A GUY!!
BUT IT'S OKAY. I DIDN'T SEE ANYTHING! NOT A DAMN THING!
SERIOUS
IN THE OTHER APARTMENT
FLUSH
GLUG GLUG GLUG
BANG
I JUST BARELY MADE IT! I'M SO GLAD CHIKA-KUN WENT HOME...! I COULDN'T HAVE GONE IF HE WAS STILL HERE!
SENSE OF FREEDOM
SIGH...!
IT'S ALL RIGHT, CHIKA-KUN! I'LL DO MY BUSINESS AS INNOCENTLY AS I CAN!!

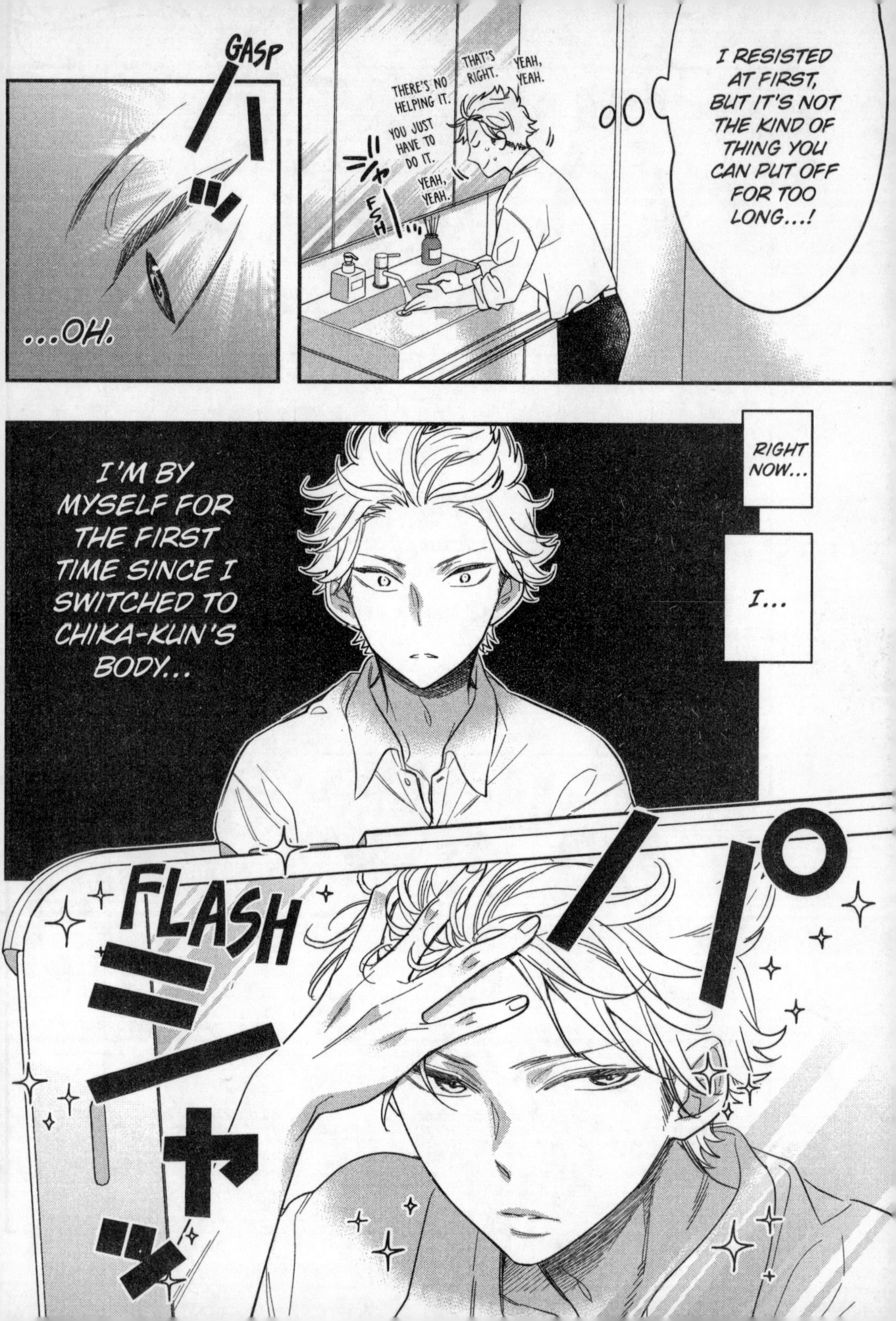
I RESISTED AT FIRST, BUT IT'S NOT THE KIND OF THING YOU CAN PUT OFF FOR TOO LONG...!
YEAH, YEAH.
THAT'S RIGHT.
THERE'S NO HELPING IT.
YOU JUST HAVE TO DO IT.
YEAH, YEAH.
FSH
GASP
...OH.
RIGHT NOW...
I...
I'M BY MYSELF FOR THE FIRST TIME SINCE I SWITCHED TO CHIKA-KUN'S BODY...
FLASH

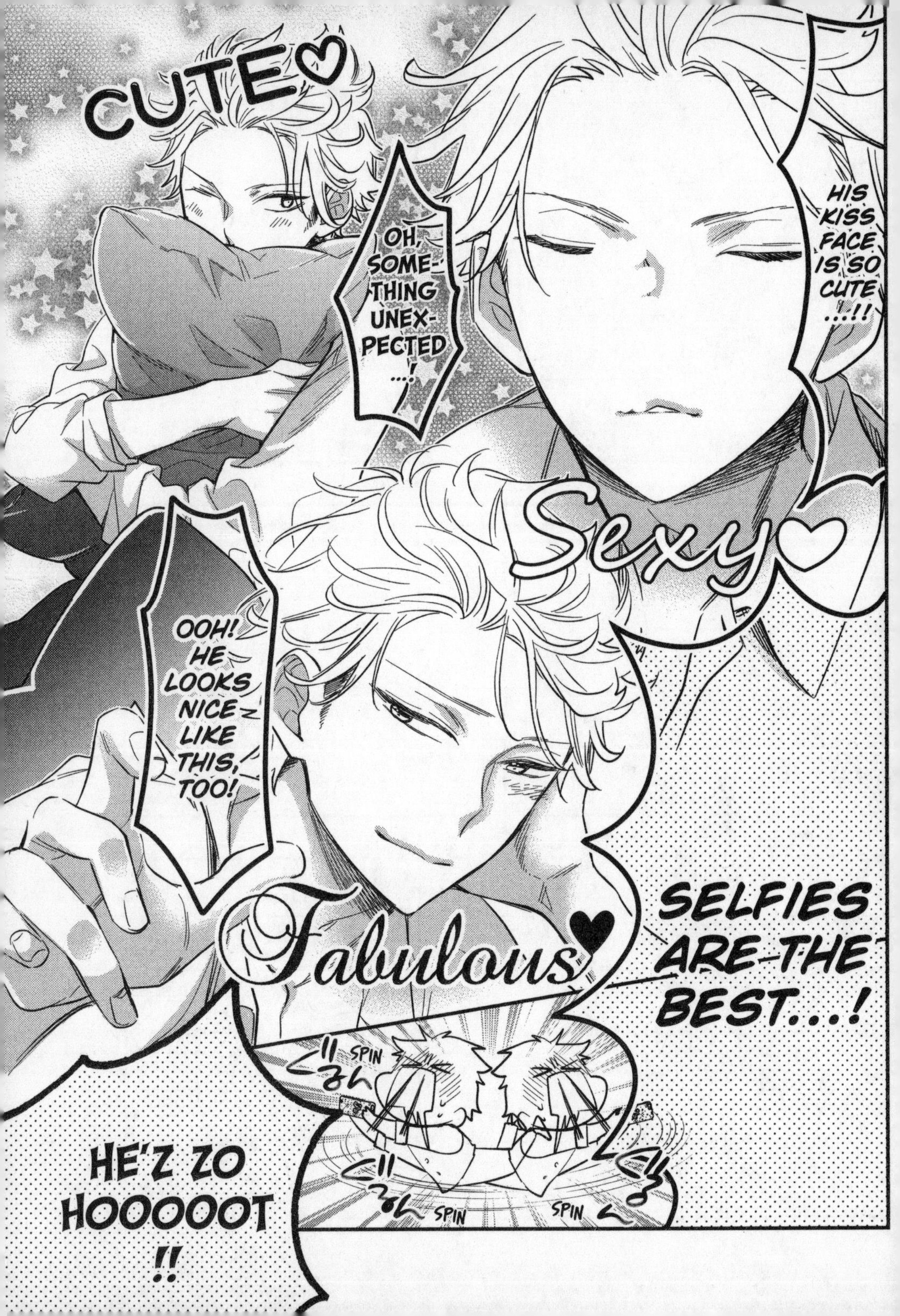
HIS KISS FACE IS SO CUTE ...!!
OH, SOMETHING UNEXPECTED ...!
CUTE♡
Sexy♡
OOH! HE LOOKS NICE LIKE THIS, TOO!
Fabulous♥
SELFIES ARE THE BEST...!
ぐるん SPIN
ぐるん SPIN
ぐるん SPIN
HE'Z ZO HOOOOOT!!

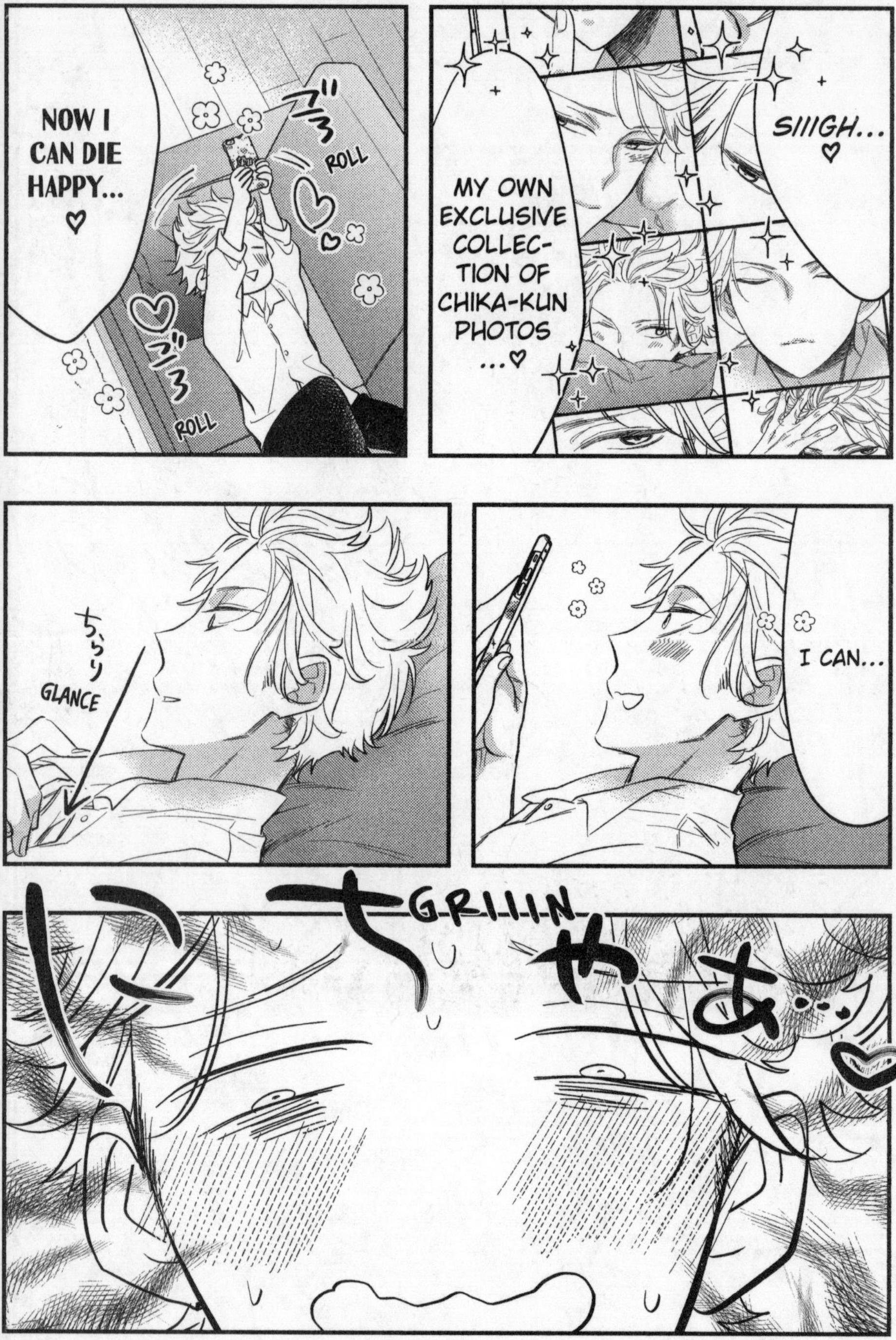
SIIIGH... ♡
MY OWN EXCLUSIVE COLLECTION OF CHIKA-KUN PHOTOS ...♡
NOW I CAN DIE HAPPY... ♡
ゴろ
ROLL
ゴろ
ROLL
I CAN...
ちらり
GLANCE
にちゃあ…♡
GRIIIN

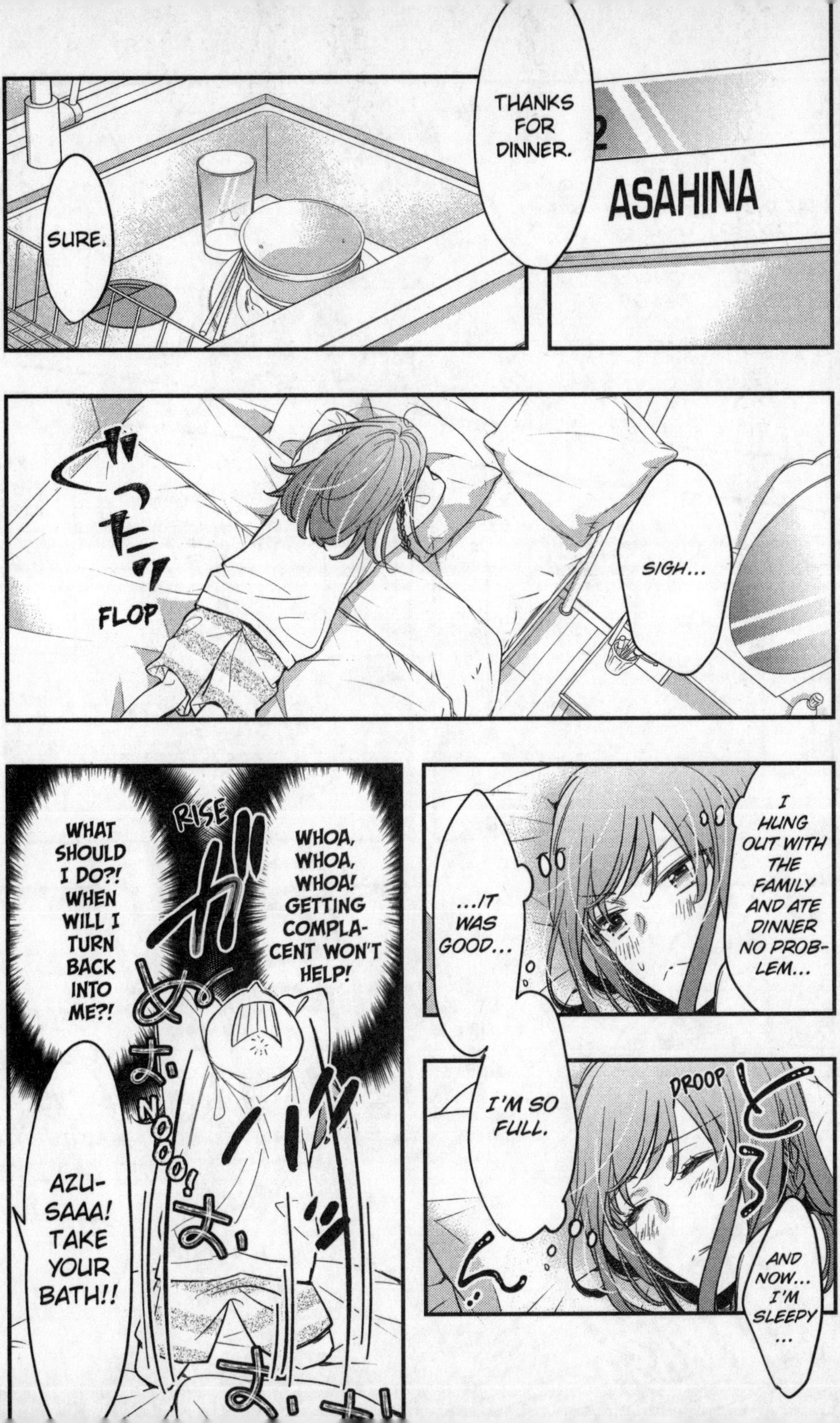
THANKS FOR DINNER.
ASAHINA
SURE.
SIGH...
FLOP
I HUNG OUT WITH THE FAMILY AND ATE DINNER NO PROBLEM...
...IT WAS GOOD...
I'M SO FULL.
DROOP
AND NOW... I'M SLEEPY...
WHOA, WHOA, WHOA! GETTING COMPLACENT WON'T HELP!
RISE
WHAT SHOULD I DO?! WHEN WILL I TURN BACK INTO ME?!
NOOO!
AZU-SAAA! TAKE YOUR BATH!!

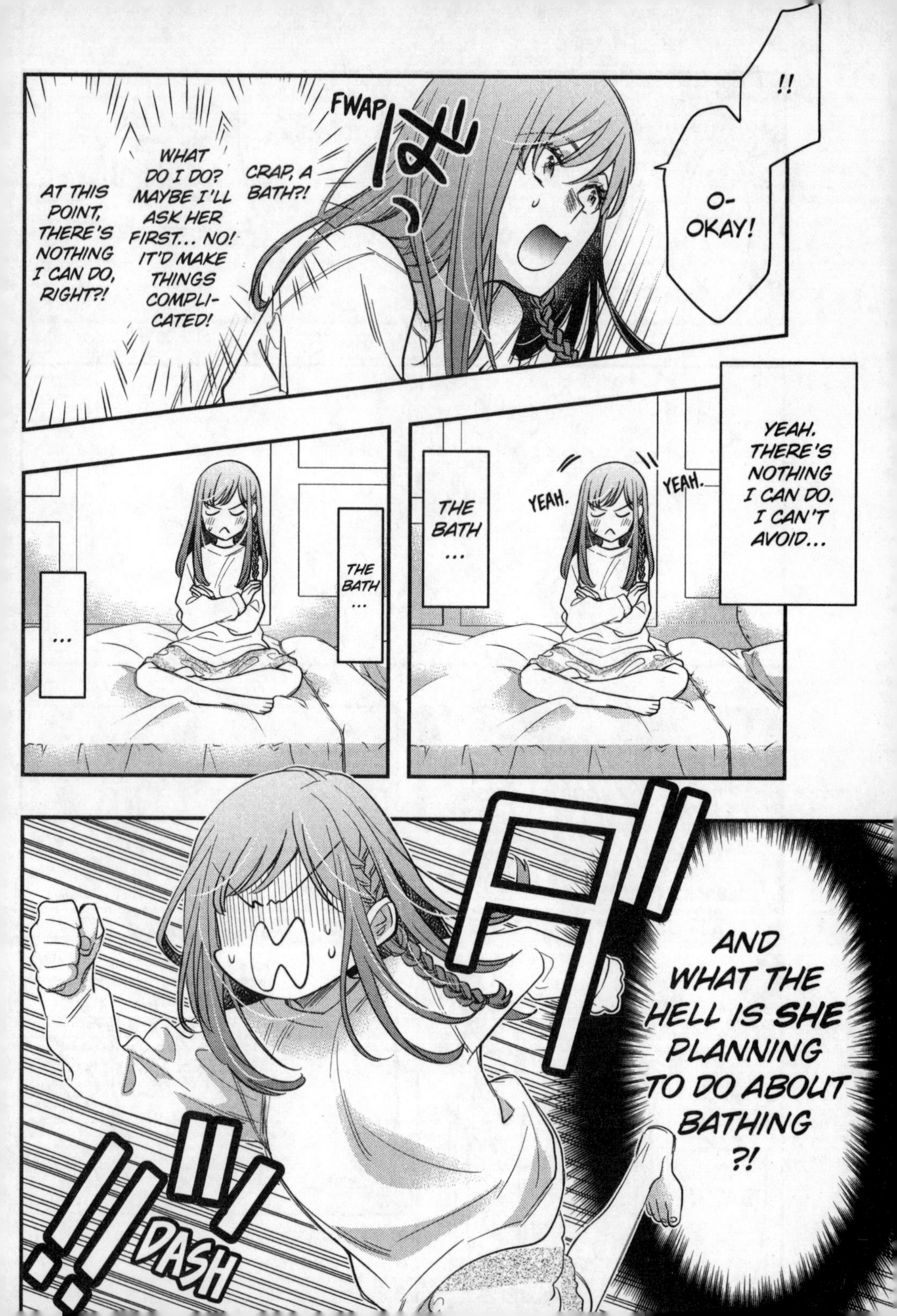
!!
O-OKAY!
FWAP
CRAP, A BATH?!
WHAT DO I DO? MAYBE I'LL ASK HER FIRST... NO! IT'D MAKE THINGS COMPLICATED!
AT THIS POINT, THERE'S NOTHING I CAN DO, RIGHT?!
YEAH. THERE'S NOTHING I CAN DO. I CAN'T AVOID...
YEAH.
YEAH.
THE BATH...
THE BATH...
...
AND WHAT THE HELL IS SHE PLANNING TO DO ABOUT BATHING?!
DASH
!!

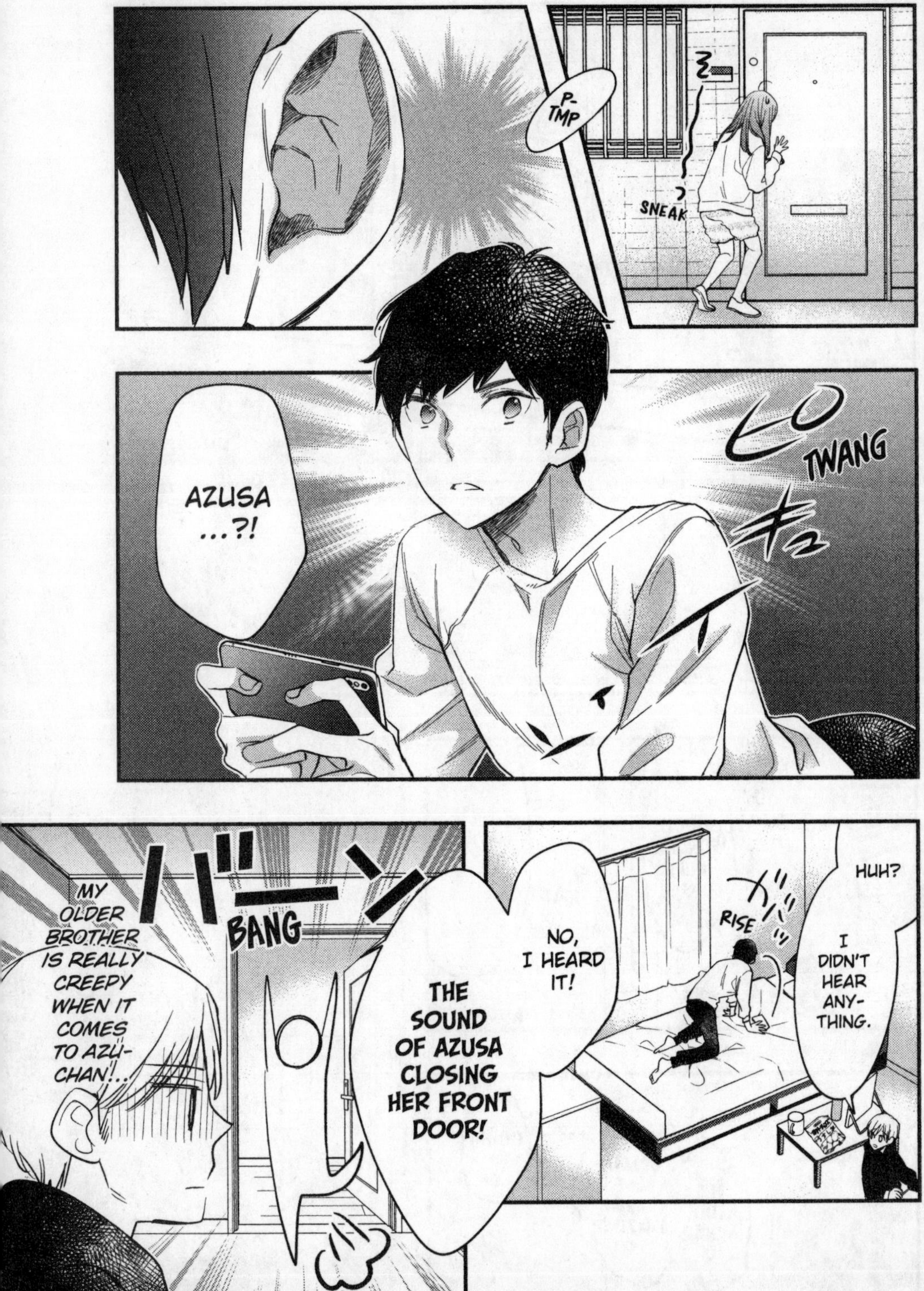
P-TMP
SNEAK
TWANG
AZUSA ...?!
HUH?
I DIDN'T HEAR ANYTHING.
RISE
NO, I HEARD IT!
THE SOUND OF AZUSA CLOSING HER FRONT DOOR!
BANG
MY OLDER BROTHER IS REALLY CREEPY WHEN IT COMES TO AZU-CHAN...

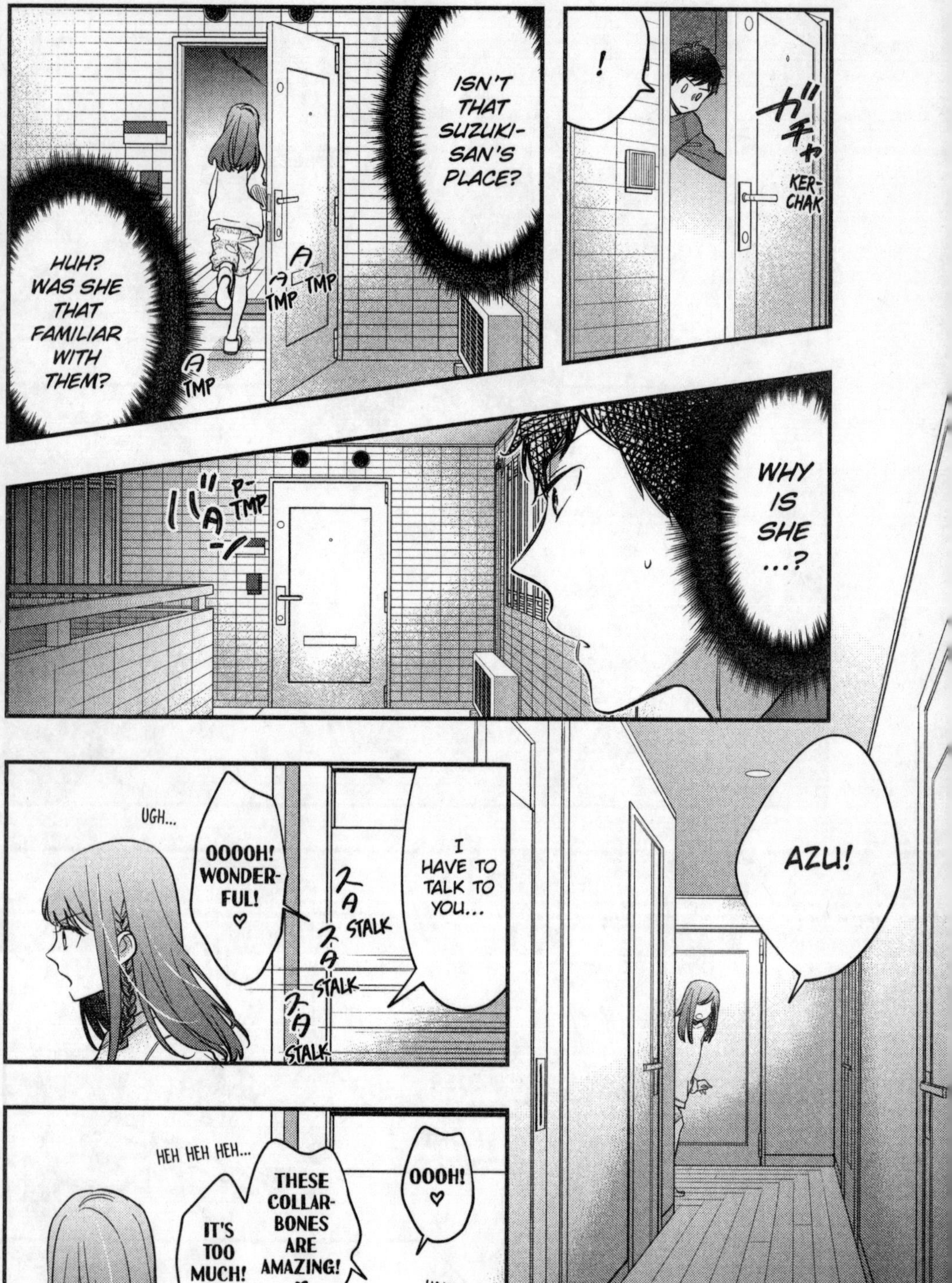
!
ガチャ
KER-CHAK
ISN'T THAT SUZUKI-SAN'S PLACE?
TMP
TMP
HUH? WAS SHE THAT FAMILIAR WITH THEM?
TMP
WHY IS SHE ...?
P-TMP
AZU!
I HAVE TO TALK TO YOU...
OOOOH! WONDERFUL! ♡
UGH...
STALK
STALK
STALK
OOOH! ♡
THESE COLLARBONES ARE AMAZING! ♡
IT'S TOO MUCH! ♡
HEH HEH HEH...
HAHA...

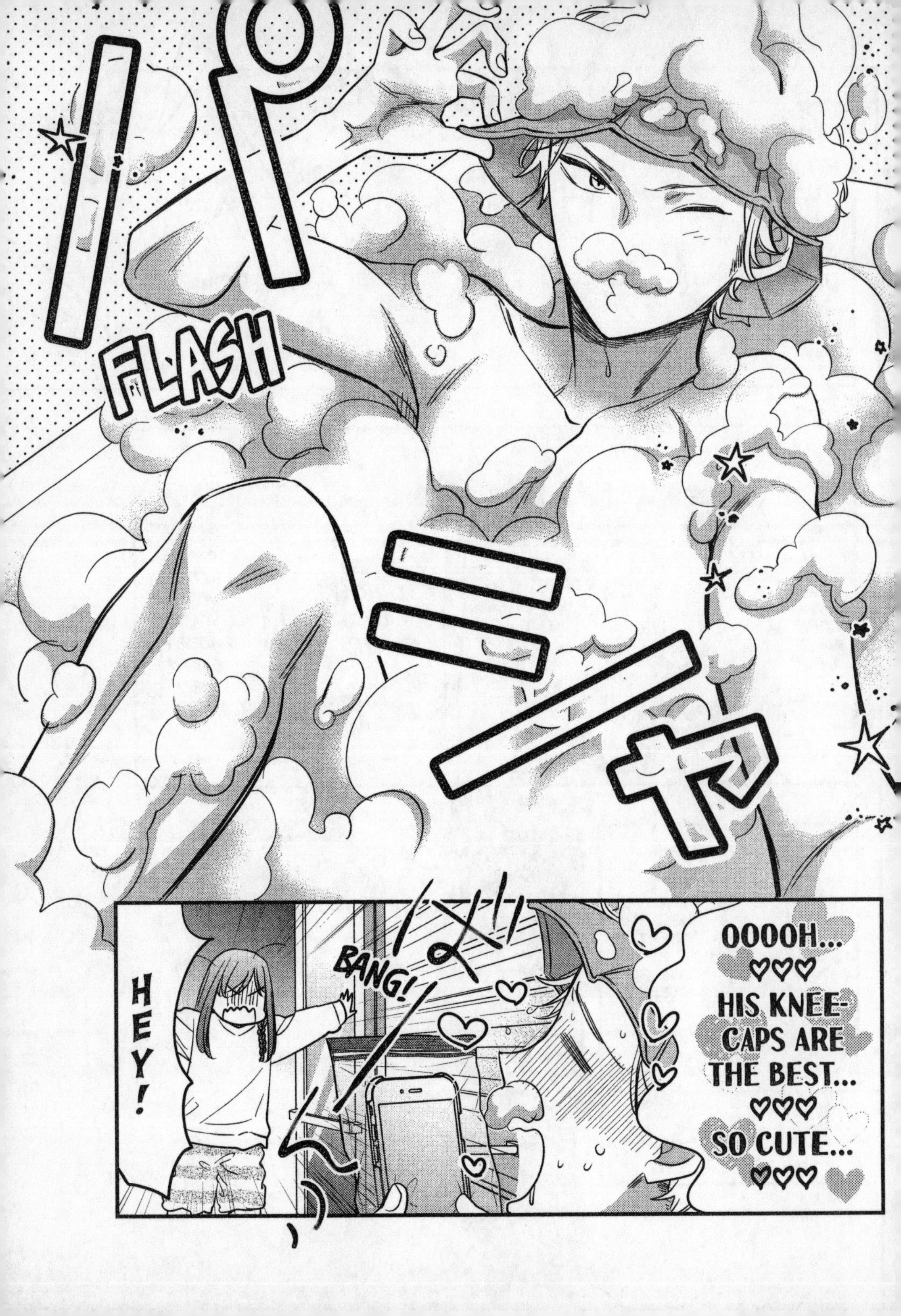
FLASH
OOOOH... ♡♡♡ HIS KNEE-CAPS ARE THE BEST... ♡♡♡ SO CUTE... ♡♡♡
BANG!
HEY!

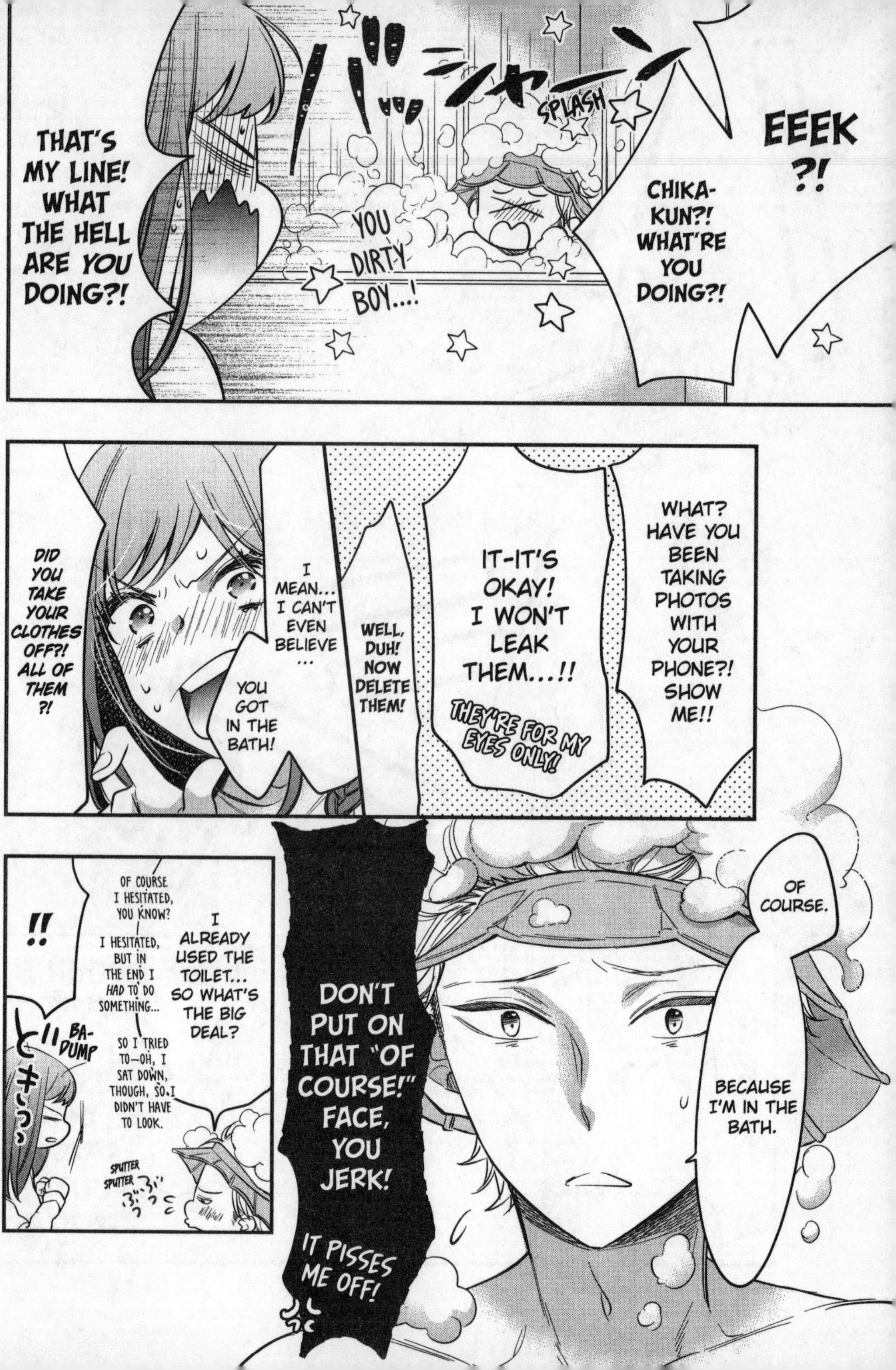
EEEK ?!
CHIKA-KUN?! WHAT'RE YOU DOING?!
SPLASH
YOU DIRTY BOY...!
THAT'S MY LINE! WHAT THE HELL ARE YOU DOING?!
WHAT? HAVE YOU BEEN TAKING PHOTOS WITH YOUR PHONE?! SHOW ME!!
IT-IT'S OKAY! I WON'T LEAK THEM...!!
THEY'RE FOR MY EYES ONLY!
WELL, DUH! NOW DELETE THEM!
I MEAN... I CAN'T EVEN BELIEVE ...
YOU GOT IN THE BATH!
DID YOU TAKE YOUR CLOTHES OFF?! ALL OF THEM ?!
OF COURSE.
BECAUSE I'M IN THE BATH.
DON'T PUT ON THAT "OF COURSE!" FACE, YOU JERK!
IT PISSES ME OFF!
I ALREADY USED THE TOILET... SO WHAT'S THE BIG DEAL?
OF COURSE I HESITATED, YOU KNOW?
I HESITATED, BUT IN THE END I HAD TO DO SOMETHING...
SO I TRIED TO—OH, I SAT DOWN, THOUGH, SO I DIDN'T HAVE TO LOOK.
!!
BA-DUMP
SPUTTER SPUTTER

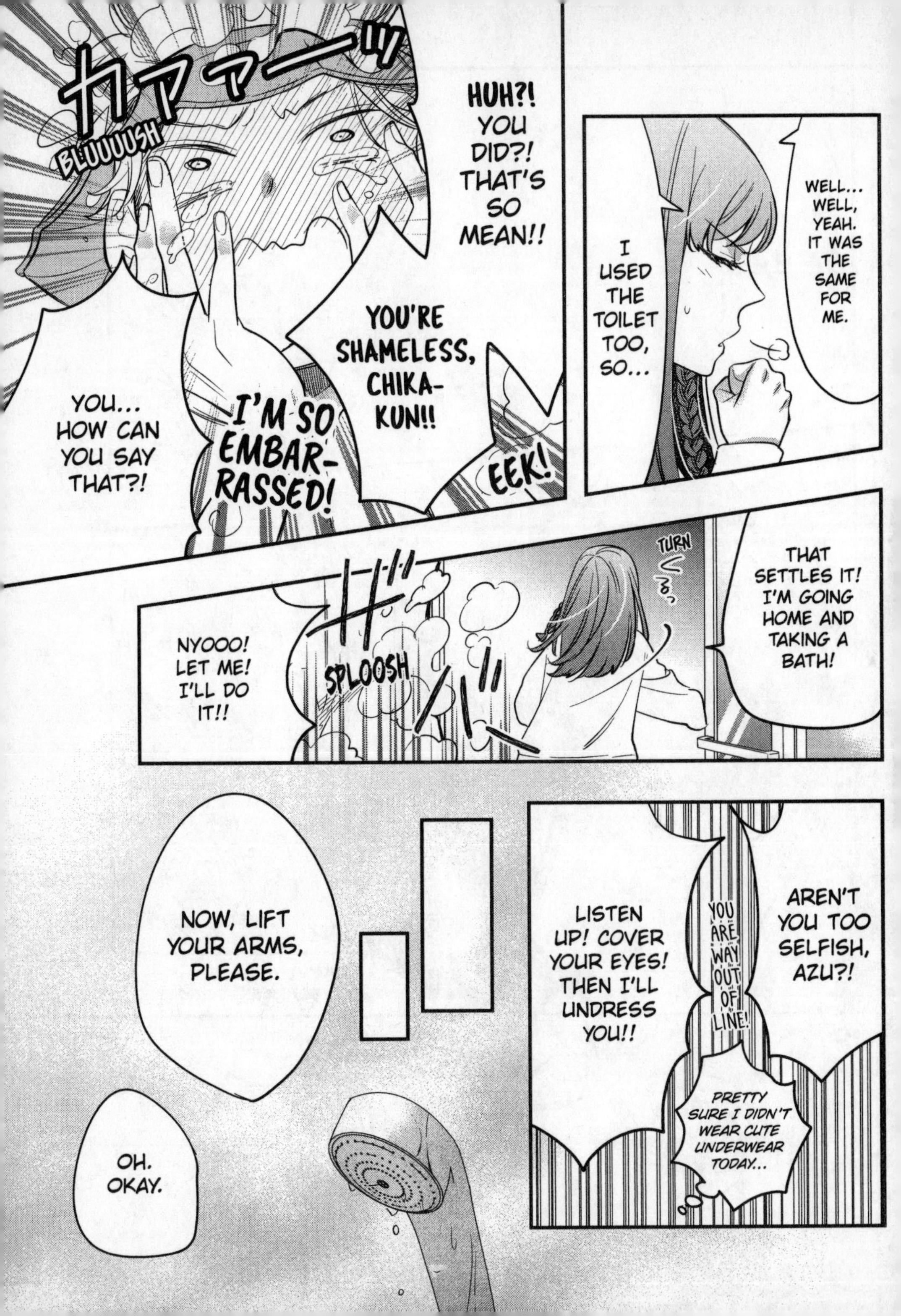

WELL... WELL, YEAH. IT WAS THE SAME FOR ME.
I USED THE TOILET TOO, SO...
HUH?! YOU DID?! THAT'S SO MEAN!!
カァァー
BLUUUUSH
YOU'RE SHAMELESS, CHIKA-KUN!!
EEK!
I'M SO EMBAR-RASSED!
YOU... HOW CAN YOU SAY THAT?!
THAT SETTLES IT! I'M GOING HOME AND TAKING A BATH!
TURN
SPLOOSH
NYOOO! LET ME! I'LL DO IT!!
AREN'T YOU TOO SELFISH, AZU?!
YOU ARE WAY OUT OF LINE!
LISTEN UP! COVER YOUR EYES! THEN I'LL UNDRESS YOU!!
PRETTY SURE I DIDN'T WEAR CUTE UNDERWEAR TODAY...
NOW, LIFT YOUR ARMS, PLEASE.
OH. OKAY.

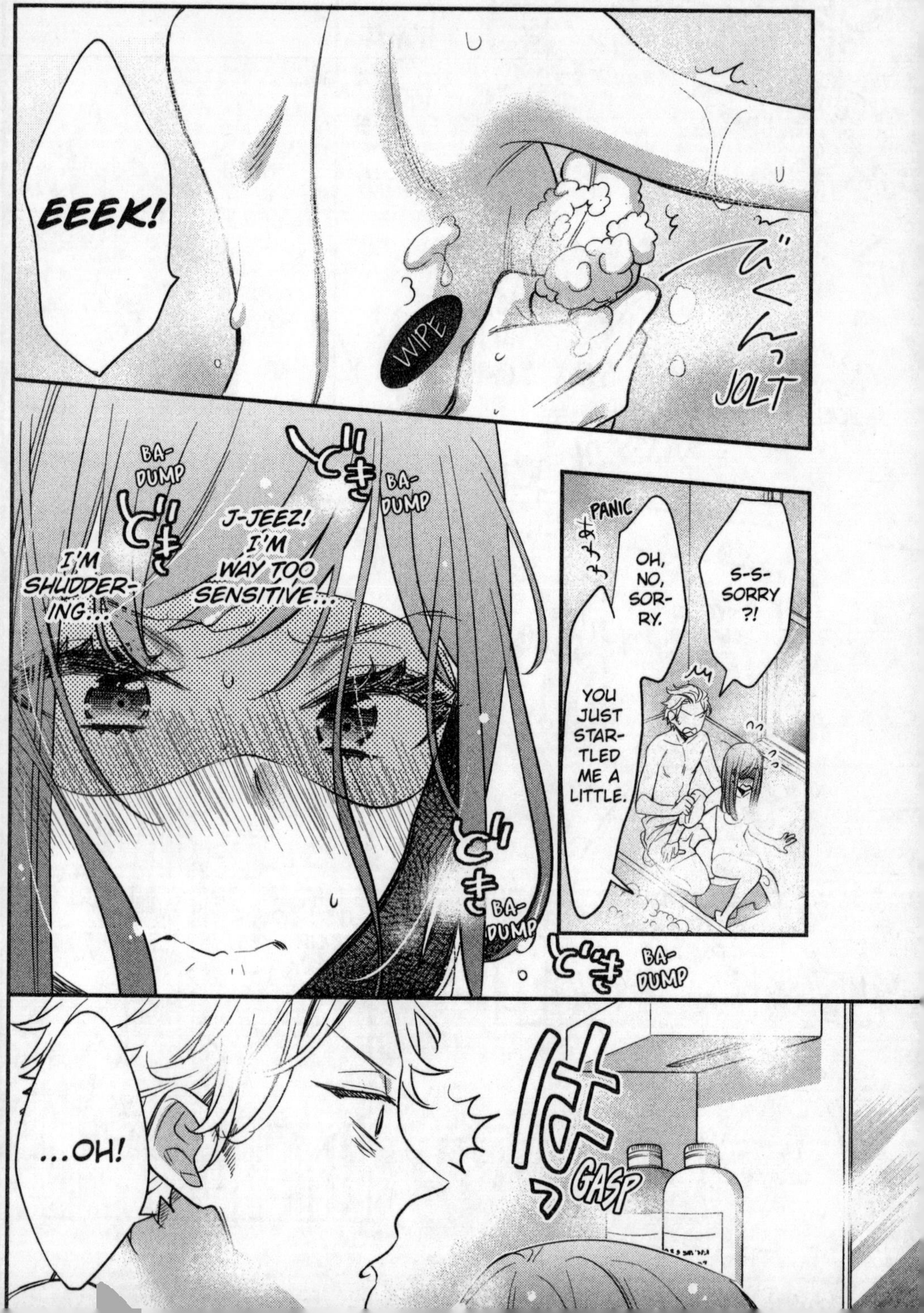
びくんっ
JOLT
WIPE
EEEK!
S-S-SORRY?!
PANIC
OH, NO, SORRY.
YOU JUST STARTLED ME A LITTLE.
どき
BA-DUMP
どき
BA-DUMP
J-JEEZ! I'M WAY TOO SENSITIVE...
I'M SHUDDERING...
どき
BA-DUMP
どき
BA-DUMP
はっ
GASP
...OH!

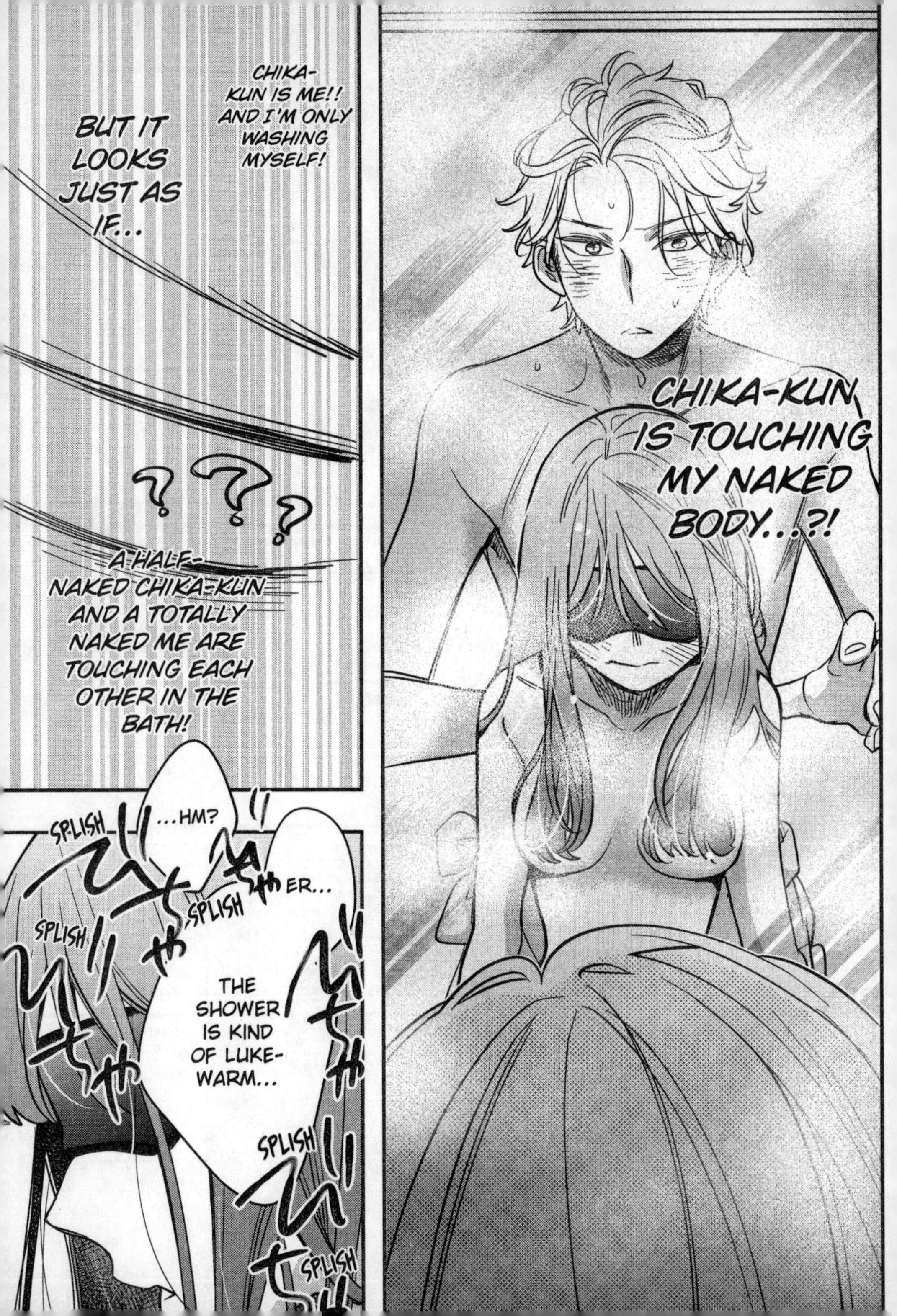
CHIKA-KUN IS TOUCHING MY NAKED BODY...?!
CHIKA-KUN IS ME!! AND I'M ONLY WASHING MYSELF!
BUT IT LOOKS JUST AS IF...
? ? ?
A HALF-NAKED CHIKA-KUN AND A TOTALLY NAKED ME ARE TOUCHING EACH OTHER IN THE BATH!
...HM?
ER...
SPLISH
SPLISH
SPLISH
THE SHOWER IS KIND OF LUKE-WARM...
SPLISH
SPLISH

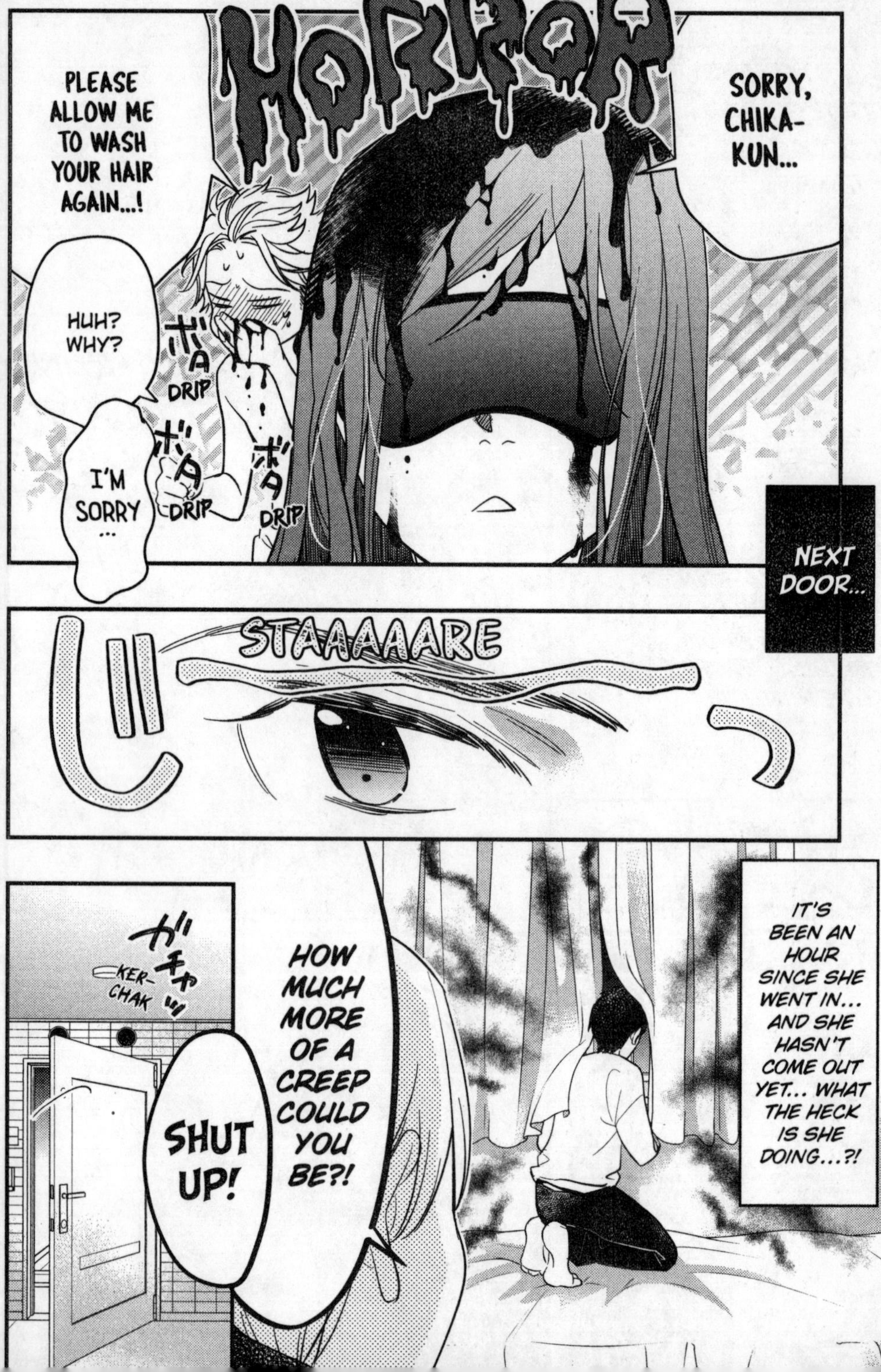

HORROR
SORRY, CHIKA-KUN...
PLEASE ALLOW ME TO WASH YOUR HAIR AGAIN...!
HUH? WHY?
ボタ DRIP
ボタ DRIP
ボタ DRIP
I'M SORRY ...
NEXT DOOR...
じー
STAAAAAARE
IT'S BEEN AN HOUR SINCE SHE WENT IN... AND SHE HASN'T COME OUT YET... WHAT THE HECK IS SHE DOING...?!
HOW MUCH MORE OF A CREEP COULD YOU BE?!
SHUT UP!
ガチャッ KER-CHAK

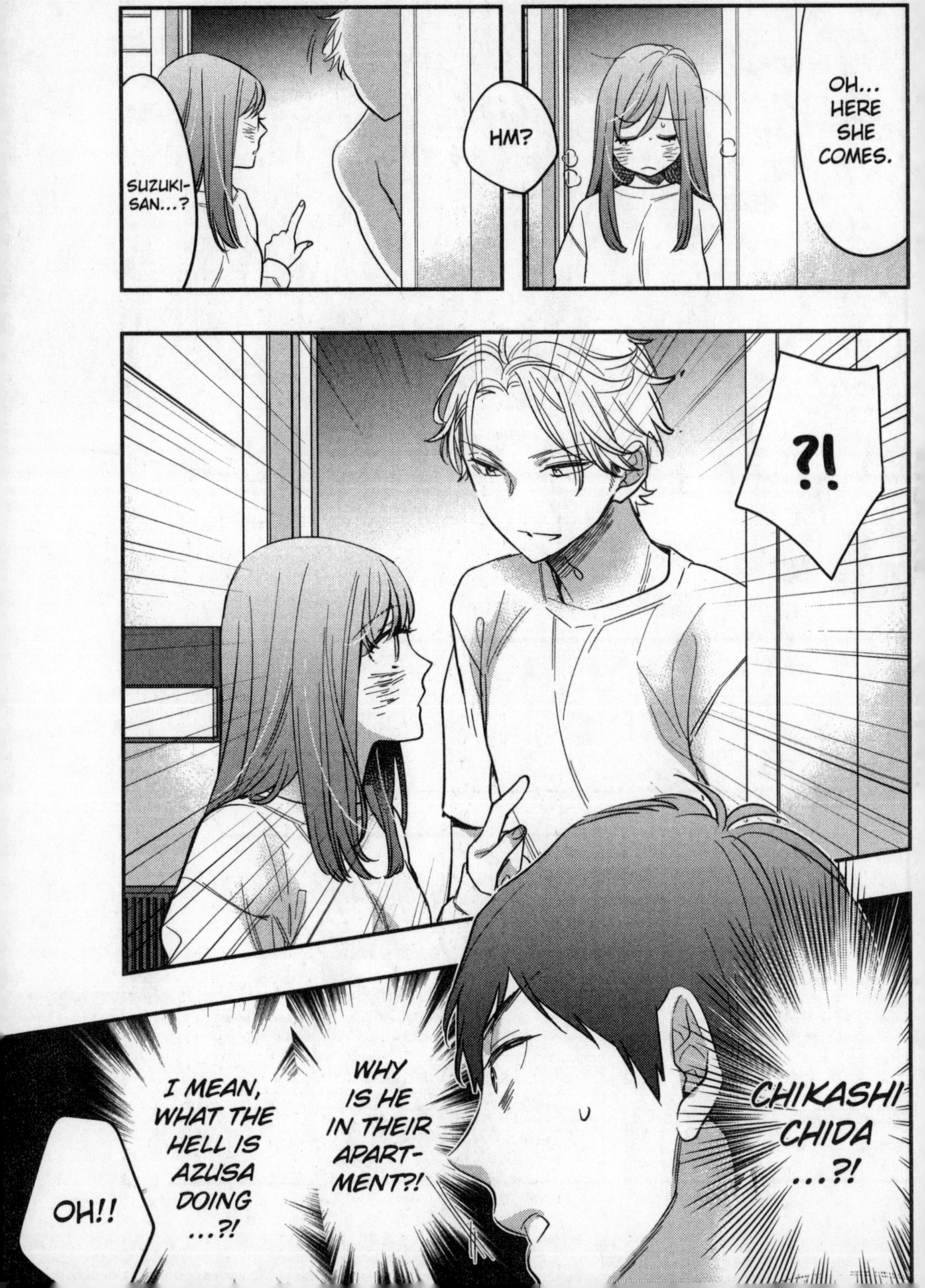
OH... HERE SHE COMES.
HM?
SUZUKI-SAN...?
?!
CHIKASHI CHIDA ...?!
WHY IS HE IN THEIR APART-MENT?!
I MEAN, WHAT THE HELL IS AZUSA DOING ...?!
OH!!

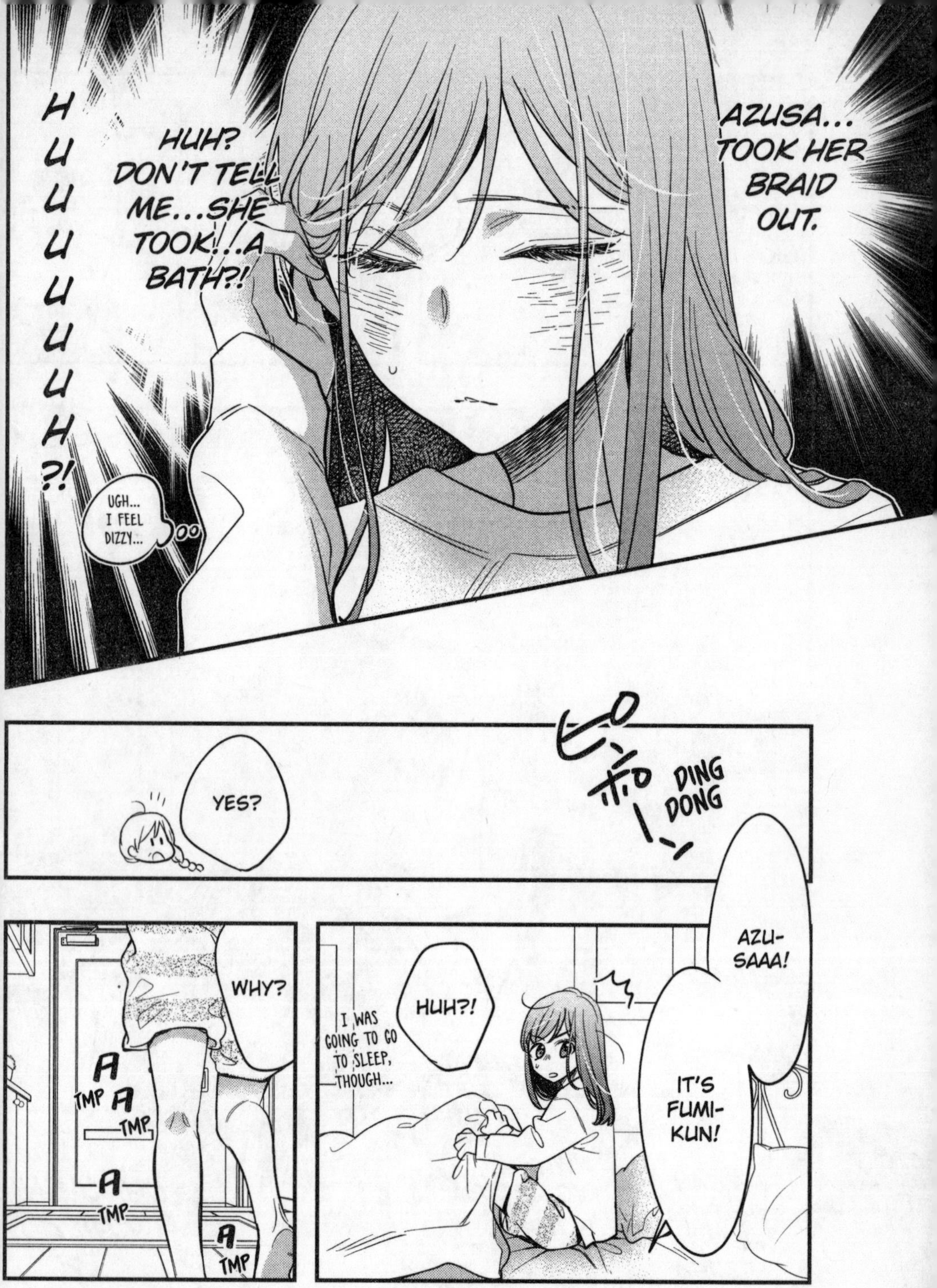
AZUSA... TOOK HER BRAID OUT.
HUH? DON'T TELL ME...SHE TOOK...A BATH?!
HUUUUUUUH?!
UGH... I FEEL DIZZY...
DING DONG
YES?
AZU-SAAA! IT'S FUMI-KUN!
HUH?!
I WAS GOING TO GO TO SLEEP, THOUGH...
WHY?
TMP
TMP
TMP
TMP

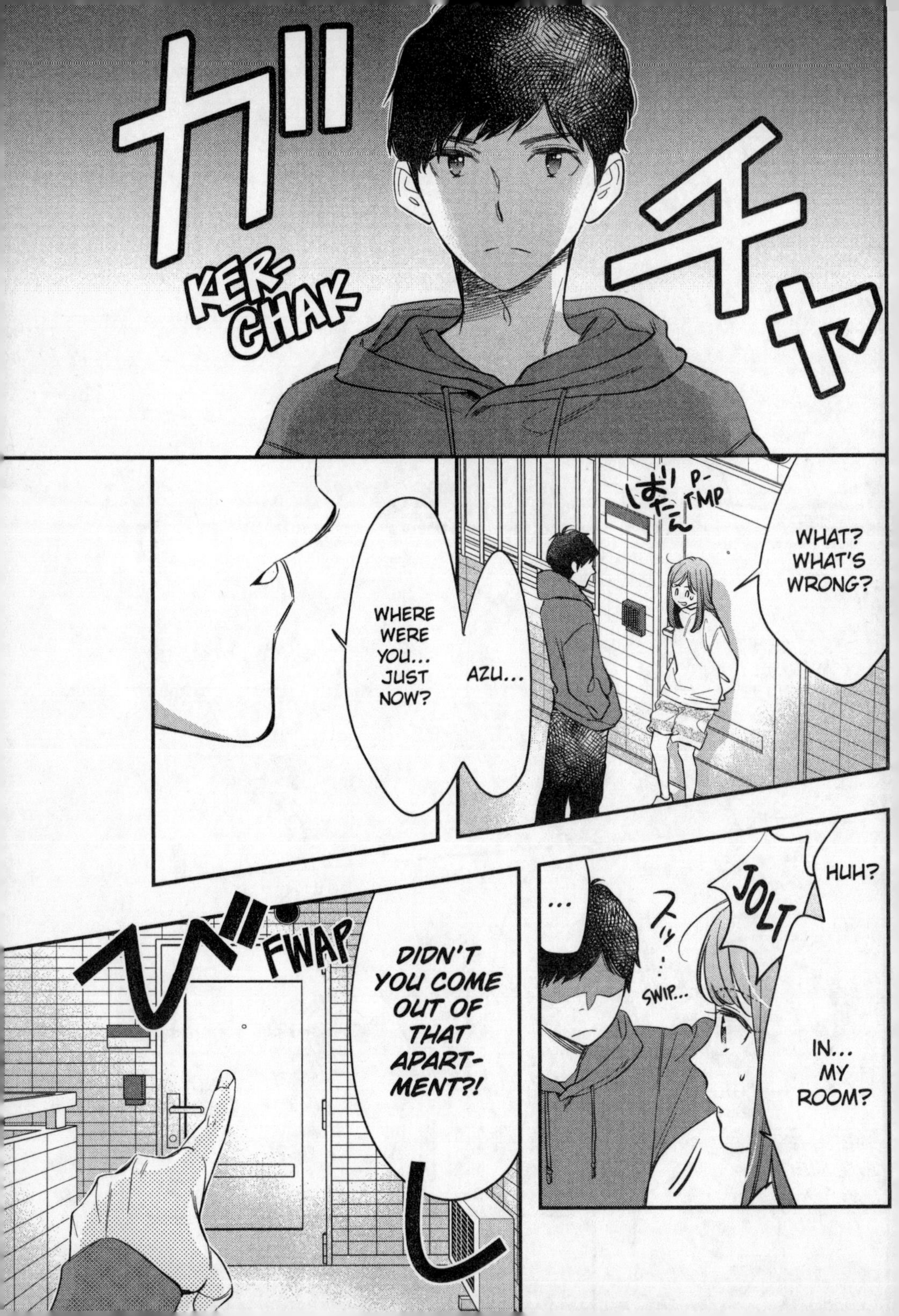
ガチャ
KER-CHAK
ばたん
P-TMP
WHAT? WHAT'S WRONG?
AZU...
WHERE WERE YOU... JUST NOW?
HUH?
JOLT
...
スッ
SWIP...
IN... MY ROOM?
へし
FWAP
DIDN'T YOU COME OUT OF THAT APART-MENT?!

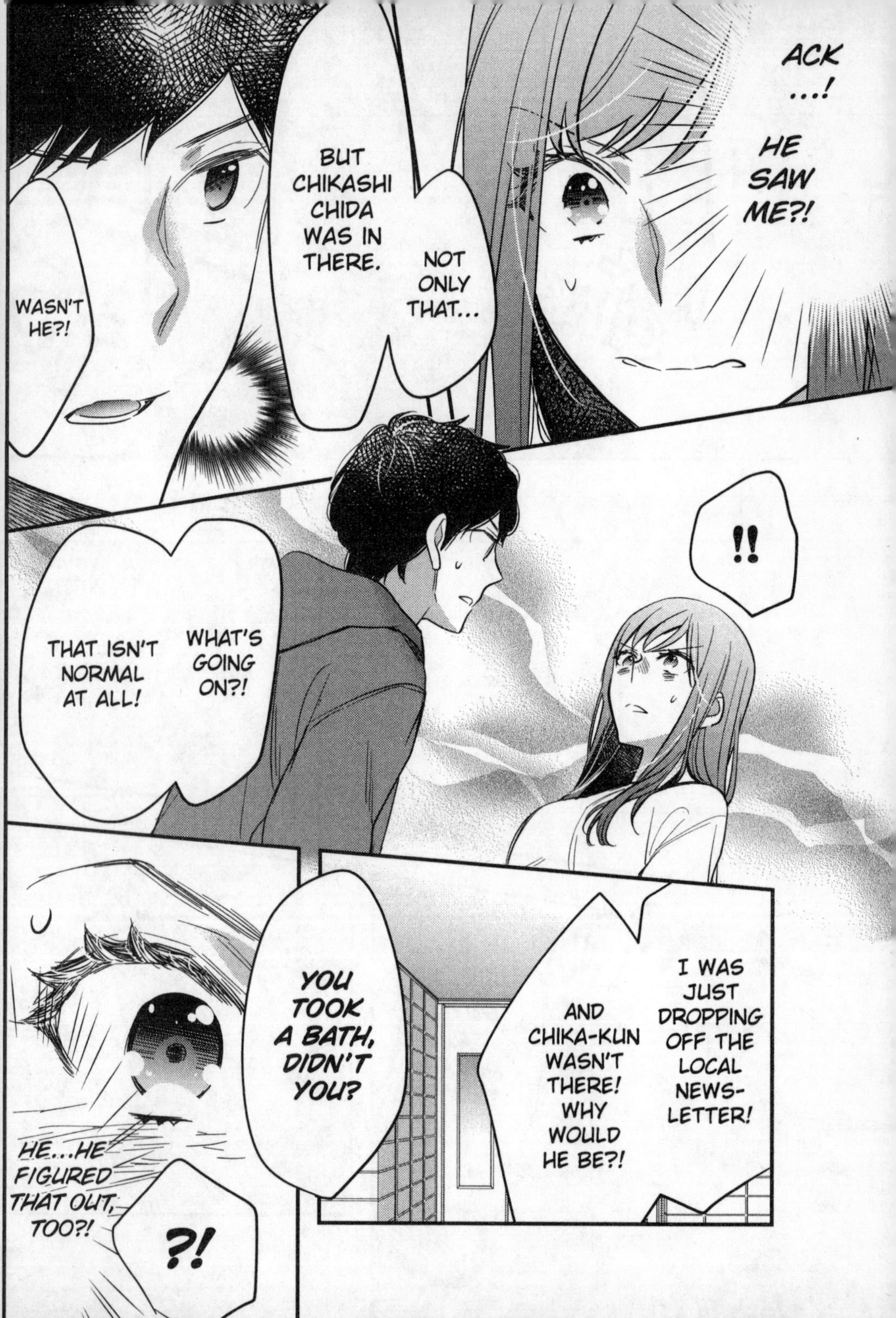
ACK ...!
HE SAW ME?!
NOT ONLY THAT...
BUT CHIKASHI CHIDA WAS IN THERE.
WASN'T HE?!
!!
WHAT'S GOING ON?!
THAT ISN'T NORMAL AT ALL!
I WAS JUST DROPPING OFF THE LOCAL NEWS-LETTER!
AND CHIKA-KUN WASN'T THERE! WHY WOULD HE BE?!
YOU TOOK A BATH, DIDN'T YOU?
?!
HE...HE FIGURED THAT OUT, TOO?!

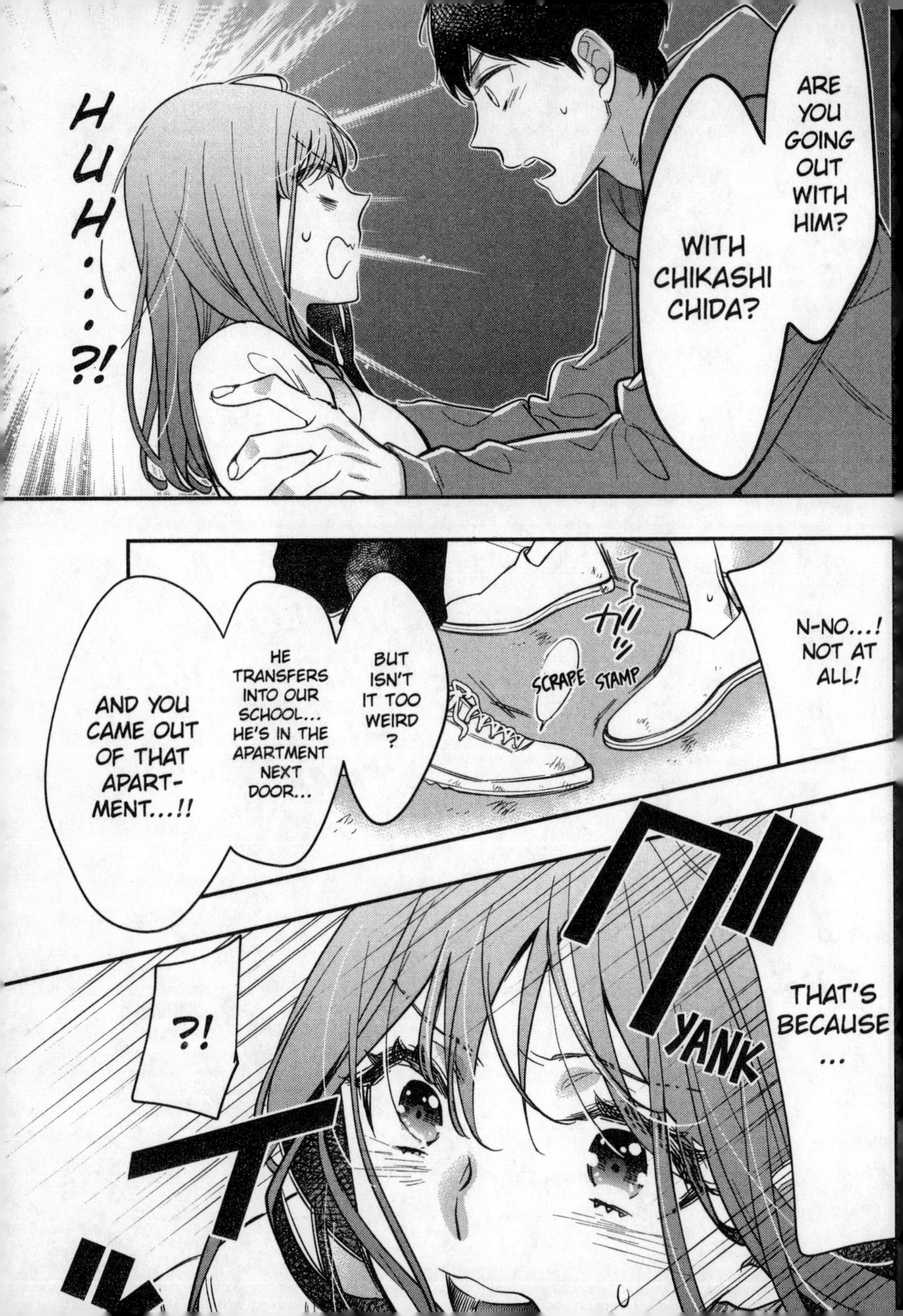

ARE YOU GOING OUT WITH HIM?
WITH CHIKASHI CHIDA?
HUH...?!
N-NO...! NOT AT ALL!
STAMP
SCRAPE
BUT ISN'T IT TOO WEIRD?
HE TRANSFERS INTO OUR SCHOOL... HE'S IN THE APARTMENT NEXT DOOR...
AND YOU CAME OUT OF THAT APART-MENT...!!
THAT'S BECAUSE ...
YANK
?!

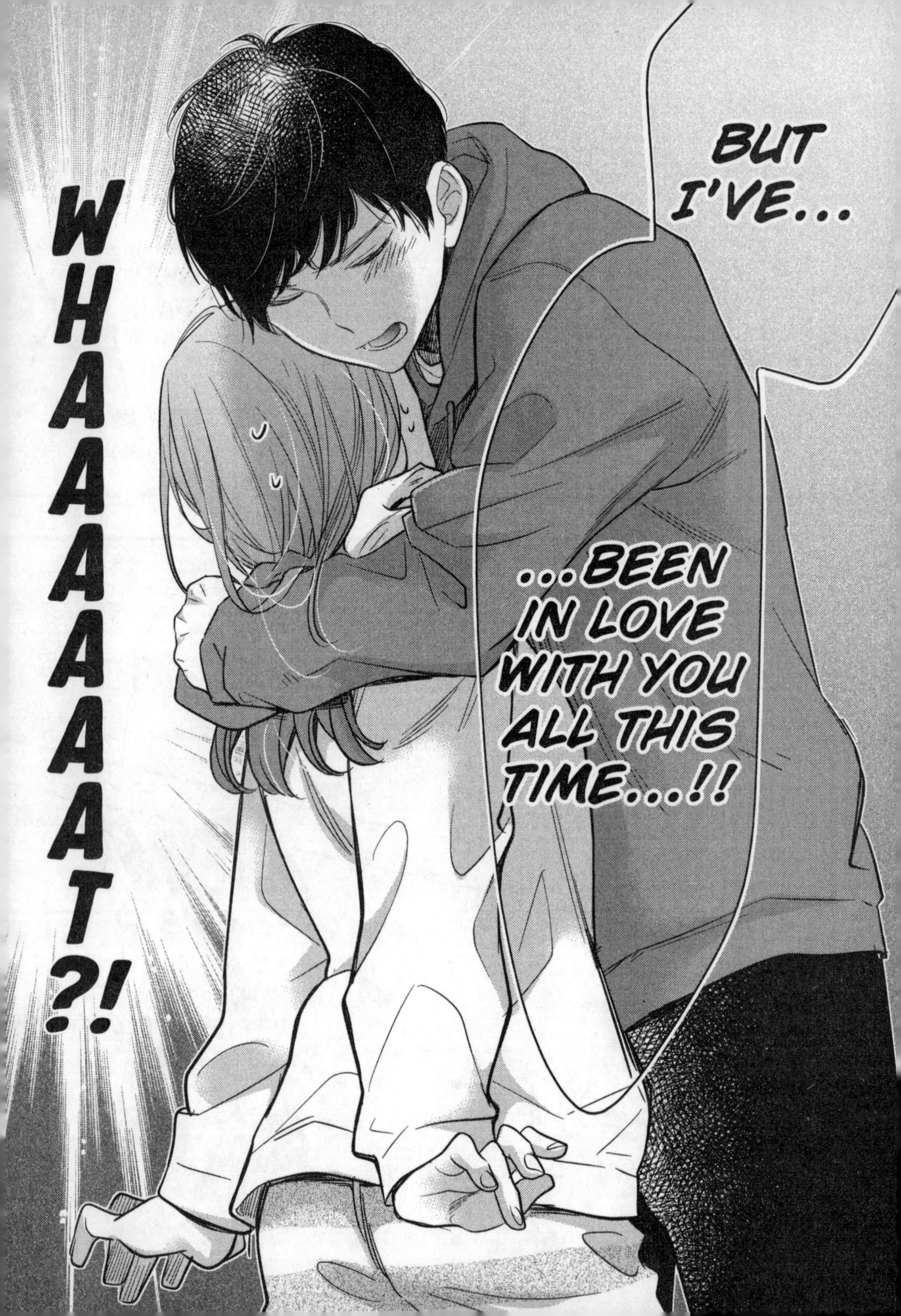
BUT I'VE...
...BEEN IN LOVE WITH YOU ALL THIS TIME...!!
WHAAAAAAT?!

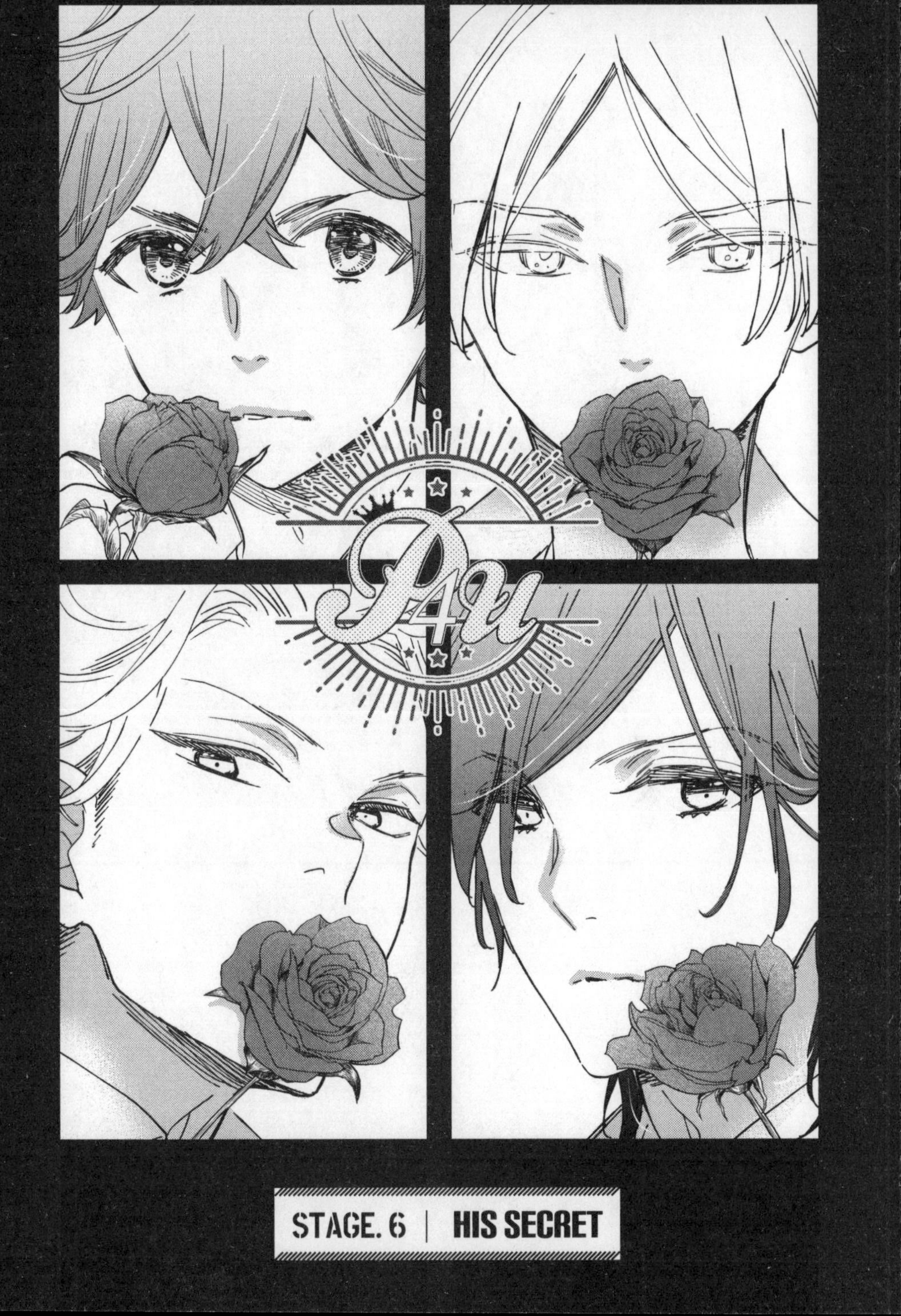

STAGE. 6 | HIS SECRET

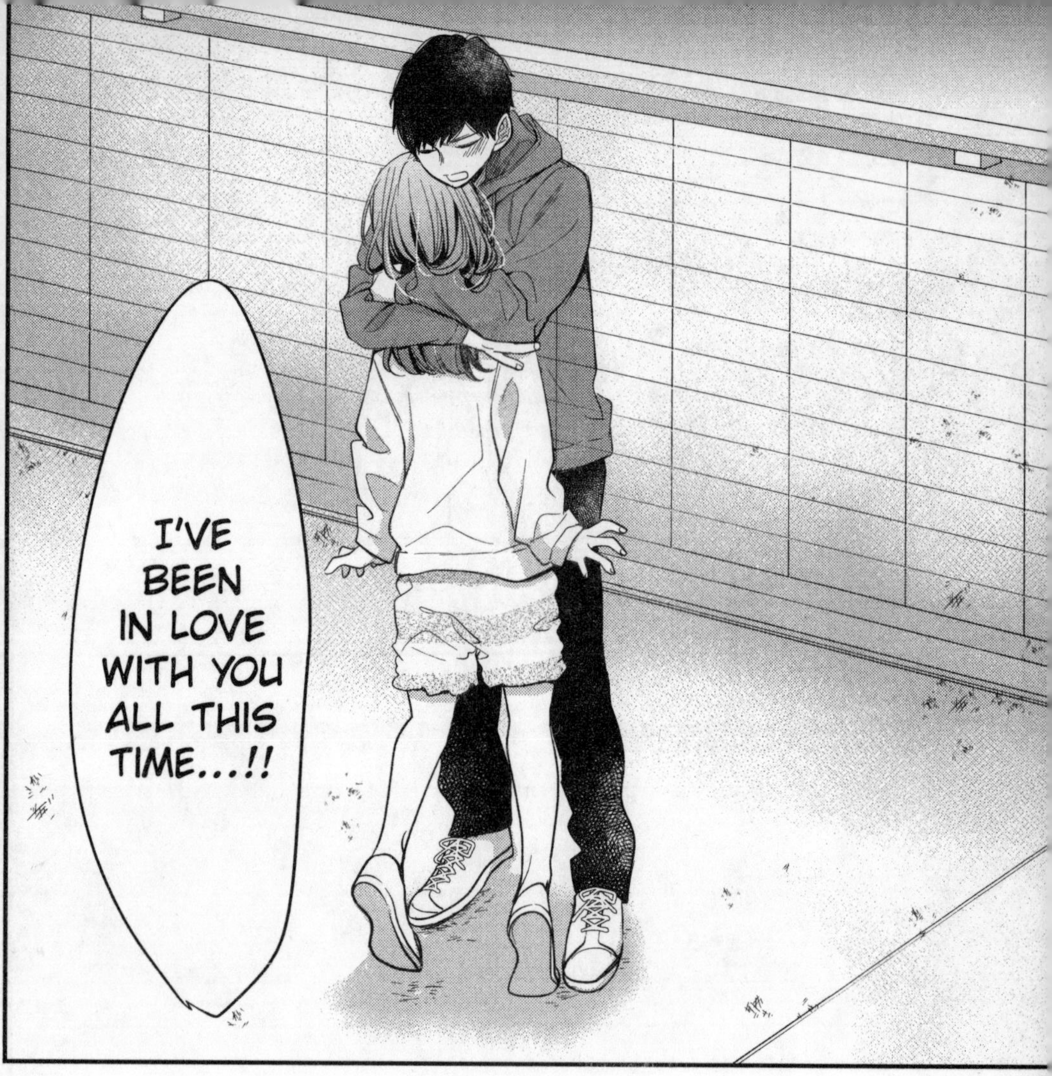
I'VE BEEN IN LOVE WITH YOU ALL THIS TIME...!!

STAR⇄CROSSED!!

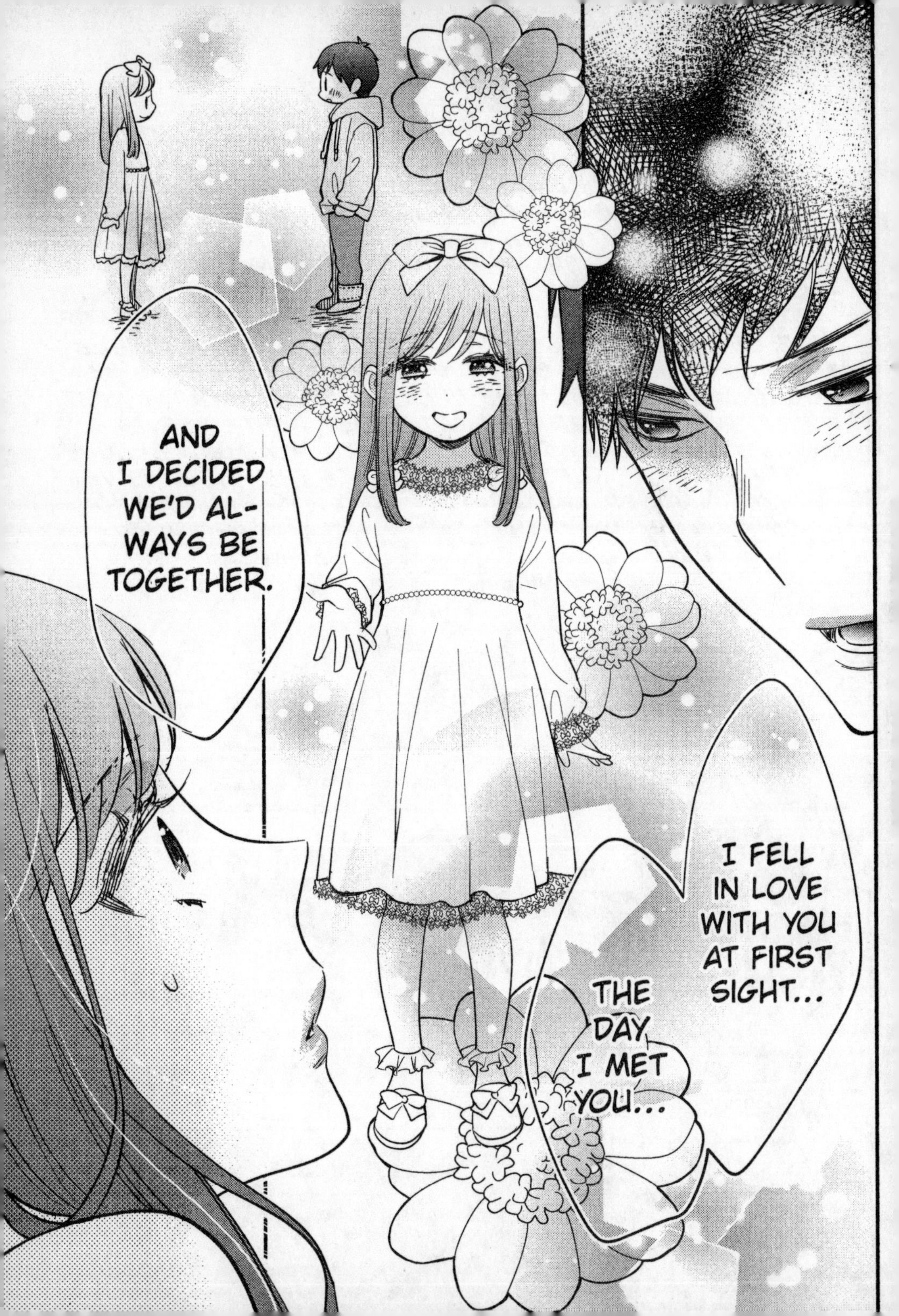
I FELL IN LOVE WITH YOU AT FIRST SIGHT...
THE DAY I MET YOU...
AND I DECIDED WE'D AL-WAYS BE TOGETHER.

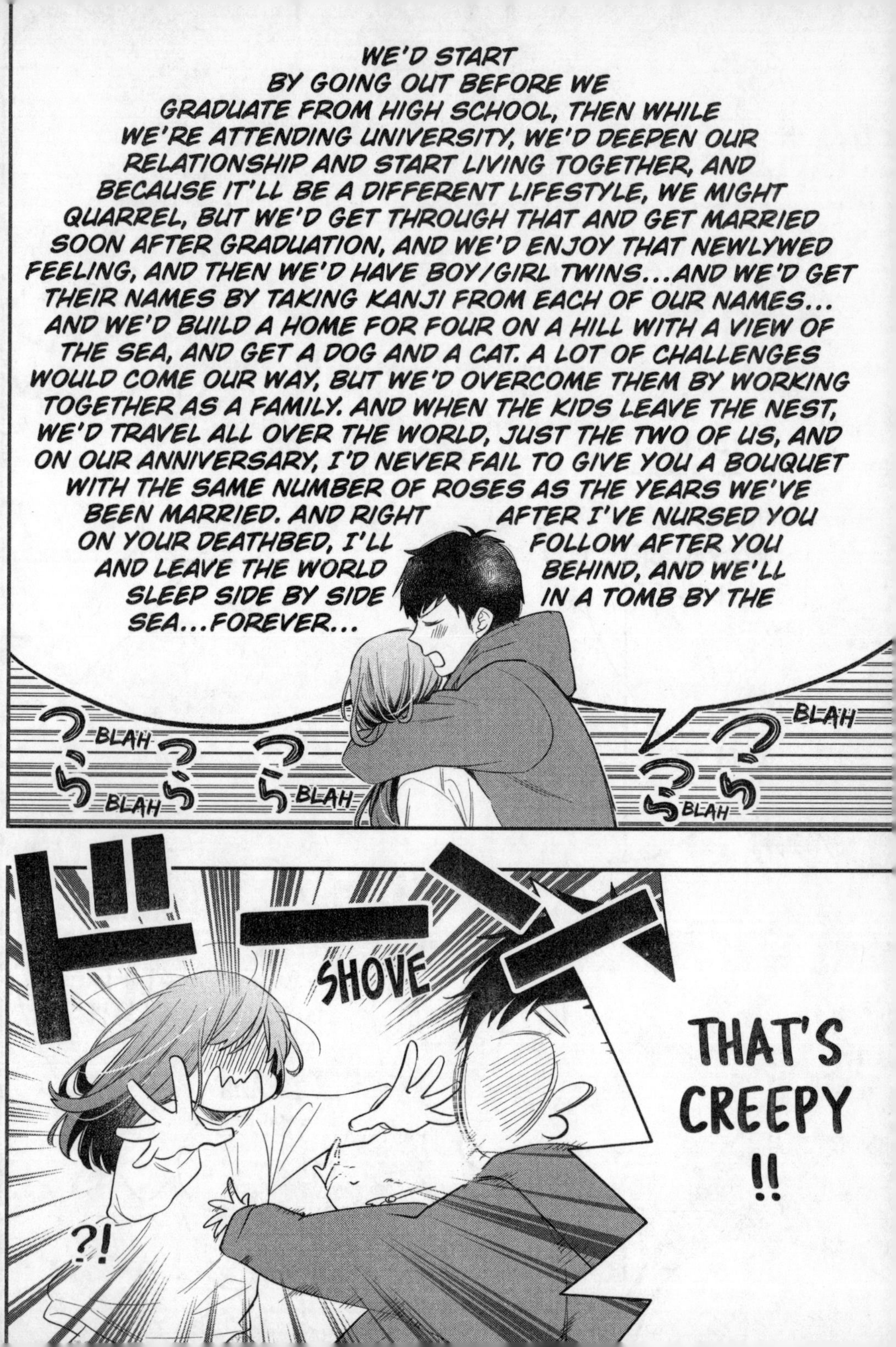
WE'D START BY GOING OUT BEFORE WE GRADUATE FROM HIGH SCHOOL, THEN WHILE WE'RE ATTENDING UNIVERSITY, WE'D DEEPEN OUR RELATIONSHIP AND START LIVING TOGETHER, AND BECAUSE IT'LL BE A DIFFERENT LIFESTYLE, WE MIGHT QUARREL, BUT WE'D GET THROUGH THAT AND GET MARRIED SOON AFTER GRADUATION, AND WE'D ENJOY THAT NEWLYWED FEELING, AND THEN WE'D HAVE BOY/GIRL TWINS...AND WE'D GET THEIR NAMES BY TAKING KANJI FROM EACH OF OUR NAMES... AND WE'D BUILD A HOME FOR FOUR ON A HILL WITH A VIEW OF THE SEA, AND GET A DOG AND A CAT. A LOT OF CHALLENGES WOULD COME OUR WAY, BUT WE'D OVERCOME THEM BY WORKING TOGETHER AS A FAMILY. AND WHEN THE KIDS LEAVE THE NEST, WE'D TRAVEL ALL OVER THE WORLD, JUST THE TWO OF US, AND ON OUR ANNIVERSARY, I'D NEVER FAIL TO GIVE YOU A BOUQUET WITH THE SAME NUMBER OF ROSES AS THE YEARS WE'VE BEEN MARRIED. AND RIGHT AFTER I'VE NURSED YOU ON YOUR DEATHBED, I'LL FOLLOW AFTER YOU AND LEAVE THE WORLD BEHIND, AND WE'LL SLEEP SIDE BY SIDE IN A TOMB BY THE SEA...FOREVER...
BLAH
BLAH
BLAH
BLAH
BLAH
THAT'S CREEPY !!
SHOVE
?!

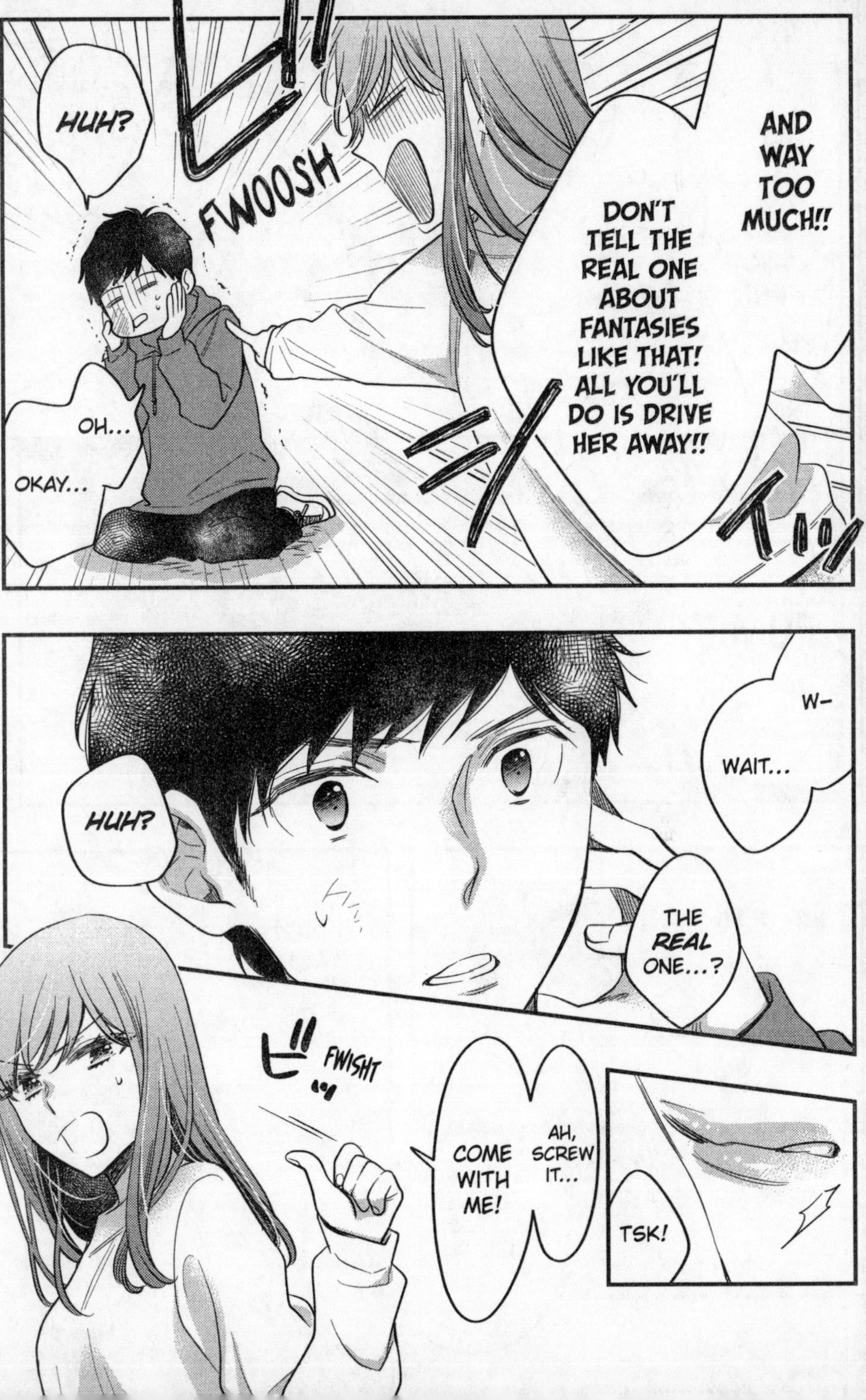
AND WAY TOO MUCH!!
DON'T TELL THE REAL ONE ABOUT FANTASIES LIKE THAT! ALL YOU'LL DO IS DRIVE HER AWAY!!
FWOOSH
HUH?
OH... OKAY...
W- WAIT...
THE REAL ONE...?
HUH?
TSK!
AH, SCREW IT...
COME WITH ME!
FWISHT

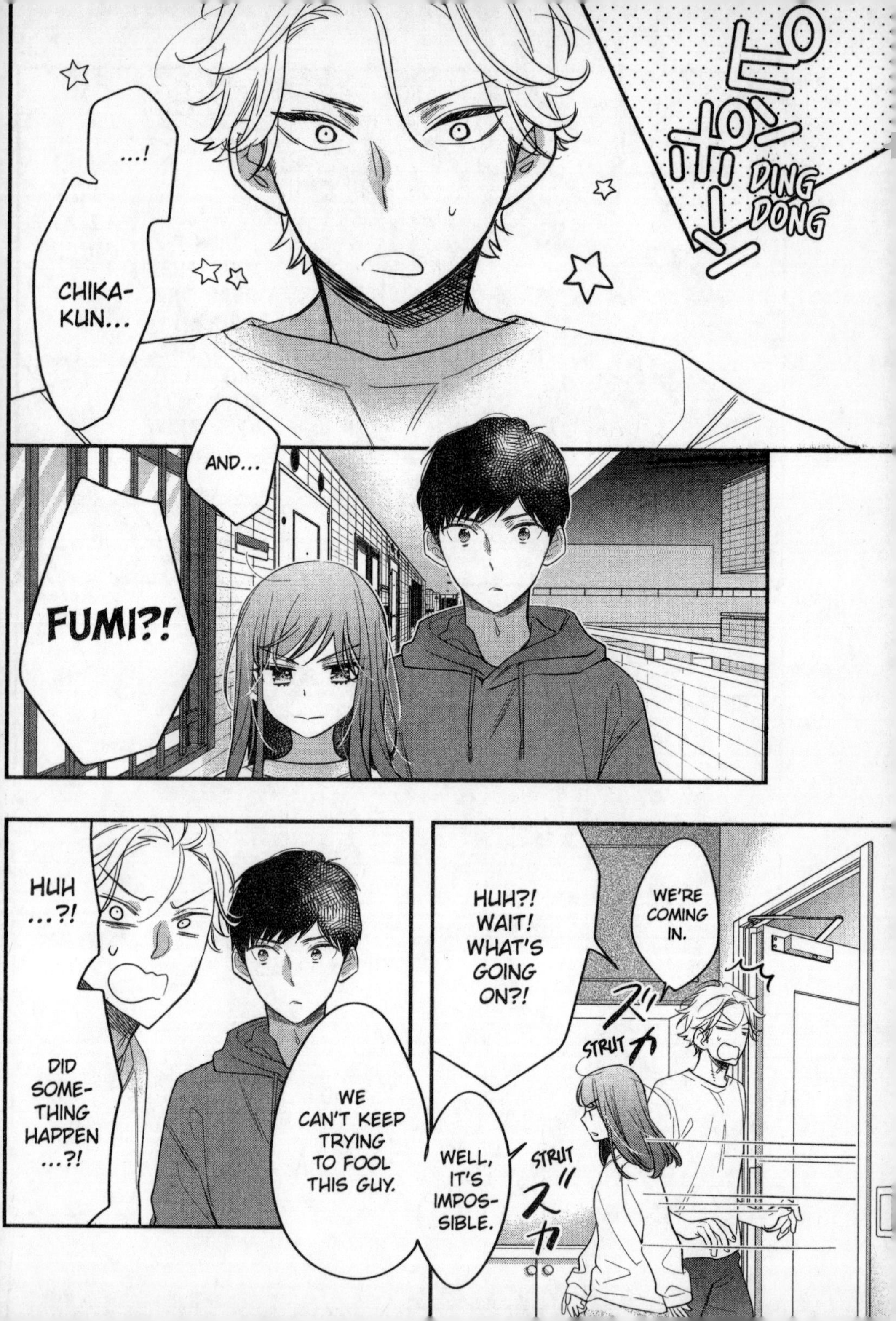
ピンポーン
DING DONG
...!
CHIKA-KUN...
AND...
FUMI?!
WE'RE COMING IN.
HUH?! WAIT! WHAT'S GOING ON?!
ズカ
STRUT
WELL, IT'S IMPOSSIBLE.
STRUT
ズカ
WE CAN'T KEEP TRYING TO FOOL THIS GUY.
HUH ...?!
DID SOMETHING HAPPEN ...?!

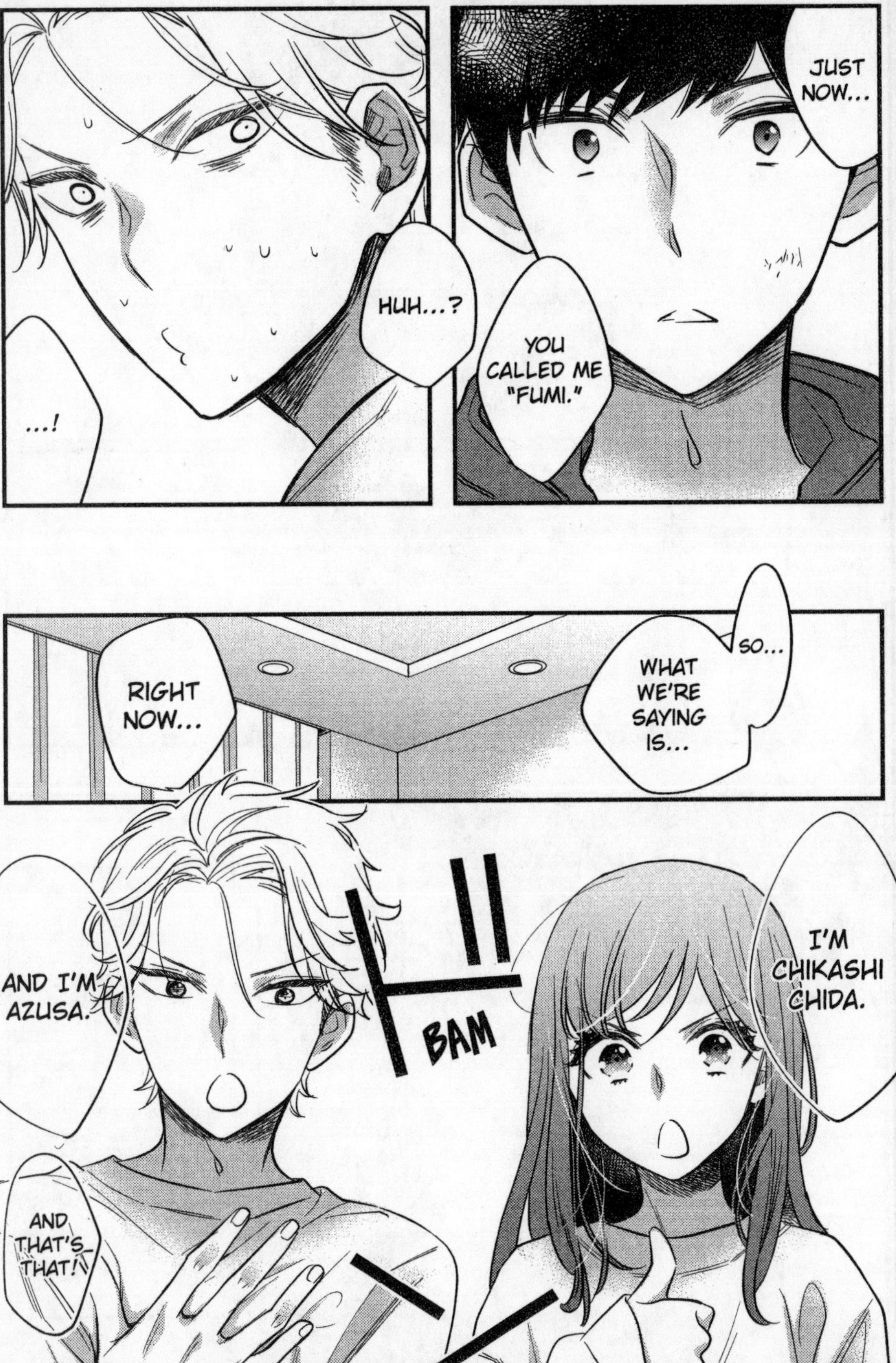
JUST NOW...
YOU CALLED ME "FUMI."
HUH...?
...!
SO...
WHAT WE'RE SAYING IS...
RIGHT NOW...
I'M CHIKASHI CHIDA.
BAM
AND I'M AZUSA.
AND THAT'S THAT!

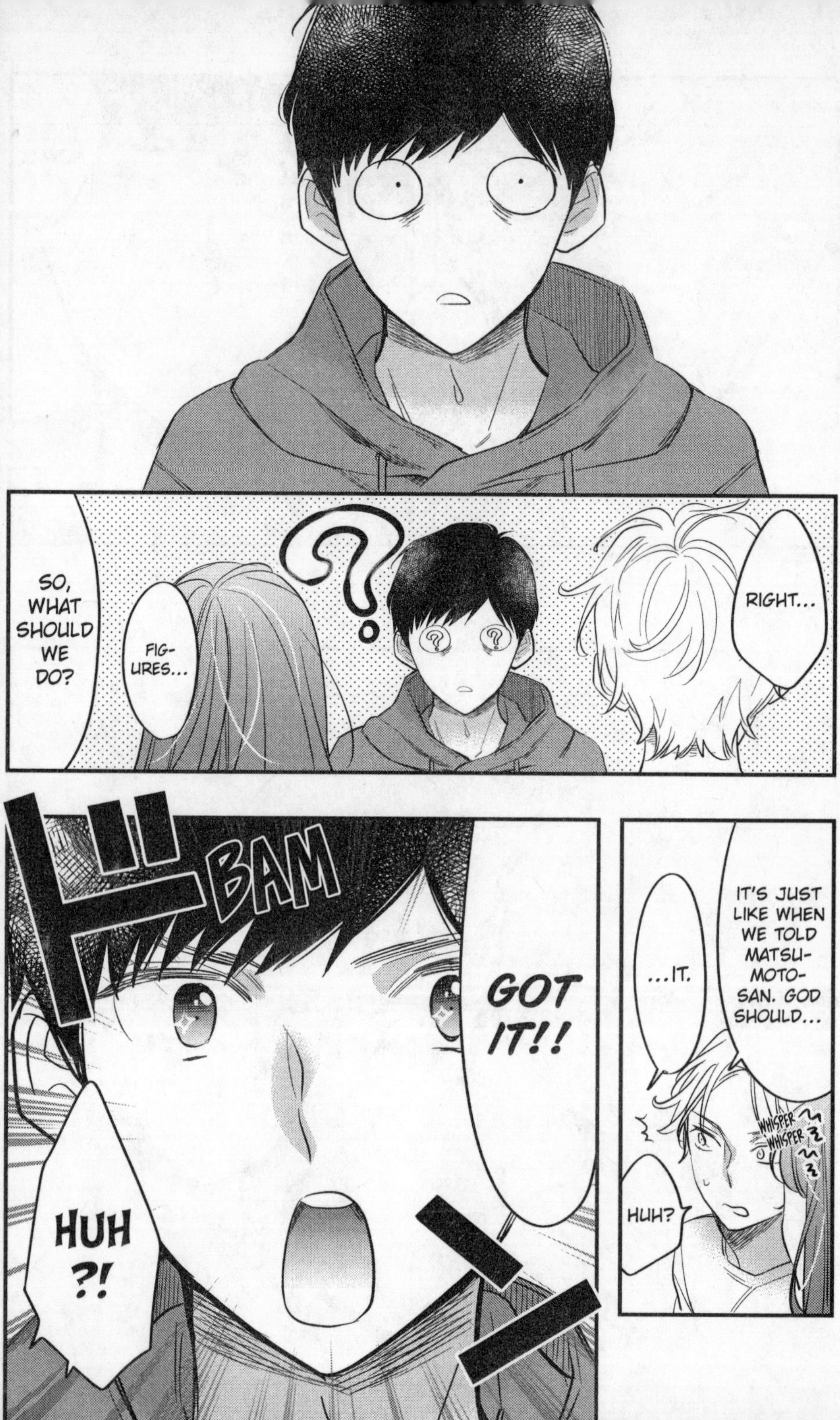
RIGHT...
FIG-URES...
SO, WHAT SHOULD WE DO?
IT'S JUST LIKE WHEN WE TOLD MATSU-MOTO-SAN. GOD SHOULD...
...IT.
WHISPER WHISPER
HUH?
BAM
GOT IT!!
HUH ?!

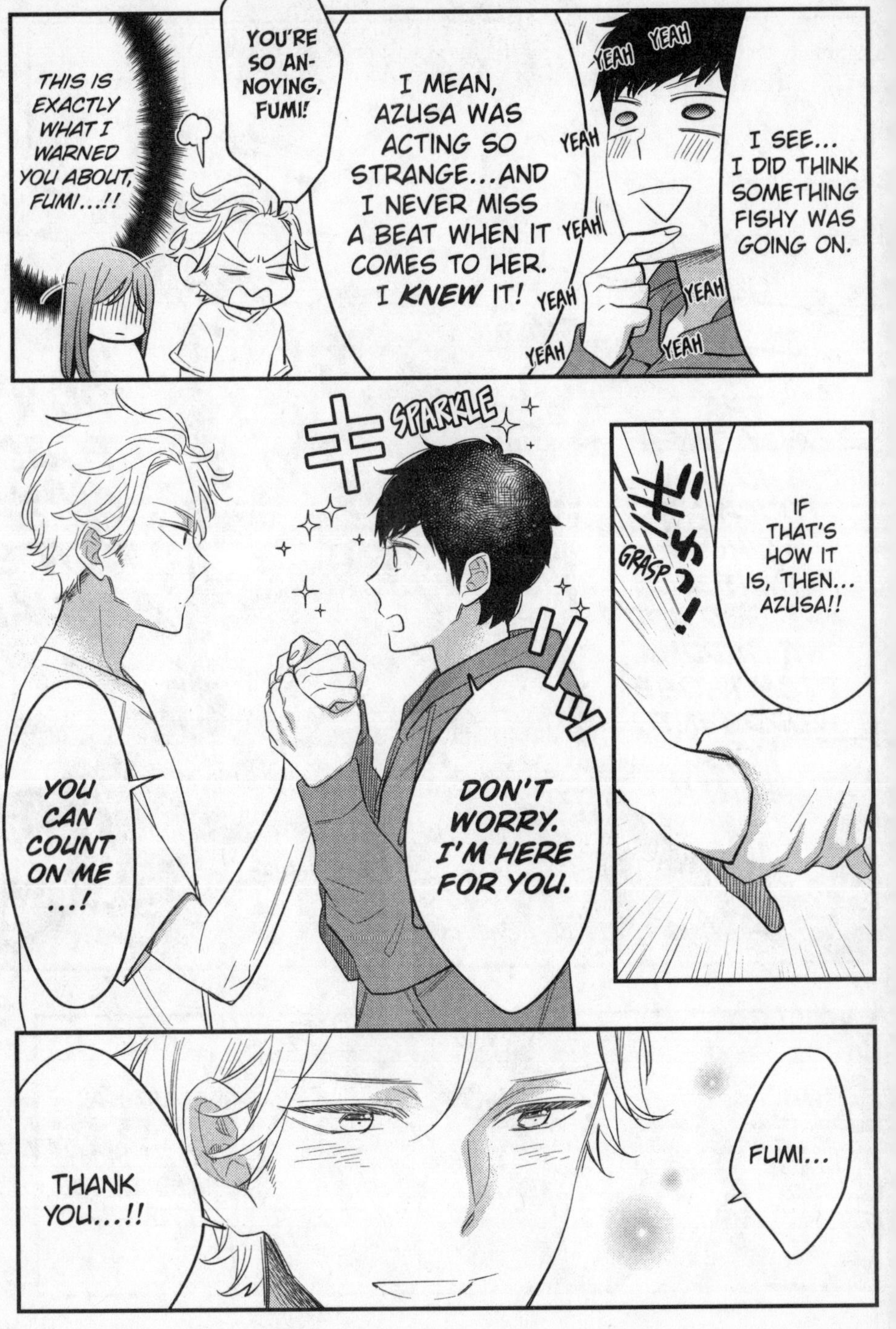
I SEE... I DID THINK SOMETHING FISHY WAS GOING ON.
YEAH YEAH YEAH YEAH YEAH YEAH YEAH YEAH
I MEAN, AZUSA WAS ACTING SO STRANGE...AND I NEVER MISS A BEAT WHEN IT COMES TO HER. I KNEW IT!
YOU'RE SO AN-NOYING, FUMI!
THIS IS EXACTLY WHAT I WARNED YOU ABOUT, FUMI...!!
GRASP
IF THAT'S HOW IT IS, THEN... AZUSA!!
SPARKLE
DON'T WORRY. I'M HERE FOR YOU.
YOU CAN COUNT ON ME ...!
FUMI...
THANK YOU...!!

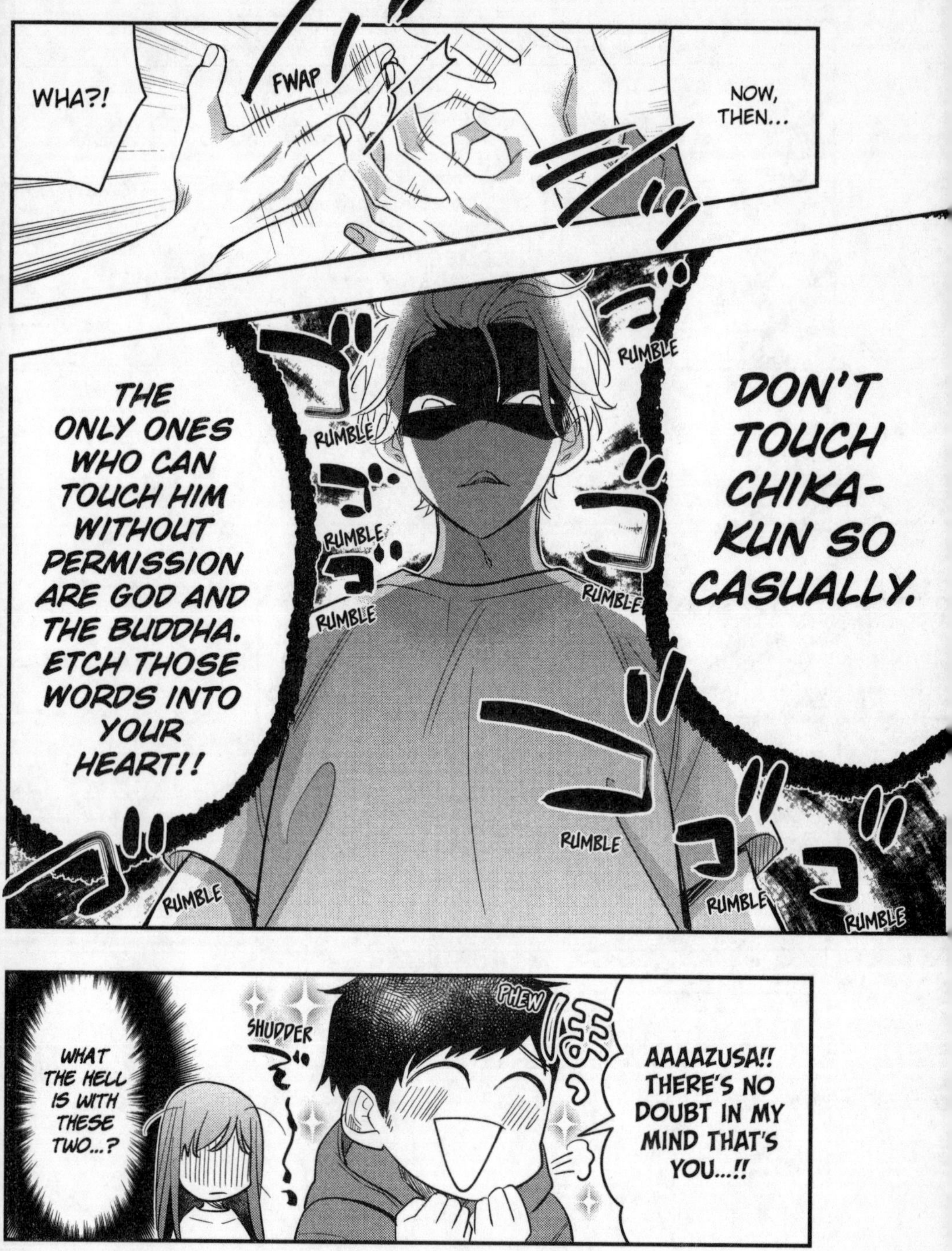
NOW, THEN...
FWAP
WHA?!
RUMBLE
DON'T TOUCH CHIKA-KUN SO CASUALLY.
RUMBLE
THE ONLY ONES WHO CAN TOUCH HIM WITHOUT PERMISSION ARE GOD AND THE BUDDHA. ETCH THOSE WORDS INTO YOUR HEART!!
RUMBLE
RUMBLE
RUMBLE
RUMBLE
RUMBLE
RUMBLE
RUMBLE
RUMBLE
AAAAZUSA!! THERE'S NO DOUBT IN MY MIND THAT'S YOU...!!
PHEW
SHUDDER
WHAT THE HELL IS WITH THESE TWO...?

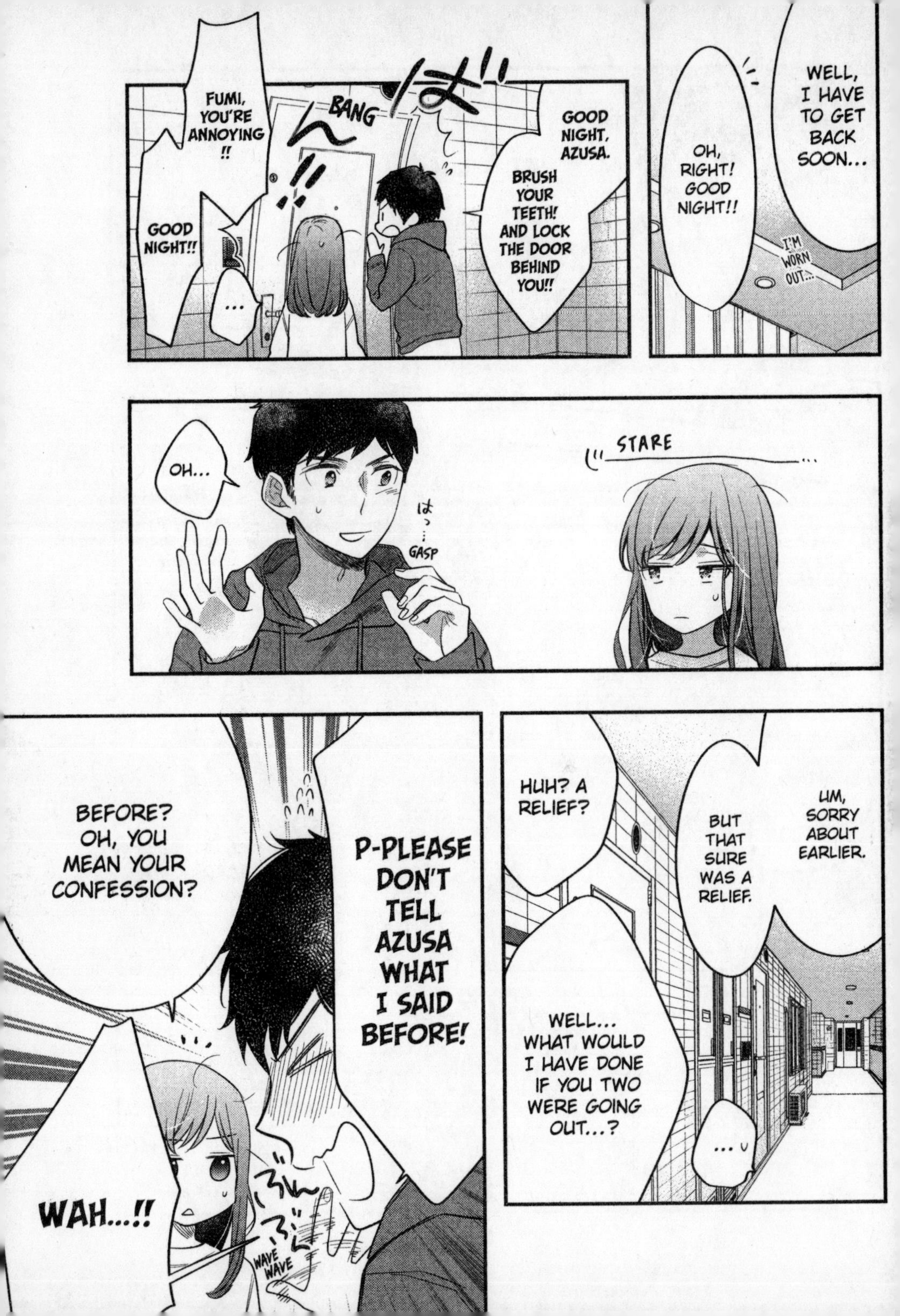
WELL, I HAVE TO GET BACK SOON...
OH, RIGHT! GOOD NIGHT!!
I'M WORN OUT...
GOOD NIGHT, AZUSA.
BRUSH YOUR TEETH! AND LOCK THE DOOR BEHIND YOU!!
BANG
FUMI, YOU'RE ANNOYING!!
GOOD NIGHT!!
...
STARE
OH...
GASP
UM, SORRY ABOUT EARLIER.
BUT THAT SURE WAS A RELIEF.
HUH? A RELIEF?
WELL... WHAT WOULD I HAVE DONE IF YOU TWO WERE GOING OUT...?
...
P-PLEASE DON'T TELL AZUSA WHAT I SAID BEFORE!
BEFORE? OH, YOU MEAN YOUR CONFESSION?
WAH...!!
WAVE WAVE

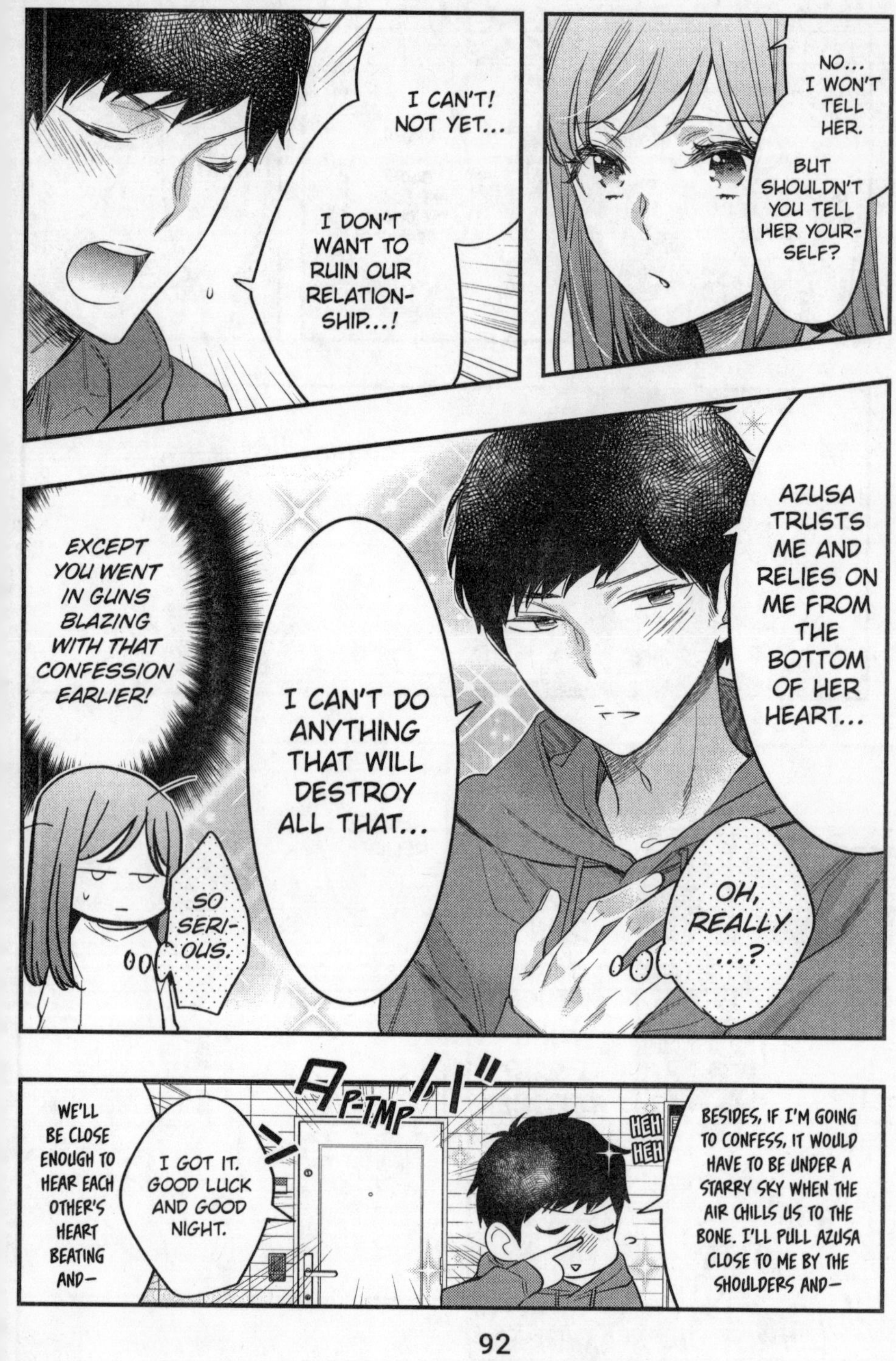
NO... I WON'T TELL HER.
BUT SHOULDN'T YOU TELL HER YOUR-SELF?
I CAN'T! NOT YET...
I DON'T WANT TO RUIN OUR RELATION-SHIP...!
AZUSA TRUSTS ME AND RELIES ON ME FROM THE BOTTOM OF HER HEART...
I CAN'T DO ANYTHING THAT WILL DESTROY ALL THAT...
OH, REALLY ...?
EXCEPT YOU WENT IN GUNS BLAZING WITH THAT CONFESSION EARLIER!
SO SERI-OUS.
BESIDES, IF I'M GOING TO CONFESS, IT WOULD HAVE TO BE UNDER A STARRY SKY WHEN THE AIR CHILLS US TO THE BONE. I'LL PULL AZUSA CLOSE TO ME BY THE SHOULDERS AND—
HEH HEH
WE'LL BE CLOSE ENOUGH TO HEAR EACH OTHER'S HEART BEATING AND—
P-TMP
I GOT IT. GOOD LUCK AND GOOD NIGHT.

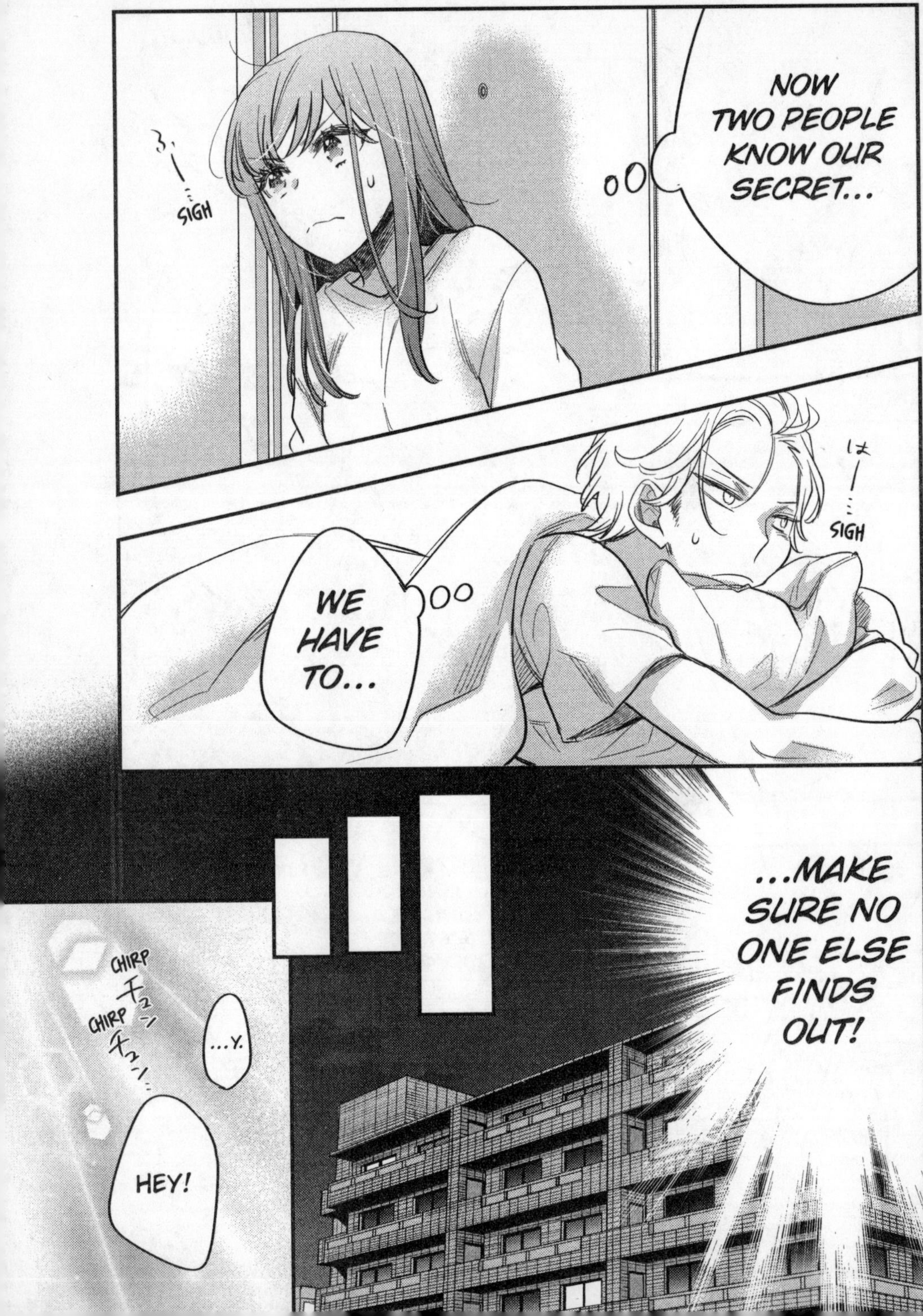
NOW TWO PEOPLE KNOW OUR SECRET...
SIGH
SIGH
WE HAVE TO...
...MAKE SURE NO ONE ELSE FINDS OUT!
CHIRP CHIRP
...Y.
HEY!

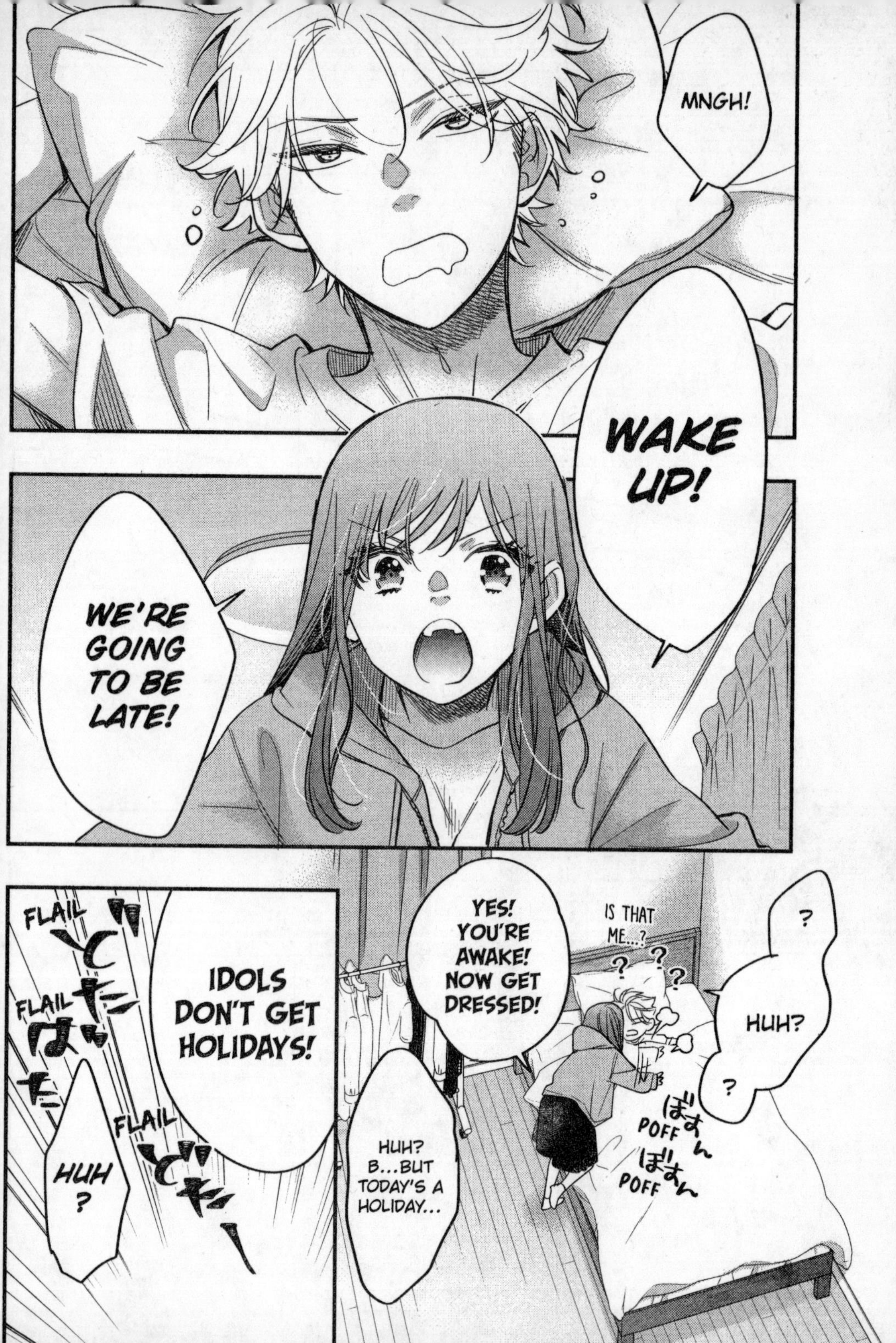
MNGH!
WAKE UP!
WE'RE GOING TO BE LATE!
?
IS THAT ME...?
HUH?
?
YES! YOU'RE AWAKE! NOW GET DRESSED!
POFF
POFF
HUH? B...BUT TODAY'S A HOLIDAY...
IDOLS DON'T GET HOLIDAYS!
FLAIL
FLAIL
FLAIL
HUH ?

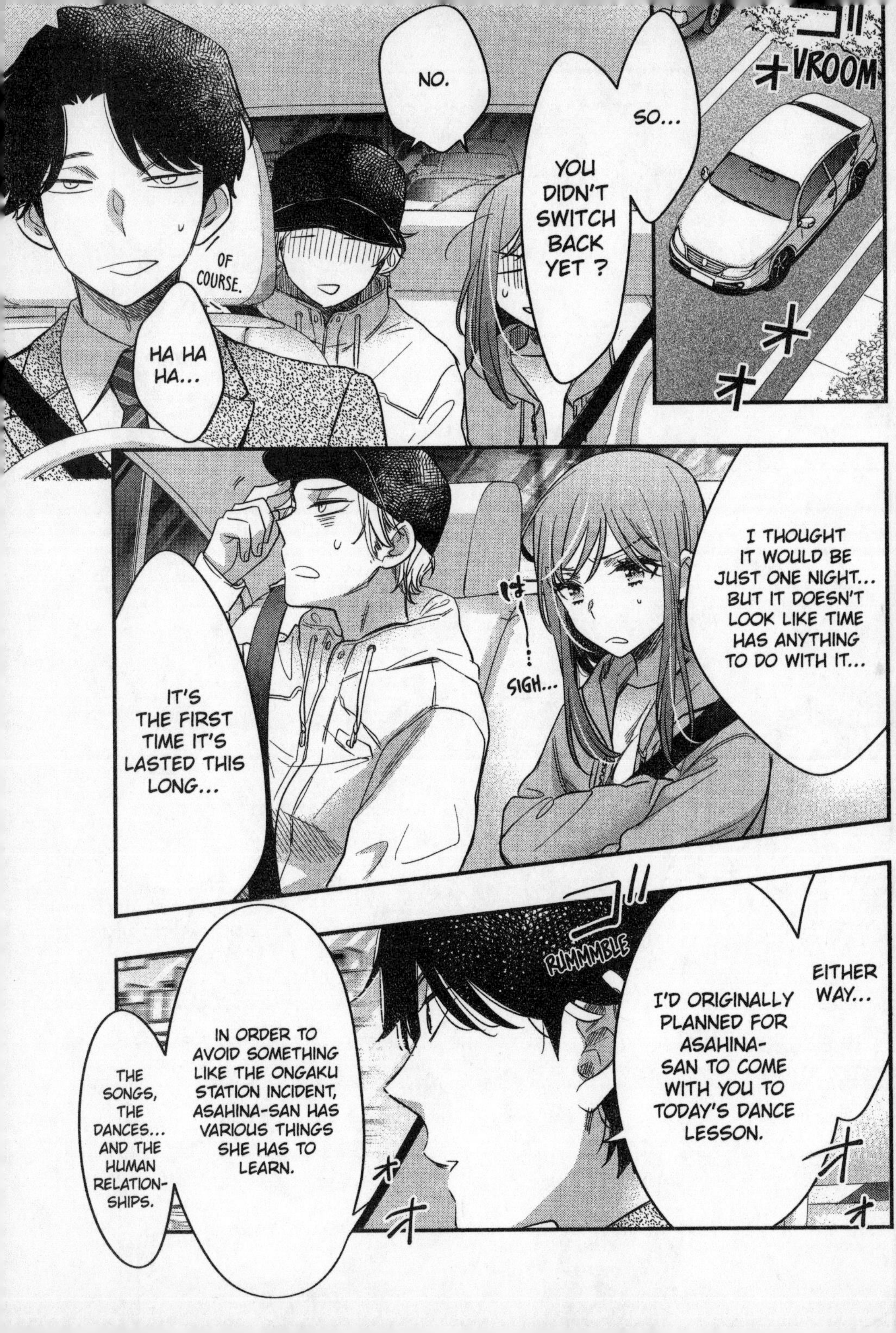
VROOM
SO...
YOU DIDN'T SWITCH BACK YET ?
NO.
OF COURSE.
HA HA HA...
I THOUGHT IT WOULD BE JUST ONE NIGHT... BUT IT DOESN'T LOOK LIKE TIME HAS ANYTHING TO DO WITH IT...
SIGH...
IT'S THE FIRST TIME IT'S LASTED THIS LONG...
RUMMMBLE
EITHER WAY...
I'D ORIGINALLY PLANNED FOR ASAHINA-SAN TO COME WITH YOU TO TODAY'S DANCE LESSON.
IN ORDER TO AVOID SOMETHING LIKE THE ONGAKU STATION INCIDENT, ASAHINA-SAN HAS VARIOUS THINGS SHE HAS TO LEARN.
THE SONGS, THE DANCES... AND THE HUMAN RELATIONSHIPS.

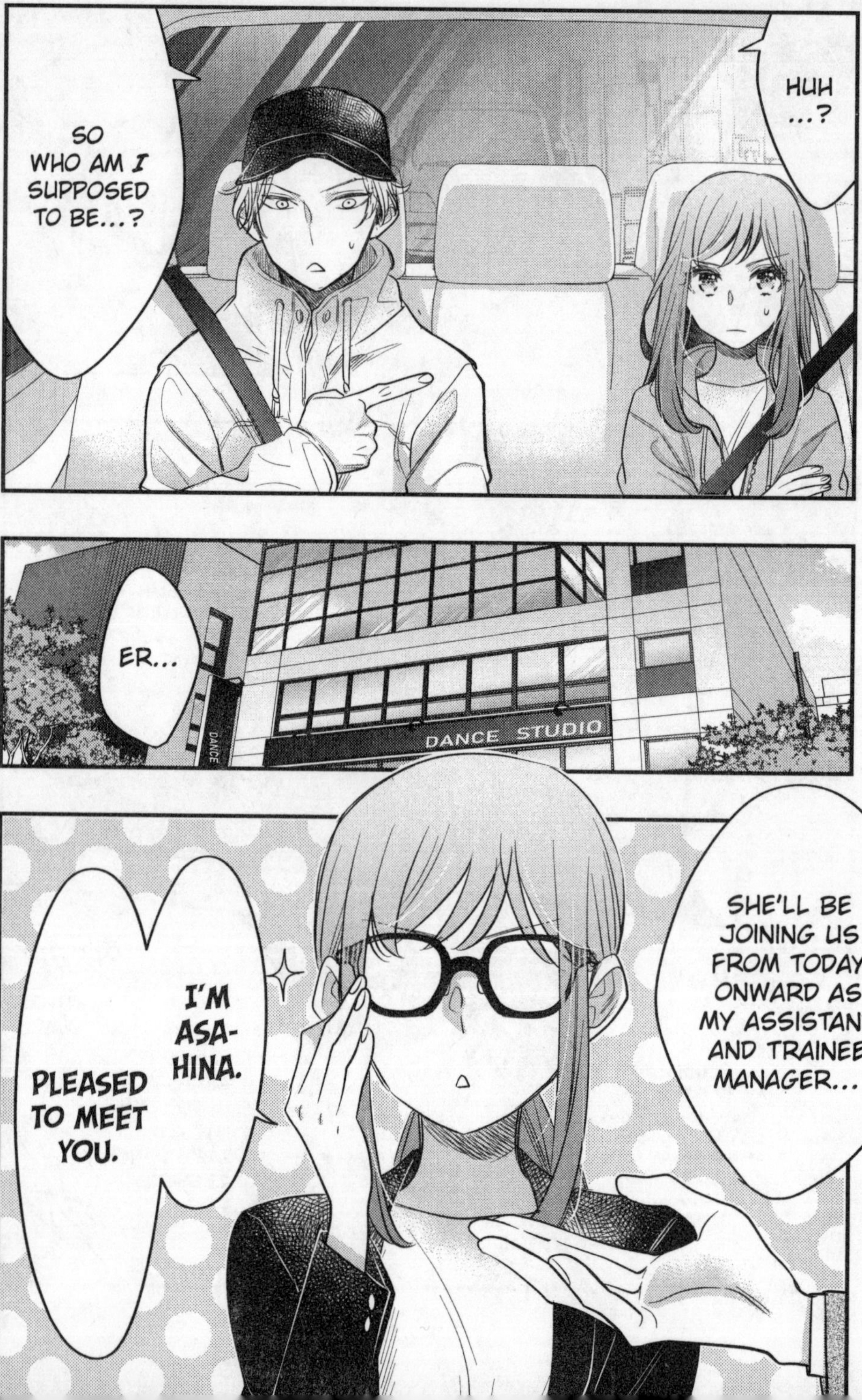
HUH ...?
SO WHO AM I SUPPOSED TO BE...?
ER...
DANCE STUDIO
DANCE
SHE'LL BE JOINING US FROM TODAY ONWARD AS MY ASSISTANT AND TRAINEE MANAGER...
I'M ASA-HINA.
PLEASED TO MEET YOU.

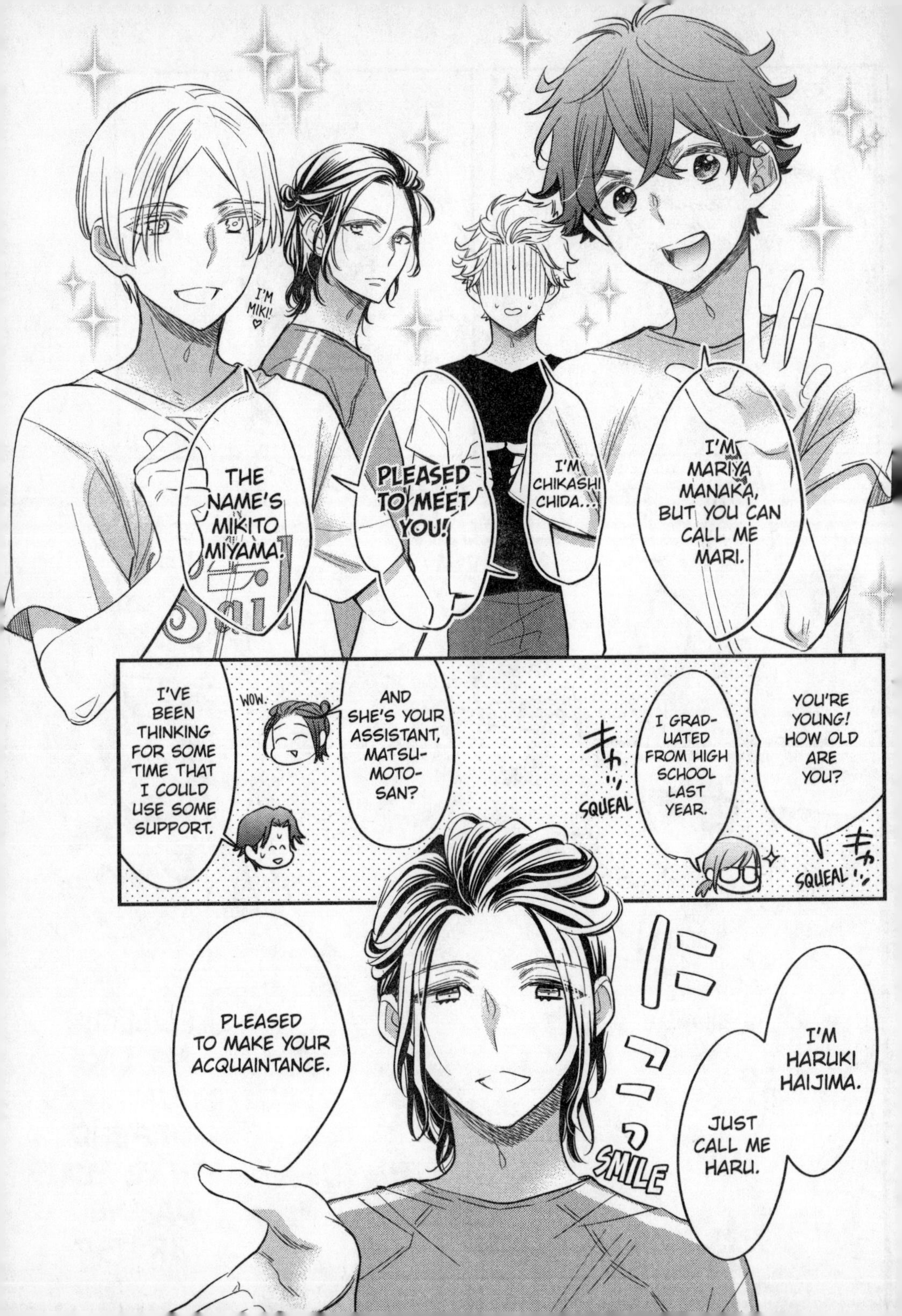
I'M MARIYA MANAKA, BUT YOU CAN CALL ME MARI.
I'M CHIKASHI CHIDA...
PLEASED TO MEET YOU!
I'M MIKI! ♡
THE NAME'S MIKITO MIYAMA!
YOU'RE YOUNG! HOW OLD ARE YOU?
SQUEAL
I GRAD-UATED FROM HIGH SCHOOL LAST YEAR.
SQUEAL
AND SHE'S YOUR ASSISTANT, MATSU-MOTO-SAN?
WOW.
I'VE BEEN THINKING FOR SOME TIME THAT I COULD USE SOME SUPPORT.
I'M HARUKI HAIJIMA.
JUST CALL ME HARU.
SMILE
PLEASED TO MAKE YOUR ACQUAINTANCE.

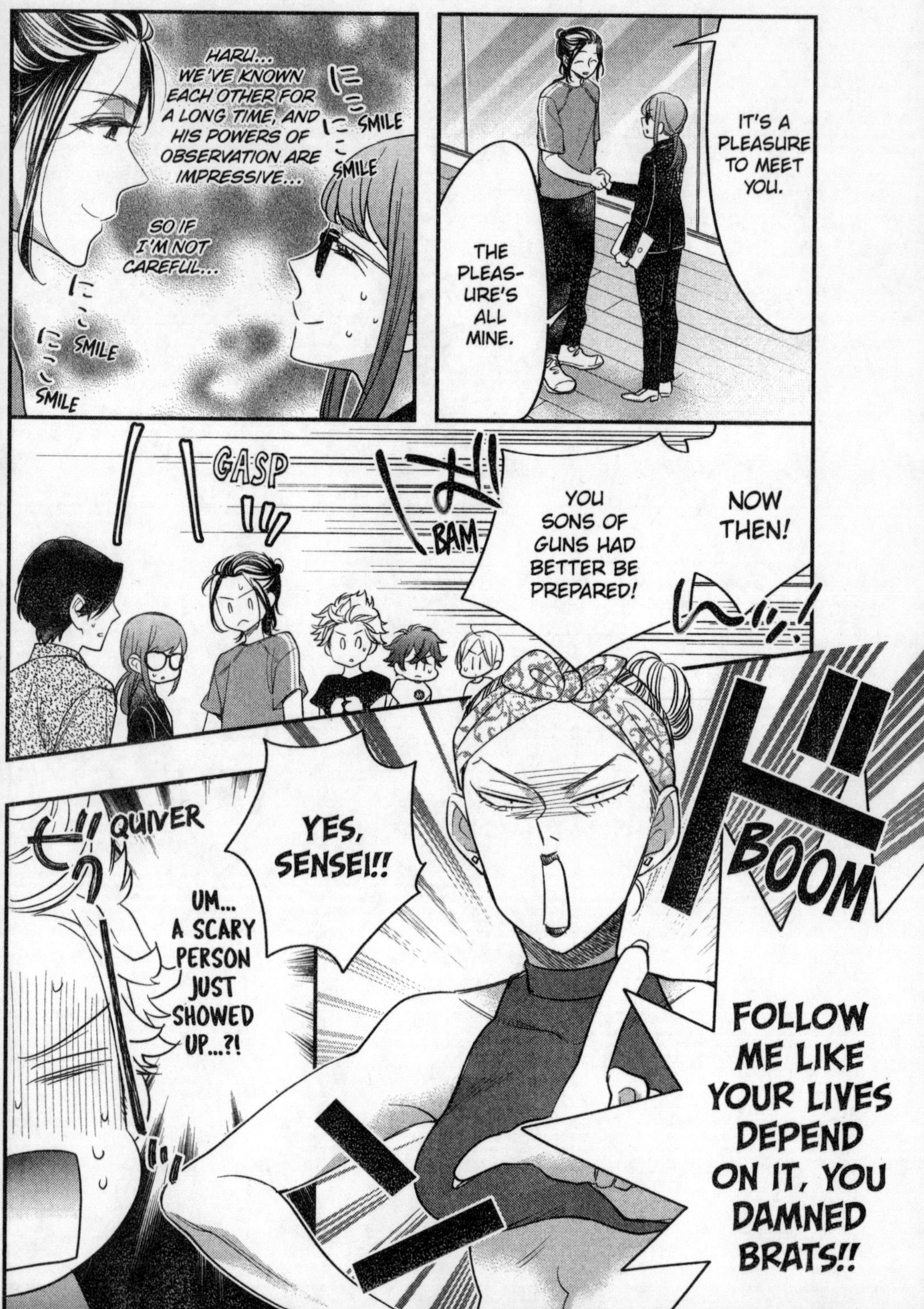
IT'S A PLEASURE TO MEET YOU.
THE PLEASURE'S ALL MINE.
HARU... WE'VE KNOWN EACH OTHER FOR A LONG TIME, AND HIS POWERS OF OBSERVATION ARE IMPRESSIVE...
SMILE
SMILE
SO IF I'M NOT CAREFUL...
SMILE
SMILE
NOW THEN!
YOU SONS OF GUNS HAD BETTER BE PREPARED!
BAM
GASP
BOOM
FOLLOW ME LIKE YOUR LIVES DEPEND ON IT, YOU DAMNED BRATS!!
YES, SENSEI!!
QUIVER
UM... A SCARY PERSON JUST SHOWED UP...?!

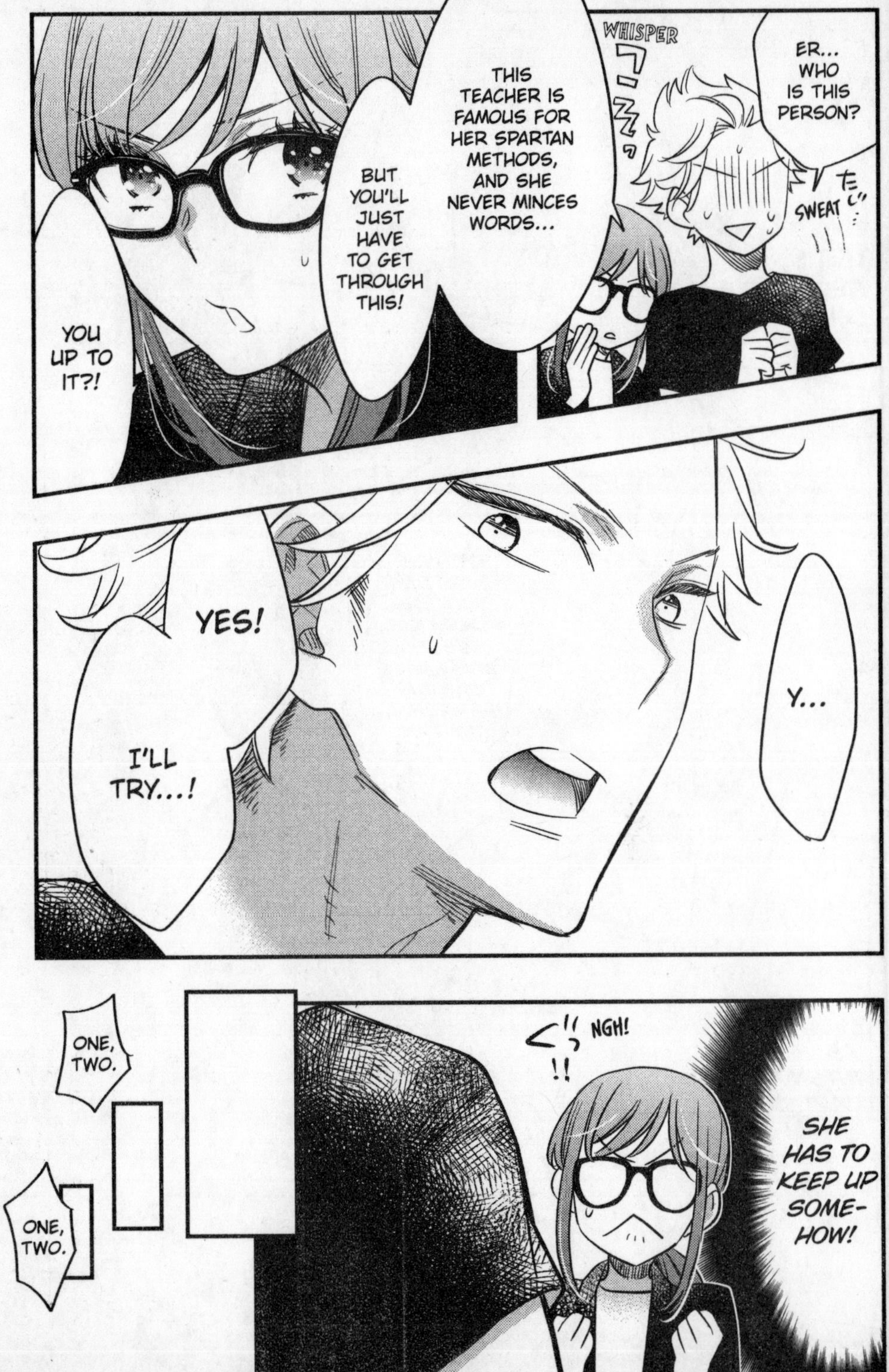
ER... WHO IS THIS PERSON?
SWEAT
WHISPER
THIS TEACHER IS FAMOUS FOR HER SPARTAN METHODS, AND SHE NEVER MINCES WORDS...
BUT YOU'LL JUST HAVE TO GET THROUGH THIS!
YOU UP TO IT?!
Y...
YES!
I'LL TRY...!
NGH!
SHE HAS TO KEEP UP SOME-HOW!
ONE, TWO.
ONE, TWO.

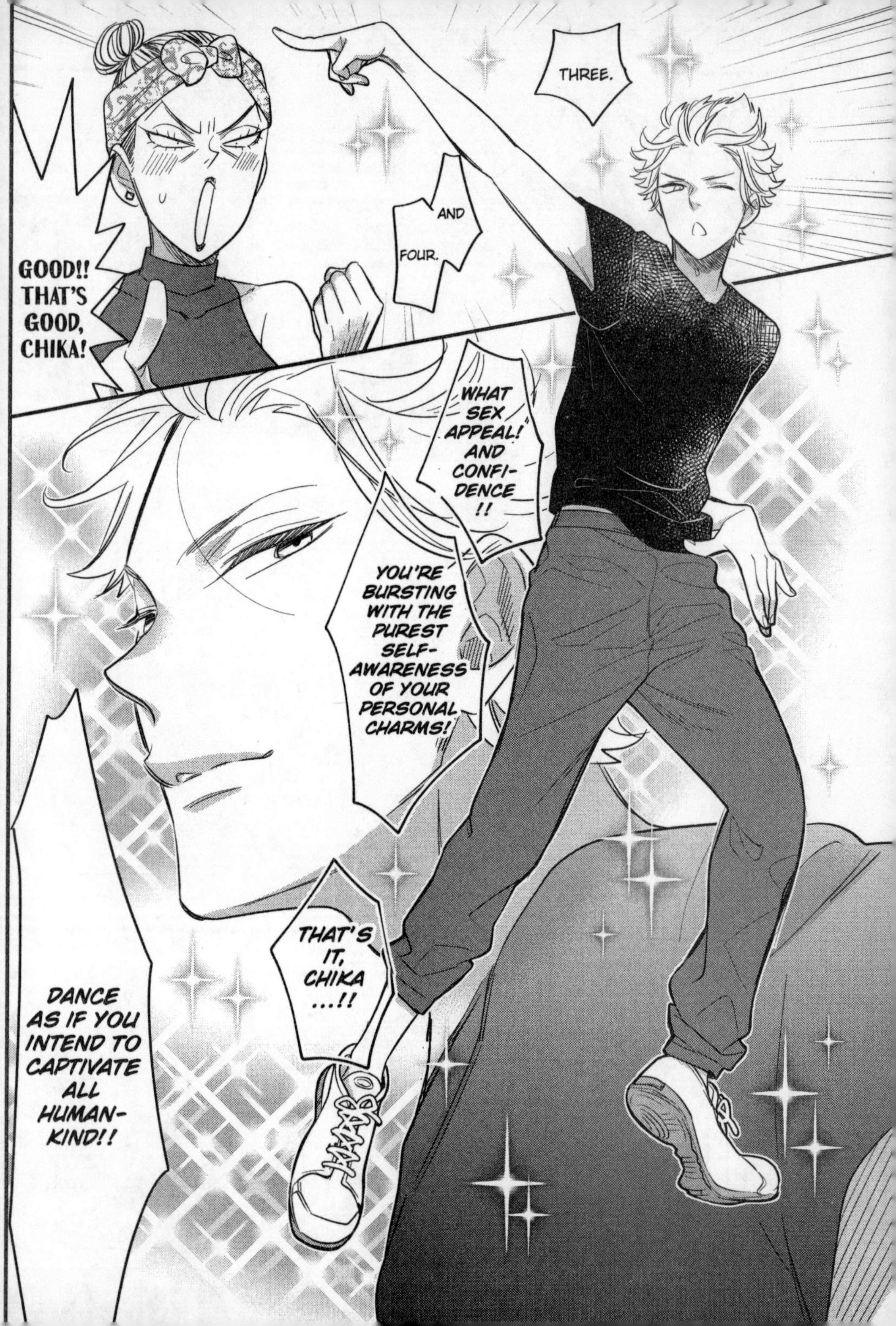
THREE.
AND FOUR.
GOOD!! THAT'S GOOD, CHIKA!
WHAT SEX APPEAL! AND CONFIDENCE!!
YOU'RE BURSTING WITH THE PUREST SELF-AWARENESS OF YOUR PERSONAL CHARMS!
THAT'S IT, CHIKA...!!
DANCE AS IF YOU INTEND TO CAPTIVATE ALL HUMANKIND!!

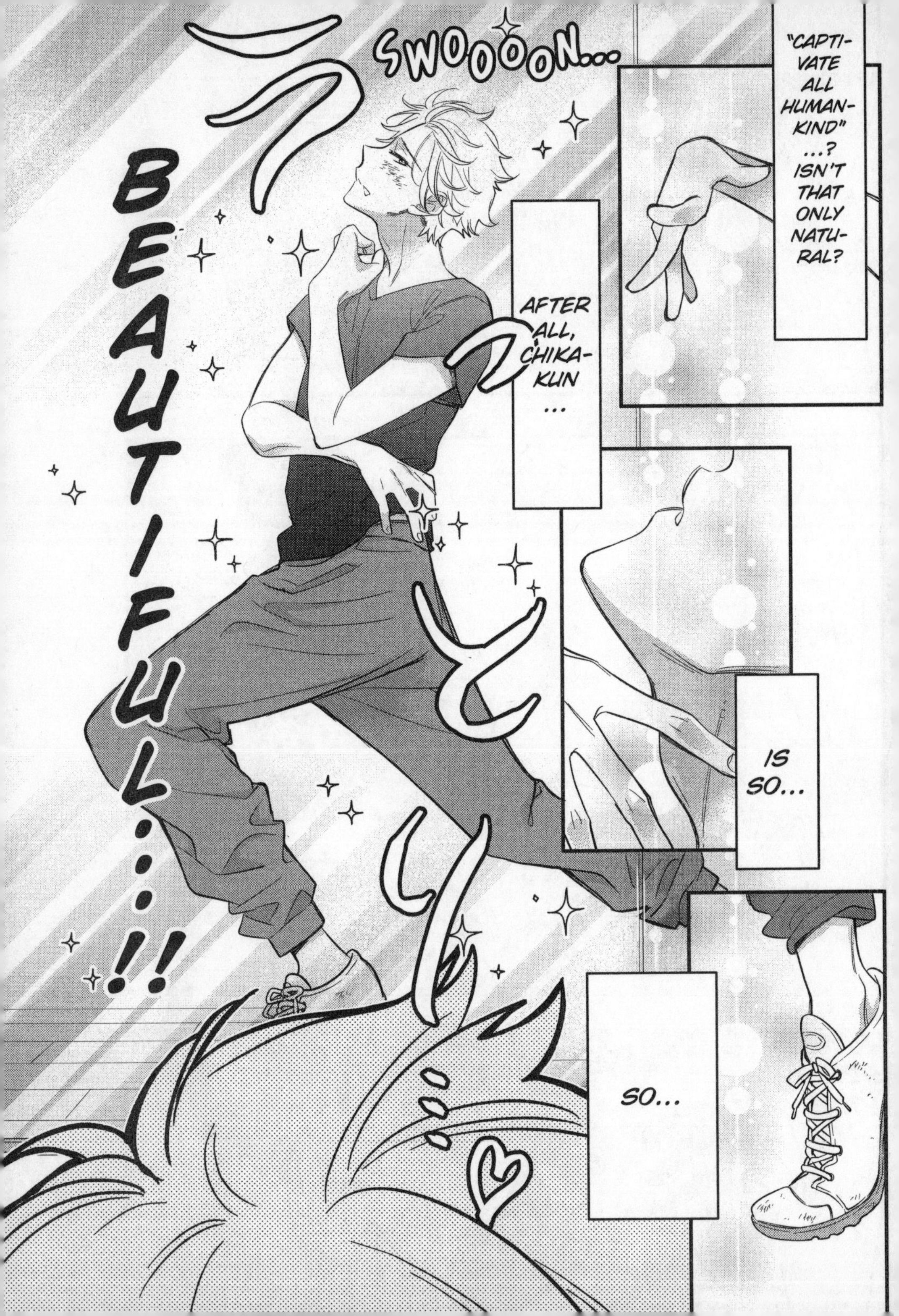
"CAPTIVATE ALL HUMANKIND" ...? ISN'T THAT ONLY NATURAL?
AFTER ALL, CHIKA-KUN ...
IS SO...
SO...
SWOOOOON...
BEAUTIFUL...!!

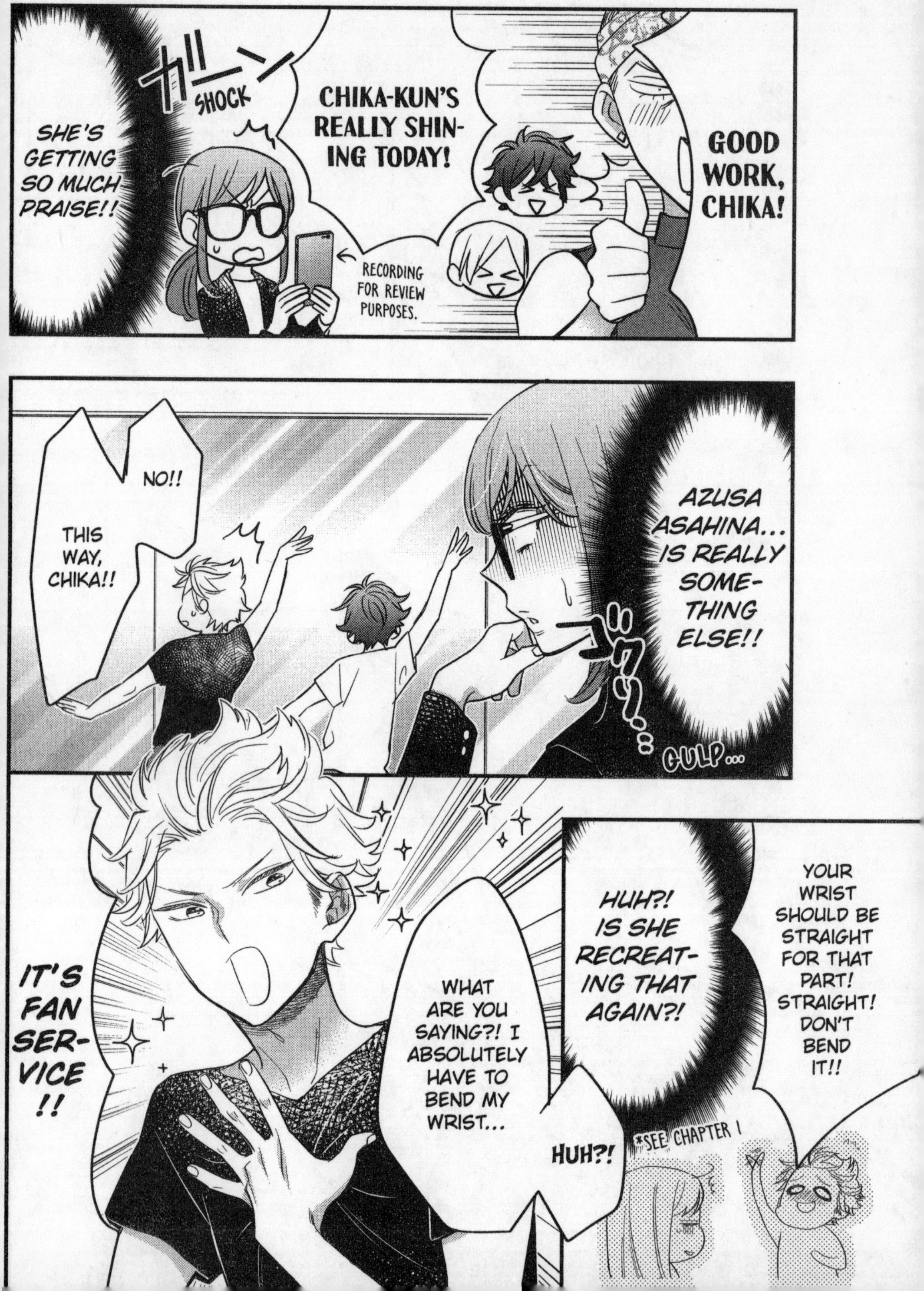
GOOD WORK, CHIKA!
CHIKA-KUN'S REALLY SHINING TODAY!
RECORDING FOR REVIEW PURPOSES.
カーン
SHOCK
SHE'S GETTING SO MUCH PRAISE!!
AZUSA ASAHINA... IS REALLY SOMETHING ELSE!!
ゴクッ...
GULP...
NO!!
THIS WAY, CHIKA!!
YOUR WRIST SHOULD BE STRAIGHT FOR THAT PART! STRAIGHT! DON'T BEND IT!!
HUH?! IS SHE RECREATING THAT AGAIN?!
*SEE CHAPTER 1
HUH?!
WHAT ARE YOU SAYING?! I ABSOLUTELY HAVE TO BEND MY WRIST...
IT'S FAN SERVICE!!

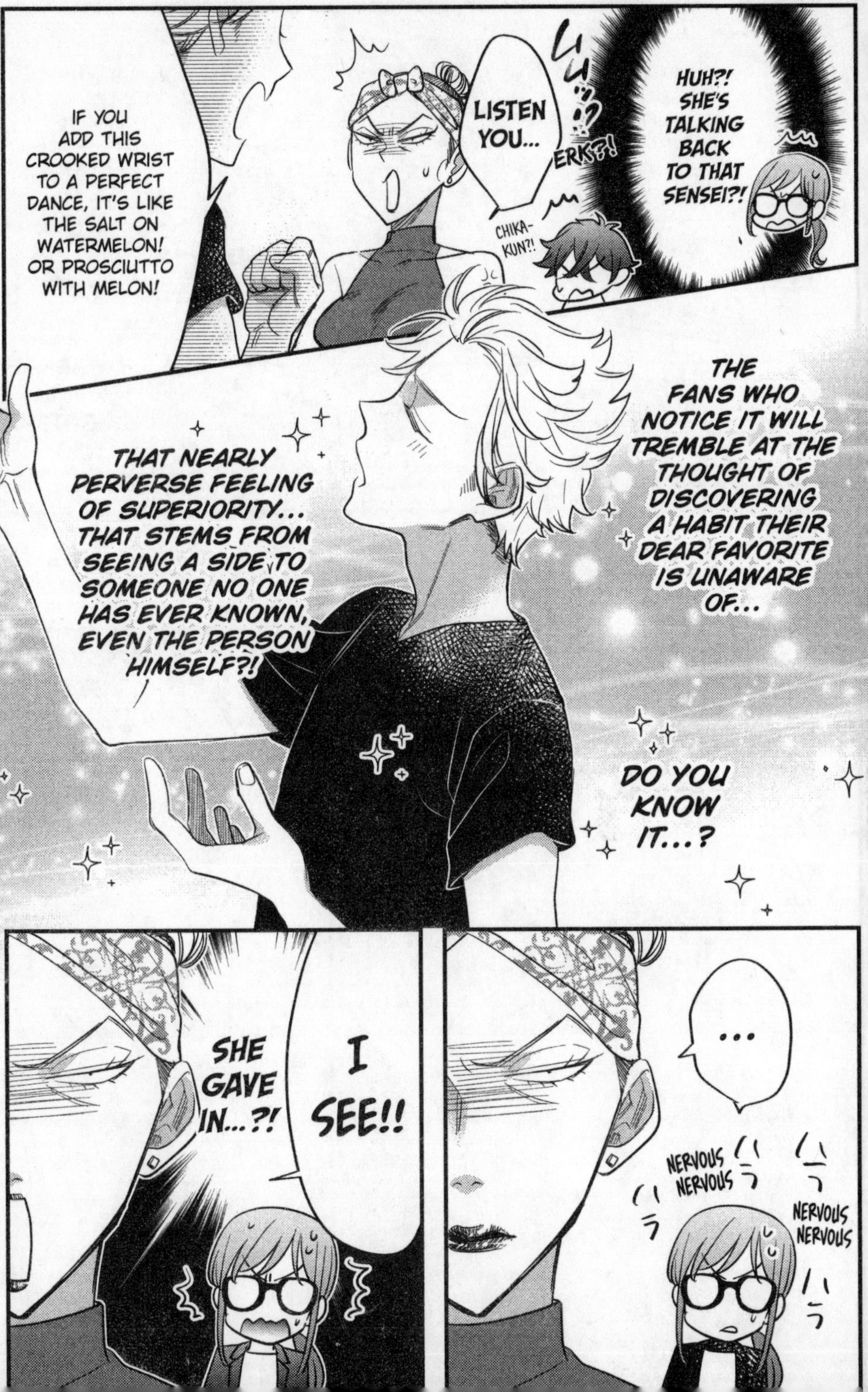
HUH?! SHE'S TALKING BACK TO THAT SENSEI?!
ERK?!
LISTEN YOU...
CHIKA-KUN?!
IF YOU ADD THIS CROOKED WRIST TO A PERFECT DANCE, IT'S LIKE THE SALT ON WATERMELON! OR PROSCIUTTO WITH MELON!
THE FANS WHO NOTICE IT WILL TREMBLE AT THE THOUGHT OF DISCOVERING A HABIT THEIR DEAR FAVORITE IS UNAWARE OF...
THAT NEARLY PERVERSE FEELING OF SUPERIORITY... THAT STEMS FROM SEEING A SIDE TO SOMEONE NO ONE HAS EVER KNOWN, EVEN THE PERSON HIMSELF?!
DO YOU KNOW IT...?
...
NERVOUS NERVOUS
NERVOUS NERVOUS
I SEE!!
SHE GAVE IN...?!

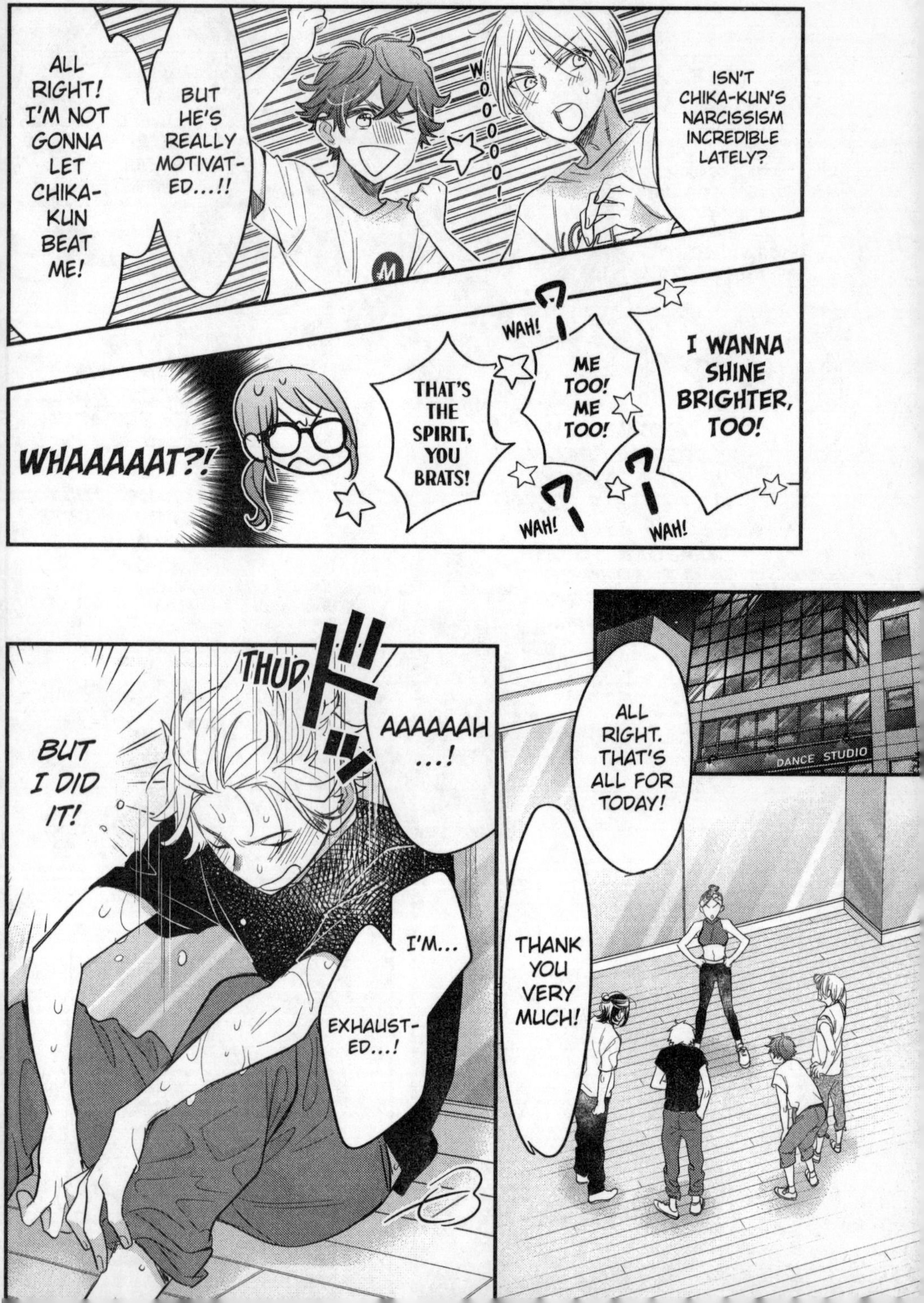
ISN'T CHIKA-KUN'S NARCISSISM INCREDIBLE LATELY?
WOOOOOOO!
BUT HE'S REALLY MOTIVAT-ED...!!
ALL RIGHT! I'M NOT GONNA LET CHIKA-KUN BEAT ME!
I WANNA SHINE BRIGHTER, TOO!
WAH!
ME TOO! ME TOO!
WAH!
WAH!
THAT'S THE SPIRIT, YOU BRATS!
WHAAAAAT?!
ALL RIGHT. THAT'S ALL FOR TODAY!
DANCE STUDIO
THANK YOU VERY MUCH!
THUD
AAAAAAH...!
BUT I DID IT!
I'M...
EXHAUST-ED...!

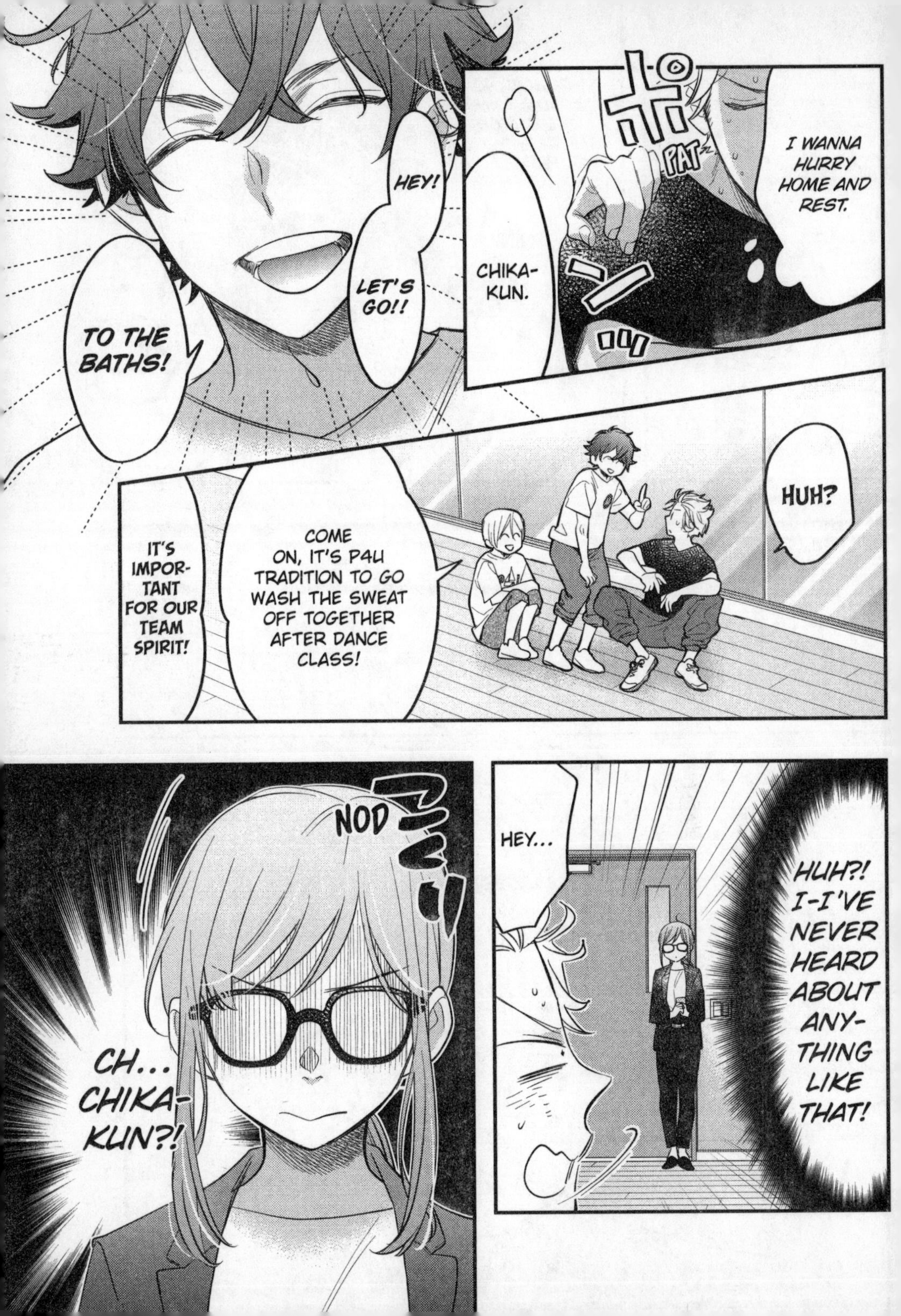
I WANNA HURRY HOME AND REST.
PAT
CHIKA-KUN.
HEY!
LET'S GO!!
TO THE BATHS!
HUH?
COME ON, IT'S P4U TRADITION TO GO WASH THE SWEAT OFF TOGETHER AFTER DANCE CLASS!
IT'S IMPORTANT FOR OUR TEAM SPIRIT!
HUH?! I-I'VE NEVER HEARD ABOUT ANYTHING LIKE THAT!
HEY...
NOD
CH... CHIKA-KUN?!

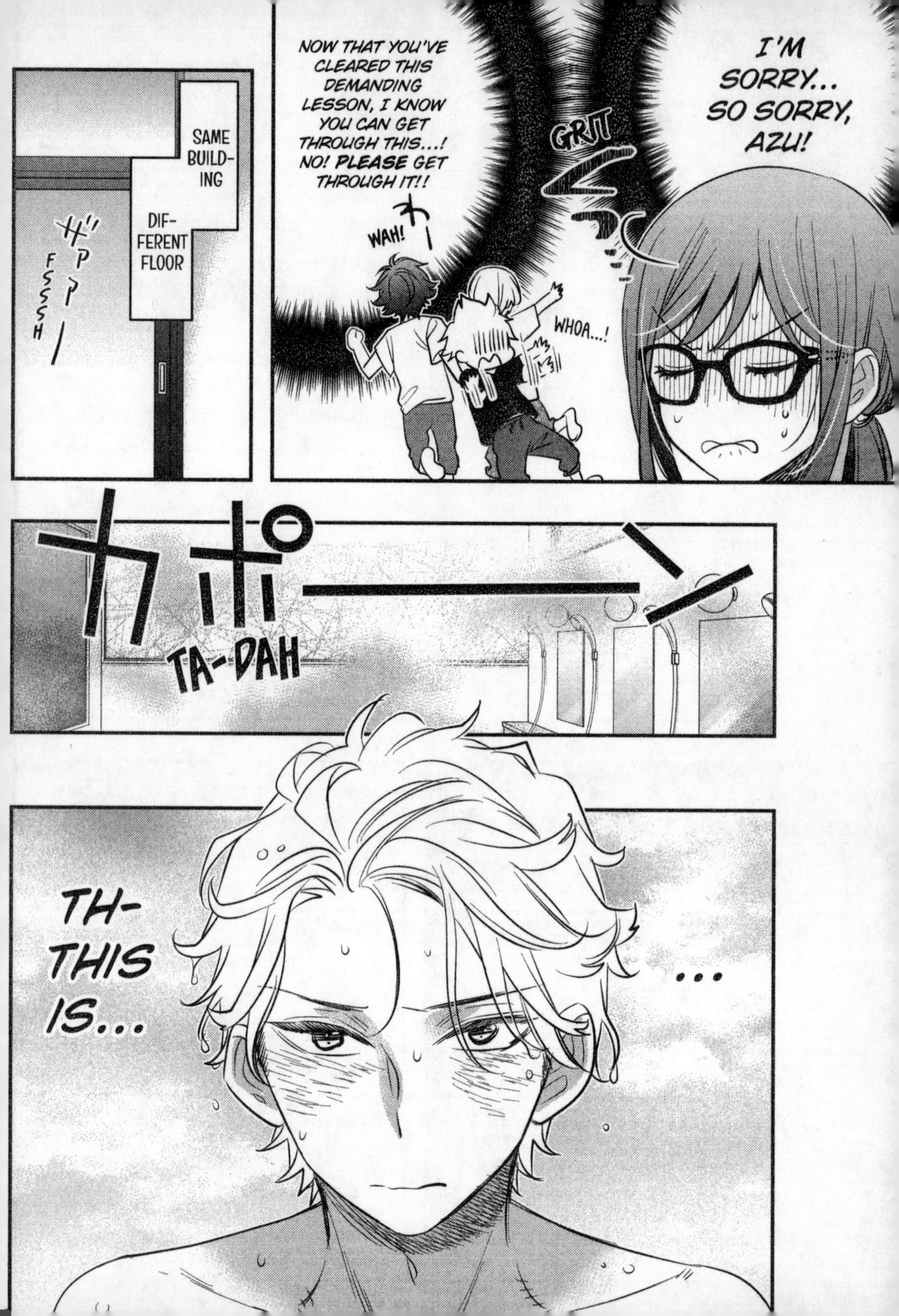

I'M SORRY... SO SORRY, AZU!
GRIT
NOW THAT YOU'VE CLEARED THIS DEMANDING LESSON, I KNOW YOU CAN GET THROUGH THIS...! NO! PLEASE GET THROUGH IT!!
WAH!
WHOA...!
SAME BUILDING-ING
DIF-FERENT FLOOR
FSSSH
カポーン
TA-DAH
...
TH-THIS IS...

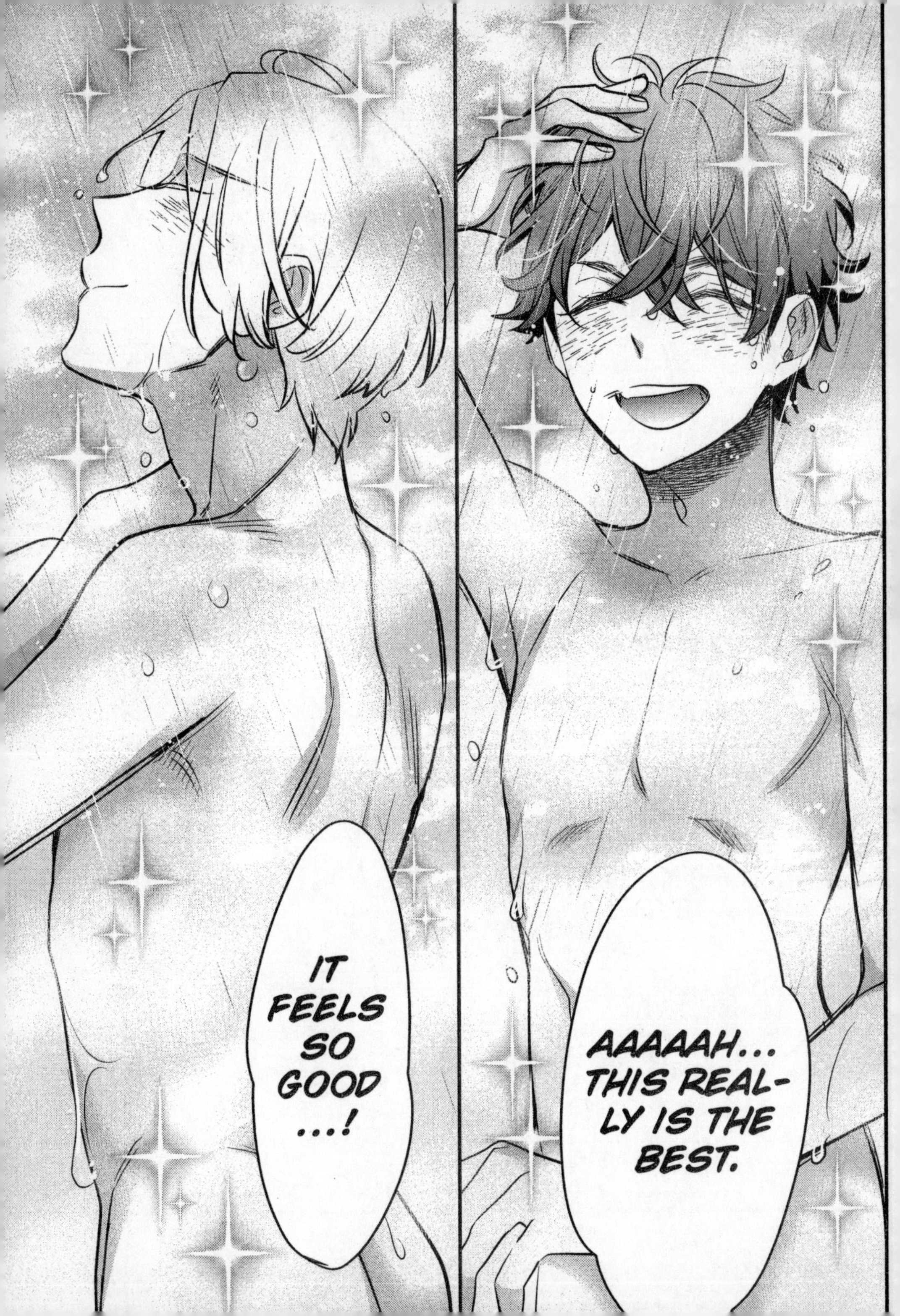
AAAAAH... THIS REAL-LY IS THE BEST.
IT FEELS SO GOOD ...!

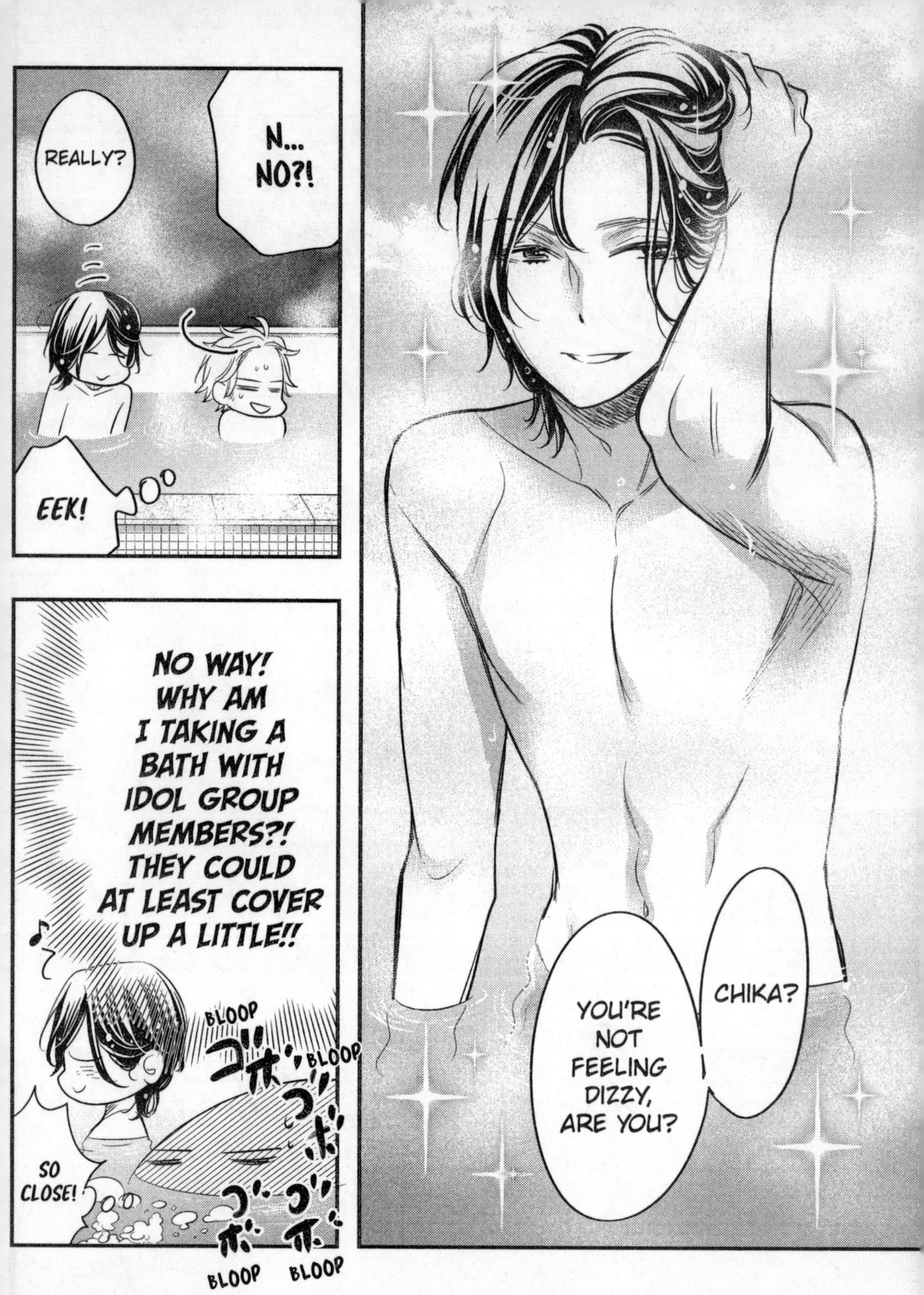
CHIKA?
YOU'RE NOT FEELING DIZZY, ARE YOU?
N... NO?!
REALLY?
EEK!
NO WAY! WHY AM I TAKING A BATH WITH IDOL GROUP MEMBERS?! THEY COULD AT LEAST COVER UP A LITTLE!!
BLOOP
BLOOP
BLOOP
BLOOP
SO CLOSE!

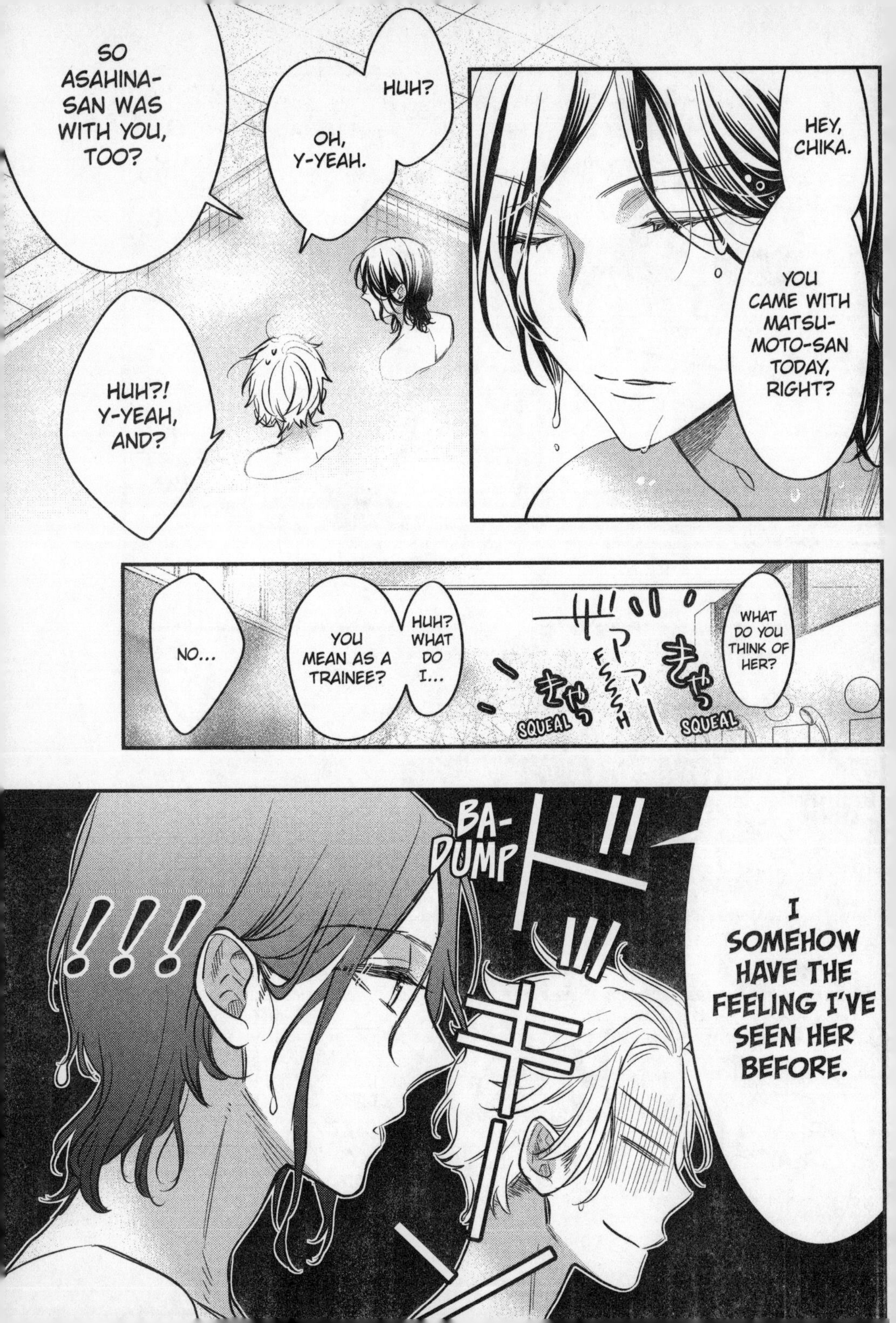
HEY, CHIKA.
YOU CAME WITH MATSU-MOTO-SAN TODAY, RIGHT?
HUH?
OH, Y-YEAH.
SO ASAHINA-SAN WAS WITH YOU, TOO?
HUH?! Y-YEAH, AND?
WHAT DO YOU THINK OF HER?
SQUEAL
FSSSH
SQUEAL
HUH? WHAT DO I...
YOU MEAN AS A TRAINEE?
NO...
I SOMEHOW HAVE THE FEELING I'VE SEEN HER BEFORE.
BA-DUMP
!!!

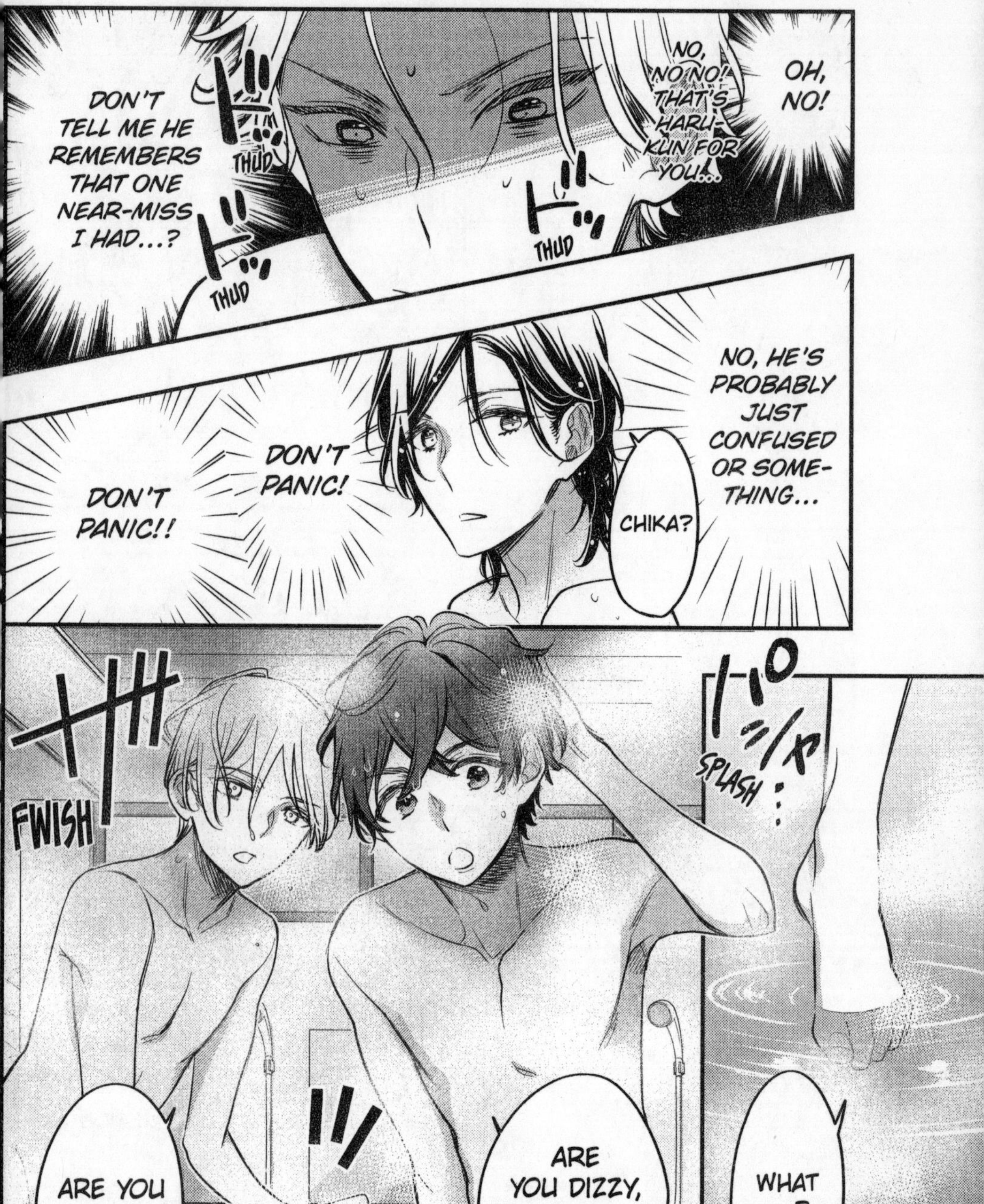
OH, NO!
NO, NO NO! THAT'S HARU-KUN FOR YOU...
THUD
DON'T TELL ME HE REMEMBERS THAT ONE NEAR-MISS I HAD...?
THUD
THUD
NO, HE'S PROBABLY JUST CONFUSED OR SOME-THING...
CHIKA?
DON'T PANIC!
DON'T PANIC!!
SPLASH
WHAT ...?
ARE YOU DIZZY, CHIKA-KUN?
FWISH
ARE YOU OKAY?

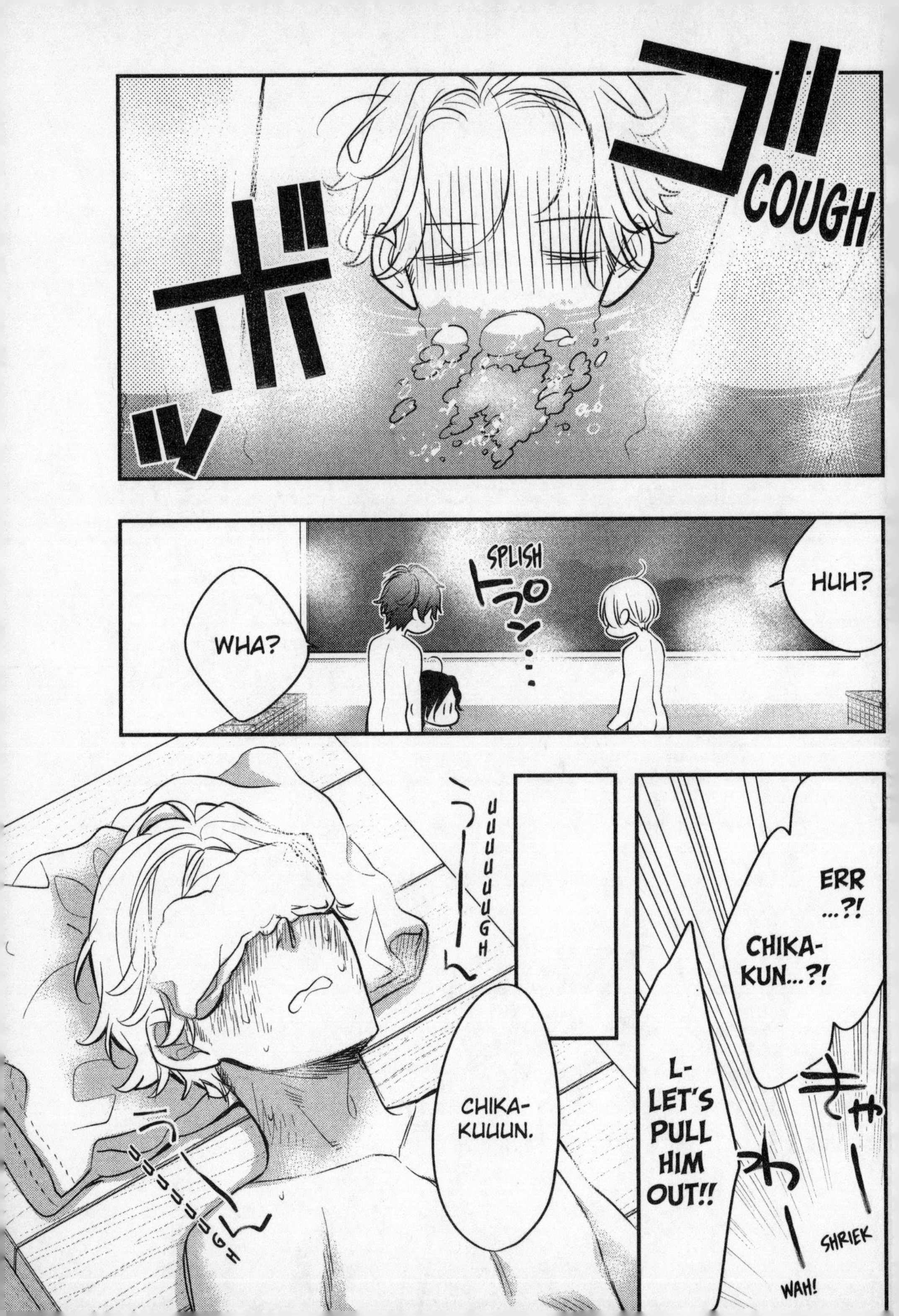
ゴボッ
COUGH
HUH?
SPLISH
トプン…
WHA?
ERR ...?!
CHIKA-KUN...?!
L- LET'S PULL HIM OUT!!
きゃー
SHRIEK
わー
WAH!
うーん
UUUUUUUGH
CHIKA-KUUUN.
うーーん
UUUUUUUUGH

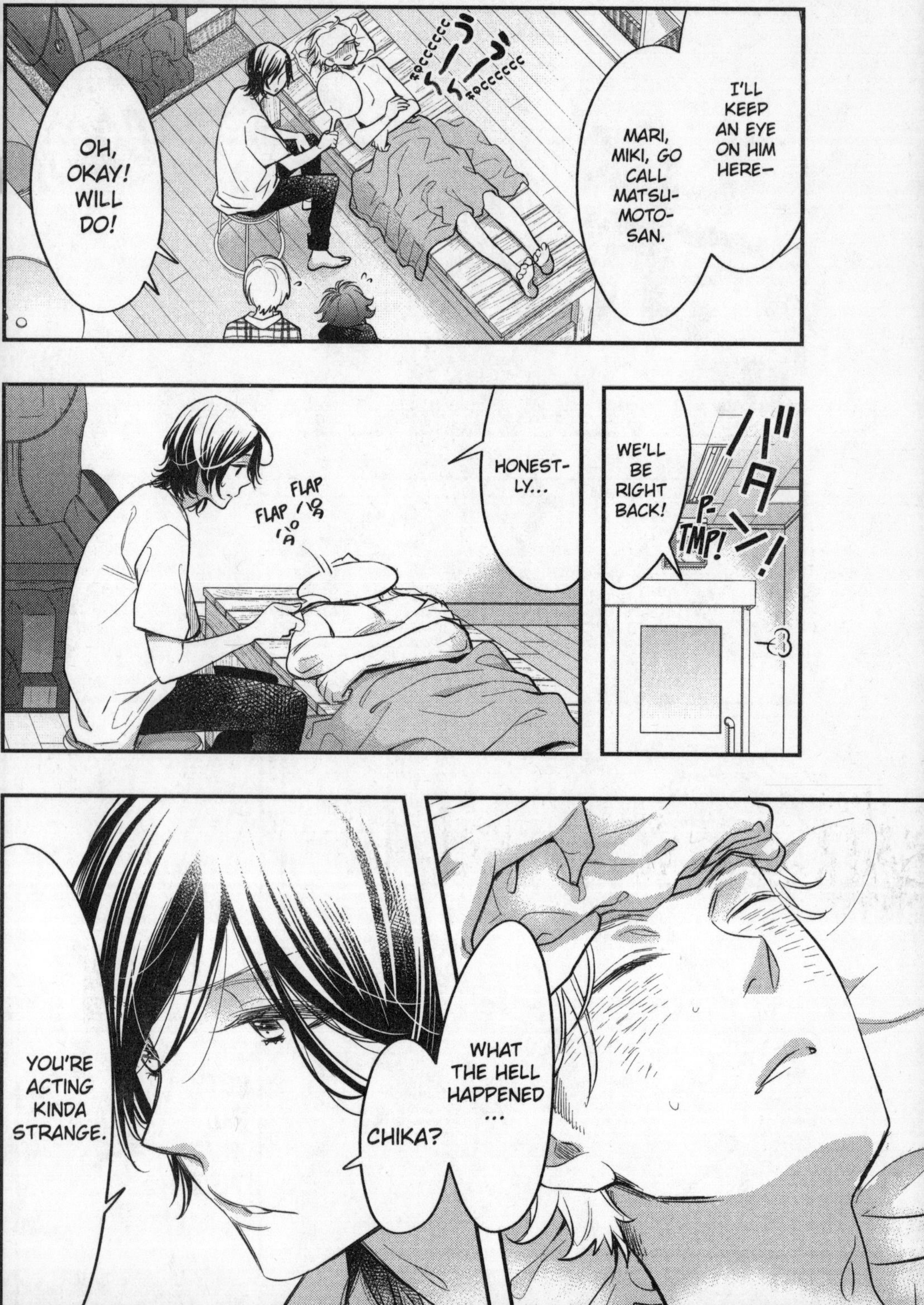
I'LL KEEP AN EYE ON HIM HERE—
MARI, MIKI, GO CALL MATSU-MOTO-SAN.
OH, OKAY! WILL DO!
WE'LL BE RIGHT BACK!
P-TMP!
HONEST-LY...
FLAP FLAP
WHAT THE HELL HAPPENED ...
CHIKA?
YOU'RE ACTING KINDA STRANGE.

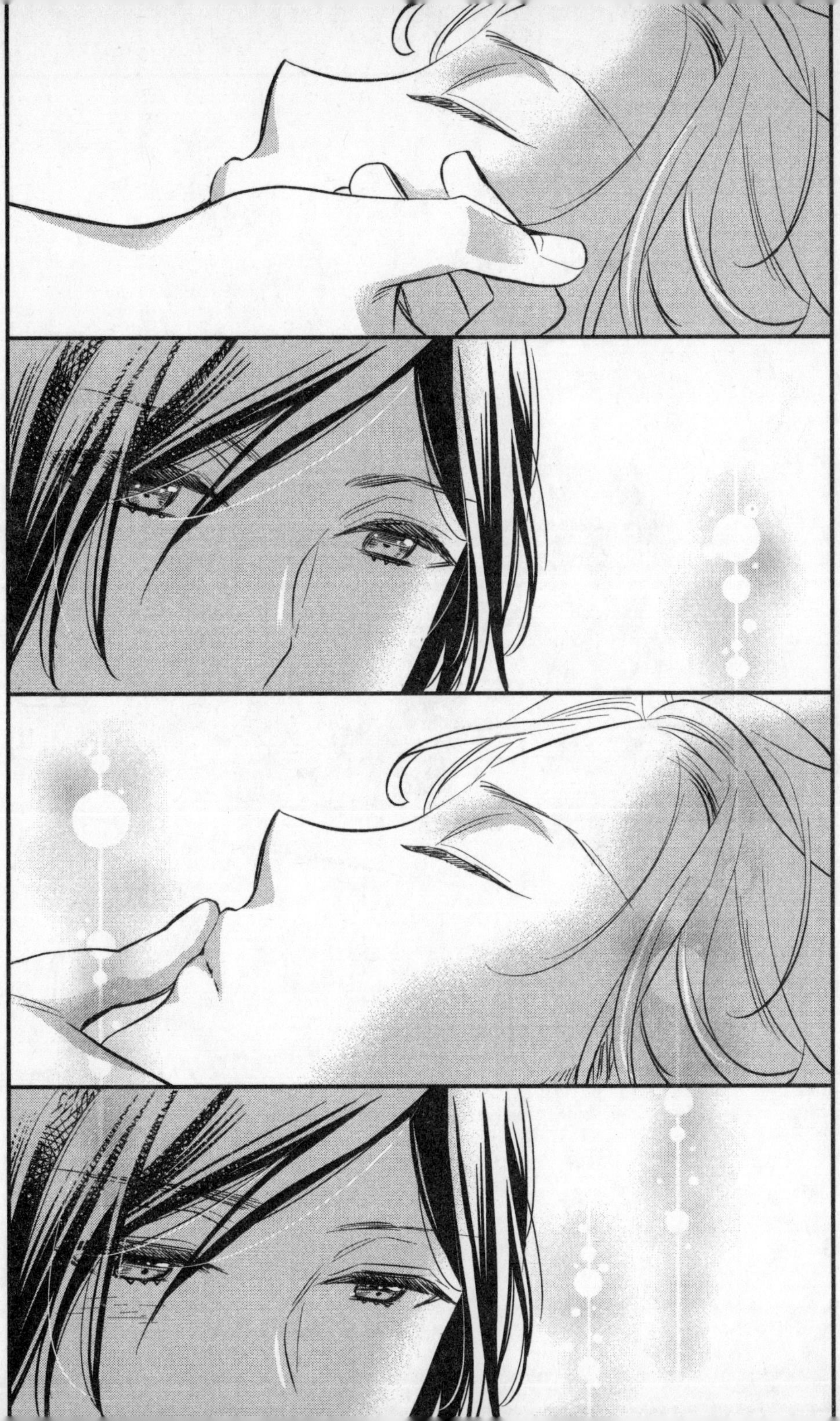

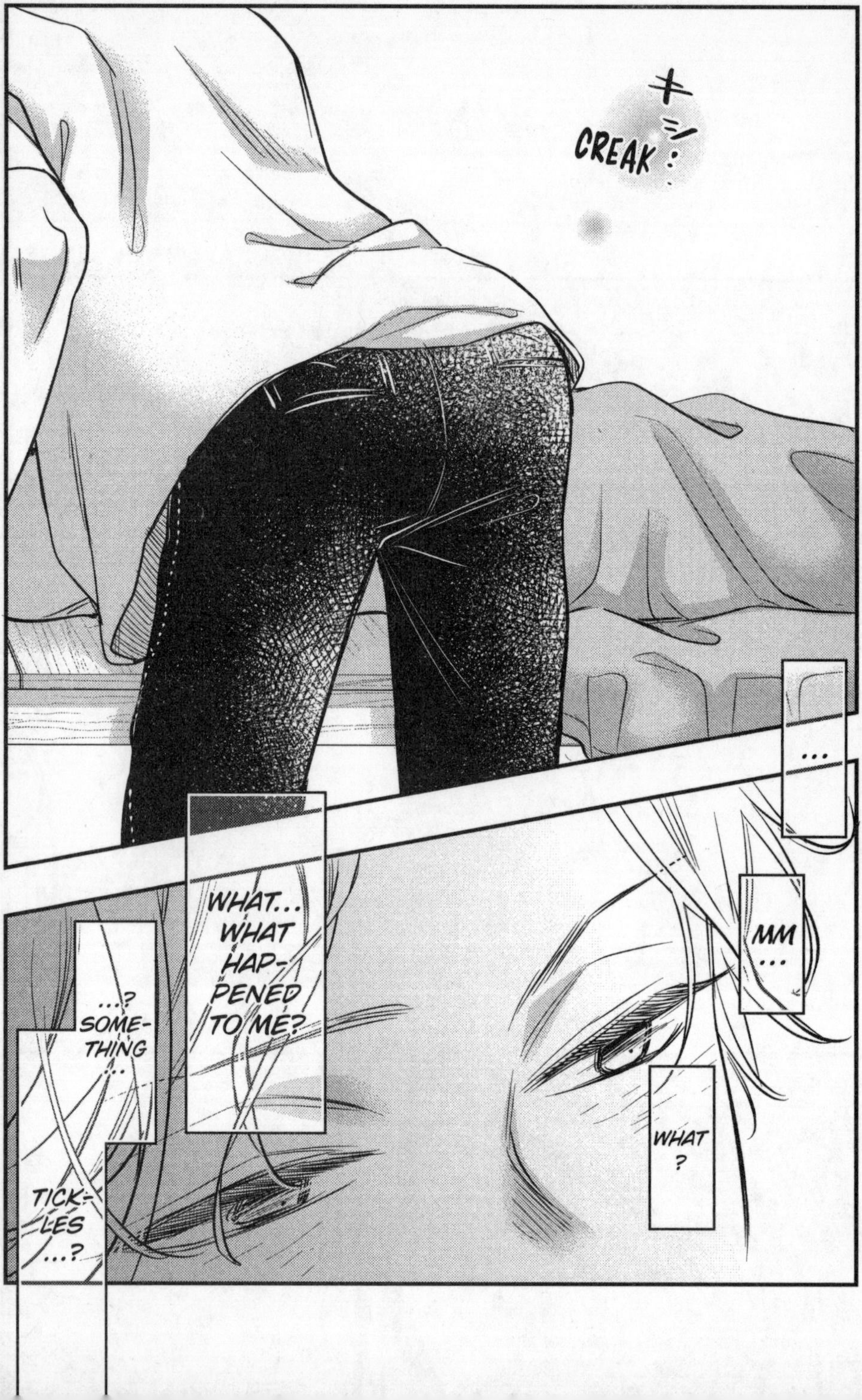
CREAK
...
MM...
WHAT?
WHAT... WHAT HAPPENED TO ME?
...? SOMETHING...
TICKLES...?

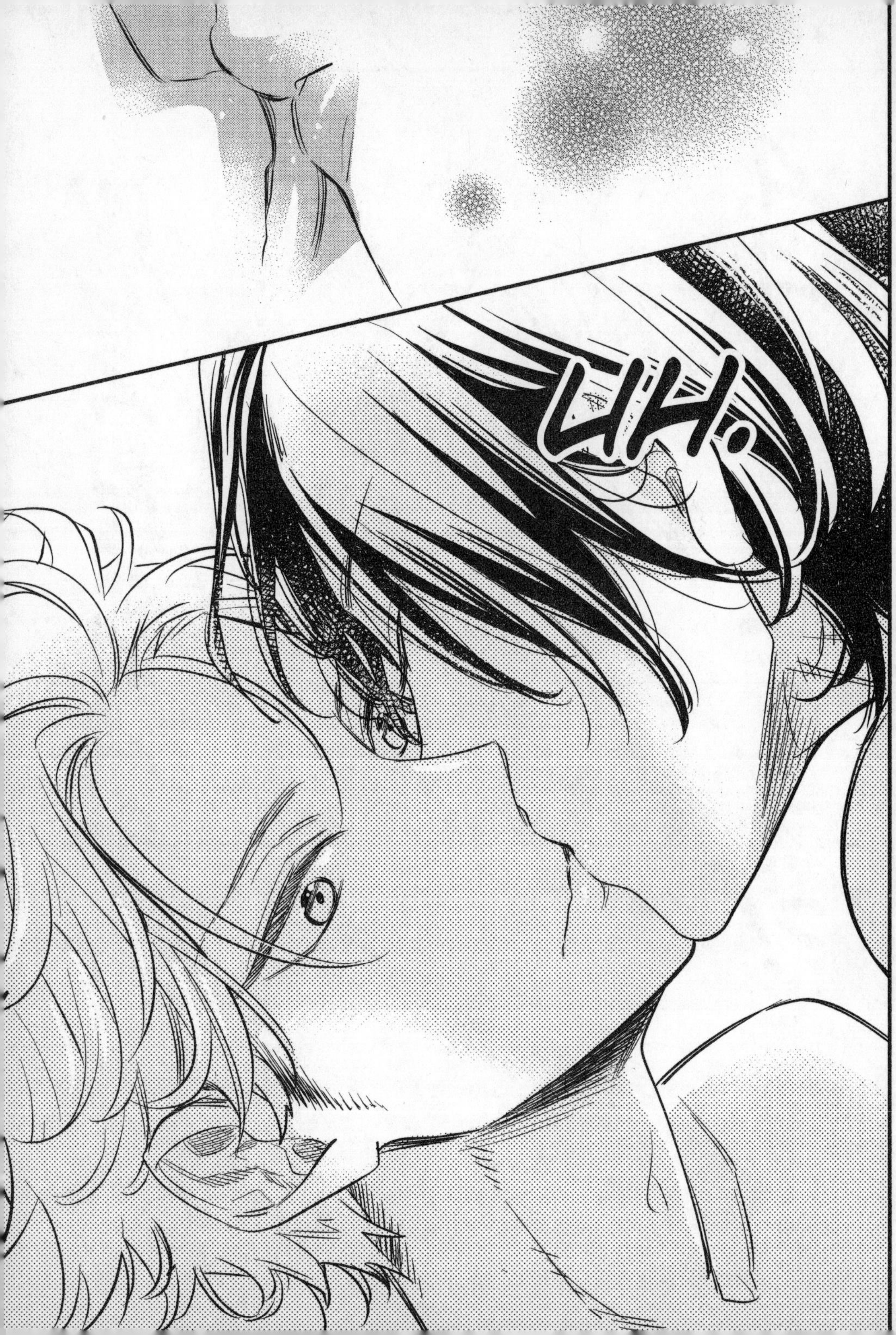
UH.

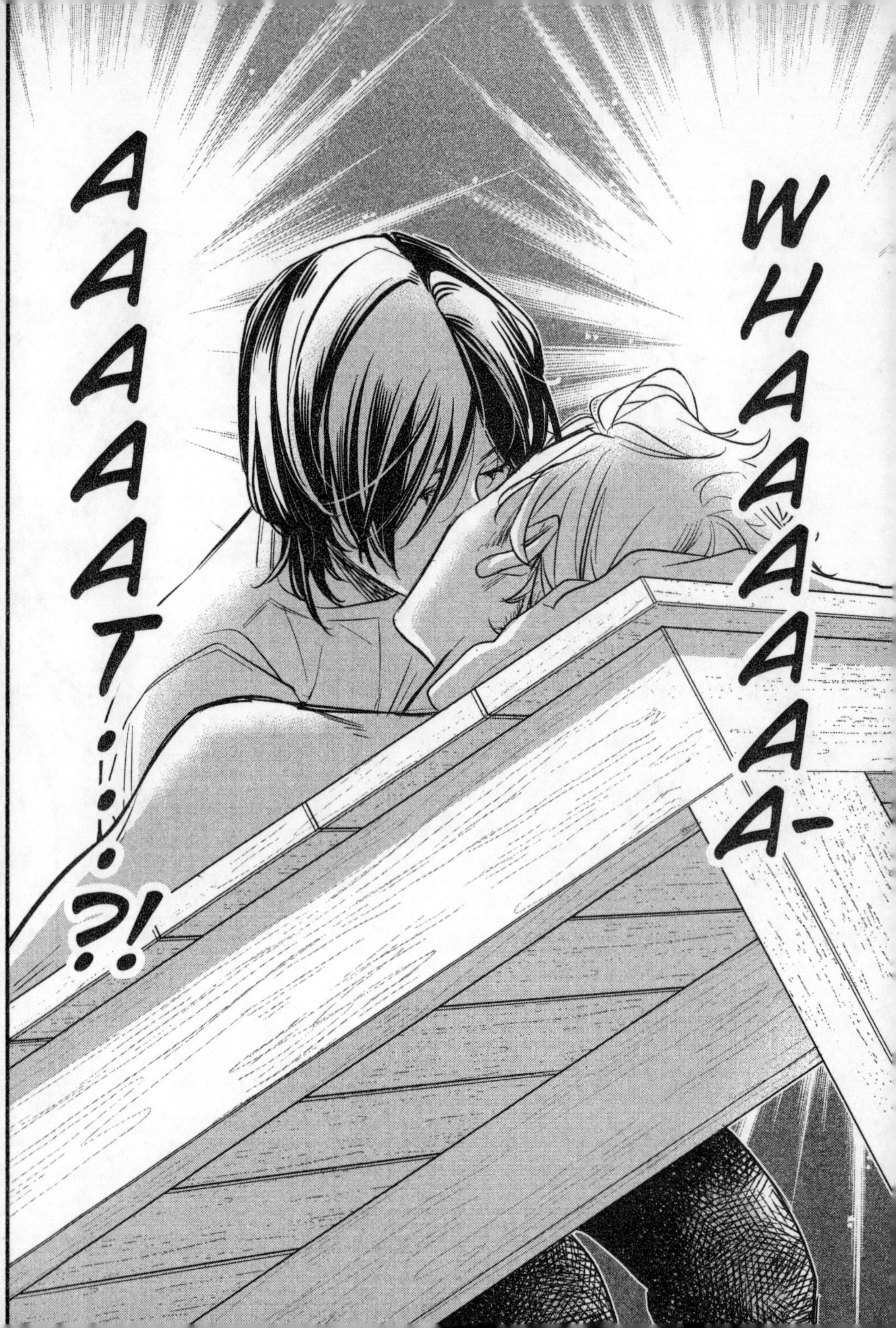
WHAAAAAAA-
AAAAAT...?!

STAR⇌CROSSED!!

← To be continued in Volume 3

R⇄CROSS

D!! STAR

AR⇄CROS

CROSSED

⇄CROSSE

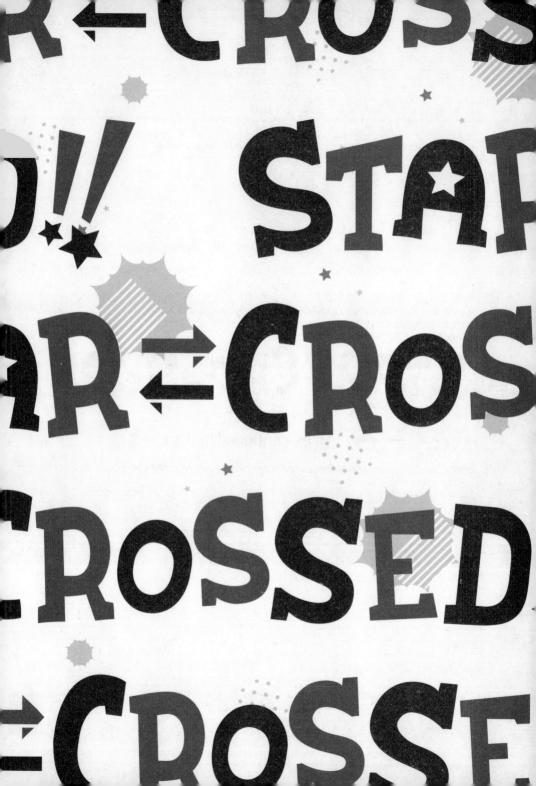

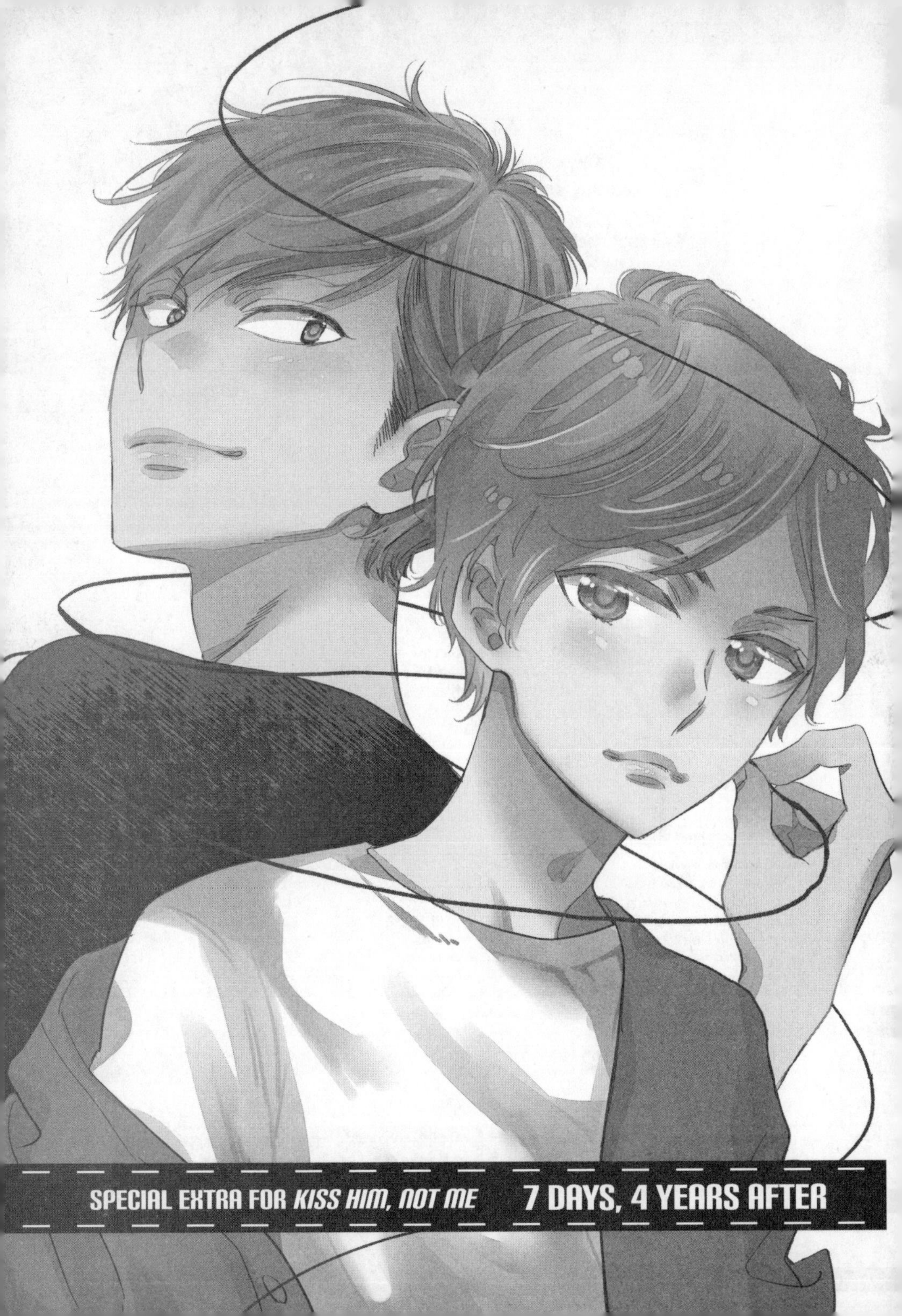
SPECIAL EXTRA FOR *KISS HIM, NOT ME*
7 DAYS, 4 YEARS AFTER

KISS HIM, NOT ME

STORY

Kae, who's what is called a "fujoshi," suddenly lost a lot of weight when her beloved anime character died! Now that she's a beautiful girl who'd turn anyone's head, she's got the attention of four hot boys?!

CHARACTER

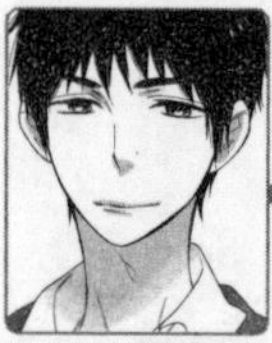

YUSUKE IGARASHI

The sporty classmate.
On the soccer team. The popular kid in class.
He's secretly taken Kae to a spot with a beautiful night view.

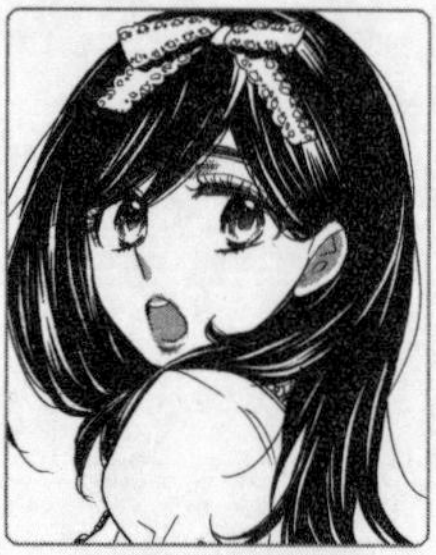

KAE SERINUMA

The main character. A fujoshi with wild fantasies.
Passionate about the anime Mirage Saga ♥
Lovey-dovey with Mutsumi-senpai.

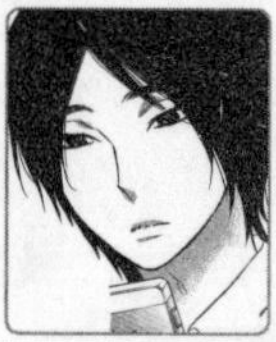

ASUMA MUTSUMI

The sub-culture senpai.
In the same history club as Kae.
Treats Kae the same way as he did in the beginning.
Kae's first boyfriend.

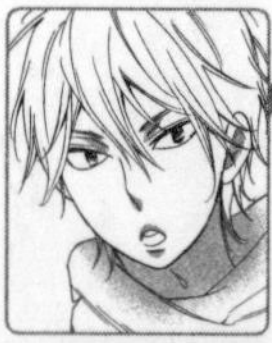

NOZOMU NANASHIMA

The frivolous classmate.
Formerly on the soccer team.
He has a smart mouth, but tells it like it is.
Stole a kiss from Kae while she was half-asleep.

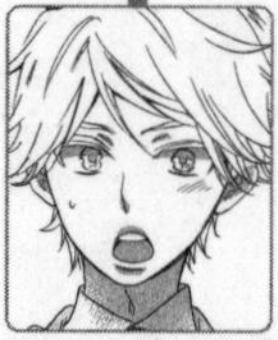

HAYATO SHINOMIYA

The hot-n-cold kohai.
A member of the health committee like Kae.
His grandfather is Norwegian.
He's fallen into Kae's chest twice.

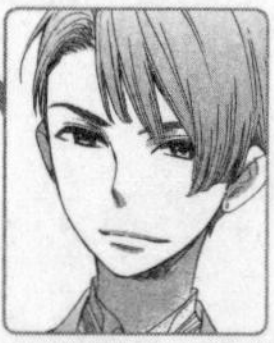

SHIMA NISHINA

The handsome female kohai and Kae's fellow fujoshi friend.
A super rich young lady.
Stole Kae's first kiss.

THIS TIME AROUND, THESE TWO ARE THE MAIN CHARACTERS.

Seven years after Kae's graduation ceremony... It comes to light that Shinomiya and Nanashima are living together! What suddenly brought these two closer? Let's turn back the clock a little and find out!

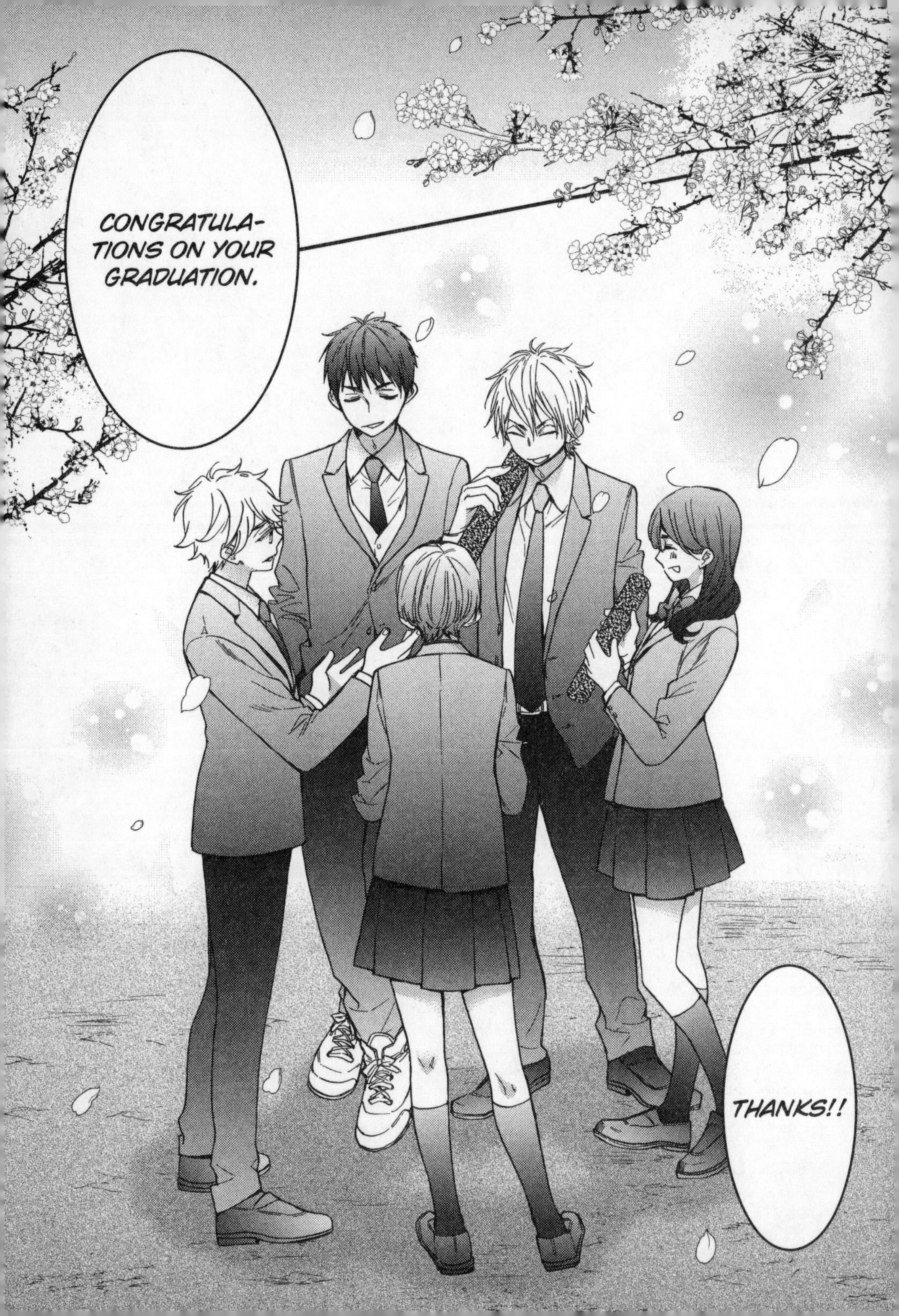
CONGRATULA-TIONS ON YOUR GRADUATION.
THANKS!!

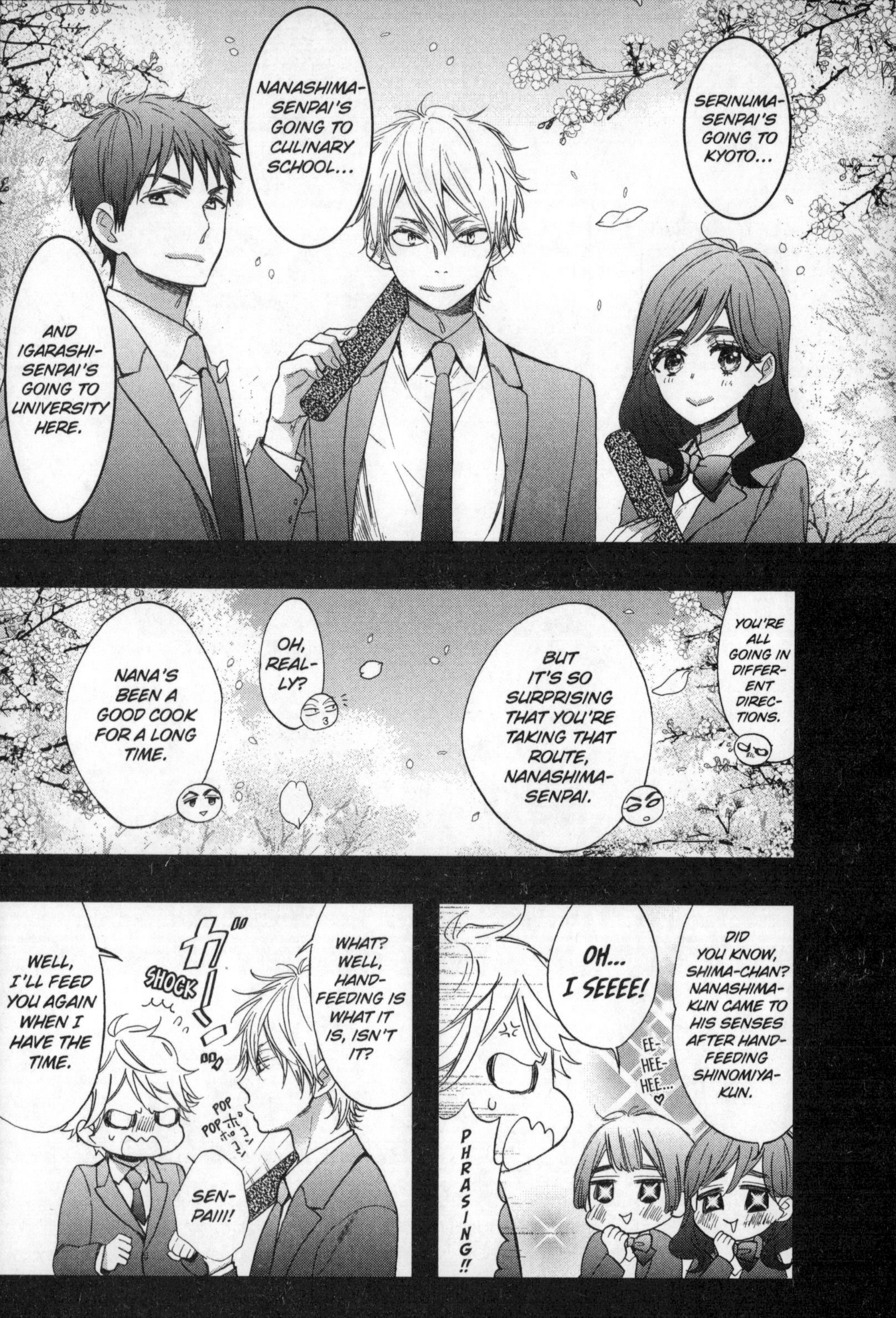
SERINUMA-SENPAI'S GOING TO KYOTO...
NANASHIMA-SENPAI'S GOING TO CULINARY SCHOOL...
AND IGARASHI-SENPAI'S GOING TO UNIVERSITY HERE.
YOU'RE ALL GOING IN DIFFERENT DIRECTIONS.
BUT IT'S SO SURPRISING THAT YOU'RE TAKING THAT ROUTE, NANASHIMA-SENPAI.
OH, REALLY?
NANA'S BEEN A GOOD COOK FOR A LONG TIME.
DID YOU KNOW, SHIMA-CHAN? NANASHIMA-KUN CAME TO HIS SENSES AFTER HAND-FEEDING SHINOMIYA-KUN.
EE-HEE-HEE...♥
OH... I SEEEE!
PHRASING!!
WHAT? WELL, HAND-FEEDING IS WHAT IT IS, ISN'T IT?
SHOCK
POP POP
SEN-PAIII!
WELL, I'LL FEED YOU AGAIN WHEN I HAVE THE TIME.

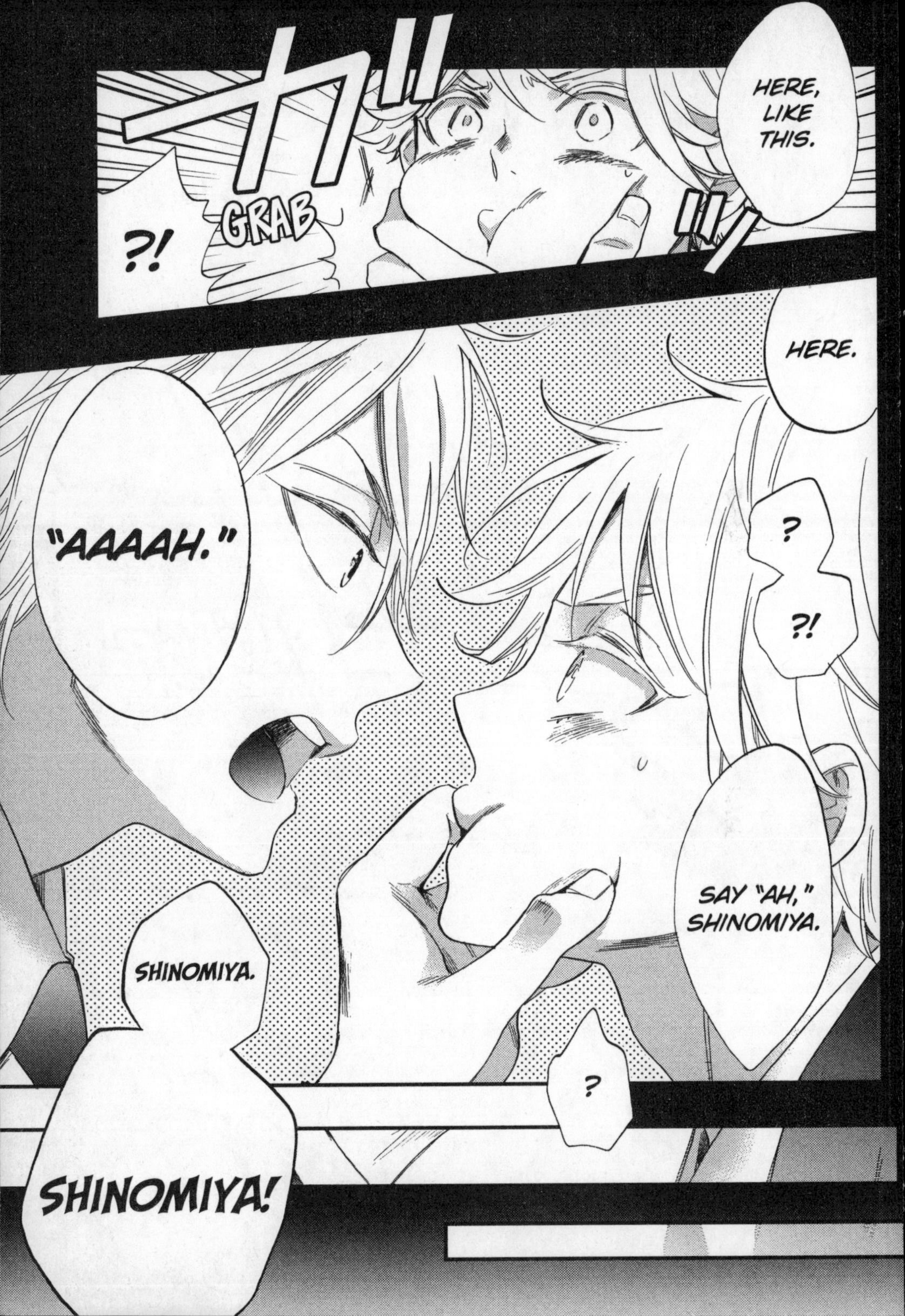
HERE, LIKE THIS.
GRAB
?!
HERE.
?
?!
SAY "AH," SHINOMIYA.
"AAAAH."
?
SHINOMIYA.
SHINOMIYA!

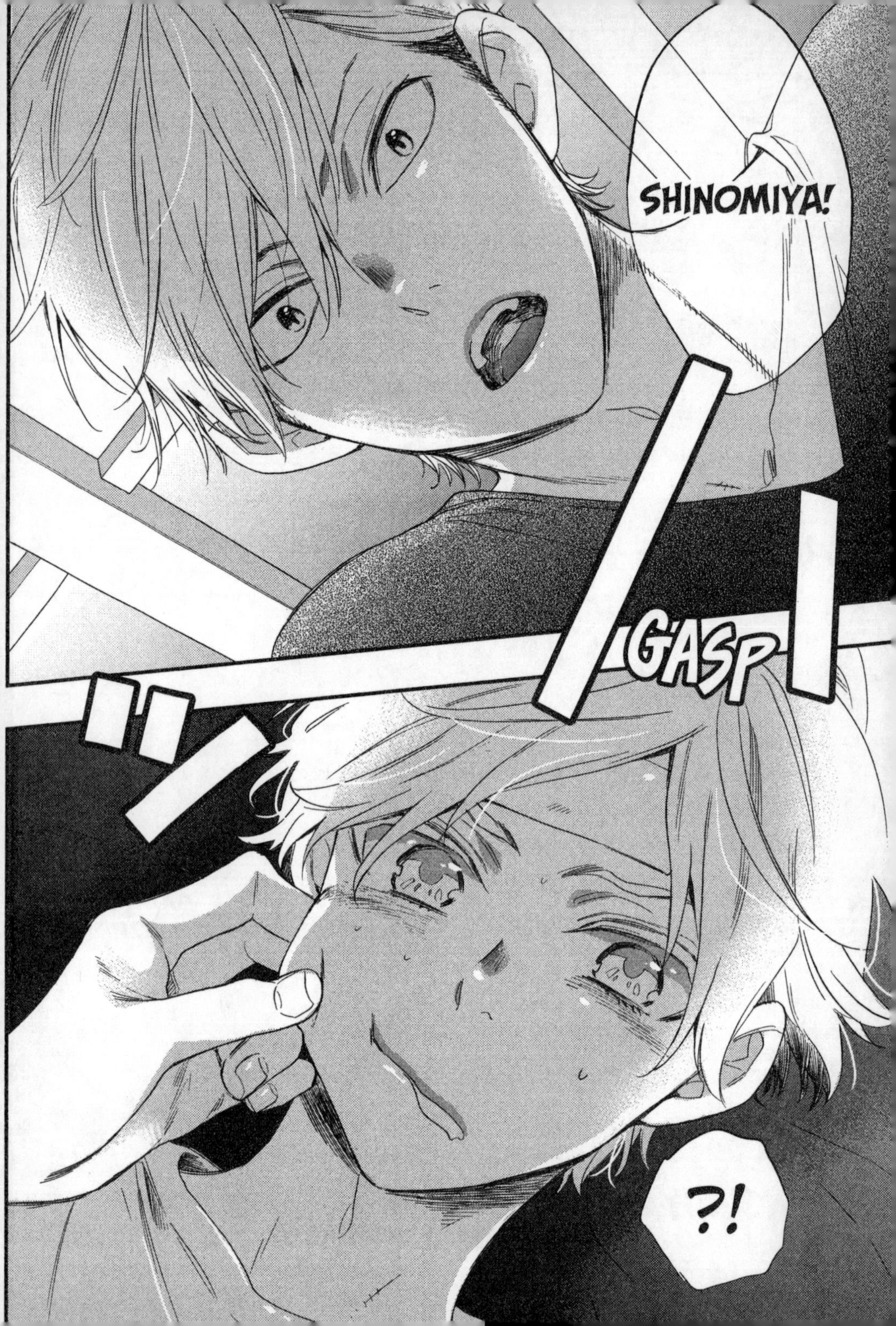
SHINOMIYA!
GASP
?!

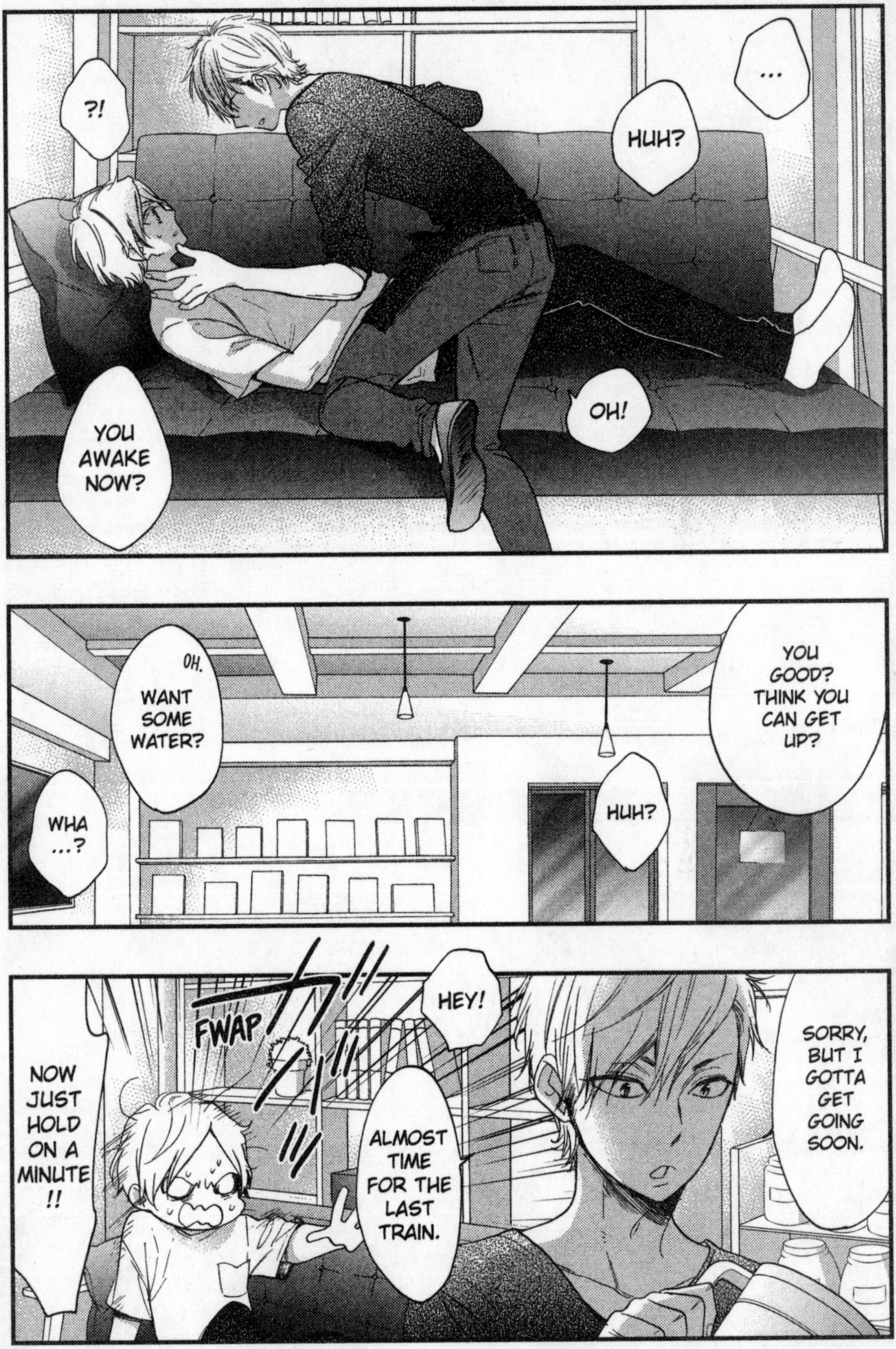
...
HUH?
?!
OH!
YOU AWAKE NOW?
YOU GOOD? THINK YOU CAN GET UP?
HUH?
OH. WANT SOME WATER?
WHA ...?
SORRY, BUT I GOTTA GET GOING SOON.
HEY!
ALMOST TIME FOR THE LAST TRAIN.
FWAP
NOW JUST HOLD ON A MINUTE !!

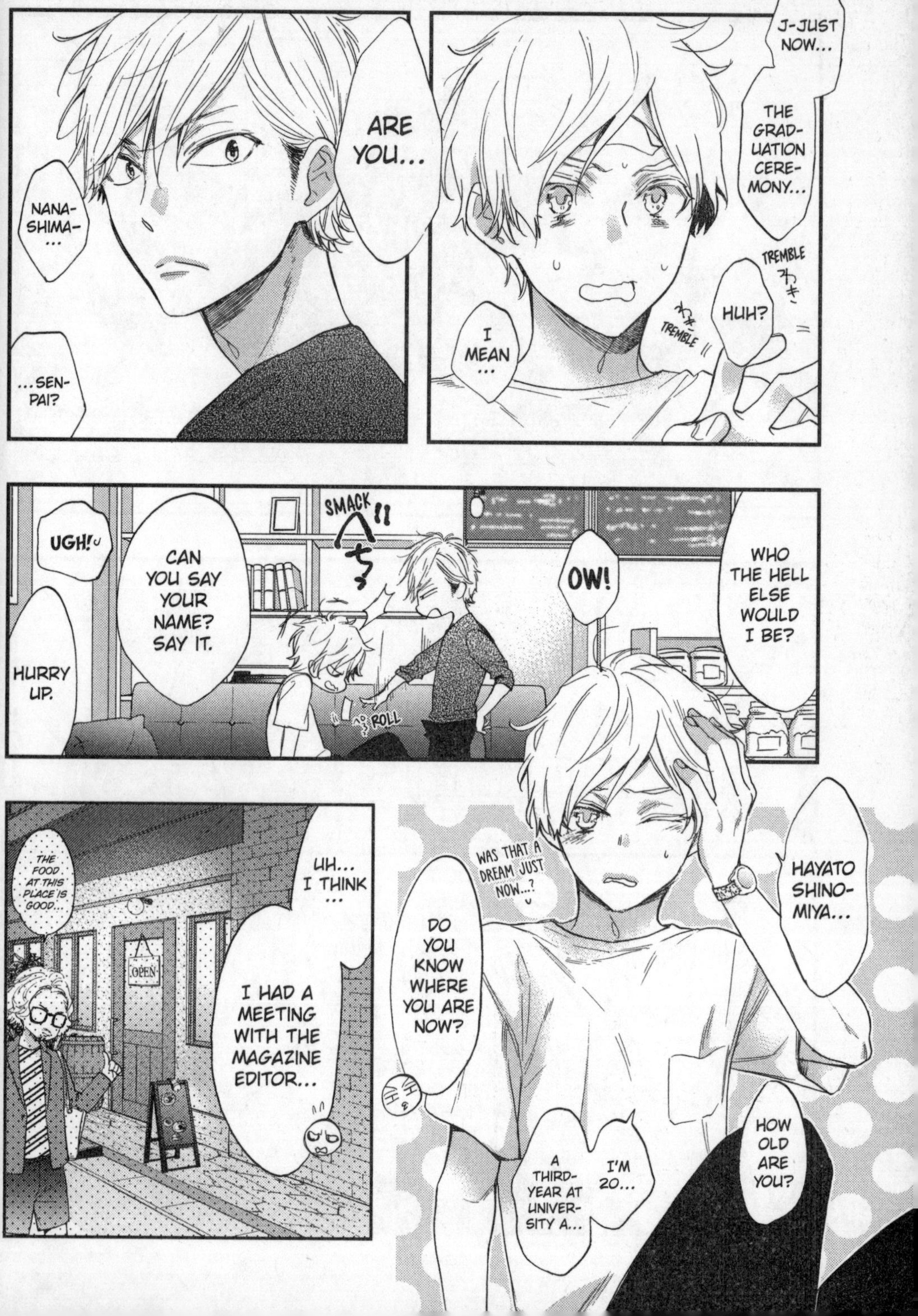
J-JUST NOW...
THE GRAD-UATION CERE-MONY...
TREMBLE
HUH?
TREMBLE
I MEAN ...
ARE YOU...
NANA-SHIMA-...
...SEN-PAI?
WHO THE HELL ELSE WOULD I BE?
OW!
SMACK!!
CAN YOU SAY YOUR NAME? SAY IT.
UGH!
ROLL
HURRY UP.
HAYATO SHINO-MIYA...
WAS THAT A DREAM JUST NOW...?
DO YOU KNOW WHERE YOU ARE NOW?
HOW OLD ARE YOU?
I'M 20...
A THIRD-YEAR AT UNIVER-SITY A...
UH... I THINK ...
I HAD A MEETING WITH THE MAGAZINE EDITOR...
THE FOOD AT THIS PLACE IS GOOD...
OPEN

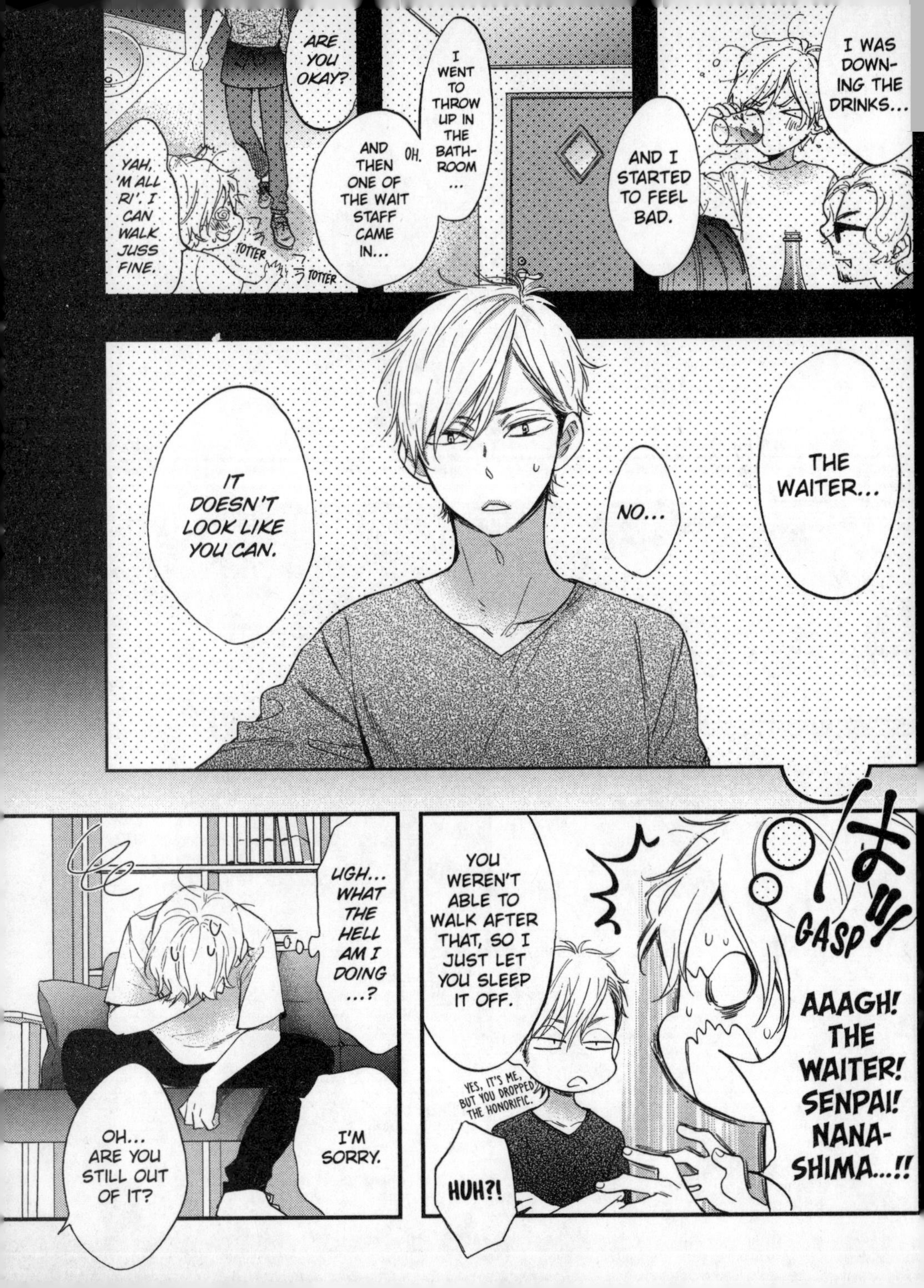
I WAS DOWNING THE DRINKS...
AND I STARTED TO FEEL BAD.
I WENT TO THROW UP IN THE BATHROOM...
OH.
AND THEN ONE OF THE WAIT STAFF CAME IN...
ARE YOU OKAY?
YAH, 'M ALL RI'. I CAN WALK JUSS FINE.
TOTTER
TOTTER
THE WAITER...
NO...
IT DOESN'T LOOK LIKE YOU CAN.
はっ!
GASP
AAAGH! THE WAITER! SENPAI! NANASHIMA...!!
YOU WEREN'T ABLE TO WALK AFTER THAT, SO I JUST LET YOU SLEEP IT OFF.
YES, IT'S ME, BUT YOU DROPPED THE HONORIFIC.
HUH?!
UGH... WHAT THE HELL AM I DOING...?
I'M SORRY.
OH... ARE YOU STILL OUT OF IT?

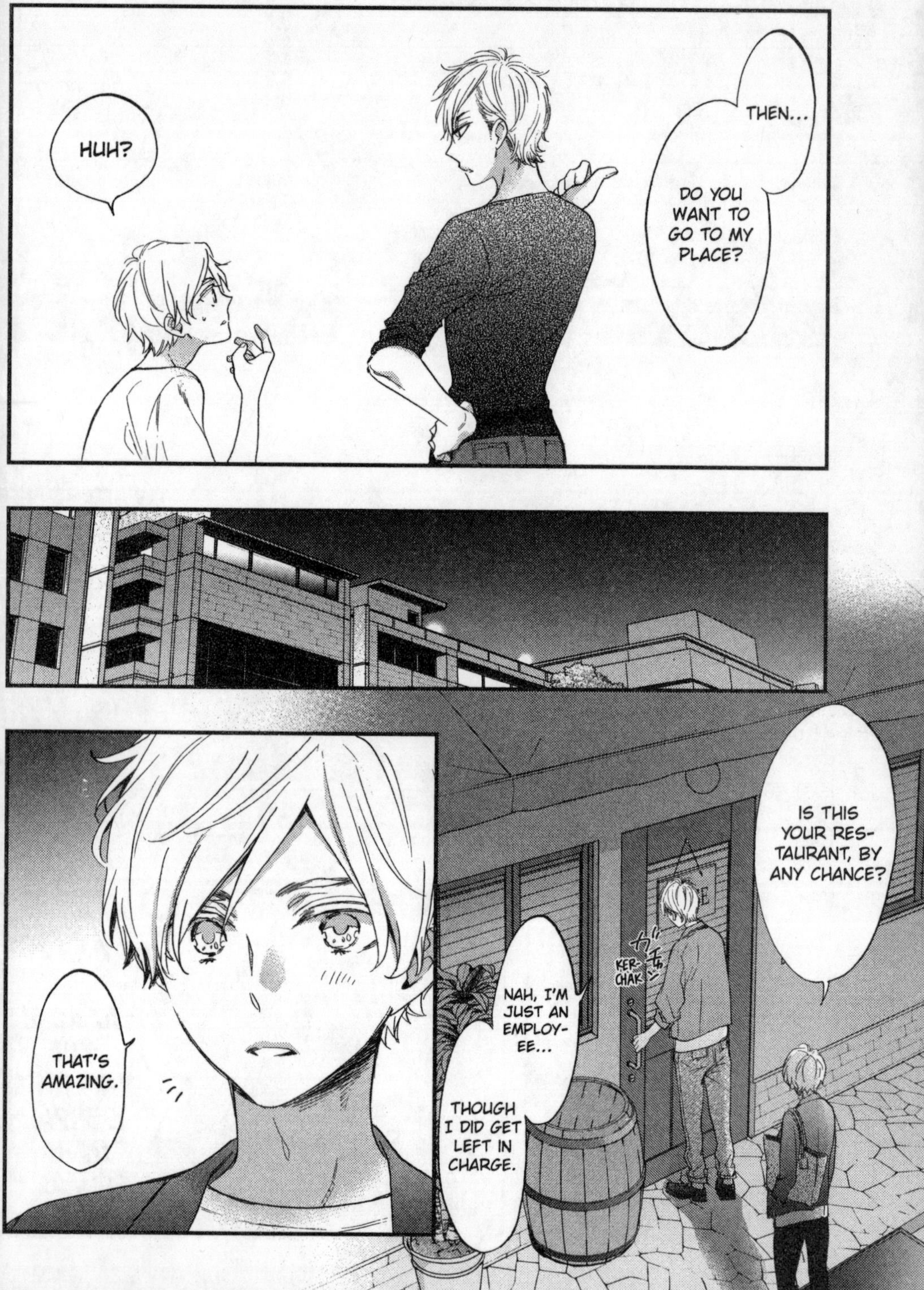
THEN... DO YOU WANT TO GO TO MY PLACE?
HUH?
IS THIS YOUR RES-TAURANT, BY ANY CHANCE?
KER-CHAK
NAH, I'M JUST AN EMPLOY-EE...
THOUGH I DID GET LEFT IN CHARGE.
THAT'S AMAZING.

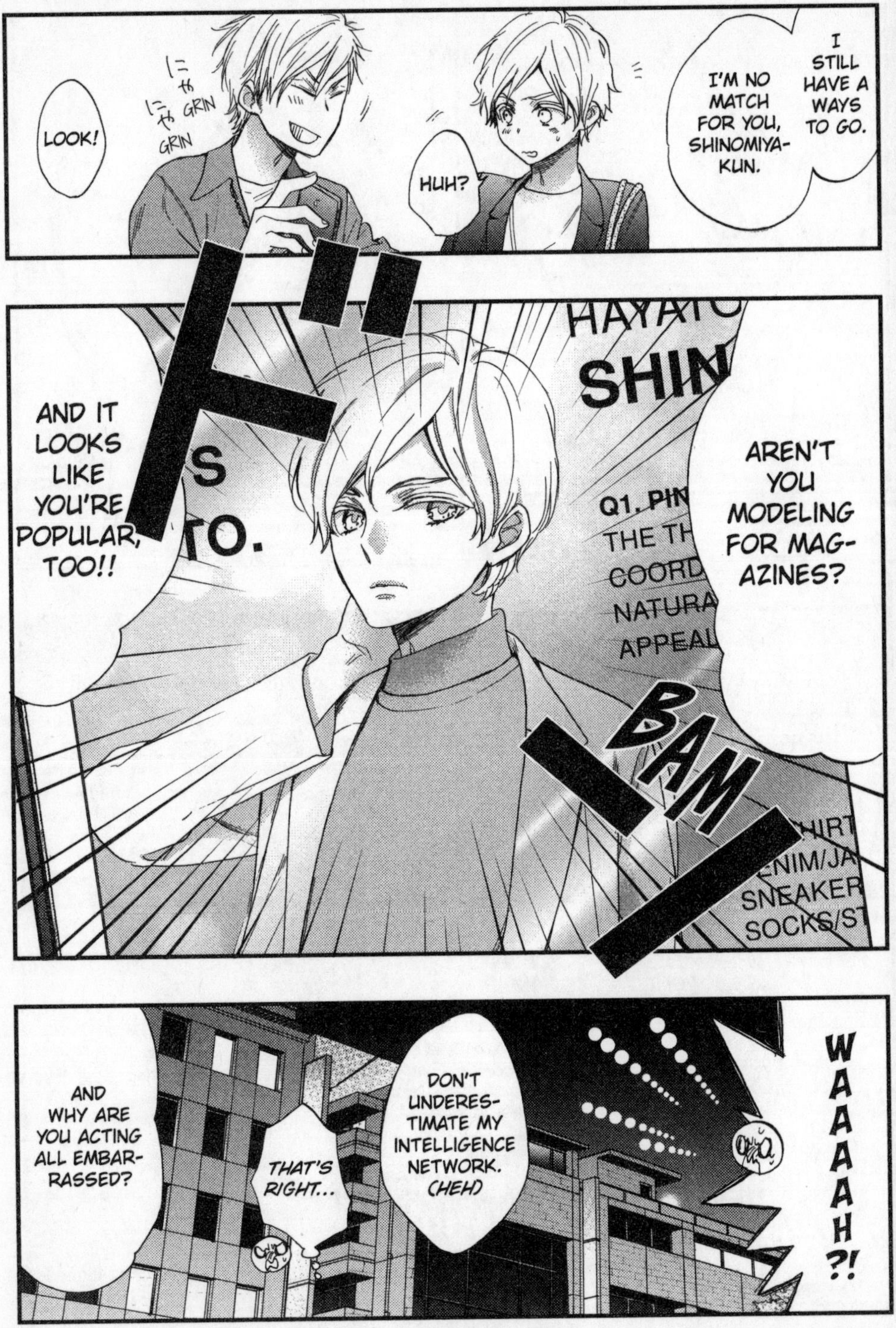
I STILL HAVE A WAYS TO GO.
I'M NO MATCH FOR YOU, SHINOMIYA-KUN.
HUH?
にや にや GRIN GRIN
LOOK!
AREN'T YOU MODELING FOR MAGAZINES?
SHIN
BAM
ド
AND IT LOOKS LIKE YOU'RE POPULAR, TOO!!
WAAAAAH?!
DON'T UNDERESTIMATE MY INTELLIGENCE NETWORK. (HEH)
THAT'S RIGHT...
AND WHY ARE YOU ACTING ALL EMBARRASSED?

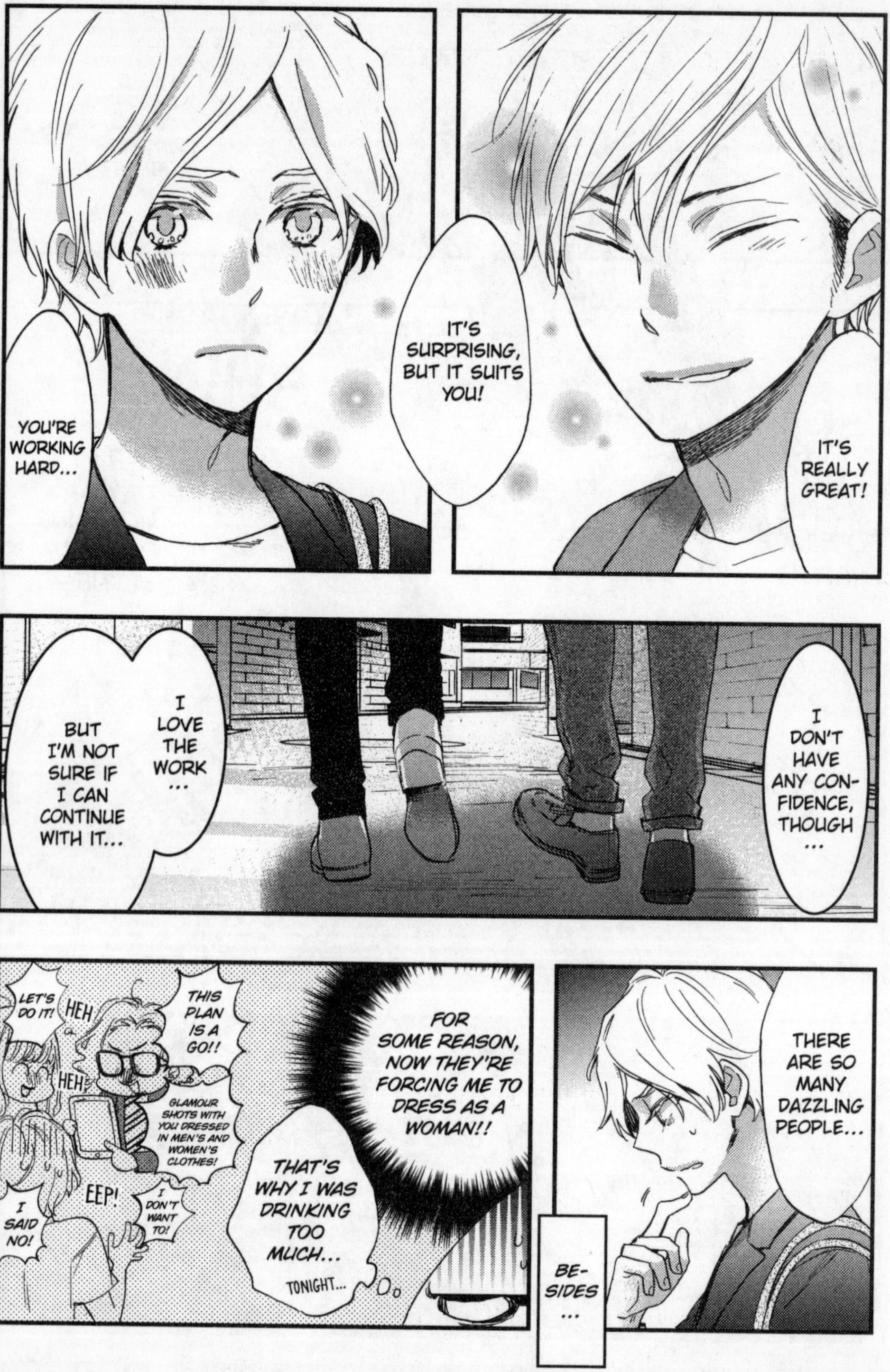
IT'S SURPRISING, BUT IT SUITS YOU!
IT'S REALLY GREAT!
YOU'RE WORKING HARD...
I DON'T HAVE ANY CON-FIDENCE, THOUGH ...
I LOVE THE WORK ...
BUT I'M NOT SURE IF I CAN CONTINUE WITH IT...
THERE ARE SO MANY DAZZLING PEOPLE...
BE-SIDES ...
FOR SOME REASON, NOW THEY'RE FORCING ME TO DRESS AS A WOMAN!!
THIS PLAN IS A GO!!
LET'S DO IT!
HEH
HEH
GLAMOUR SHOTS WITH YOU DRESSED IN MEN'S AND WOMEN'S CLOTHES!
I DON'T WANT TO!
EEP!
I SAID NO!
THAT'S WHY I WAS DRINKING TOO MUCH...
TONIGHT...

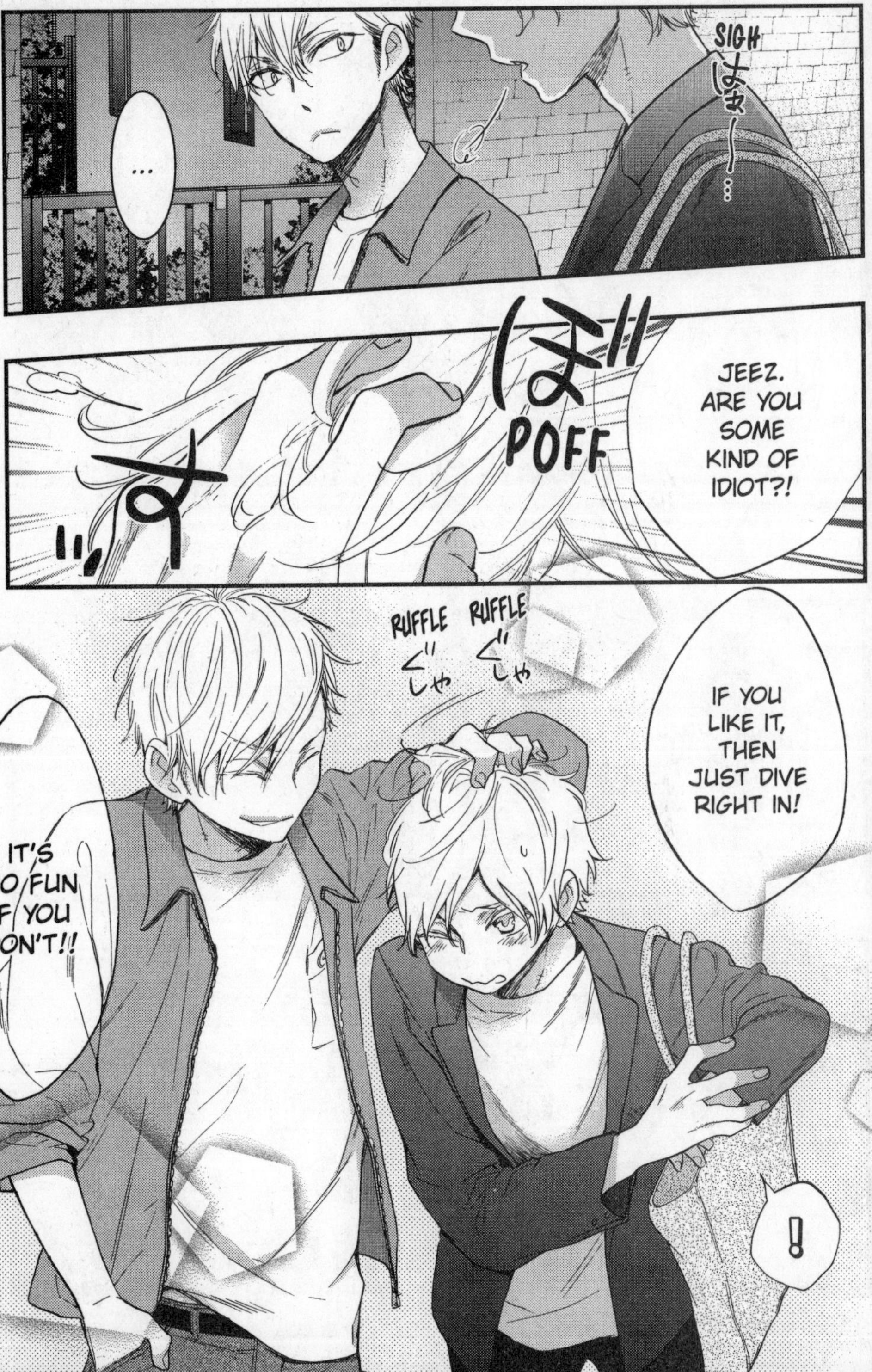
SIGH
はぁ〜…
…
JEEZ. ARE YOU SOME KIND OF IDIOT?!
ぼ
POFF
すッ
IF YOU LIKE IT, THEN JUST DIVE RIGHT IN!
RUFFLE
ぐしゃ
RUFFLE
ぐしゃ
IT'S NO FUN IF YOU DON'T!!
!

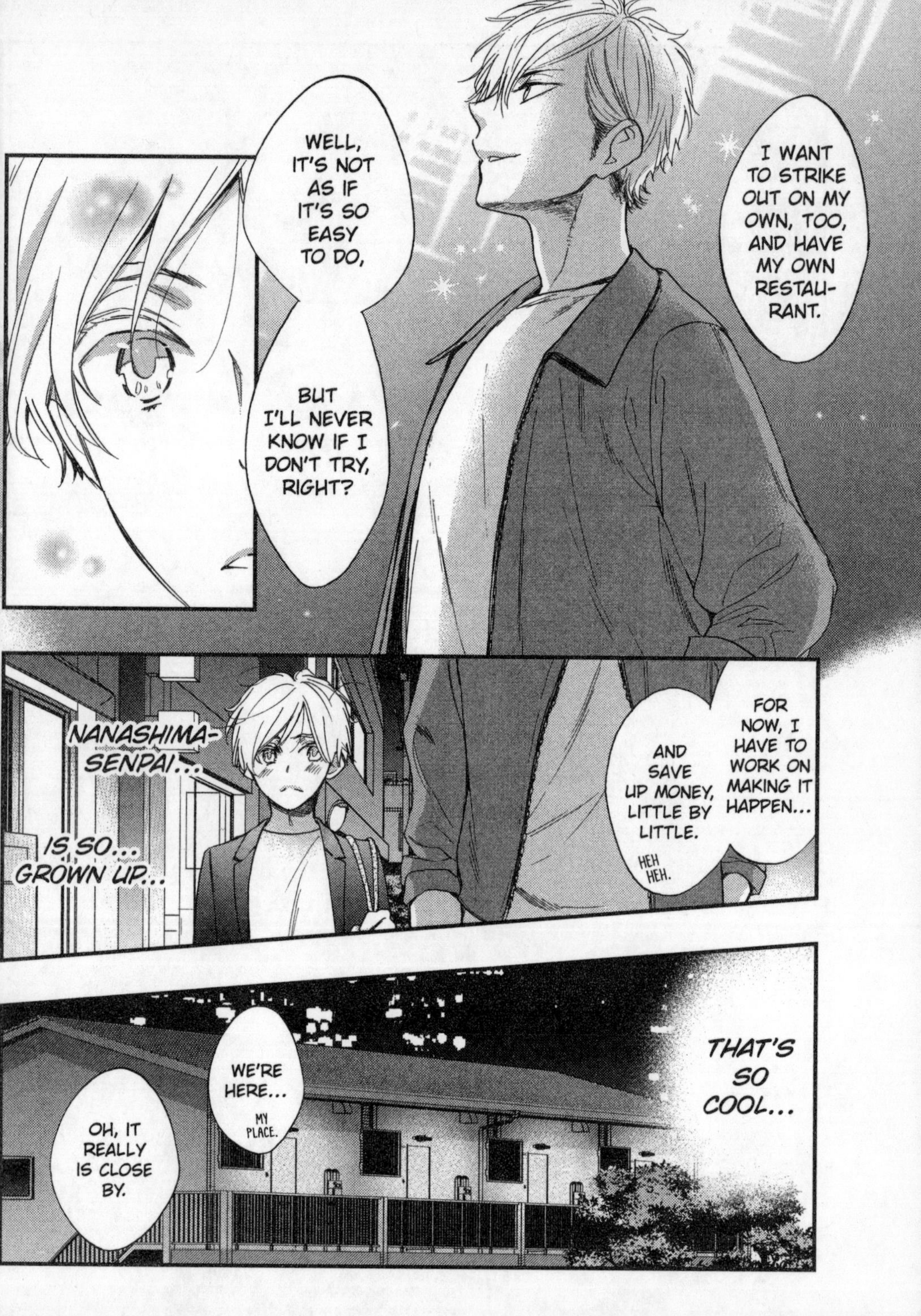
I WANT TO STRIKE OUT ON MY OWN, TOO, AND HAVE MY OWN RESTAU-RANT.
WELL, IT'S NOT AS IF IT'S SO EASY TO DO,
BUT I'LL NEVER KNOW IF I DON'T TRY, RIGHT?
FOR NOW, I HAVE TO WORK ON MAKING IT HAPPEN...
AND SAVE UP MONEY, LITTLE BY LITTLE.
HEH HEH.
NANASHIMA-SENPAI...
IS SO... GROWN UP...
THAT'S SO COOL...
WE'RE HERE...
MY PLACE.
OH, IT REALLY IS CLOSE BY.

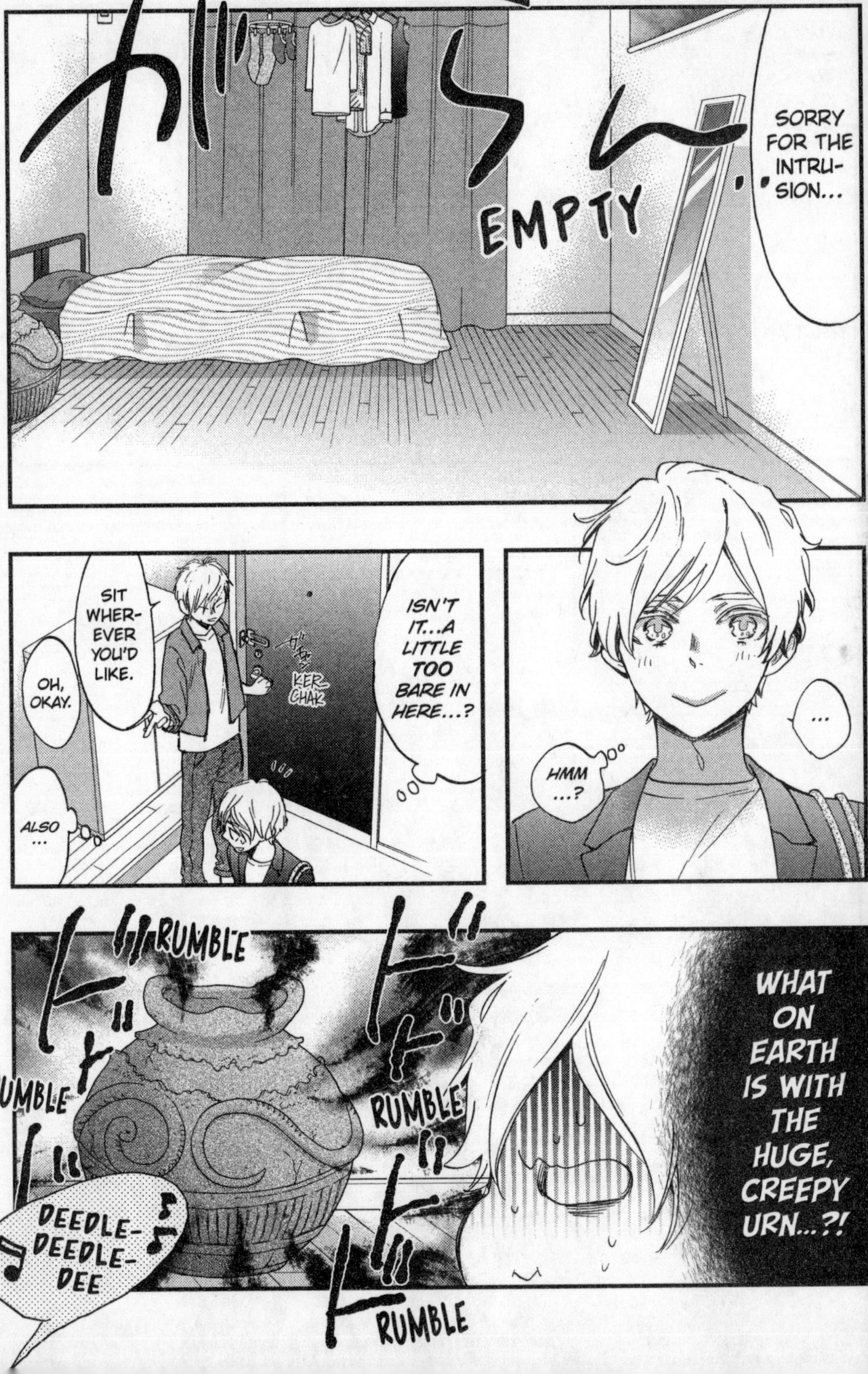
SORRY FOR THE INTRUSION...
がらん
EMPTY
...
HMM ...?
ISN'T IT...A LITTLE TOO BARE IN HERE...?
KER-CHAK
SIT WHEREVER YOU'D LIKE.
OH, OKAY.
ALSO ...
WHAT ON EARTH IS WITH THE HUGE, CREEPY URN...?!
RUMBLE
RUMBLE
RUMBLE
RUMBLE
DEEDLE-DEEDLE-DEE

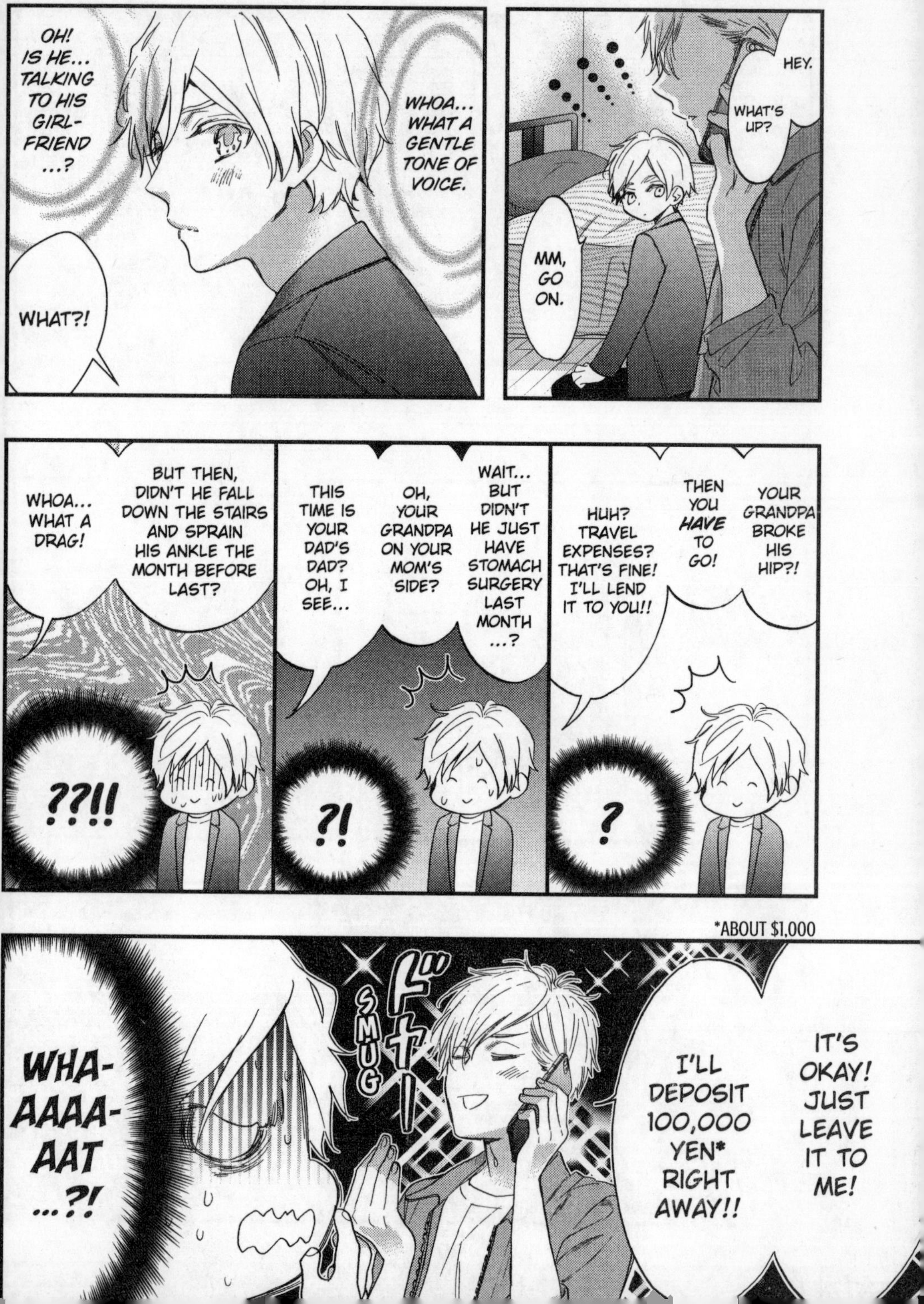
HEY.
WHAT'S UP?
MM, GO ON.
WHOA... WHAT A GENTLE TONE OF VOICE.
OH! IS HE... TALKING TO HIS GIRL-FRIEND ...?
WHAT?!
YOUR GRANDPA BROKE HIS HIP?!
THEN YOU *HAVE* TO GO!
HUH? TRAVEL EXPENSES? THAT'S FINE! I'LL LEND IT TO YOU!!
?
WAIT... BUT DIDN'T HE JUST HAVE STOMACH SURGERY LAST MONTH ...?
OH, YOUR GRANDPA ON YOUR MOM'S SIDE?
THIS TIME IS YOUR DAD'S DAD? OH, I SEE...
?!
BUT THEN, DIDN'T HE FALL DOWN THE STAIRS AND SPRAIN HIS ANKLE THE MONTH BEFORE LAST?
WHOA... WHAT A DRAG!
??!!
*ABOUT $1,000
IT'S OKAY! JUST LEAVE IT TO ME!
I'LL DEPOSIT 100,000 YEN* RIGHT AWAY!!
SMUG
WHA-AAAA-AAT ...?!

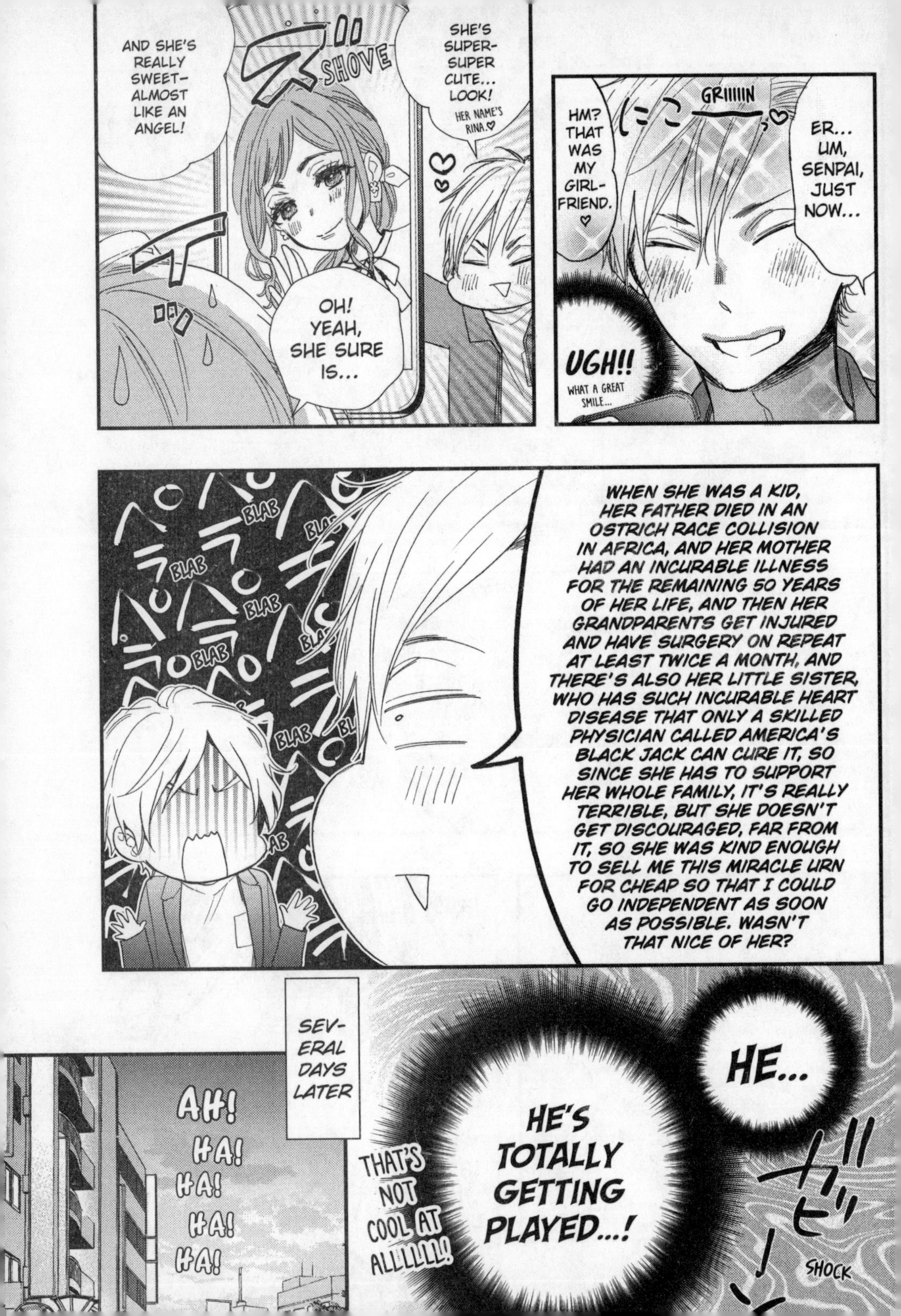
ER... UM, SENPAI, JUST NOW...
GRIIIIIN
HM? THAT WAS MY GIRLFRIEND. ♡
UGH!!
WHAT A GREAT SMILE...
SHE'S SUPER-SUPER CUTE... LOOK!
HER NAME'S RINA.♡
SHOVE
AND SHE'S REALLY SWEET—ALMOST LIKE AN ANGEL!
OH! YEAH, SHE SURE IS...
WHEN SHE WAS A KID, HER FATHER DIED IN AN OSTRICH RACE COLLISION IN AFRICA, AND HER MOTHER HAD AN INCURABLE ILLNESS FOR THE REMAINING 50 YEARS OF HER LIFE, AND THEN HER GRANDPARENTS GET INJURED AND HAVE SURGERY ON REPEAT AT LEAST TWICE A MONTH, AND THERE'S ALSO HER LITTLE SISTER, WHO HAS SUCH INCURABLE HEART DISEASE THAT ONLY A SKILLED PHYSICIAN CALLED AMERICA'S BLACK JACK CAN CURE IT, SO SINCE SHE HAS TO SUPPORT HER WHOLE FAMILY, IT'S REALLY TERRIBLE, BUT SHE DOESN'T GET DISCOURAGED, FAR FROM IT, SO SHE WAS KIND ENOUGH TO SELL ME THIS MIRACLE URN FOR CHEAP SO THAT I COULD GO INDEPENDENT AS SOON AS POSSIBLE. WASN'T THAT NICE OF HER?
BLAB
BLAB
BLAB
BLAB
BLAB
HE...
HE'S TOTALLY GETTING PLAYED...!
SHOCK
THAT'S NOT COOL AT ALLLLLL!
SEV-ERAL DAYS LATER
AH! HA! HA! HA! HA!

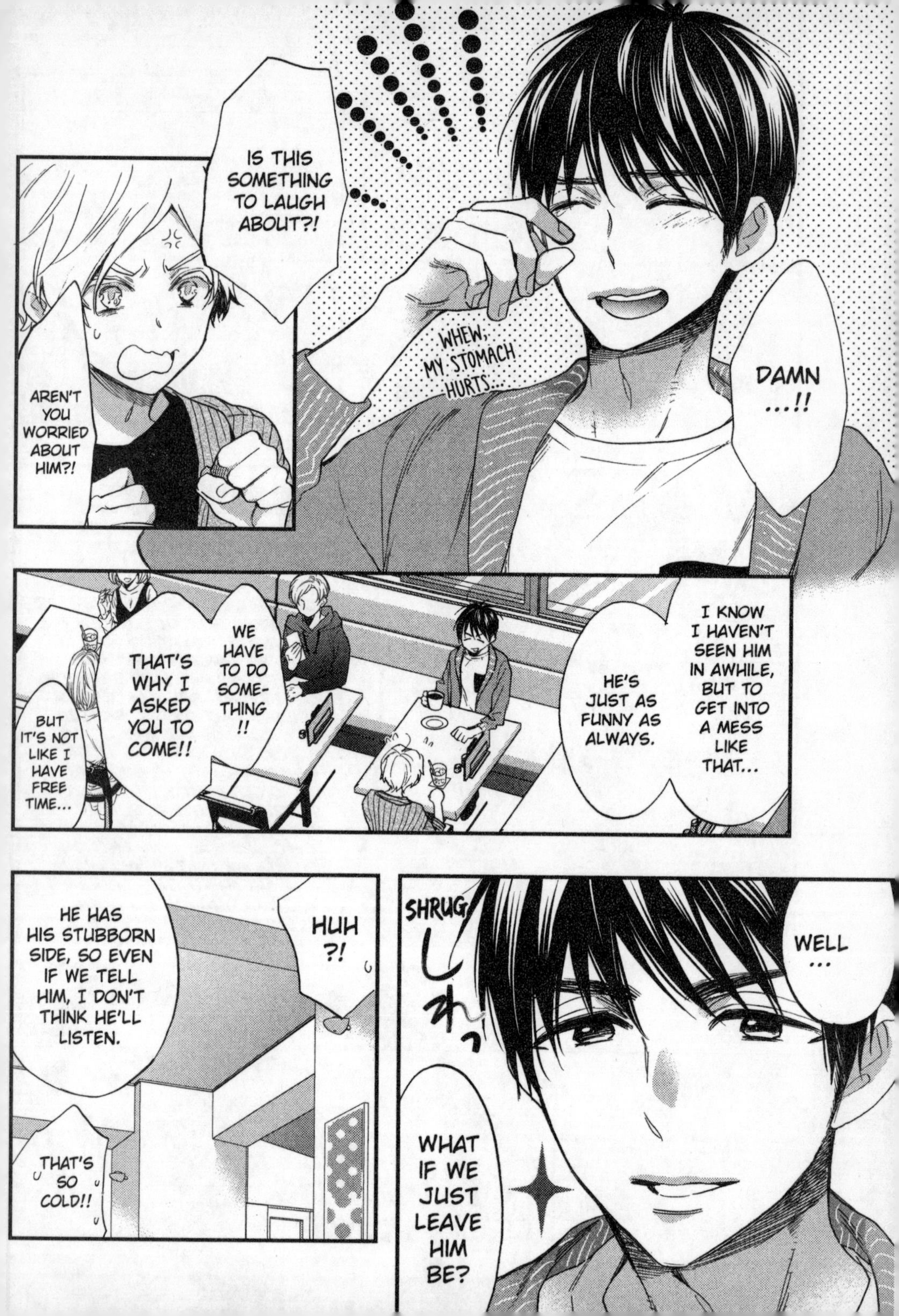

DAMN ...!!
WHEW, MY STOMACH HURTS...
IS THIS SOMETHING TO LAUGH ABOUT?!
AREN'T YOU WORRIED ABOUT HIM?!
I KNOW I HAVEN'T SEEN HIM IN AWHILE, BUT TO GET INTO A MESS LIKE THAT...
HE'S JUST AS FUNNY AS ALWAYS.
WE HAVE TO DO SOME-THING!!
THAT'S WHY I ASKED YOU TO COME!!
BUT IT'S NOT LIKE I HAVE FREE TIME...
WELL ...
SHRUG
しれっ
WHAT IF WE JUST LEAVE HIM BE?
HUH ?!
HE HAS HIS STUBBORN SIDE, SO EVEN IF WE TELL HIM, I DON'T THINK HE'LL LISTEN.
THAT'S SO COLD!!

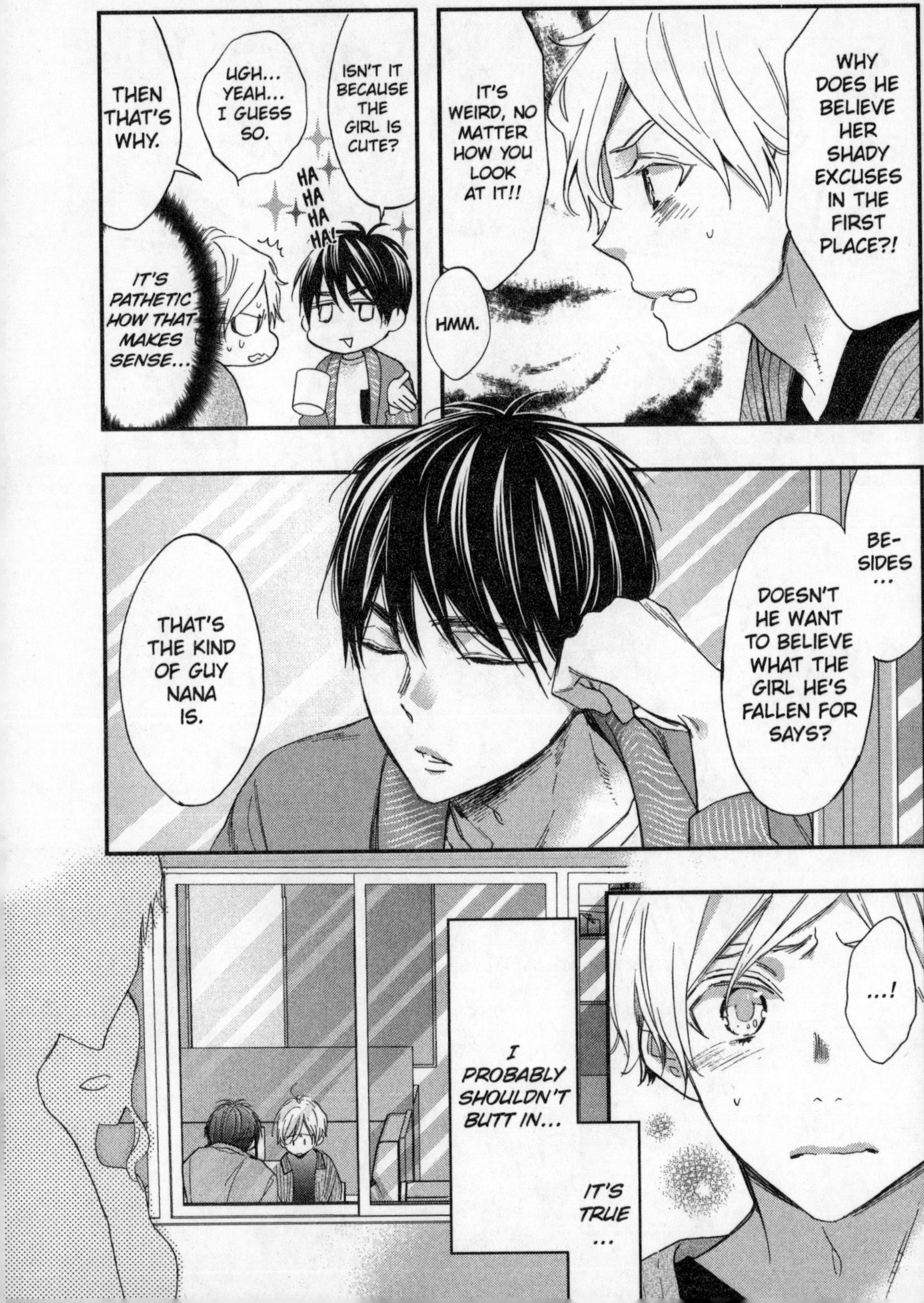
WHY DOES HE BELIEVE HER SHADY EXCUSES IN THE FIRST PLACE?!
IT'S WEIRD, NO MATTER HOW YOU LOOK AT IT!!
HMM.
ISN'T IT BECAUSE THE GIRL IS CUTE?
HA HA HA HA!
UGH... YEAH... I GUESS SO.
THEN THAT'S WHY.
IT'S PATHETIC HOW THAT MAKES SENSE...
BE-SIDES...
DOESN'T HE WANT TO BELIEVE WHAT THE GIRL HE'S FALLEN FOR SAYS?
THAT'S THE KIND OF GUY NANA IS.
...!
I PROBABLY SHOULDN'T BUTT IN...
IT'S TRUE...

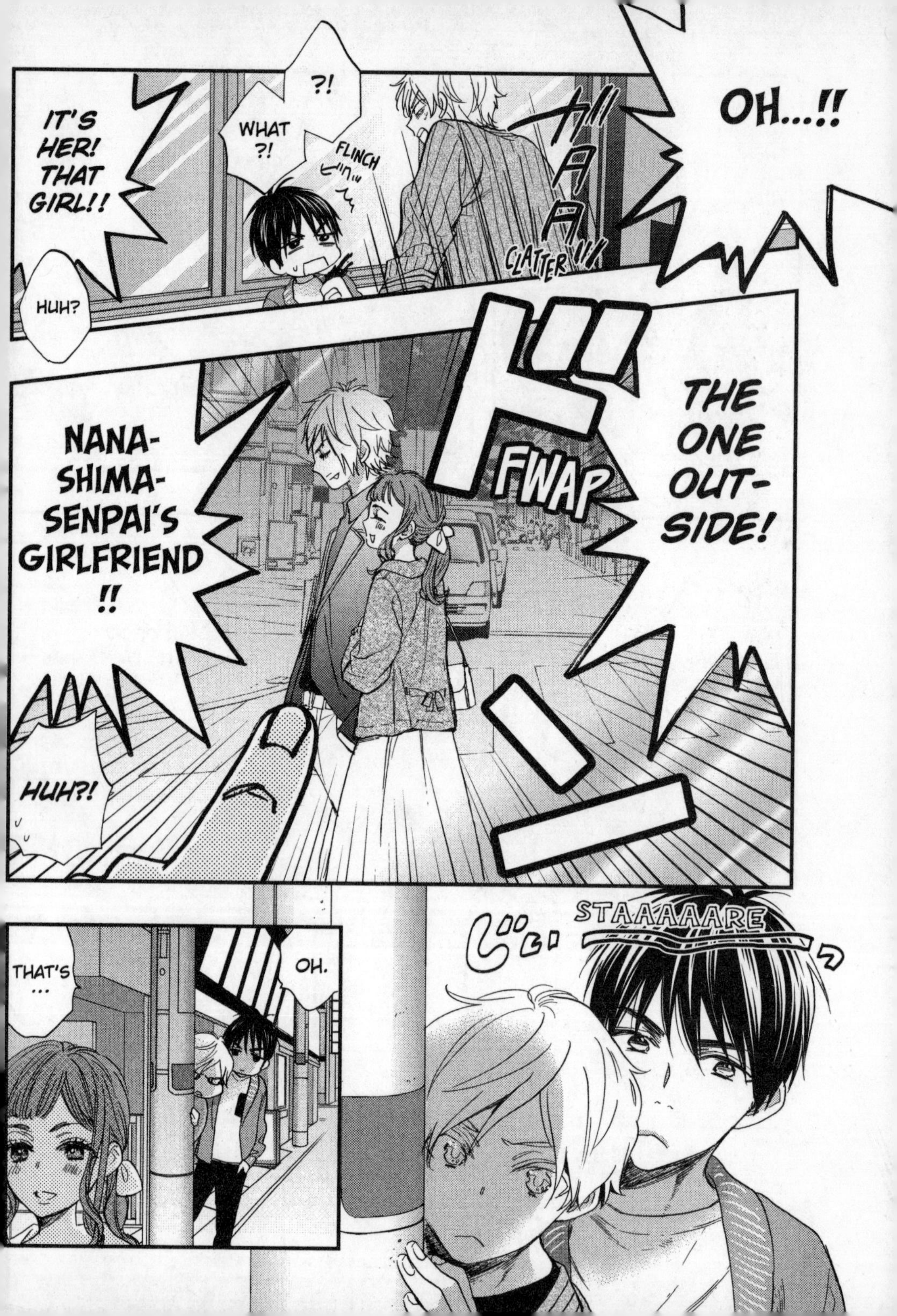
OH...!!
CLATTER
?!
WHAT ?!
FLINCH
IT'S HER! THAT GIRL!!
HUH?
THE ONE OUT-SIDE!
FWAP
NANA-SHIMA-SENPAI'S GIRLFRIEND !!
HUH?!
STAAAAAARE
OH.
THAT'S ...

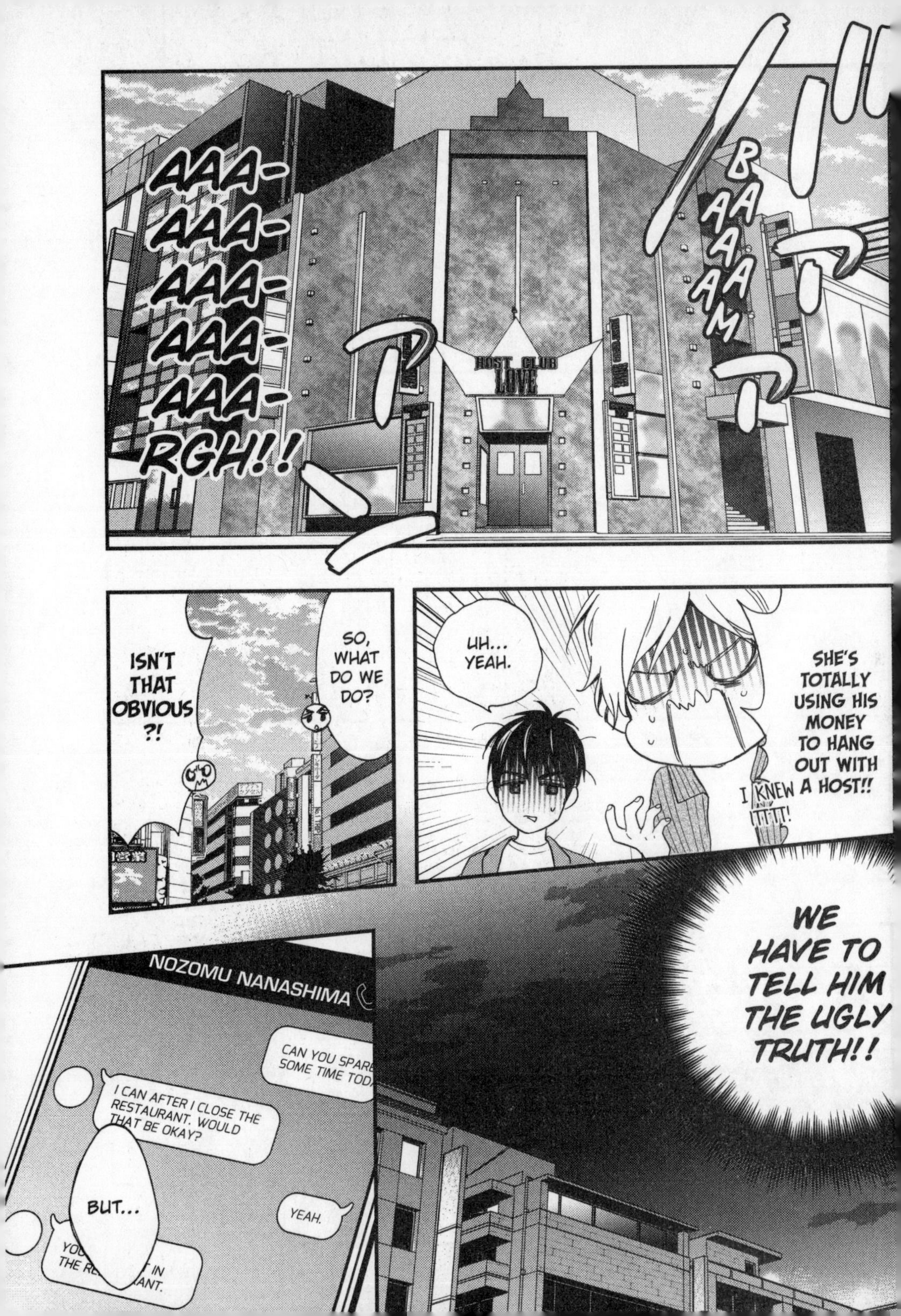
BAAAAM
AAA-AAA-AAA-AAA-AAA-RGH!!
HOST CLUB LOVE
SHE'S TOTALLY USING HIS MONEY TO HANG OUT WITH A HOST!!
I KNEW IT!
UH... YEAH.
SO, WHAT DO WE DO?
ISN'T THAT OBVIOUS?!
WE HAVE TO TELL HIM THE UGLY TRUTH!!
NOZOMU NANASHIMA
CAN YOU SPARE SOME TIME TODA
I CAN AFTER I CLOSE THE RESTAURANT. WOULD THAT BE OKAY?
YEAH.
BUT...

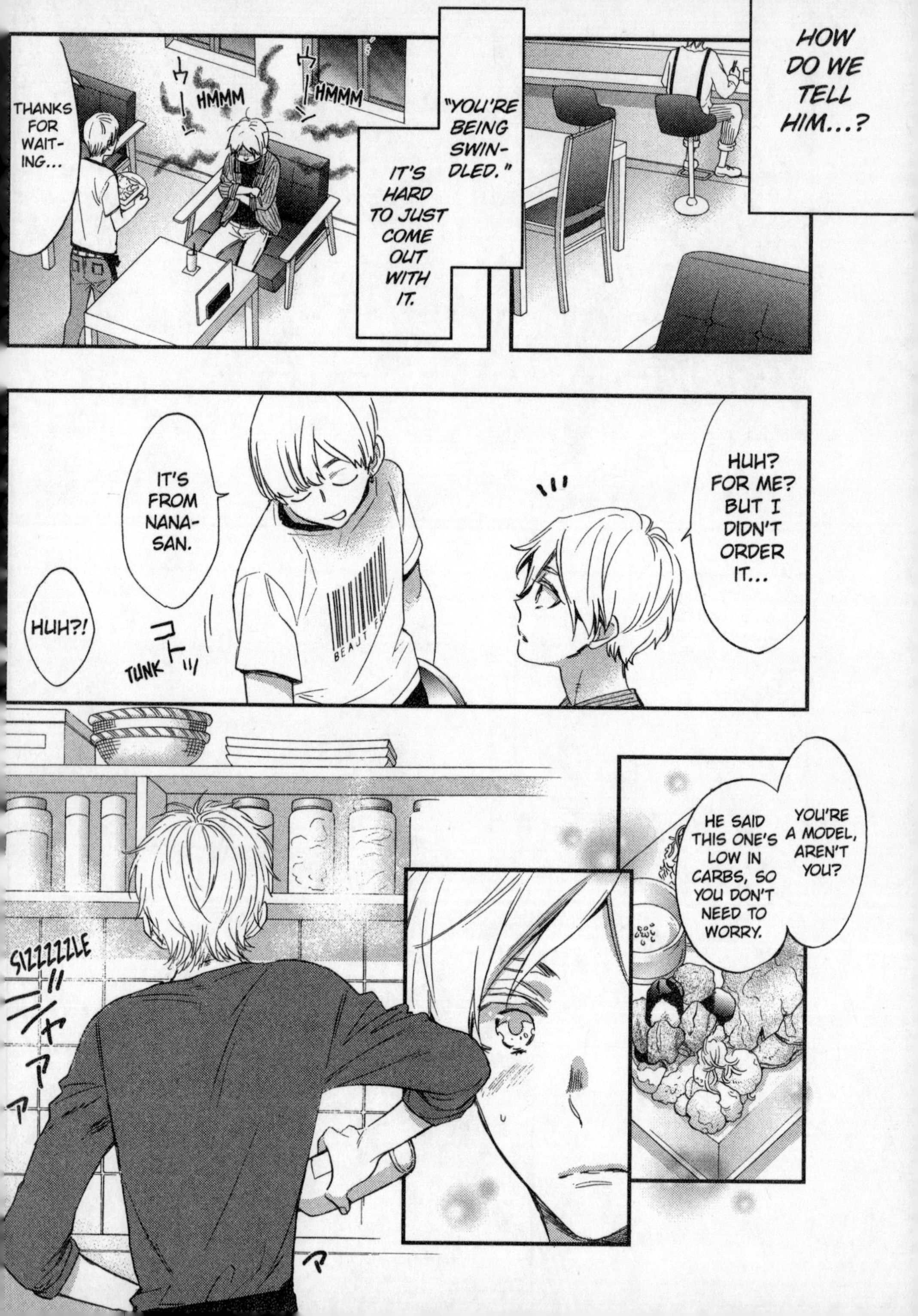
HOW DO WE TELL HIM...?
"YOU'RE BEING SWINDLED."
IT'S HARD TO JUST COME OUT WITH IT.
HMMM
HMMM
THANKS FOR WAITING...
HUH? FOR ME? BUT I DIDN'T ORDER IT...
IT'S FROM NANA-SAN.
HUH?!
TUNK
YOU'RE A MODEL, AREN'T YOU?
HE SAID THIS ONE'S LOW IN CARBS, SO YOU DON'T NEED TO WORRY.
SIZZZZZLE

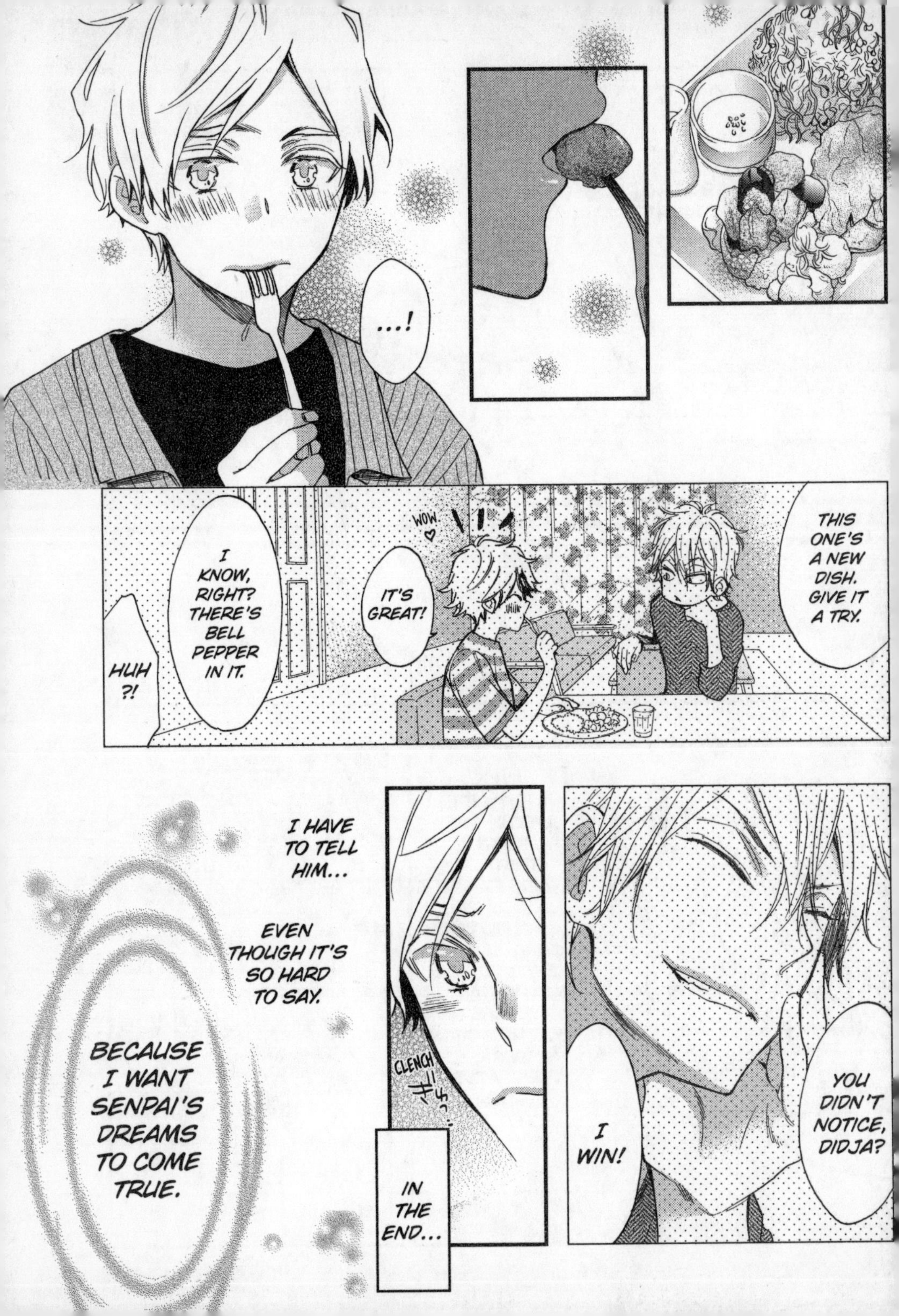
...!
THIS ONE'S A NEW DISH. GIVE IT A TRY.
WOW ♥
IT'S GREAT!
I KNOW, RIGHT? THERE'S BELL PEPPER IN IT.
HUH?!
YOU DIDN'T NOTICE, DIDJA?
I WIN!
CLENCH
IN THE END...
I HAVE TO TELL HIM...
EVEN THOUGH IT'S SO HARD TO SAY.
BECAUSE I WANT SENPAI'S DREAMS TO COME TRUE.

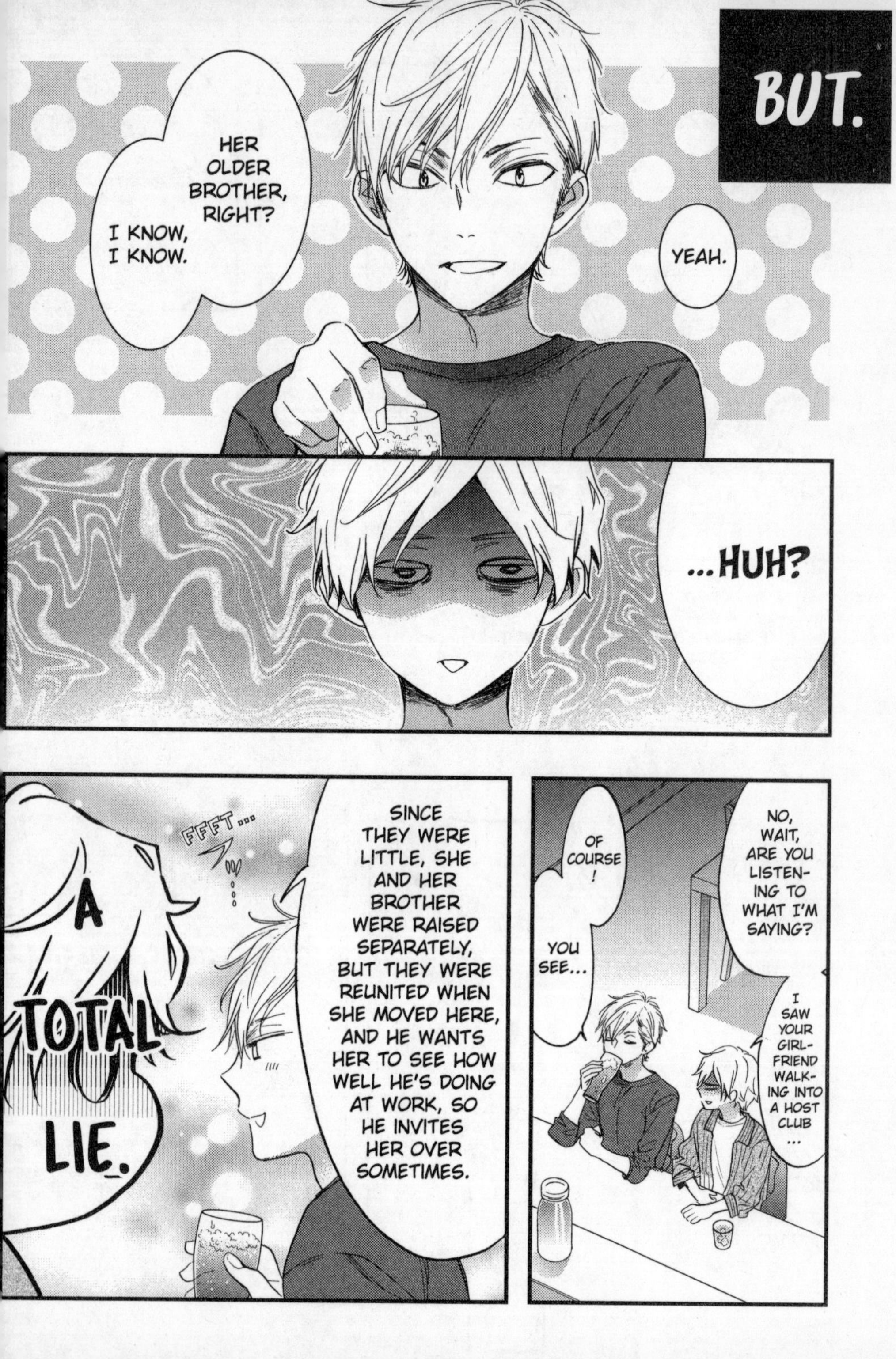
BUT.
HER OLDER BROTHER, RIGHT? I KNOW, I KNOW.
YEAH.
...HUH?
NO, WAIT, ARE YOU LISTEN-ING TO WHAT I'M SAYING?
OF COURSE!
YOU SEE...
I SAW YOUR GIRL-FRIEND WALK-ING INTO A HOST CLUB...
SINCE THEY WERE LITTLE, SHE AND HER BROTHER WERE RAISED SEPARATELY, BUT THEY WERE REUNITED WHEN SHE MOVED HERE, AND HE WANTS HER TO SEE HOW WELL HE'S DOING AT WORK, SO HE INVITES HER OVER SOMETIMES.
FFFT...
A TOTAL LIE.

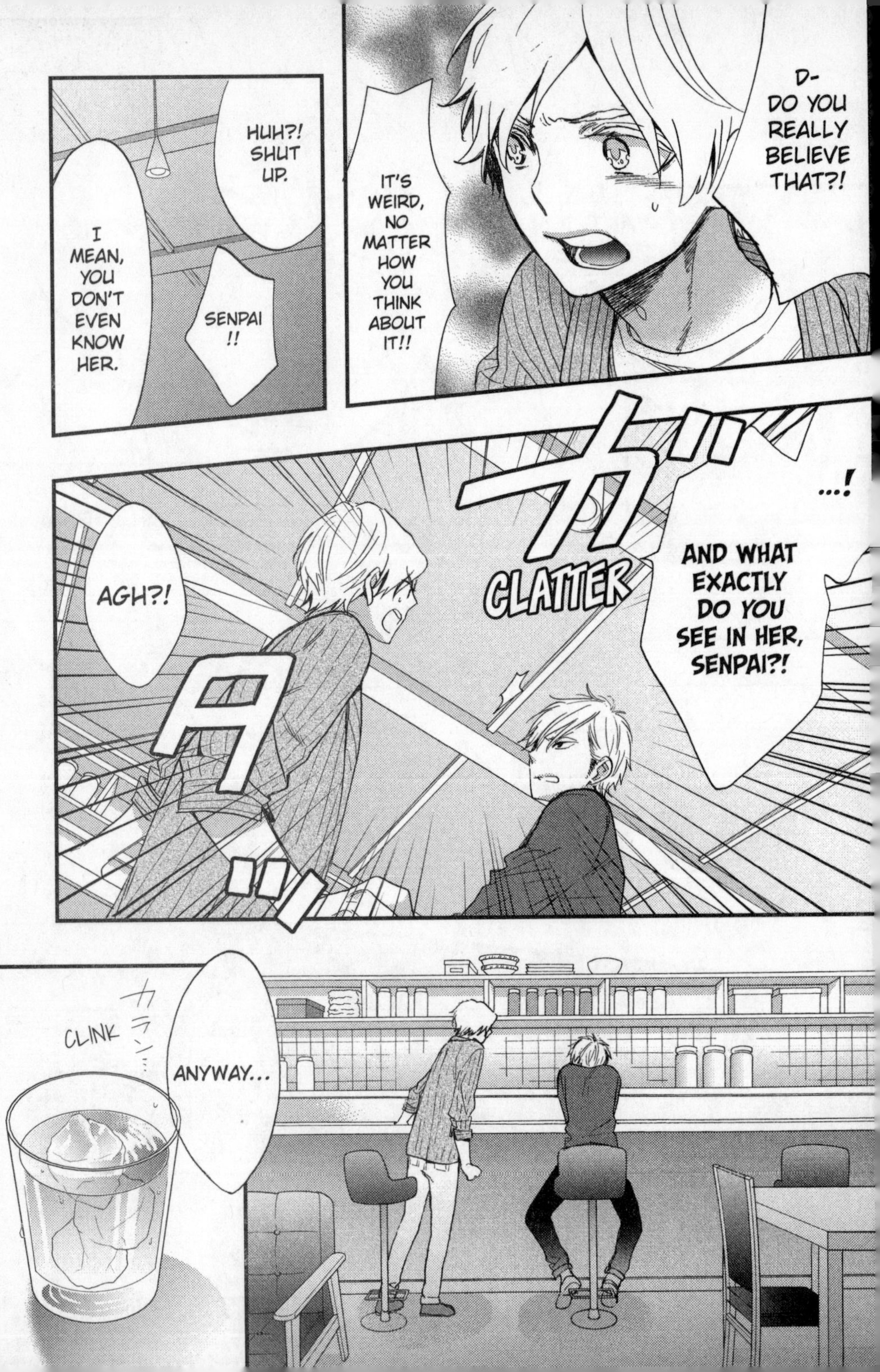
D- DO YOU REALLY BELIEVE THAT?!
IT'S WEIRD, NO MATTER HOW YOU THINK ABOUT IT!!
HUH?! SHUT UP.
SENPAI!!
I MEAN, YOU DON'T EVEN KNOW HER.
...!
AND WHAT EXACTLY DO YOU SEE IN HER, SENPAI?!
CLATTER
AGH?!
ANYWAY...
CLINK

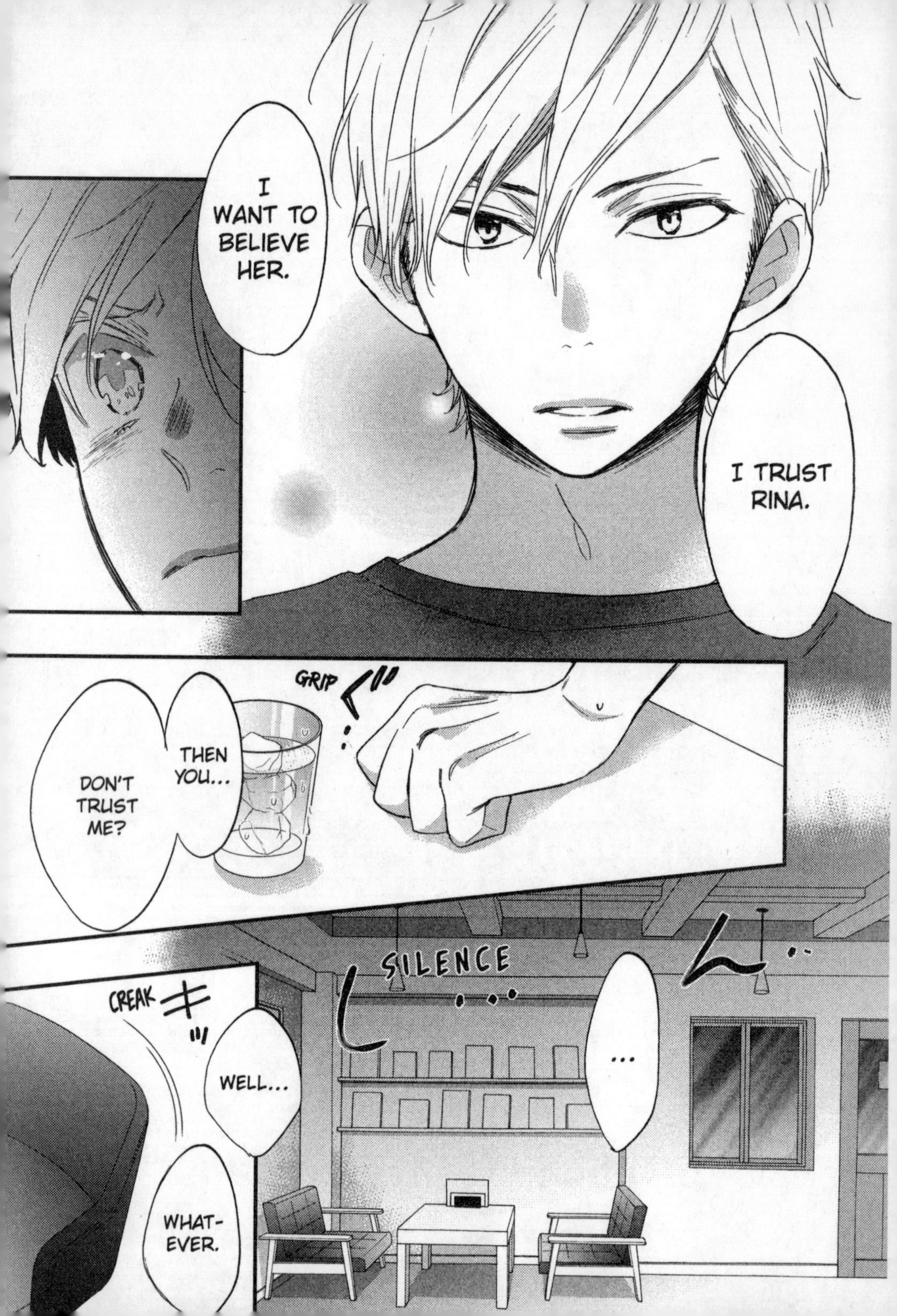
I WANT TO BELIEVE HER.
I TRUST RINA.
GRIP
THEN YOU...
DON'T TRUST ME?
SILENCE
...
CREAK
WELL...
WHAT-EVER.

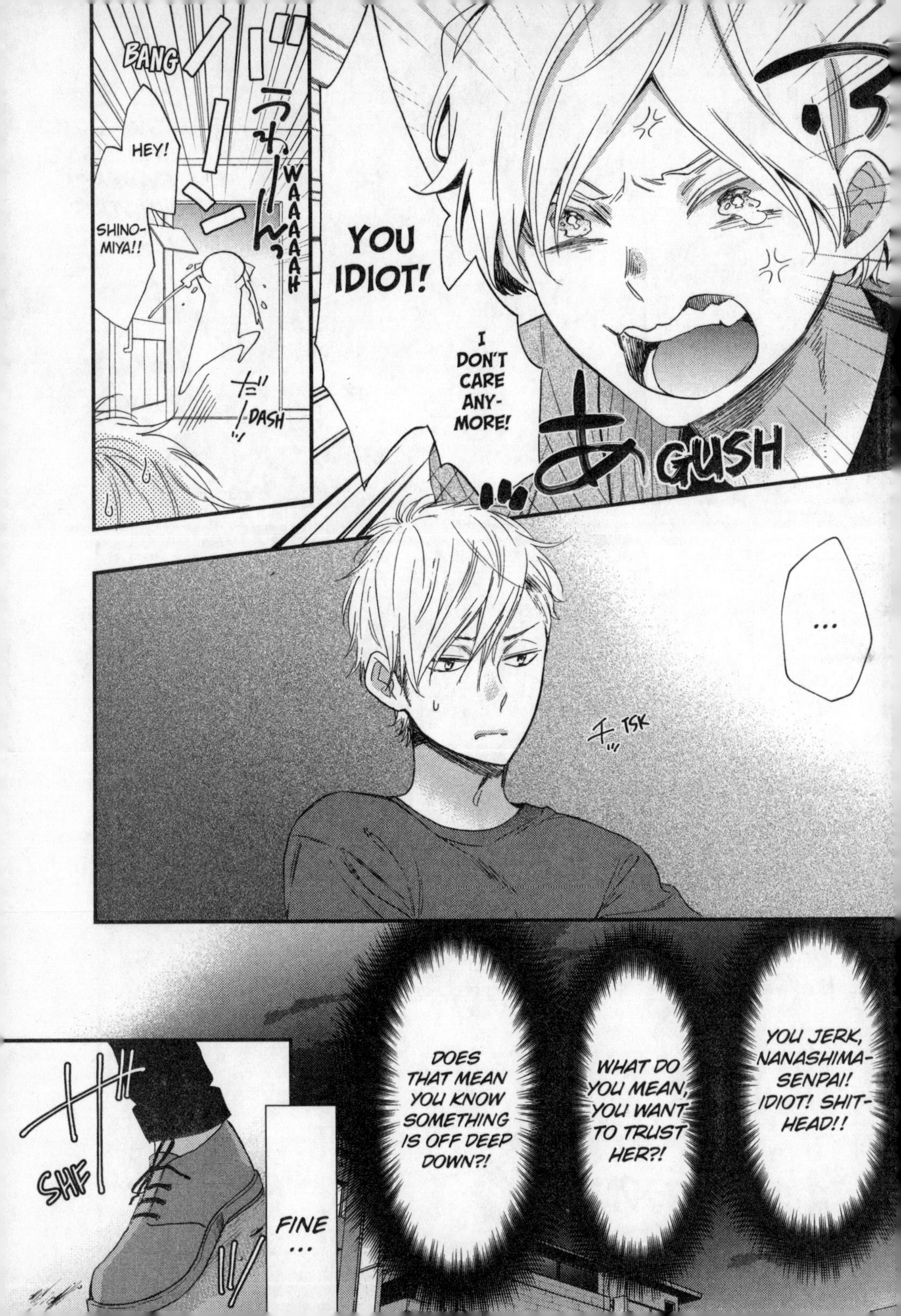
YOU IDIOT!
I DON'T CARE ANY-MORE!
GUSH
BANG
HEY!
SHINO-MIYA!!
WAAAAAAAH
DASH
...
TSK
YOU JERK, NANASHIMA-SENPAI! IDIOT! SHIT-HEAD!!
WHAT DO YOU MEAN, YOU WANT TO TRUST HER?!
DOES THAT MEAN YOU KNOW SOMETHING IS OFF DEEP DOWN?!
FINE...
SHF

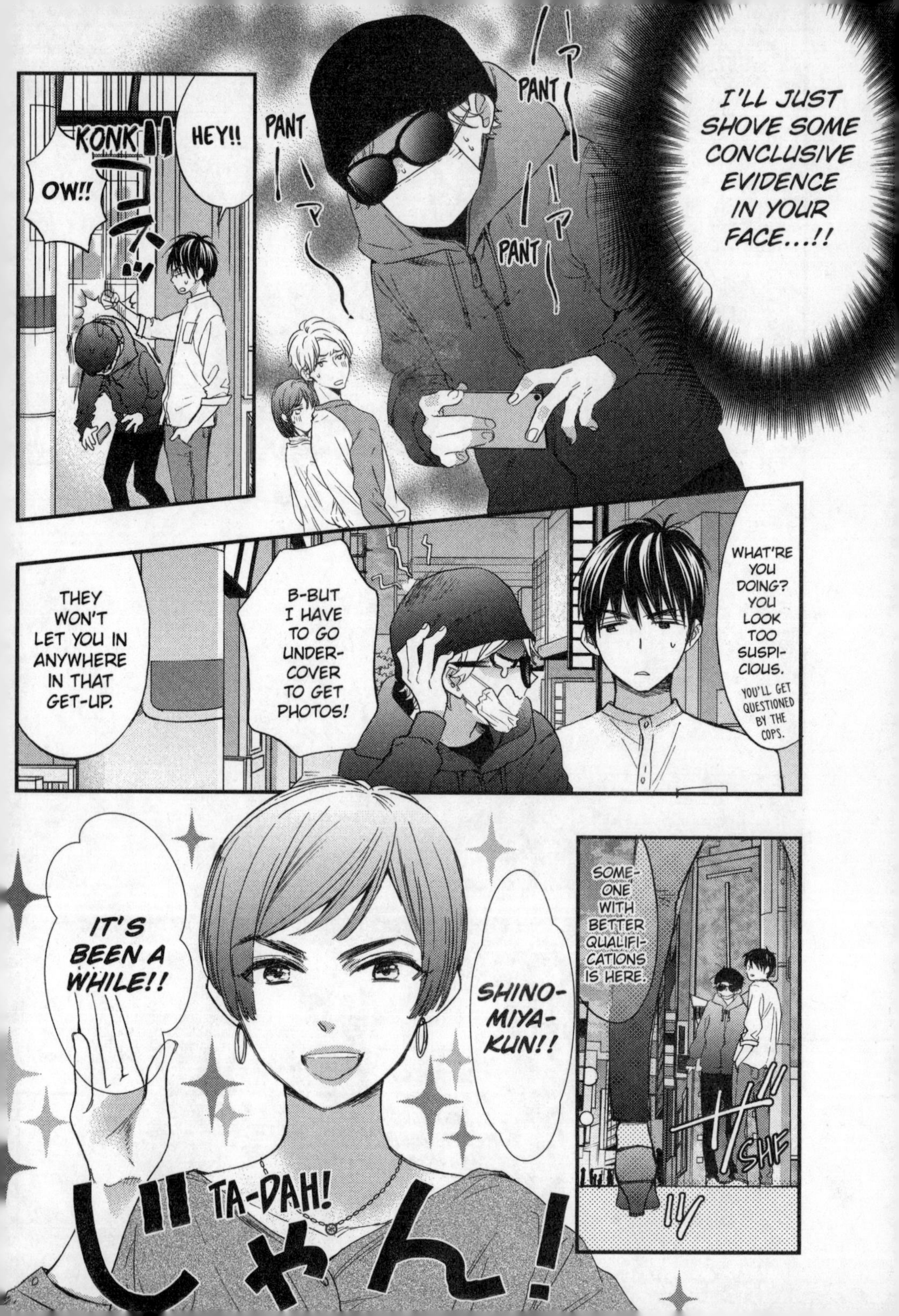

I'LL JUST SHOVE SOME CONCLUSIVE EVIDENCE IN YOUR FACE...!!
PANT
PANT
PANT
HEY!!
KONK
OW!!
WHAT'RE YOU DOING? YOU LOOK TOO SUSPICIOUS.
YOU'LL GET QUESTIONED BY THE COPS.
B-BUT I HAVE TO GO UNDERCOVER TO GET PHOTOS!
THEY WON'T LET YOU IN ANYWHERE IN THAT GET-UP.
SOMEONE WITH BETTER QUALIFICATIONS IS HERE.
SHF
SHINOMIYA-KUN!!
IT'S BEEN A WHILE!!
TA-DAH!
じゃん!

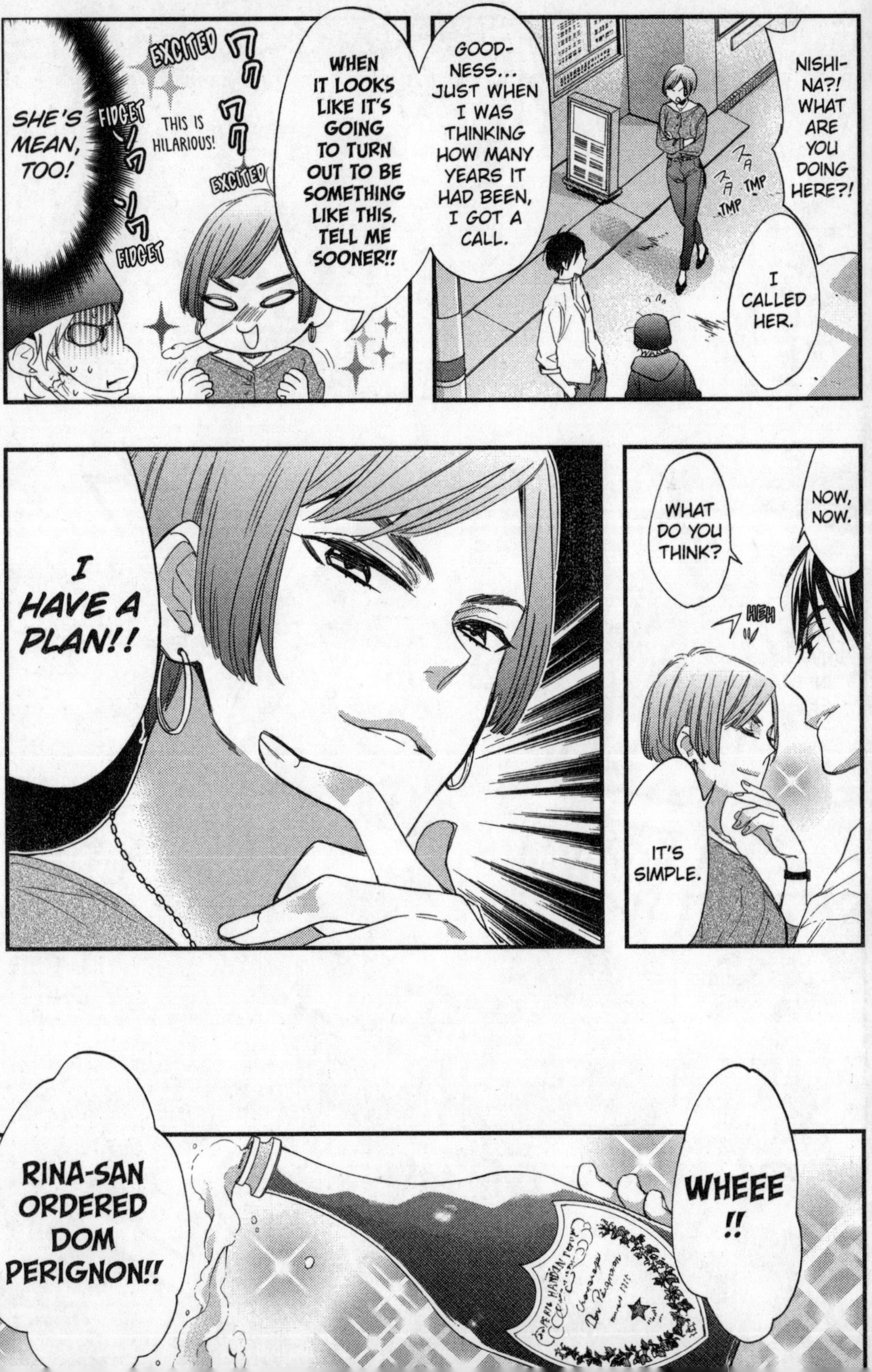
NISHINA?! WHAT ARE YOU DOING HERE?!
TMP
TMP
I CALLED HER.
GOODNESS... JUST WHEN I WAS THINKING HOW MANY YEARS IT HAD BEEN, I GOT A CALL.
WHEN IT LOOKS LIKE IT'S GOING TO TURN OUT TO BE SOMETHING LIKE THIS, TELL ME SOONER!!
EXCITED
EXCITED
THIS IS HILARIOUS!
FIDGET
FIDGET
SHE'S MEAN, TOO!
NOW, NOW.
WHAT DO YOU THINK?
HEH
IT'S SIMPLE.
I HAVE A PLAN!!
WHEEE!!
RINA-SAN ORDERED DOM PERIGNON!!

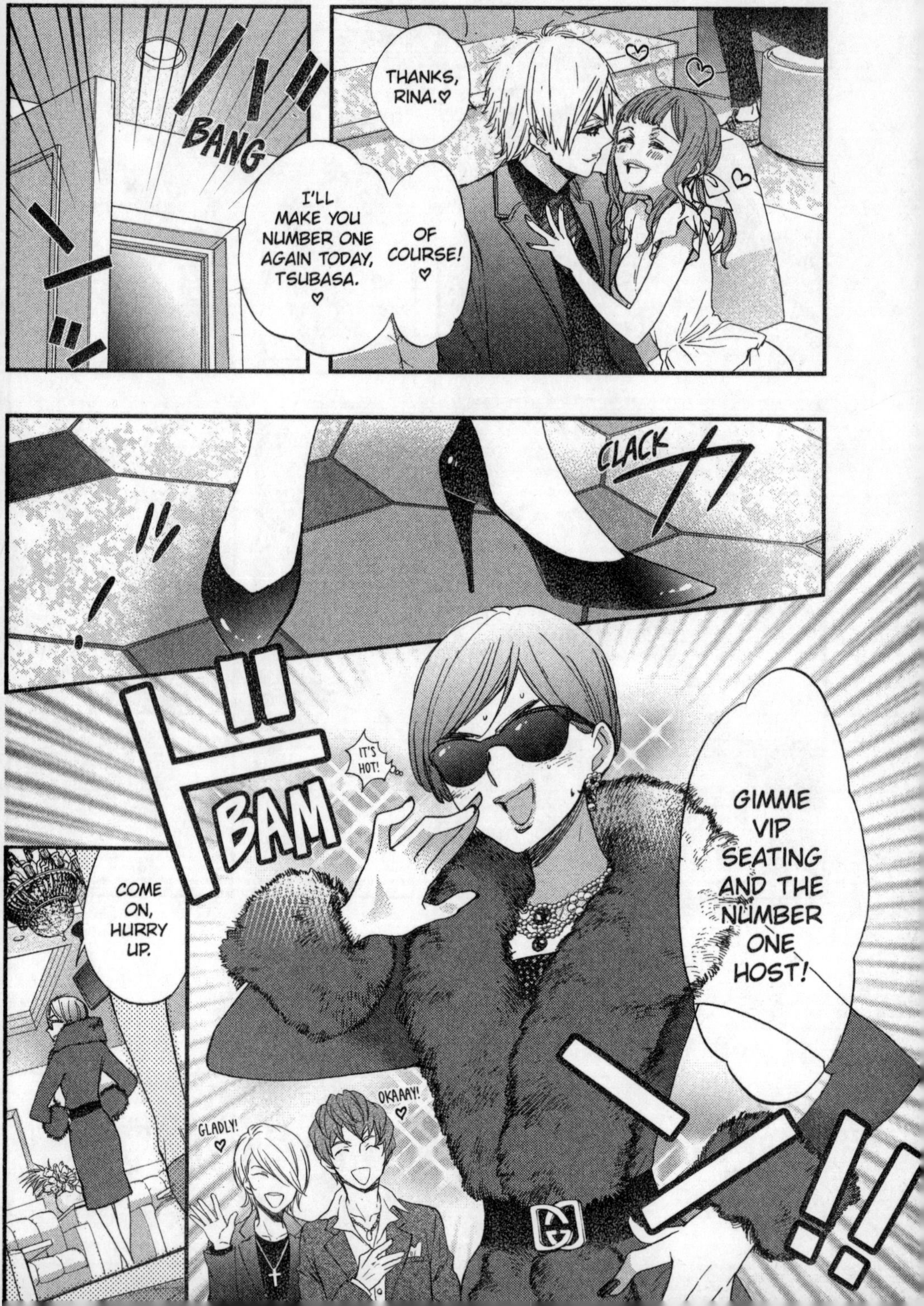
THANKS, RINA.♡
OF COURSE! ♡
I'LL MAKE YOU NUMBER ONE AGAIN TODAY, TSUBASA. ♡
BANG
CLACK
GIMME VIP SEATING AND THE NUMBER ONE HOST!
IT'S HOT!
BAM
COME ON, HURRY UP.
OKAAAY! ♡
GLADLY! ♡

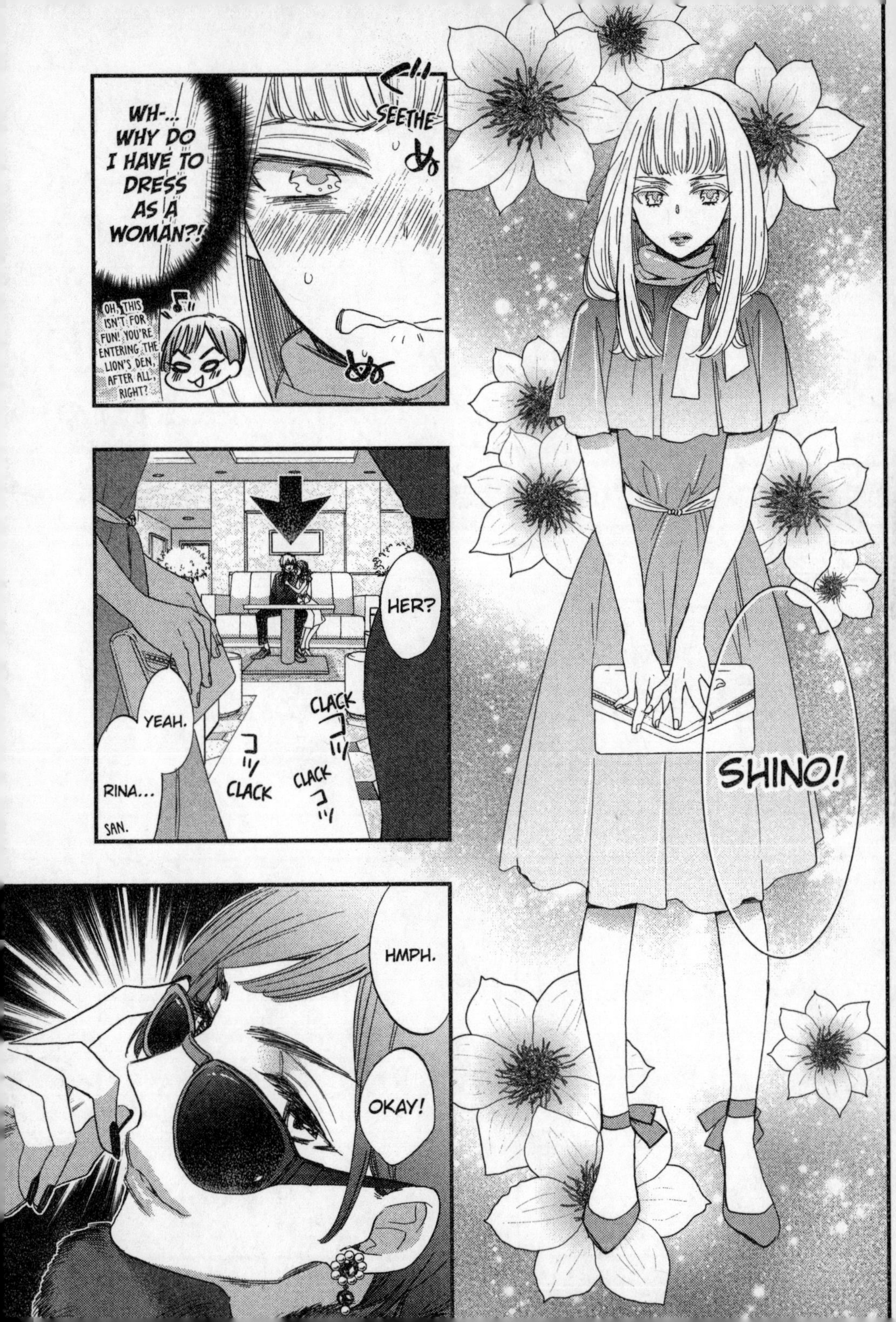
SHINO!
SEETHE
WH-... WHY DO I HAVE TO DRESS AS A WOMAN?!
OH, THIS ISN'T FOR FUN! YOU'RE ENTERING THE LION'S DEN, AFTER ALL, RIGHT?
HER?
CLACK
CLACK
YEAH.
CLACK
RINA... SAN.
HMPH.
OKAY!

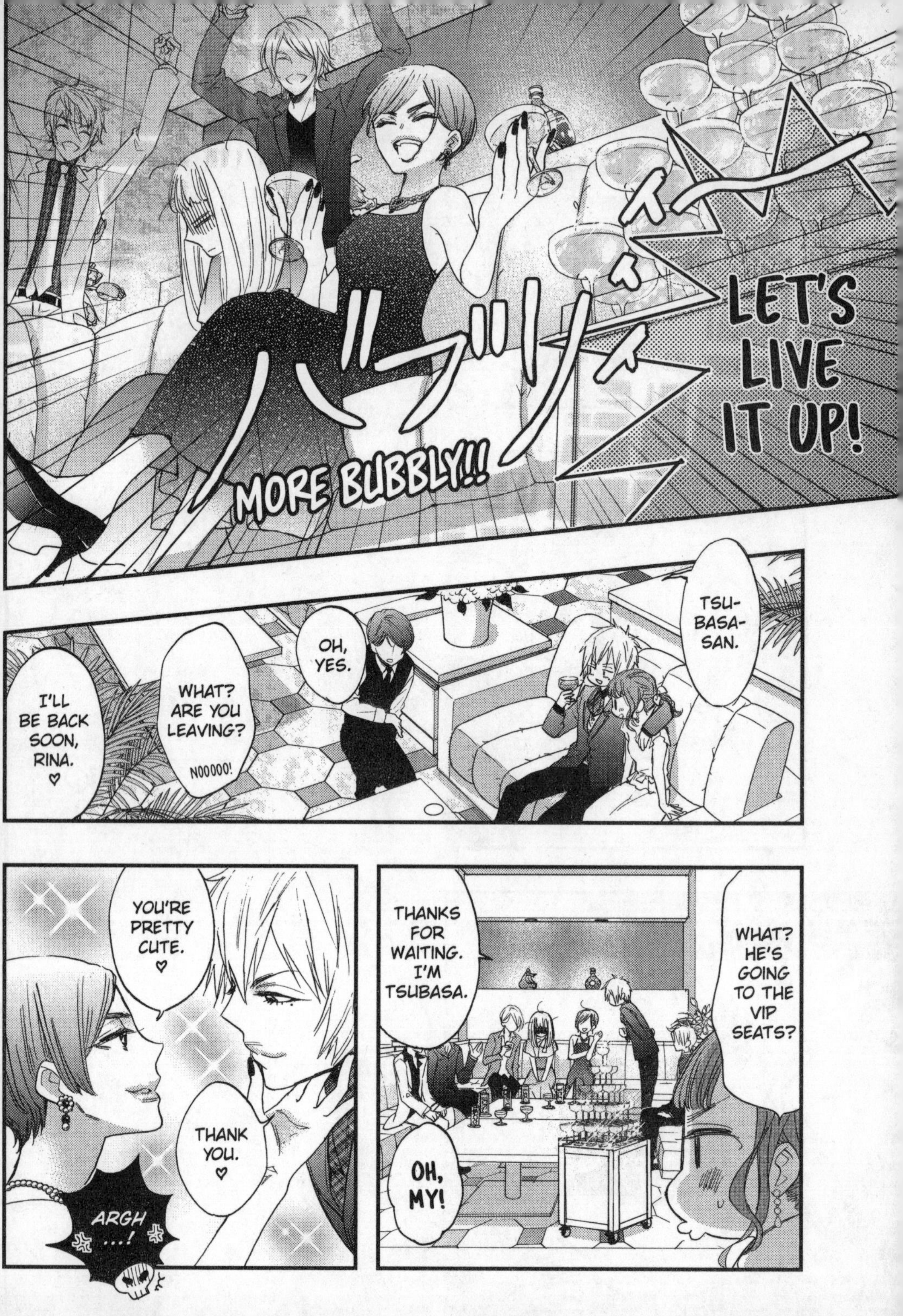
LET'S LIVE IT UP!
MORE BUBBLY!!!
TSU-BASA-SAN.
OH, YES.
WHAT? ARE YOU LEAVING?
NOOOOO!
I'LL BE BACK SOON, RINA. ♡
WHAT? HE'S GOING TO THE VIP SEATS?
THANKS FOR WAITING. I'M TSUBASA.
OH, MY!
YOU'RE PRETTY CUTE. ♡
THANK YOU. ♡
ARGH ...!

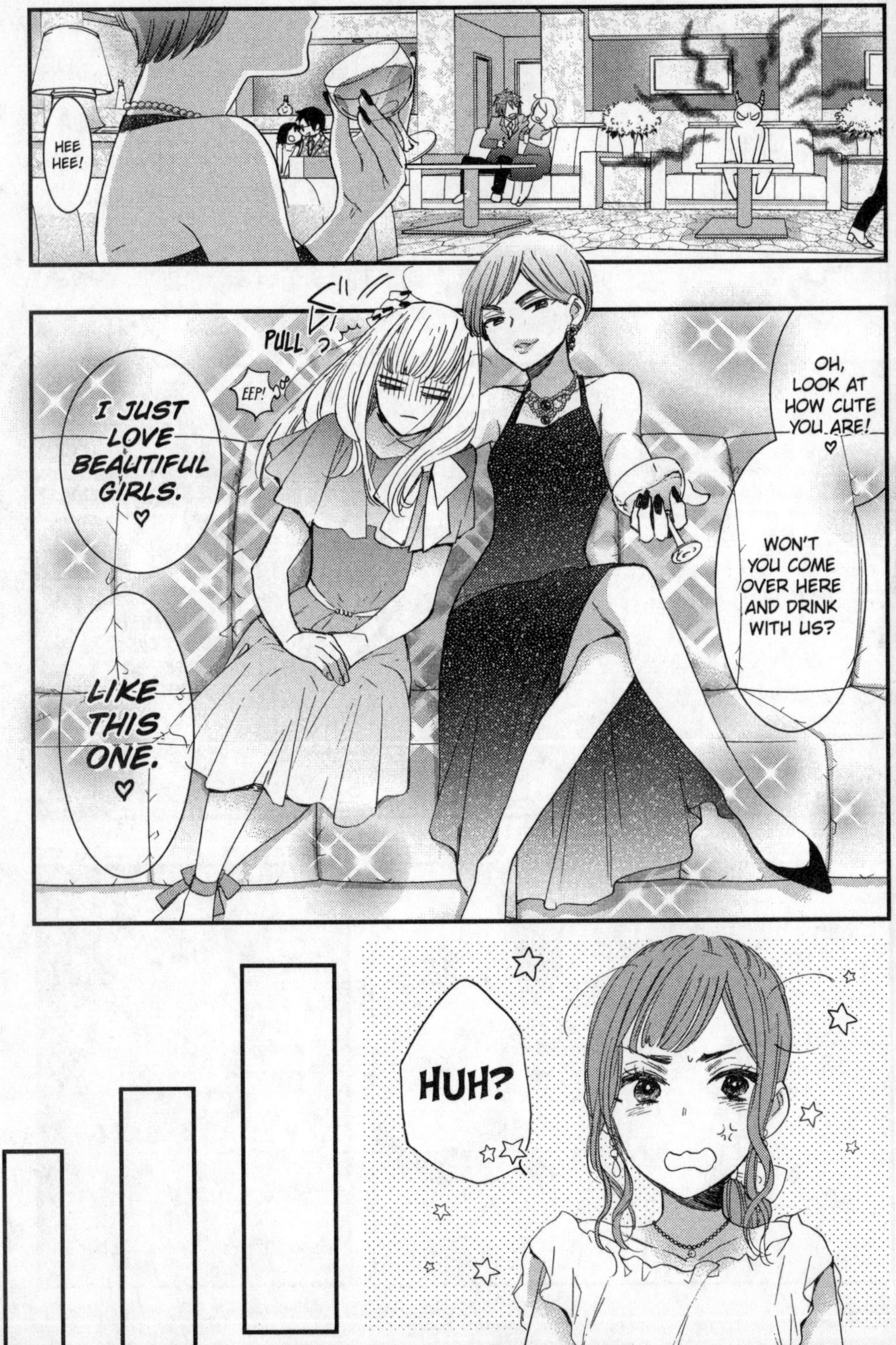
HEE HEE!
OH, LOOK AT HOW CUTE YOU ARE! ♡
WON'T YOU COME OVER HERE AND DRINK WITH US?
PULL
EEP!
I JUST LOVE BEAUTIFUL GIRLS. ♡
LIKE THIS ONE. ♡
HUH?

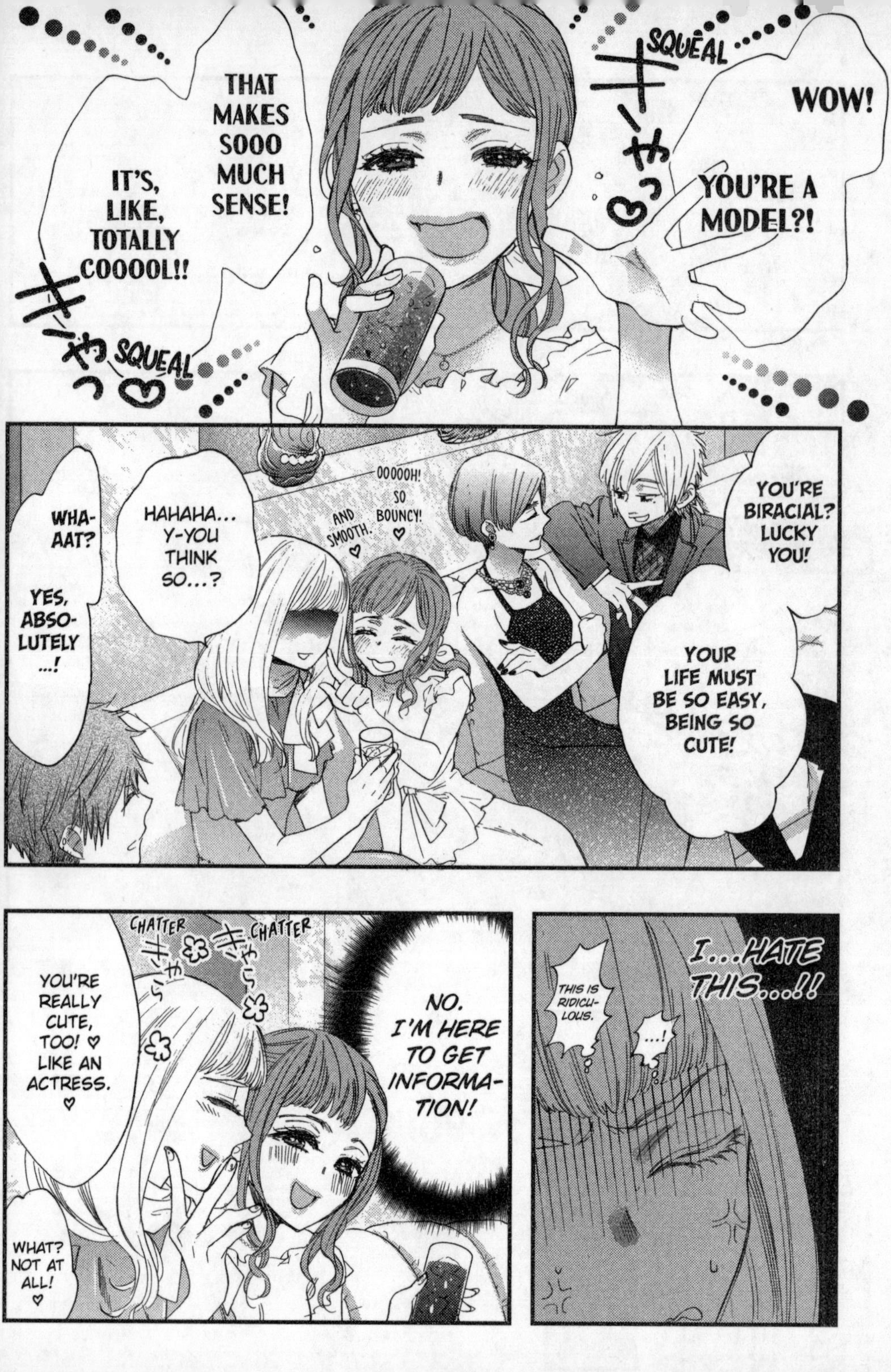
SQUEAL
WOW!
YOU'RE A MODEL?!
THAT MAKES SOOO MUCH SENSE!
IT'S, LIKE, TOTALLY COOOOL!!
SQUEAL
YOU'RE BIRACIAL? LUCKY YOU!
YOUR LIFE MUST BE SO EASY, BEING SO CUTE!
OOOOOH! SO BOUNCY! ♡
AND SMOOTH. ♡
HAHAHA... Y-YOU THINK SO...?
WHA-AAT?
YES, ABSOLUTELY...!
I...HATE THIS...!!
THIS IS RIDICULOUS.
...!
CHATTER CHATTER
NO. I'M HERE TO GET INFORMATION!
YOU'RE REALLY CUTE, TOO! ♡ LIKE AN ACTRESS. ♡
WHAT? NOT AT ALL! ♡

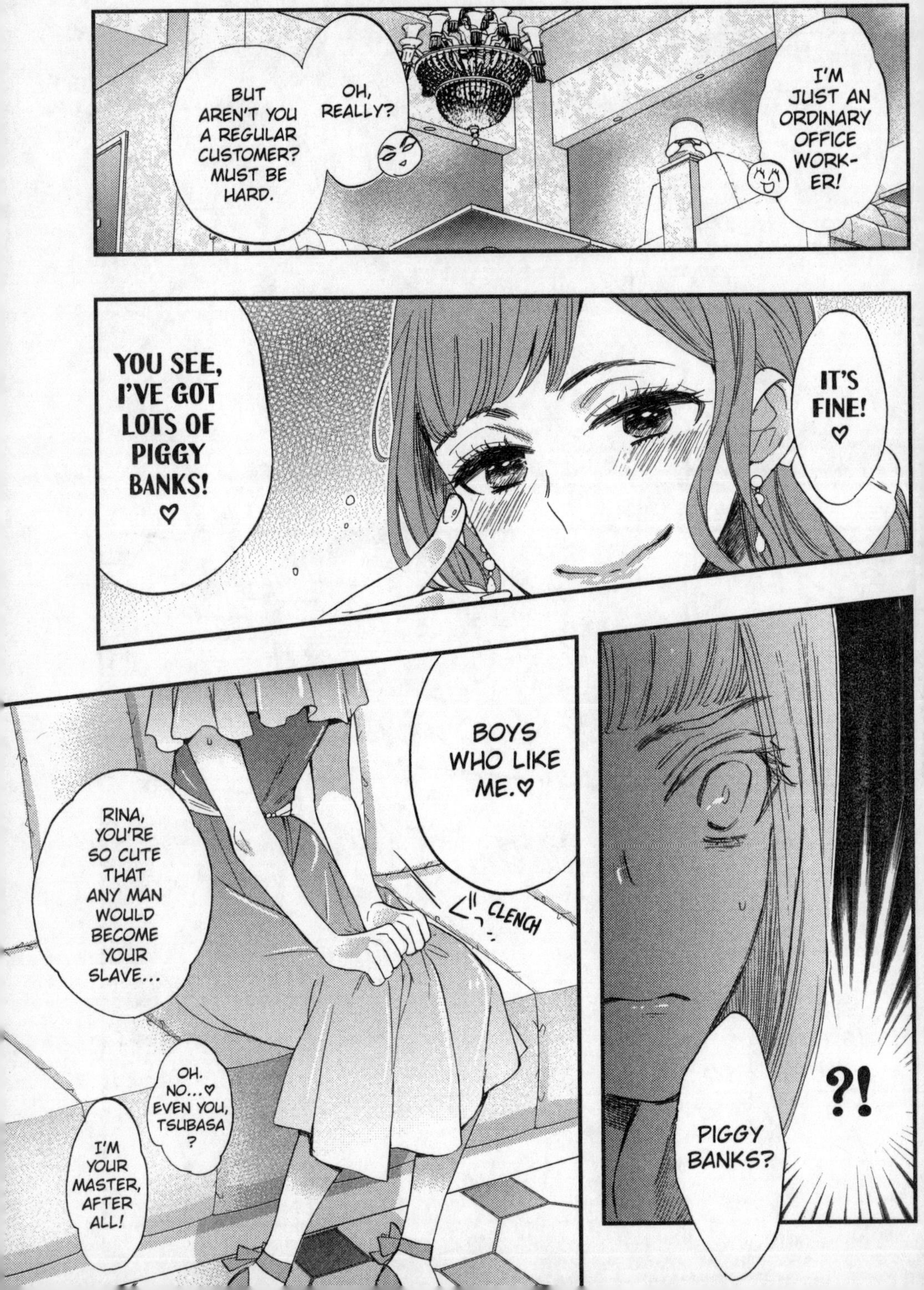
I'M JUST AN ORDINARY OFFICE WORKER!
OH, REALLY?
BUT AREN'T YOU A REGULAR CUSTOMER? MUST BE HARD.
IT'S FINE! ♡
YOU SEE, I'VE GOT LOTS OF PIGGY BANKS! ♡
?!
PIGGY BANKS?
BOYS WHO LIKE ME.♡
CLENCH
RINA, YOU'RE SO CUTE THAT ANY MAN WOULD BECOME YOUR SLAVE...
OH. NO...♡ EVEN YOU, TSUBASA?
I'M YOUR MASTER, AFTER ALL!

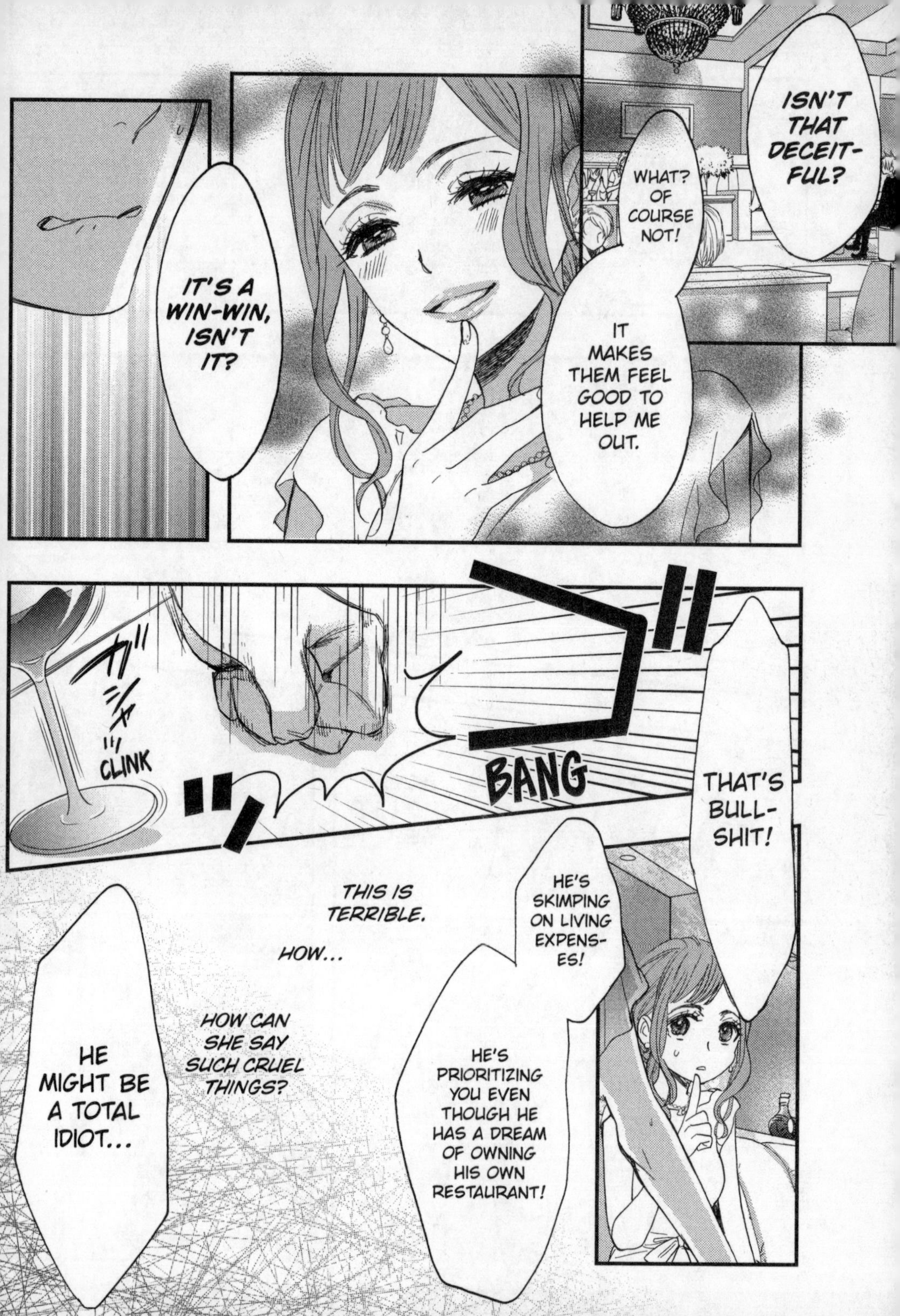
ISN'T THAT DECEIT-FUL?
WHAT? OF COURSE NOT!
IT MAKES THEM FEEL GOOD TO HELP ME OUT.
IT'S A WIN-WIN, ISN'T IT?
THAT'S BULL-SHIT!
BANG
CLINK
HE'S SKIMPING ON LIVING EXPENS-ES!
HE'S PRIORITIZING YOU EVEN THOUGH HE HAS A DREAM OF OWNING HIS OWN RESTAURANT!
THIS IS TERRIBLE.
HOW...
HOW CAN SHE SAY SUCH CRUEL THINGS?
HE MIGHT BE A TOTAL IDIOT...

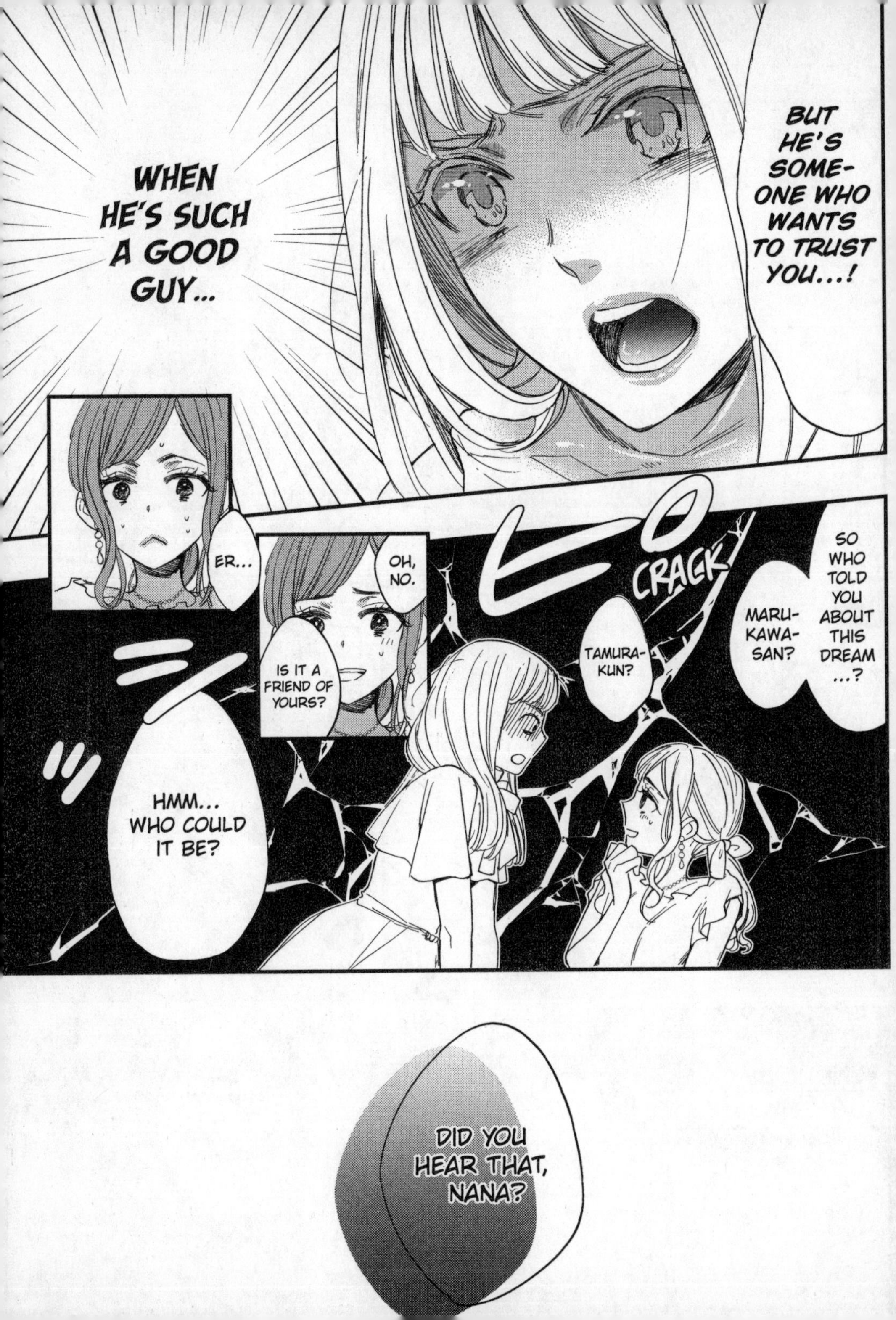
BUT HE'S SOME-ONE WHO WANTS TO TRUST YOU...!
WHEN HE'S SUCH A GOOD GUY...
SO WHO TOLD YOU ABOUT THIS DREAM ...?
MARU-KAWA-SAN?
CRACK
TAMURA-KUN?
ER...
OH, NO.
IS IT A FRIEND OF YOURS?
HMM... WHO COULD IT BE?
DID YOU HEAR THAT, NANA?

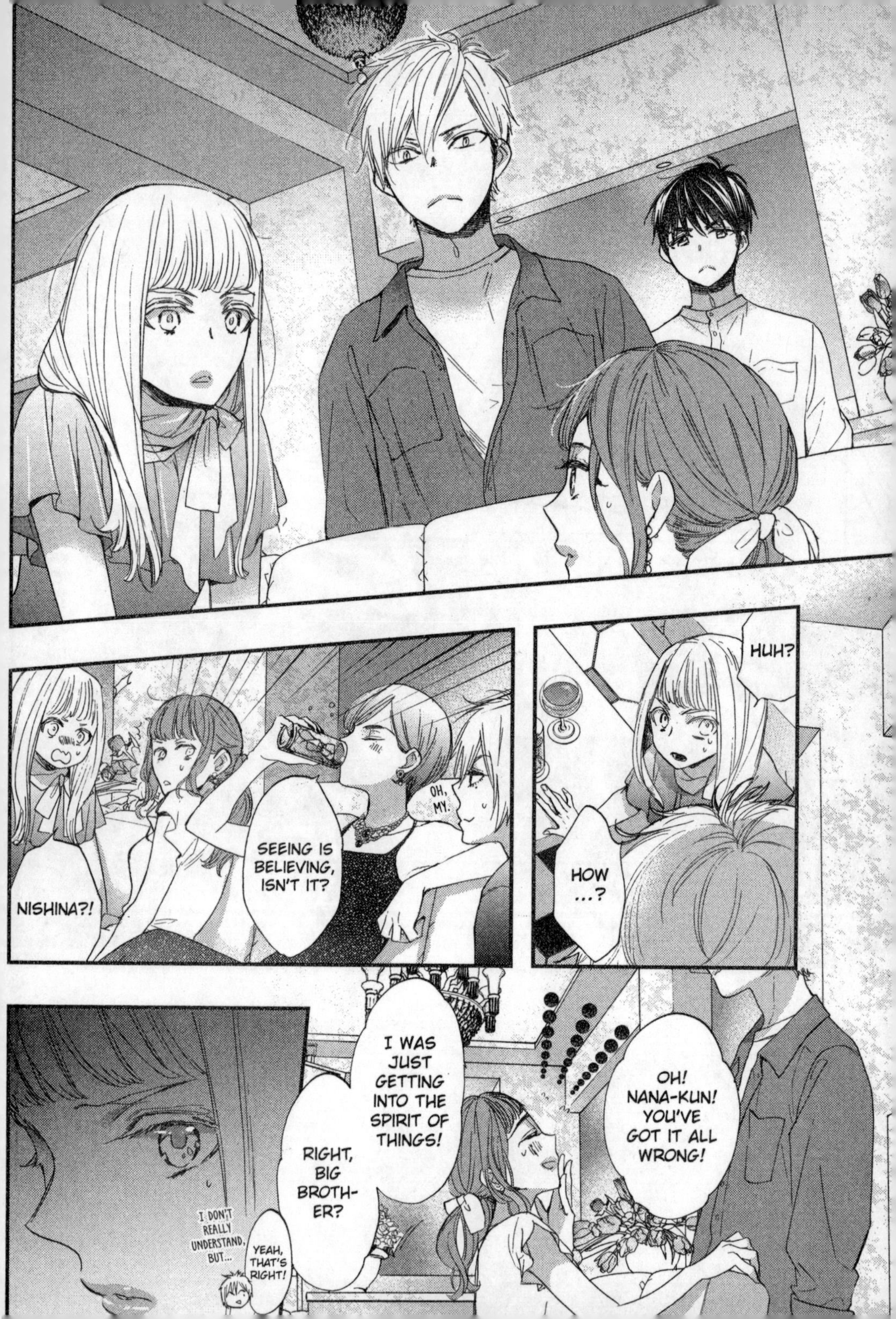
HUH?
HOW ...?
OH, MY.
SEEING IS BELIEVING, ISN'T IT?
NISHINA?!
OH! NANA-KUN! YOU'VE GOT IT ALL WRONG!
I WAS JUST GETTING INTO THE SPIRIT OF THINGS!
RIGHT, BIG BROTHER?
YEAH, THAT'S RIGHT!
I DON'T REALLY UNDERSTAND, BUT...

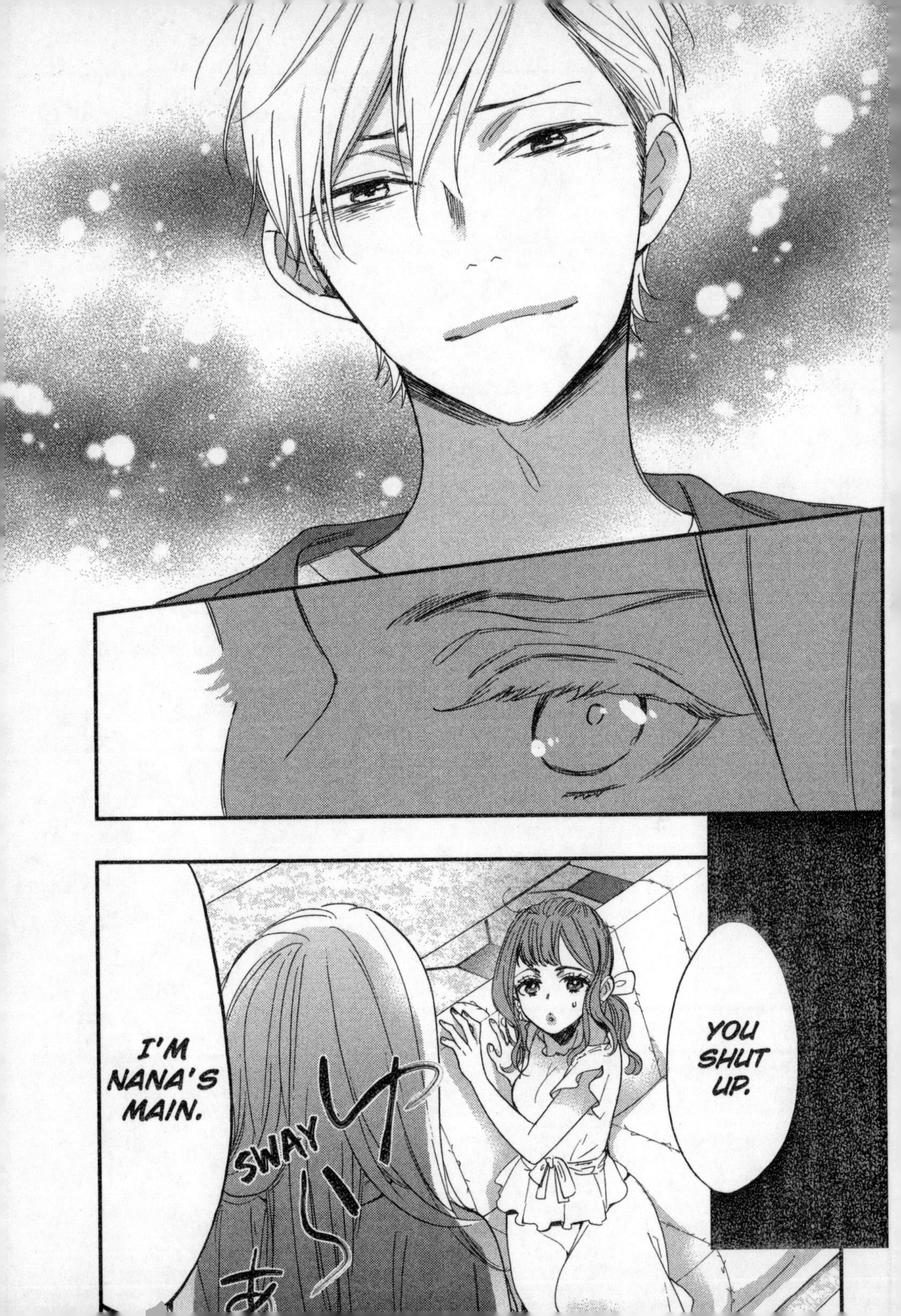
YOU SHUT UP.
I'M NANA'S MAIN.
SWAY

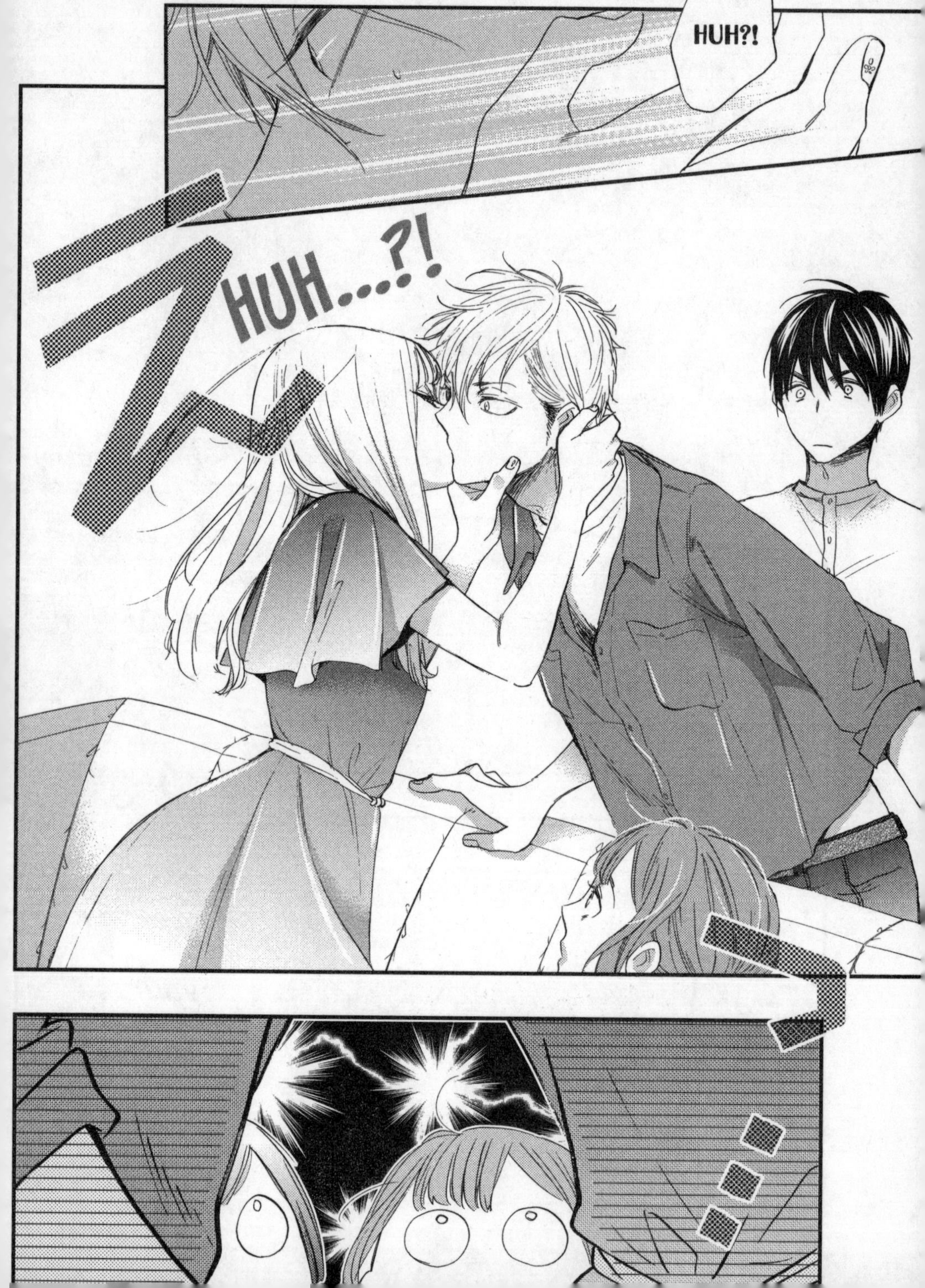
HUH?!
HUH...?!

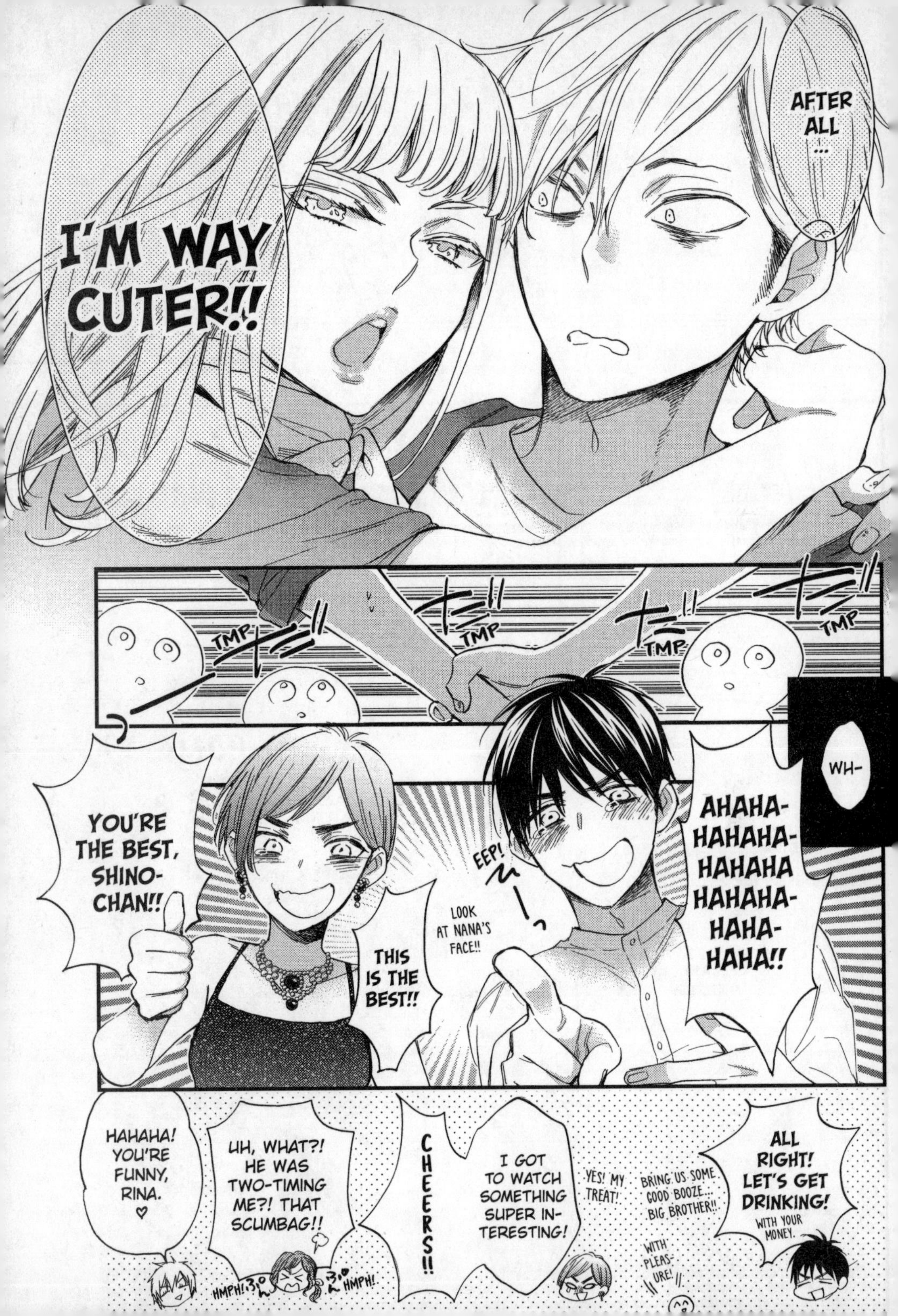
AFTER ALL ...
I'M WAY CUTER!!
TMP TMP TMP TMP
WH-
AHAHA-HAHAHA-HAHAHA HAHAHA-HAHA-HAHA!!
EEP!
LOOK AT NANA'S FACE!!
THIS IS THE BEST!!
YOU'RE THE BEST, SHINO-CHAN!!
ALL RIGHT! LET'S GET DRINKING!
WITH YOUR MONEY.
BRING US SOME GOOD BOOZE... BIG BROTHER!!
WITH PLEASURE!
YES! MY TREAT!
I GOT TO WATCH SOMETHING SUPER INTERESTING!
CHEERS!!
UH, WHAT?! HE WAS TWO-TIMING ME?! THAT SCUMBAG!!
HMPH! HMPH!
HAHAHA! YOU'RE FUNNY, RINA. ♡

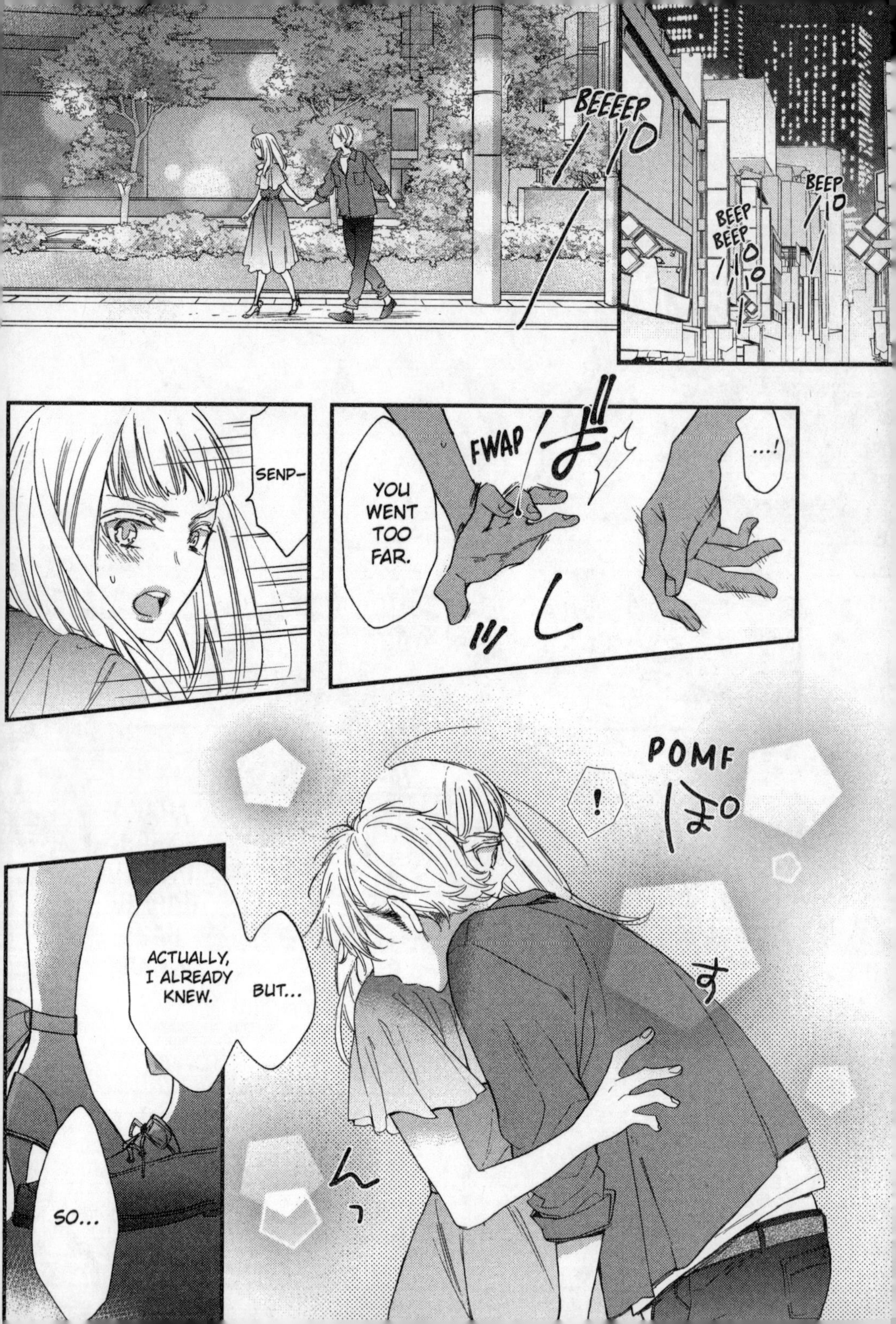
BEEP
BEEP BEEP
BEEEEP
...!
FWAP
YOU WENT TOO FAR.
SENP-
POMF
!
ACTUALLY, I ALREADY KNEW.
BUT...
SO...

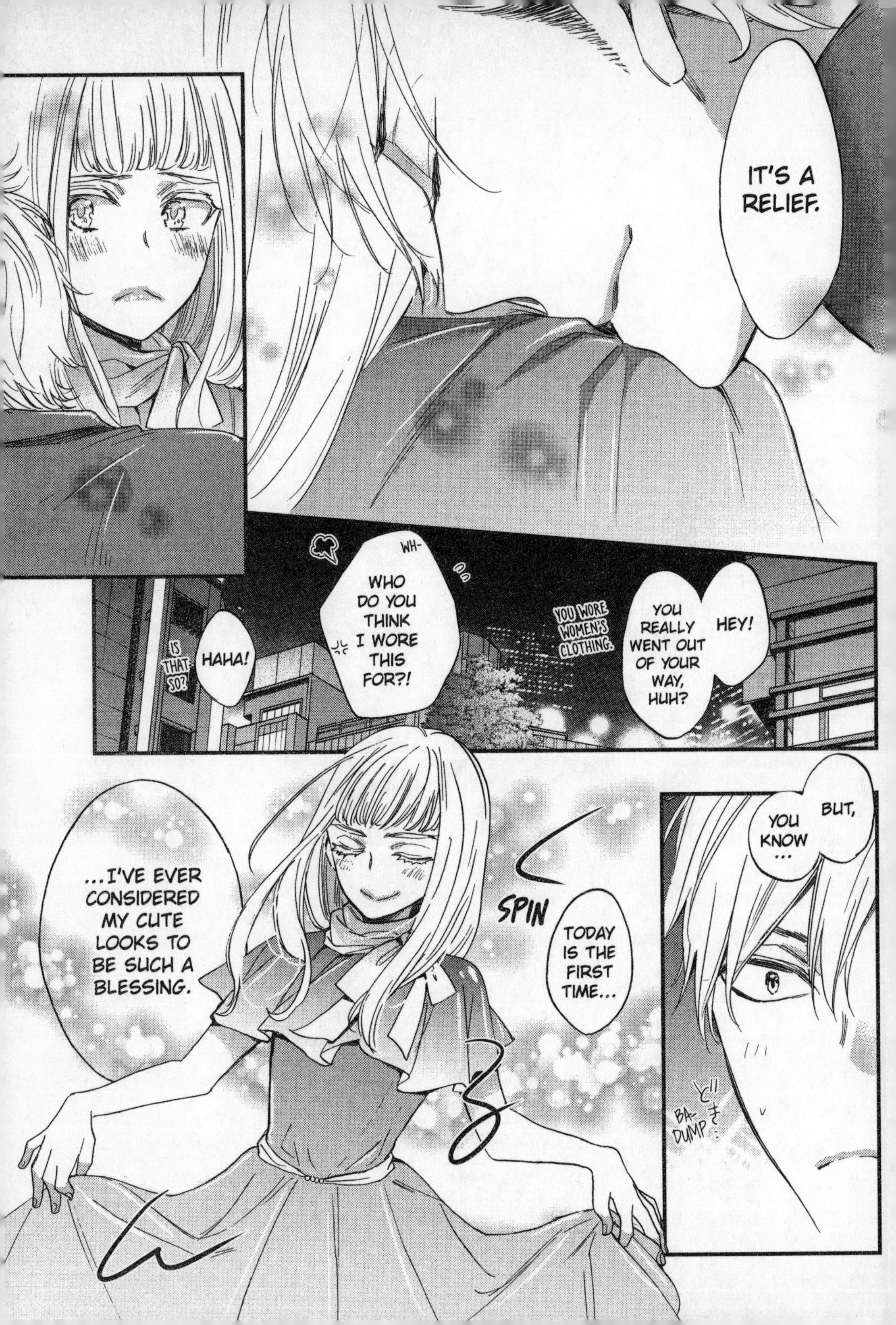
IT'S A RELIEF.
HEY!
YOU REALLY WENT OUT OF YOUR WAY, HUH?
YOU WORE WOMEN'S CLOTHING.
WH-
WHO DO YOU THINK I WORE THIS FOR?!
HAHA!
IS THAT SO?
BUT, YOU KNOW ...
BA-DUMP
TODAY IS THE FIRST TIME...
SPIN
...I'VE EVER CONSIDERED MY CUTE LOOKS TO BE SUCH A BLESSING.

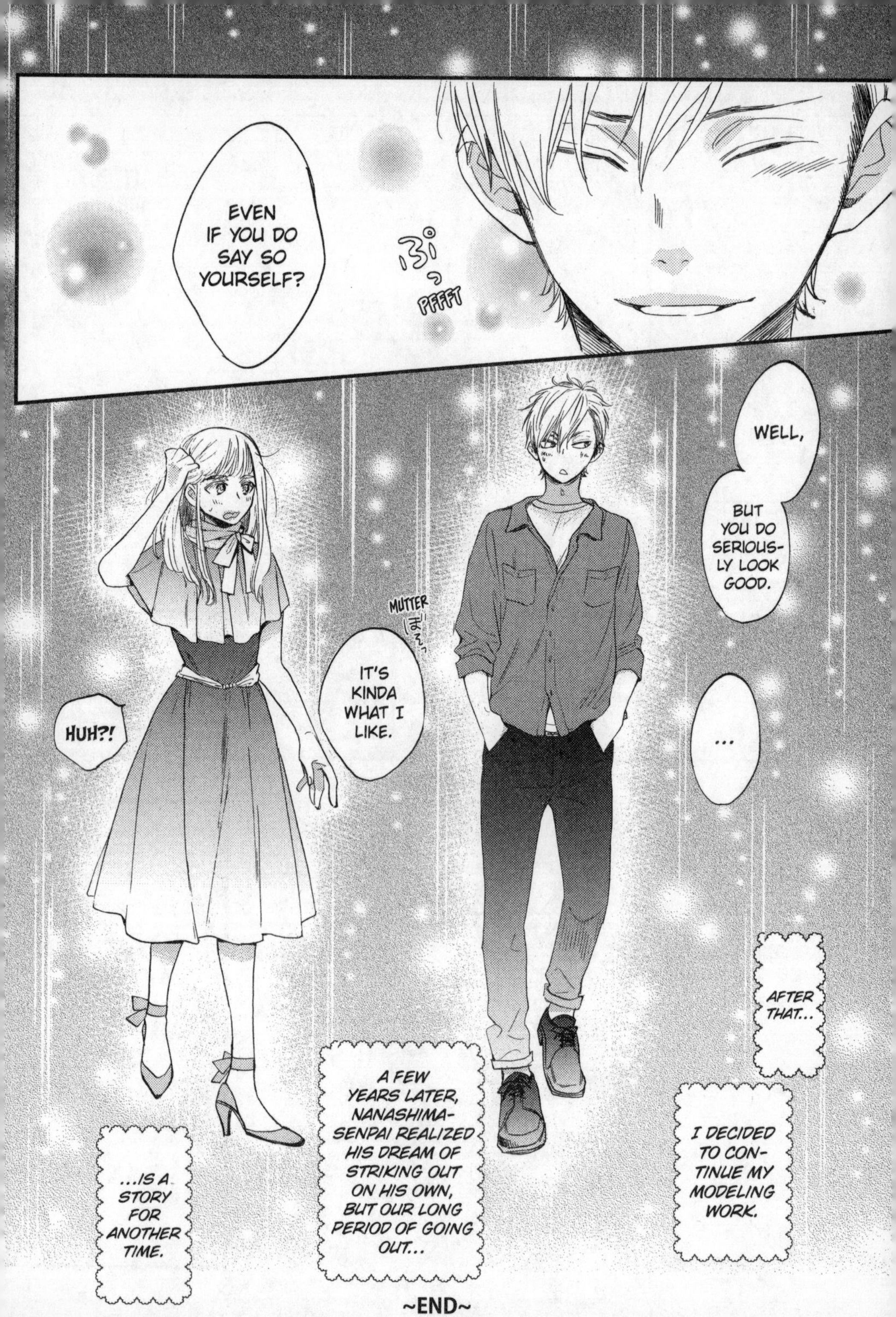
ぷっ
PFFFT
EVEN IF YOU DO SAY SO YOURSELF?
WELL,
BUT YOU DO SERIOUS-LY LOOK GOOD.
...
MUTTER
ぼそっ
IT'S KINDA WHAT I LIKE.
HUH?!
AFTER THAT...
I DECIDED TO CON-TINUE MY MODELING WORK.
A FEW YEARS LATER, NANASHIMA-SENPAI REALIZED HIS DREAM OF STRIKING OUT ON HIS OWN, BUT OUR LONG PERIOD OF GOING OUT...
...IS A STORY FOR ANOTHER TIME.

~END~

AFTERWORD
HELLO. I'M JUNKO. THIS IS THE SECOND VOLUME! THAT WAS FAST!
IT WAS A BIT CHAOTIC WITH GLIMPSES OF SCHOOL LIFE AND IDOL WORK LIFE, AND FUMI AND HARU GETTING MORE INVOLVED, BUT HOPEFULLY YOU ALL ENJOYED IT?
'CUZ I SURE DID!
ALTHOUGH HE WAS SHARPER THAN AZU THOUGHT, FUMI HAS TAKEN THE STORY IN AN UNEXPECTED BUT WELCOME DIRECTION.
LOOKING AFTER AZU REQUIRES A FORCE TO BE RECK-ONED WITH.
PLEASE LET ME HEAR YOUR IMPRESSIONS AND SUCH IF YOU'D CARE TO! THEY INSPIRE ME.
TWITTER*
@WANKONYANKO
SEE YOU IN VOLUME 3...!
THANK YOU VERY MUCH FOR THE LETTERS AND SUCH.

*TWITTER ACCOUNT IS IN JAPANESE ONLY

THANKS!

SPECIAL ADVISER/EIKI EIKI-SENSEI

ASSISTANTS/UZUKI-SAN, AKI-SAN, MIKAN-SAN, SHIROE-SAN, YUUGE-SAN (FOR COLLABORATION IN COLORING THE COVER ART)

DESIGN/HASE-PRO

SUPERVISING EDITOR/SATO-SAN

EVERYONE ELSE WHO WAS INVOLVED, AND YOU!

TRANSLATION NOTES

Idol otaku, page 2

The concept of "otaku" in Japan goes beyond the typical idea of "nerds" or "geeks" in Western understanding, and more broadly refers to obsessive fans who hoard information or merchandise of their favorite things, whether it be trains, anime/manga, or in Azusa's case, idols/pop stars.

THE SUPER-SPECIAL ULTRA-FABULOUS GOD IDOL SSR CHIKA-KUN IS HERE! RIGHT NOW!

SSR, page 15

In mobile games that feature collectible in-game resources such as character cards, these resources tend to be classified according to their rarity, which then determines their value. Ranking systems vary from game to game, but a general example of one using the "SSR" classification may rank resources as: R (Rare) < SR (Super Rare) < SSR (Super Super Rare).

I WAS JUST DROPPING OFF THE LOCAL NEWS-LETTER!
AND CHIKA-KUN WASN'T THERE! WHY WOULD HE BE?!

Newsletter, page 78

Chikashi (in Azusa's body) uses the word "kairanban," which refers to a newsletter-type document that is meant to be circulated among residents in a single complex or community, and may contain information from local official bodies like government offices. The newsletter or notice may be accompanied by a form listing the names associated with each household in the community, where residents will mark off their name to confirm receipt, then pass the material on to the next household, until it's been seen by everyone.

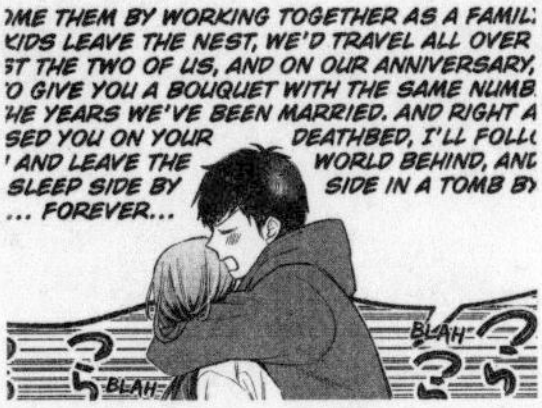
THEM BY WORKING TOGETHER AS A
LEAVE THE NEST, WE'D TRAVEL ALL OVER
THE TWO OF US, AND ON OUR ANNIVERSARY,
GIVE YOU A BOUQUET WITH THE SAME
YEARS WE'VE BEEN MARRIED. AND RIGHT
YOU ON YOUR DEATHBED,
AND LEAVE THE WORLD BEHIND,
SLEEP SIDE BY SIDE IN A TOMB
... FOREVER...
BLAH
BLAH

Kanji in names, page 84

"Kanji" refers to the ideographical character set used in Japanese, which was based on the Chinese writing system, and name meanings are derived from what kanji are used to compose them. Choosing kanji for names can thus be a very involved affair, but in this context, Fumi's desire to use characters from his and Azusa's names is meant to have a corny edge to it.

Fujoshi, senpai, kohai, page 120

Fujoshi: most commonly refers to passionate anime/manga fangirls who objectify male characters and male-to-male sexuality. Literally means "rotten woman."

Senpai: Someone who is relatively more experienced in a school or work setting.

Kohai: Someone who is relatively less experienced in a school or work setting.

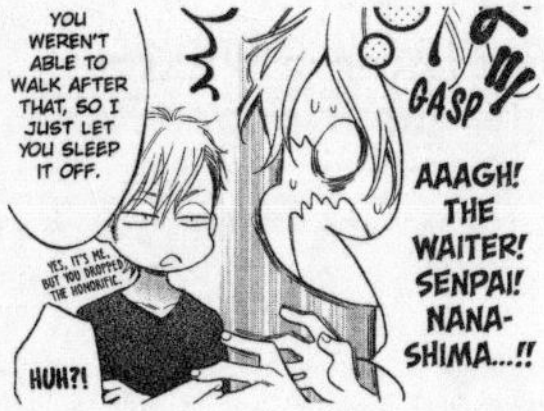
GASP!
AAAGH! THE WAITER! SENPAI! NANA-SHIMA...!!
YOU WEREN'T ABLE TO WALK AFTER THAT, SO I JUST LET YOU SLEEP IT OFF.
YES, IT'S ME. BUT YOU DROPPED THE HONORIFIC.
HUH?!

Dropped honorific, page 127

Addressing someone without an honorific is considered to be particularly intimate, and could be seen as a sign of disrespect, especially when done in a semi-hierarchical relationship like between senpai and kohai. Nanashima understands Shinomiya's only slipped up, but perhaps wants to make sure he doesn't get carried away.

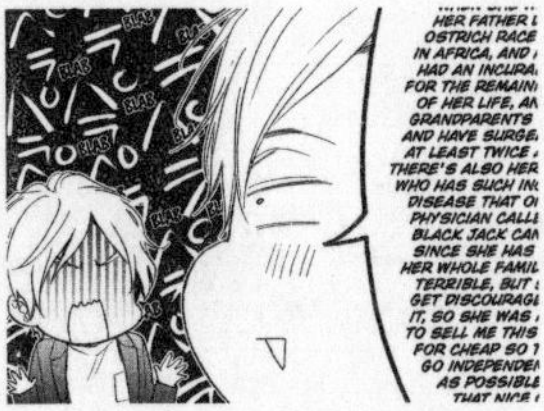
HER FATHER
OSTRICH RACE
IN AFRICA, AND
HAD AN
FOR THE
OF HER LIFE,
GRANDPARENTS
AND HAVE
AT LEAST TWICE
THERE'S ALSO
WHO HAS SUCH
DISEASE THAT
PHYSICIAN
BLACK JACK
SINCE SHE HAS
HER WHOLE
TERRIBLE, BUT
GET
IT, SO SHE WAS
TO SELL ME THIS
FOR CHEAP SO
GO
AS
BLAB

America's Black Jack, page 135

A reference to the Black Jack character created by Osamu Tezuka. He is a genius surgeon with exceptional medical prowess, but chooses to operate from the shadows rather than as a licensed doctor. Ironically, Black Jack has been known to treat patients without charging fees, which casts some doubt on Rina's story…

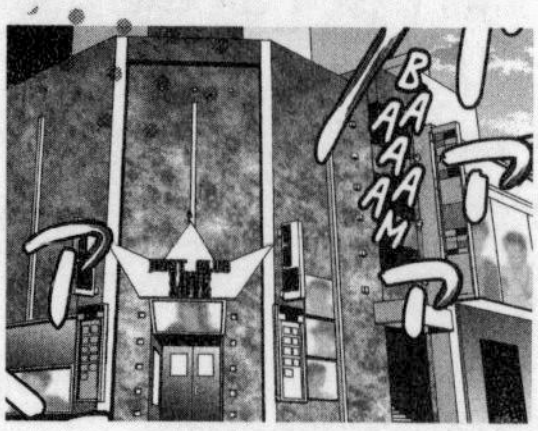
BAAAAM

Host club, page 139

A leisure establishment where clients can pay to spend time with male staff who are generally good looking and skilled at conversation. Rankings among male hosts within a club are determined by how much money in tips and alcohol sales they can rake in, hence Rina's efforts of spending as much as possible on Tsubasa's company and the alcohol they drink together.

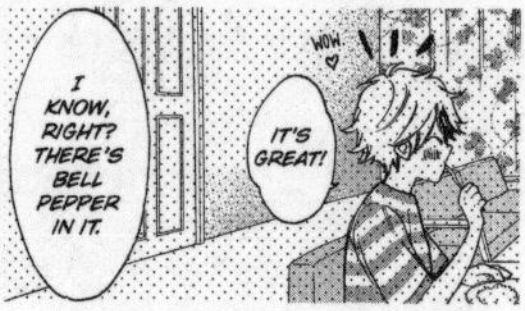
WOW
IT'S GREAT!
I KNOW, RIGHT? THERE'S BELL PEPPER IN IT.

Bell peppers, page 141

The reputation of bell peppers, specifically green ones, in Japan is very similar to that of broccoli in the West: kids love to hate them. Nanashima's effort to hide the bell peppers in Shinomiya's dish seems to suggest that the latter still has an immature palate.

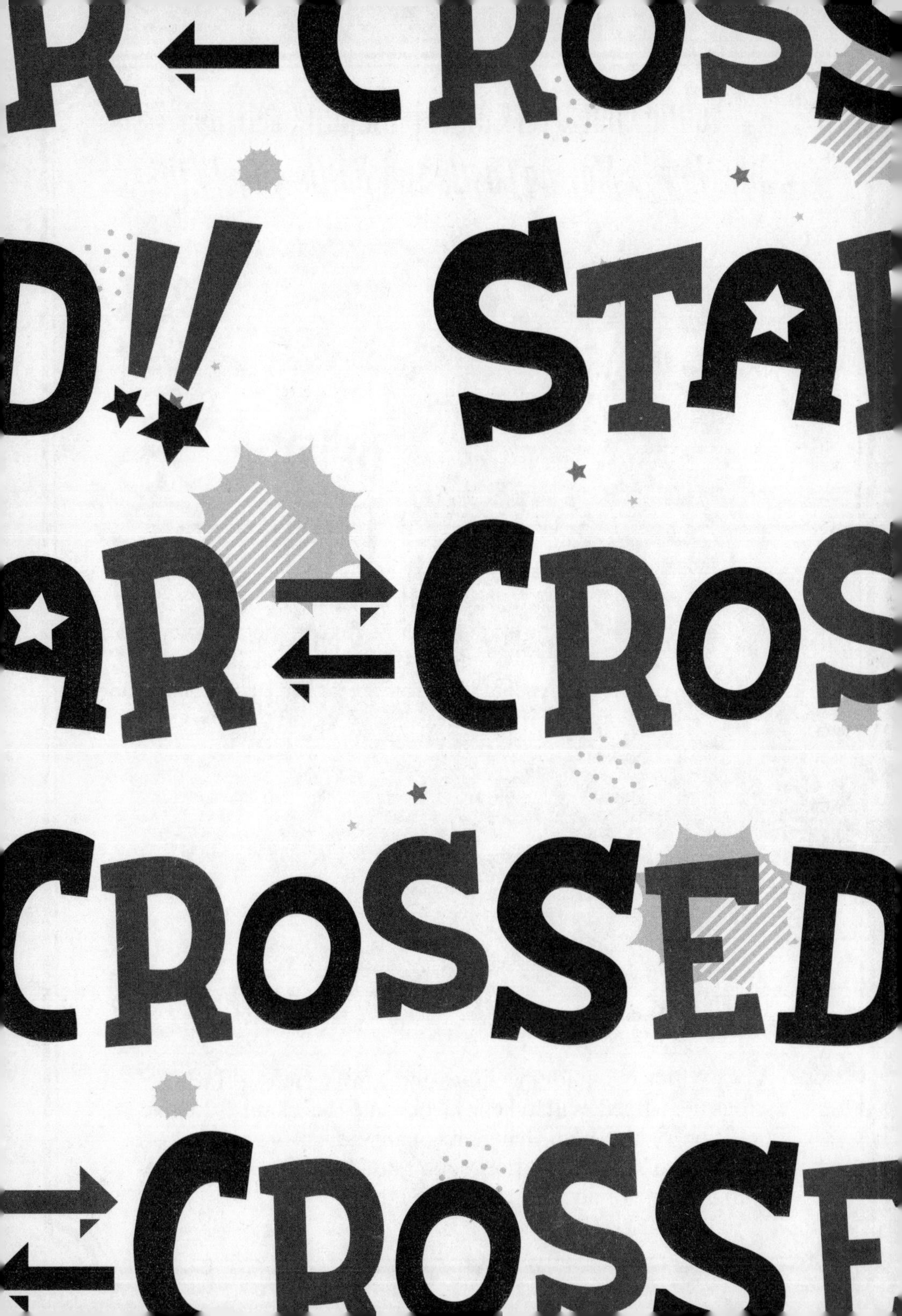
R⇄CROSS
D!! STAR
AR⇄CROS
CROSSED
⇄CROSSE

Young characters and steampunk setting, like *Howl's Moving Castle* and *Battle Angel Alita*

Beyond the Clouds © 2018 Nicke / Ki-oon

A boy with a talent for machines and a mysterious girl whose wings he's fixed will take you beyond the clouds! In the tradition of the high-flying, resonant adventure stories of Studio Ghibli comes a gorgeous tale about the longing of young hearts for adventure and friendship!

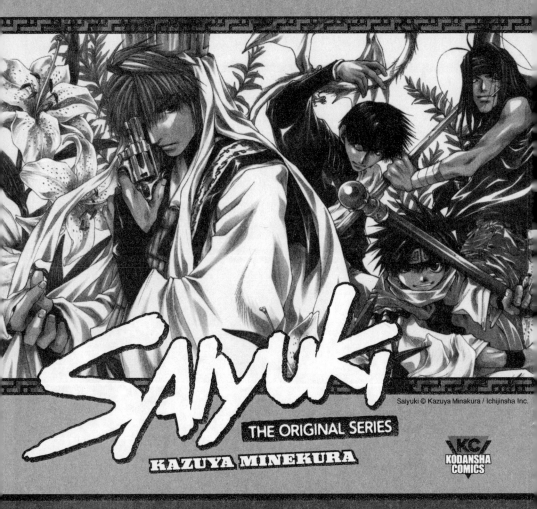

A SMART, NEW ROMANTIC COMEDY FOR FANS OF *SHORTCAKE CAKE* AND *TERRACE HOUSE*!

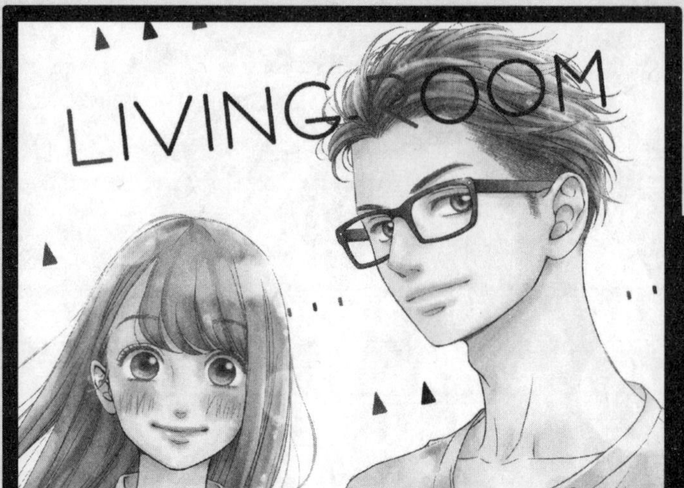
LIVING-ROOM
1
Keiko Iwashita
MATSUNAGA-SAN

A romance manga starring high school girl Meeko, who learns to live on her own in a boarding house whose living room is home to the odd (but handsome) Matsunaga-san. She begins to adjust to her new life away from her parents, but Meeko soon learns that no matter how far away from home she is, she's still a young girl at heart — especially when she finds herself falling for Matsunaga-san.

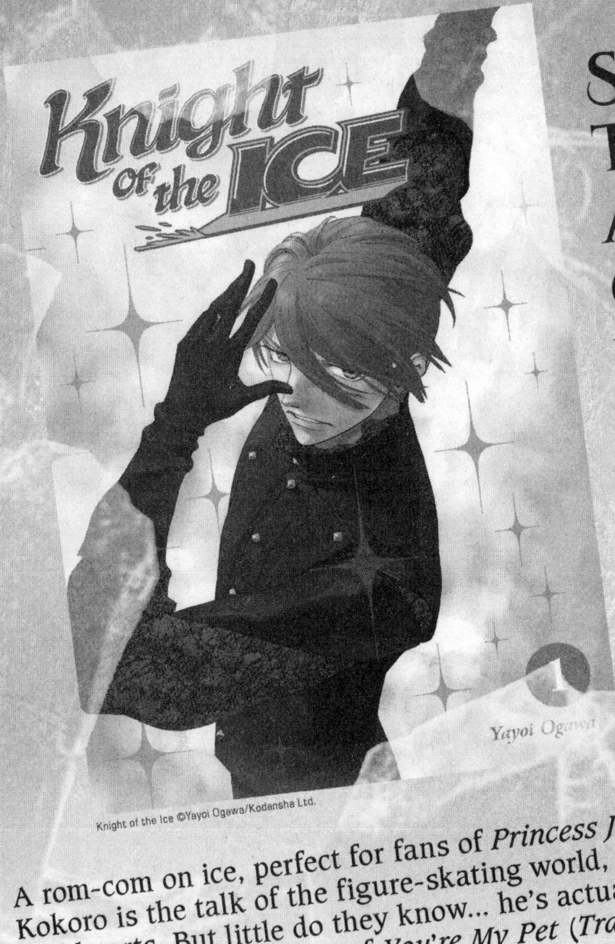
Knight of the ICE
1
Yayoi Ogawa

Knight of the Ice ©Yayoi Ogawa/Kodansha Ltd.

SKATING THRILLS AND ICY CHILLS WITH THIS NEW TINGLY ROMANCE SERIES!

A rom-com on ice, perfect for fans of *Princess Jellyfish* and *Wotakoi*. Kokoro is the talk of the figure-skating world, winning trophies and hearts. But little do they know... he's actually a huge nerd! From the beloved creator of *You're My Pet* (*Tramps Like Us*).

Chitose is a serious young woman, working for the health magazine *SASSO*. Or at least, she would be, if she wasn't constantly getting distracted by her childhood friend, international figure skating star Kokoro Kijinami! In the public eye and on the ice, Kokoro is a gallant, flawless knight, but behind his glittery costumes and breathtaking spins lies a secret: He's actually a hopelessly romantic otaku, who can only land his quad jumps when Chitose is on hand to recite a spell from his favorite magical girl anime!

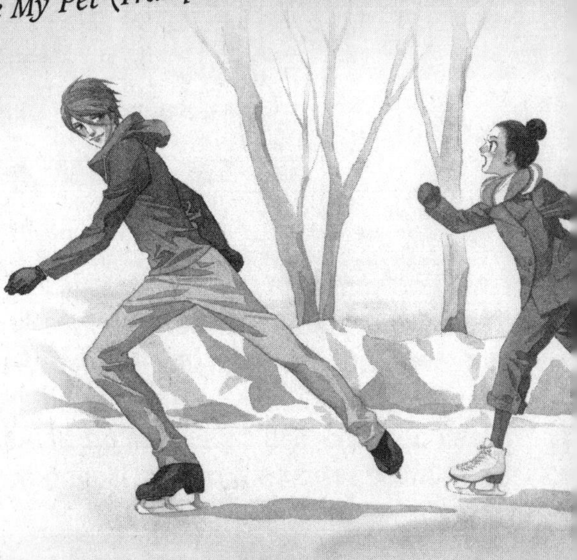

KC KODANSHA COMICS

THE SWEET SCENT OF LOVE IS IN THE AIR! FOR FANS OF OFFBEAT ROMANCES LIKE *WOTAKO!*

Sweat and Soap © Kintetsu Yamada / Kodansha Ltd.

In an office romance, there's a fine line between sexy and awkward... and that line is where Asako — a woman who sweats copiously — meets Koutarou — a perfume developer who can't get enough of Asako's, er, scent. Don't miss a romcom manga like no other!

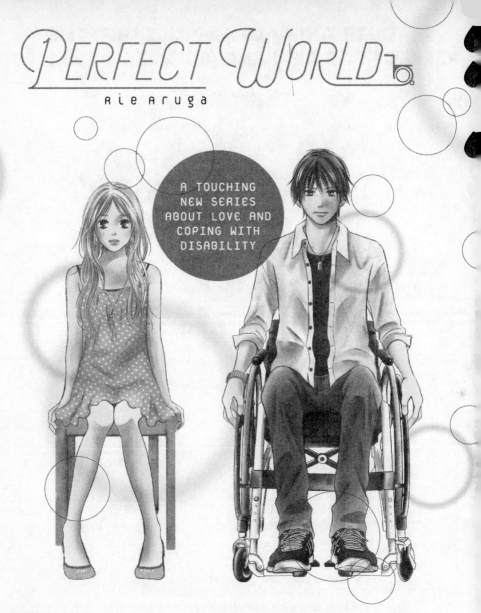

PERFECT WORLD

Rie Aruga

A TOUCHING NEW SERIES ABOUT LOVE AND COPING WITH DISABILITY

An office party reunites Tsugumi with her high school crush Itsuki. He's realized his dream of becoming an architect, but along the way, he experienced a spinal injury that put him in a wheelchair. Now Tsugumi's rekindled feelings will butt up against prejudices she never considered — and Itsuki will have to decide if he's ready to let someone into his heart...

"Depicts with great delicacy and courage the difficulties some with disabilities experience getting involved in romantic relationships... Rie Aruga refuses to romanticize, pushing her heroine to face the reality of disability. She invites her readers to the same tasks of empathy, knowledge and recognition."
—Slate.fr

"An important entry [in manga romance]... The emotional core of both plot and characters indicates thoughtfulness... [Aruga's] research is readily apparent in the text and artwork, making this feel like a real story."
—Anime News Network

KC KODANSHA COMICS

A Kodansha Comics Trade Paperback Original
Star-Crossed!! 2 copyright © 2019 Junko
English translation copyright © 2021 Junko

All rights reserved.

Published in the United States by Kodansha Comics, an imprint of Kodansha USA Publishing, LLC, New York.

Publication rights for this English edition arranged through Kodansha Ltd., Tokyo.

First published in Japan in 2019 by Kodansha Ltd., Tokyo as *Wota Doru, Oshiga watashide watashiga oshide*, volume 2.

ISBN 978-1-64651-189-1

Original cover design by HASEPRO

Printed in the United States of America.

www.kodanshacomics.com

3rd Printing
Translation: Barbara Vincent / amimaru
Lettering: Mohit Dhiman / amimaru
Production assistants: Dani Brockman, Monika Hegedusova, Adam Jankowski / amimaru
Additional lettering and layout: Sara Linsley
Editing: Vanessa Tenazas
Kodansha Comics edition cover design by Phil Balsman

Publisher: Kiichiro Sugawara

Director of publishing services: Ben Applegate
Associate director of operations: Stephen Pakula
Publishing services managing editors: Alanna Ruse, Madison Salters
Assistant production managers: Emi Lotto, Angela Zurlo
Logo and character art ©Kodansha USA Publishing, LLC